Through the tumultous times of the 1913 Lock-Out, the 1916 Rebellion, the War of Independence and the Civil War, Seán O'Casey, more than any other writer, illuminated the colourful stories and concerns of the people. Now his daughter Shivaun provides us with the full story of Seán's and Eileen's family life – all the trials, tribulations and struggles in times of war and peace in Britain. It's a story of labour and love, told with great integrity and sensitivity. As we now live in a world, truly "in a state of chassis", we all remember better times and hope for a better year, but also remember Seán's view that "Every action of our lives touches on some chord that will vibrate in eternity"

DES GERAGHTY, former President of SIPTU, the original trade union of Larkin and Connolly

In *Next Year Will be a Good One*, Shivaun O'Casey offers an intimate and absorbing portrait of life within the O'Casey household, richly illustrated with personal letters and family photographs that reflect the deep bond they shared throughout their lives. Sean emerges as a devoted father and husband, and the narrative also reveals the personal side of his life in the theatre – highlighting the loyal friendships he formed and the many memorable anecdotes. Together, these elements make for a compelling and heartfelt read.

ANNE KRAUSE

True to the heritage of her family, Shivaun O' Casey's book is a joy. It is gold dust.

DAVID GOTHARD CBE, artistic director, producer and teacher

Next Year Will Be a Good One describes a very full life – two very full lives. There's the man who fell in love, who became the loving father of three children – after he left Dublin. There's the isolation, familiar to any artist. There's the anxiety – also familiar. There's the 1930s, the War years – the bombing, the deprivation. There is the joy and the grief. There are the adventures – the new plays or new productions of old ones, in Sean's case; the setting out, leaving home and England, to tour the USA as an actor, in Shivaun's. The book is packed with life. And love.

RODDY DOYLE

This intimate memoir, interweaving her own recollections with letters from family and friends, some published here for the first time, lets the story tell itself, and draws us closer to the O'Casey family. Shivaun also reflects on her life as an actor and director as she makes her first tentative steps to move out from the shadow of her famous father.

PAUL O'BRIEN, author, *Seán O'Casey: Political Activist and Writer*

To my son Ruben, daughter-in-law Sarah
and my grandchildren Agnes and Esther.
With thanks, admiration and
deep everlasting love.

Next Year will be a Good One

Life with Sean O'Casey, my family and theatre

SHIVAUN O'CASEY

EDITED BY JOHN WILSON FOSTER
FOREWORD BY RODDY DOYLE

BELCOUVER PRESS

NOTE:
The letters from my father Sean to my mother Eileen, my brother Breon and me include letters seeing print for the first time. His letters to my brother Niall were lost in the move that Eileen made to London from St Marychurch after Sean's death. In the early 2000s, letters from Eileen and also my brothers Breon and Niall had written to Mina and Jack Carney were returned to me. Some of the letters to Sean that I quote are in my father's archive in the National Library of Ireland, Dublin. I have reproduced for the first time whimsical pen sketches which often accompanied Sean's letters to me. The first sketch, however, is by young Niall in the early years of the war.

FRONTISPIECE PAGE 6: Shivaun O'Casey. PHOTOGRAPH: Mark Burley

PAGE 232: Niall O'Casey. PHOTOGRAPH: Gjon Mili

PAGE 428: Sean, 1954, PHOTOGRAPH: Gjon Mili

Published 2025
by Belcouver Press
info@belcouverpress.com

Except as otherwise permitted under the Copyright, Designs and Patents Act 1988, this publication may only be reproduced, stored or transmitted in any form or by any means with the prior permission in writing of the publisher or, in the case of reprographic reproduction, in accordance with the terms of a licence issued by The Copyright Licensing Agency. Enquiries concerning reproduction outside those terms should be sent to the publisher.

Preface and text © Shivaun O'Casey, 2025
Foreword © Roddy Doyle, 2025
Notes © John Wilson Foster, 2025

PHOTOGRAPHS: © Shivaun O'Casey unless otherwise credited

ISBN 978-0-9935607-7-4

Printed by Biddles Ltd
Design and production by Wendy Dunbar, Dunbar Design

Contents

PREFACE BY SHIVAUN O'CASEY 7
FOREWORD BY RODDY DOYLE 9

PART ONE
A Family Tree

1 The War Years, 1938–1941 15
2 The War Years, 1942–1945 47
3 Back to Peace, 1945–1948 76
4 A Few Trying Things, 1948–1952 111
5 Foxhole and Call-Up, 1952–1953 141
6 Bivouacs, Beaches and Bonfires, 1953–1955 160
7 Niall to University, Paris and London for Me, 1955–1956 187
8 Niall's Last Fight, 1956 210

PART TWO
The Tree Splintered 233

1 RADA and My Prospects, 1957 234
2 Fare Thee Well, America, 1958 276
3 Now What? 1958 294
4 At Home in Bristol, 1959–1960 313
5 Last Days in Bristol, 1960–1961 344
6 Another Bash at Acting School, 1961–1962 362
7 The Last Lap, 1962–1963 383
8 Sixteen Red Admirals, 1963–1964 405

Preface

This story is like a necklace of many-coloured beads of variable sizes. I have been wanting to write an account of the O'Casey family for some time. The crucial incentive was the sudden shock on May 22, 2011 of seeing my brother Breon's handsome body in front of me against the cold, white hospital sheets, emptied of all life, a red rose placed carefully in the centre of his chest by the nurses who had laid him out so carefully for the family to view; he was still warm. Our past together crumpled around me: all our shared memories over seventy-odd years, all the ups and downs, the searing sadness and often uncontrollable laughter, all sharing of these things gone now. All that was left was for me to mull over the memories alone .

They come – memories from moments ago – like the muffled echoes that answered my shouts in the old quarry where I played with my friends. When we heard an echo we would shout our names and rude words and wait to hear the mysterious voice repeat our calls, ghost-like; a repeat of a moment ago.

Of course, during my very early years I understood little or nothing of what was going on around me, so "The War Years" in the first Part of my book is told from things I heard as I grew up, helped by a recorded interview I made with Breon a few years before he died; also by letters from Breon and my father Sean O'Casey's published letters. But the main voice in "The War Years" is my mother Eileen O'Casey's from letters she wrote to her friend Mina Carney and her husband Jack during the war. As the book goes on, letters from all the family join in. The voices throughout are those of the whole family, swelled by Sean's autobiographies, his letters to me, and his Notebook, together with Eileen's two memoirs, *Sean* (1971) and *Eileen* (1976).

It was my mother Eileen who amidst tribulations would declare optimistically: "Next year will be a good one!"

SHIVAUN O'CASEY
ASHBURTON, DEVON, 2025

Foreword

When I'm writing, when I'm working on, say, a novel, I'm often aware that the work of other writers is influencing – inspiring, infecting – what I do. I read Joyce Carol Oates' novel, *Black Water*, at the time when I was writing my own novel, *The Woman Who Walked Into Doors*. In *Black Water*, Oates keeps revisiting a key episode, re-examining it, altering the wording slightly but significantly. I thought that my narrator, Paula Spencer, could do that, revisit the moment when her husband, Charlo, hits her for the first time. I'd still have written the book, but reading *Black Water* when I did, added to it – a bit – for the better.

I could go through all of my books and point out moments when other writers and film makers came to mind. I was thinking of Fellini's *Amarcord* – a year in the life of a young boy – when I was working out the structure of *Paddy Clarke Ha Ha Ha*. I re-read James Plunkett's *Strumpet City* as I started to write *A Star Called Henry*.

Other writers hover. Two, in particular. Dickens and O'Casey. They are always there, in the room with me. They are why I wanted to become a writer. I've loved Dickens since I was a child and someone gave me *Oliver Twist* for my birthday. I've read and re-read Dickens ever since. Explaining why I love him seems unnecessary, but what I like most about his work is that every character matters. Every character lives. Every character, no matter how minor, gets at least one great line. The fat boy in *Pickwick Papers* might not be one of Dickens' more important characters but he gets to say, 'I wants to make your flesh creep', one of his most memorable lines. I try to make sure that every character I create has a line and a life.

The other constant is Sean O'Casey.

I was a secondary school teacher, between 1979 and 1993, in a school on the Northside of Dublin. Kilbarrack, where the school was located and where I'd grown up, is about eight kilometres from No. 442 North Circular Road, where O'Casey wrote his great Dublin plays. Very soon into my new job, it began to occur to me that the kids I was listening to all day were the grandchildren of the characters who populated *The*

Plough and the Stars and *Juno and the Paycock*. The council estate surrounding the school had been built to house the people coming out from the Georgian tenements – 'the slums' – of the north inner city. I was hearing the voices that O'Casey had heard. O'Casey's world was here, in the Northside suburbs. I was loving the new job but this realisation – or, more accurately, the decision: these are O'Casey's grandkids – made me even happier.

Because I loved Sean O'Casey. I think I'm being accurate when I say that I'd seen only one of his plays onstage, the Abbey's production of *The Plough and the Stars*, with Cyril Cusack as Fluther Good, when I started teaching. But I'd read everything I could find, all the plays, the six volumes of autobiography, the essays, his pamphlet on the Irish Citizen Army. It was O'Casey on the page that I loved first, the plays on paper, and the autobiographies. But it was some years before I realised that I could allow myself to be creatively inspired by the people surrounding me, in the same way that O'Casey had been.

I wrote *The Commitments* in 1986, seven years after I started teaching. A character, Outspan Foster, the band's soon-to-be guitarist, speaks on the very first line.

– We'll ask Jimmy, said Outspan. – Jimmy'll know.

I decided against quotation marks: dialogue would be announced by a dash, the way O'Casey had done it in *I Knock on the Door* and *Pictures in the Hallway*. The dialogue was blunter that way. It seemed to make more of what the character said, and brought his words closer to the telling of the story. It looked better too, I thought, and I've been using the dashes – O'Casey's dashes – ever since.

What I loved about O'Casey – besides the dashes – was the humanity of his people, their flaws and glories, their wit, their courage, their vanity, delusions, loudness. And they were so near. I felt that from the beginning they were only up the road, a few stops away on the bus. Art – drama, fiction – was outside the school window, or in the bedsit next door, right in front of me.

How do you thank the writer who helped you on your way, decades after you started, so long ago that you'd forgotten that there was a debt? By keeping in touch, by going to new productions of the plays, by re-reading the books, by reading the biographies and – now – by picking up and reading this book, *Next Year Will Be a Good One*, Shivaun O'Casey's memoir.

O'Casey was born in 1880. Shivaun, his daughter, has finished writing this book in 2025. Look at those dates again and do the subtraction: one hundred and forty-five years. It's extraordinary, it's wonderful, even before you open the book and start reading.

There's often a sense that O'Casey stopped living when he left Dublin, that his later work, contrasted to the Dublin plays, is of less value, so the life is of less value, not worth examining or recording. But *Next Year Will Be a Good One* makes a nonsense of that thought. The book describes a very full life – two very full lives. There's the man who fell in love, who became the loving father of three children – after he left Dublin. There's the isolation, familiar to any artist. There's the anxiety – also familiar. There's the 1930s, the War years – the bombing, the deprivation. There is the joy and the grief. There are the adventures – the new plays or new productions of old ones, in Sean's case; the setting out, leaving home and England, to tour the USA as an actor, in Shivaun's. The book is packed with life.

And love.

The father loved his daughter and the daughter loved her father. They learnt from each other, shaped one another. That love – father for daughter, daughter for Dad – is rarely well captured on the page or on screen. It's often corny, even dishonest. But this book's greatest strength is that love, and how Shivaun O'Casey manages to capture the complexity of it, and the joy. In telling her story, she's telling her father's. In telling her father's story, she's telling her own. It's deeply moving, and fascinating and entertaining – and just plain good.

RODDY DOYLE

PART ONE
A FAMILY TREE

1
The War Years
1938–1941

A BLACK-OUT BABY

I was born in a blacked-out hospital in Devon as the Second World War revved up its engine. I can imagine my mother in the last stages of her labour; she would have made a lot of noise: groans, shouts, maybe some expletives. Eileen was free from inhibitions; she was a natural spirit who had survived people trying to restrain her. She was on her back with her legs wide apart and her feet strapped into stirrups: a convenient position for the doctor but not the best position for the labouring mother. She would have pushed hard when she was told to and tried to stop when told to; pushed and pushed until suddenly the huge last contraction took over her whole body, as muscles she never knew she had convulsed and grabbed and fiercely pushed me out as she collapsed backwards and heard my first cry. That's how I imagine it.

Many times my mother and I sat together on sofas, at tables, or more comfortably on her bed leaning against cushions. We were the two females of the close-knit family and this bound us together. From childhood to middle age Eileen grew from being my mother to being my closest friend. Her three births were a frequent topic and sometimes my birth got an airing. She began: "I always blow up from the word 'go'. Of course I blow up now if I get worried, it's nerves you know. You were the most beautiful of my babies, you were carried around the ward by the nurses to show you off; the first black-out baby born in Torbay Hospital. First you had black curls, then blonde curls and finally straight brown hair. Breon was slightly premature. Dr Waller, the famous paediatrician who looked after me in London, was worried about me as the baby was getting so big and so he decided to induce him at home.[1] We lived in Woronzow Road, St John's Wood then. Sean was sent away for the night so he didn't fuss. It was a long labour and little Breon's eyes ran because the tear ducts hadn't yet been formed; they righted themselves and he was a beautiful

[1] Dr Harold Waller (1881–1955), who became a family friend, was consultant physician to the British Hospital for Mothers and Babies in Woolwich. His father, Rev. Horace Waller, accompanied David Livingstone on some of his later expeditions. There are several letters between Sean and Dr Waller in the Sean O'Casey Papers in the National Library of Ireland. A letter from Sean to Waller discussing communism and drama is in the University of Delaware Library Special Collections.

baby. Now, Niall was different looking, he was a very long baby and didn't have black hair. I gave birth to him on my own in the nursing home as everyone was off duty and Niall wasn't expected so soon – he was out by the time a nurse appeared. Sean was irate but he kept it in because of me.

You won't mind me saying darling, will you? – you know Niall was the closest to me, we understood each other. When he grew up he liked going out with me, he liked having a good time.

I went a bit dotty while I was pregnant with you, dearest. During the last month I started sleep-walking again. I had slept walked in the convent; no one told me it would happen and when I bled from my middle I was severely shocked. I was told I had started 'the Curse' and nothing more, except how to make sanitary towels from bits of old sheet and cotton wool, and how to wash, boil and dry them for use again. With my imagination I thought I was cursed and would go to hell, that I was very sinful and so I started not to sleep properly and to sleepwalk: once I walked along the stair banister. Finally I had a complete breakdown and was sent to a nursing home near Brighton and most of the girls there were from convents or Roedean School for Girls – you know, a posh school for girls.

So now, pregnant with you, Sean was more and more concerned about me wandering about at night making pots of tea and leaving a terrible mess. You see he was afraid I might hurt myself by falling down the stairs or I might set the house on fire, so he slept on the floor across my door at night so he could tell if I tried to get out and he could coax me back to bed. You know it is very dangerous to wake someone up if they are sleepwalking – they can go mad or die.

Anyway I managed to get past him without waking him and the whole thing became so bad that they decided to take me into hospital two weeks before you were due, to keep an eye on me: although I was allowed out during the day. They gave me injections every day to calm me and at night they tied spoons on a string all around my bed to alert them if I should climb out of bed. I managed to get past the spoons; I must have been very canny, and they found me washing the dirty nappies in the washroom and you can imagine the mess I had made, and what the smell must have been like. They had to clean me up as well as the room, and I can tell you they were not pleased. Matron decided that someone had to watch me all night. Maybe that's why you are a bit odd dear, like me". (She would chortle here).

"No. I have no idea what the injections were, do you think it could have been morphine? I always wanted to play the part of Mrs Tyrone in *Long Day's Journey into Night*." (Mrs Tyrone's morphine addiction was caused by her son's difficult birth.) "They did make me less anxious and made me sleep better.

Sean always wanted a girl. I had been in labour for hours and hours when you finally burst out. I was lying there with my feet strapped up and the doctor delivering you cried out, 'It's a girl!' and rushed off to phone Sean with the good news. Just left me there with the nurses.

Yes, of course Sean asked how I was. If there was ever any decision about who should be saved the mother or the baby it was always me. By the time the doctor got back my legs were numb and hurting.

You weren't an easy birth my darling, you were big you see, even bigger than Breon, 8 lbs or more. The doctor told me how delighted Sean was to have a little girl and congratulated me as he stitched me up. The nurses had done all the other business. I was very happy; you were so beautiful and I was glad to have a girl with two boys already. Yes, I fed you for about six months. Dr Waller and I believed in breastfeeding, we all did then, especially with war breaking out. Dr Waller always said that a baby gets all it needs from the breast.[2]

I was never the same after you, I never got my figure back and my milk went all wrong. My legs swelled up as if I had elephantiasis, you see my milk went all over my body so finally I had to stop feeding you. There you are, my dear, but you were worth it. I love you very much. We do row, but we really love each other don't we? I do worry about you, though.

You were the first black-out baby at Torbay Hospital, they put a plaque up that said 'Baby O'Casey, First black-out baby born 28th September 1939 at (just after midnight)'. They had to put 'baby' because we couldn't decide what to call you for months. All your ration books had Baby O'Casey written in them."

Sean was holding the fort at home.

---

[2] Harold Waller was a breast-feeding advocate and author of *Clinical Studies in Lactation* (1938) and *The Breasts and Breast Feeding* (1957).

Wednesday 22nd September 1939

My dearest Eily,

Everything is quiet here. Niall went to bed calmly, but he seemed subdued in some way, quietly shaking hands with me, & saying good night. He obviously feels it strange that you aren't with us. Brian, too, said "it feels lonely without mammy."[3] and, truth to tell, I feel rotten, a full up feeling in the belly and a strange sense of being by myself. But I've always felt so; even when you were absent for only a day, & sometimes, even when you go to the pictures. I do hope you may have a restful night, though it must be damned strange in a strange place. However, I'm sure, you'll soon get friendly with the nurses. Don't fret anyway; and don't try to suppress 'the fidgets' too much, because I don't happen to be with you, or because you aren't in your own home. ... Anyway, both of us worry too much.

It was a pity we couldn't have gone to the hospital together. ... I'll look up the times of the Torquay buses, with the forms [timetables] , & see if I can come down on odd days – early, say twelve or so, & come back in the afternoon. I don't think I'd like to stop for "bed and Breakfast." I'd feel rotten in the morning with my eyes and unshaven face. ...

Rest as much as you can; read your stories; play your patience; and don't worry about us. We'll crawl along till you get back. "It's funny to think" said Brian, "that in a short time there'll be another in the family."
    God be with you
    All my love
    Sean

October 7th 1939

Dearest Eily,

Nothing new to report: all going as usual here. Had rather a partly boring evening with the McNally's [neighbours]. Present: a Professor of Phenology[4] & his lady, in trousers & evening-cut bodice, & they

---

[3] Sean in letters sometimes called his son Brian instead of Breon.
[4] Phenology is "the study of cyclic and seasonal natural phenomena, especially in relation to climate and plant and animal life" (*OED*).

having to go home in a car on a dark night in the pelting rain. I am still very fond of McNally himself.

I hope everything is well with you & Shivaun: & that the feeding is nearly exact now.

Brian & I will probably come down on the 2.15 bus, and be with you about 3.15 or so.

What the result of Hitler's speech may be, few can say. I still believe that the conference is bound to come, & the war postponed sine die.

Anyhow, as he says, [Hitler] two powers can't win, tho two may be vanquished – exactly what will happen – both will be wiped out. But neither can afford that, so I daresay there'll be a settlement of some kind.[5]

I hope so.
All my love
Sean

THE DEVON MOVE

In 1938 Sean and Eileen had decided to go down to Devon to live, to be near a "progressive" school called Dartington Hall, the school that George Bernard Shaw told them "was the only school for the O'Casey children," and when Eileen exclaimed, "We could never afford it" had said, "Nonsense, you will find the money somehow." Which they did.

They were looking for a school for Breon who was eleven and the school he was attending stopped at that age. They found nothing in London that they liked and so had looked to George Bernard Shaw for his advice that was duly given. Shaw knew the school because the Fabian Society held its Summer Schools on the Dartington Estate.[6] So Sean and Eileen visited the school and stayed at the Hall with its founders, Dorothy and Leonard

---

[5] In his speech to the Reichstag on October 6, 1939, the day after the German invasion of Poland was completed, Hitler said that both sides in the Great War had been losers and Sean may have seized on this as a deterrent to world war. But Hitler also said that there can ever be only one victor, and he intended Germany to be that victor in any conflict.

[6] "The credit for originating the political summer school in Great Britain belongs to the Fabian Society": Joseph R. Starr, "Foreign Governments and Politics; The Summer Schools and Other Educational Activities of British Socialist Groups," *The American Political Science Review* 30.5 (October 1936): 958. The Fabian Society, formed in 1884, held its first summer school in 1906, two decades before Leonard and Dorothy Elmhirst bought Dartington Hall.

Elmhirst.[7] Eileen in particular fell in love with the school and immediately accepted its child-centred philosophy; Sean approved of the outspoken and confident pupils he met and talked to; on asking one child what he thought of him the child answered – "I think you are quite ugly." An honest answer to a pompous question, Sean decided.

Both Sean and Eileen had disliked their schooling in different ways. Eileen's had been in strict Catholic Ursuline convents in England, mainly London, stuck there during term and holidays while her mother worked as a nurse to old people in their homes. Eileen generally found school miserable, although by nature she was a jolly child and made the very best of it all. Sean had visited school rarely due to a serious eye disease he contracted when a little boy of five called trachoma (the disease that usually leaves you blind and with your eyelashes growing inwards and needing to be plucked out). His sister Ella was a schoolmistress and taught Sean the rudiments of reading, writing and spelling; the rest he learned himself when he was twelve and was desperate to educate himself and to read books.

So they took Shaw's advice and decided to move down to Devon to be near enough the school for the boys to be day pupils and hence the "community of the home" would continue, something dear to Sean's heart. The Head of the School was William Burnlee Curry and at that time the only day pupils were the children of the teachers and those who worked on the Estate.[8] Eileen pleaded with Curry to take her two boys on as day pupils and won; and opened the door for other local children to attend who weren't the children of Estate workers or teachers.

---

[7] Leonard Elmhirst (b. 1893) married Dorothy Payne Whitney, an American, when he was living in the U.S. Dartington Hall was to be the hub of the rural utopia they envisioned. The Elmhirsts were anti-capitalist and said to be "in active and articulate revolt against the values and conventions of their class while at the same time inescapably imbued with many of them": Ian Britain, quoted in a review of Michael Young's 1982 biography of the Elmhirsts: David Cannadine, "Utopia Limited," *London Review of Books* 14.13 (1982).

[8] A science teacher, W.B. Curry (1900–1962) was Headmaster of Dartington Hall from 1930 to 1957. Under his leadership, the school grew from 51 to 194 pupils, with a lengthening waiting list. Curry was a committed educational and political liberal and pacifist who published an influential book, *The School and a Changing Civilization* (1934). He was also a committed democratic federalist and in 1939 he published *The Case for Federal Union*. Among the alumni of the school, which closed in 1987, were the children of Ernest Freud (son of Sigmund), Victor Gollancz and Bertrand Russell.

THE WAR YEARS 1938-1941

In 1938 Sean came down first on the train from London with Breon, Niall and Helen, the nanny who helped Eileen look after Niall. Breon had to start the term at school. Breon remembered the red earth of south-west Devon as he looked out of the train window as they approached Exeter. They all stayed with the Markhams at The Lodge on the Dartington Estate. Les Markham was the market gardener on the Estate and grew all the vegetables. Eileen was left behind at Battersea to pack the O'Casey belongings and store them with Harrods until they found a new home to rent. A little later Eileen followed on down to Devon and the little Lodge became very full indeed. It was important to get a place of their own so Sean could start work and, hopefully, bring in some money. So, Eileen, helped by the Elmhirsts, looked for a home.

After much searching Eileen found a house to rent on the outside rim of the market town of Totnes, the side nearest to Dartington Hall, that would do as a home and where they were to live for about sixteen years. This house stood solid and firm in front of the Totnes police station, part of a row of similar detached Edwardian houses. Ours was called Tingrith, and was, I suppose, a pompous house, although I always loved it. The front of the house had two sets of bays reaching the two stories, with floor to ceiling windows on the ground floor and the windows upstairs starting about two feet from the floor. The door was on the side through a rather nice old conservatory, with some coloured glass adorning it. The police station, it was said by the tramps who passed our way, did the best breakfast, and many tramps tried to get apprehended for the night.

Eileen had a way with colour and making a house a home: here she made the front room, one of the bay-windowed downstairs rooms, into the "posh room", one that was used only for high days and holidays. When you wanted to play the piano on a cold day, you had to light a very small electric fire to give a pretence of heat; the upright Bechstein stood in there, bought for Eileen from Harrods by a rich friend when she was a chorus girl. In this room Sean and Eileen hung their two Augustus John paintings, one a portrait of Sean given to them by John for a wedding present, the other the most beautiful *Head of a Gitana*: this was hung over the divan and I often lay on the divan and looked at the beautiful face; and this was the one I hated most to part with after Eileen's death, but we had to sell them both to meet her large tax bill that had gathered moss for years to reach a very large amount. Also over a display cabinet full of bits of china was a picture by Adrian Maurice Daintrey, a man who was famous for a while in the 1920s and admired by Shaw, whom Breon thought didn't have great taste in art.[9] Beside the piano was the lithograph of a church by Utrillo. On the wall opposite the fireplace was an oak sideboard and in front if it stood a dining-set from Heal's.[10] The rugs were modern art deco, and so were the glass vases and bowls. Here stood the only radio, a piece of freestanding furniture like a walnut cabinet. This room was where all the "good" furniture and things lived, on hold for holidays and visitors.

The room we all lived in was the kitchen that had an old black cast-iron range that when lit with its coal fire let out a great heat; next to it was the most comfortable chair I have ever sat in, an old stuffed armchair with no legs nestling on the floor. Off the kitchen, through a little hallway where the back stairs went up, was a cold scullery where the cooking was done on a gas stove and with an old butler's sink for washing up in. Eileen usually had a jug of flowers on the kitchen-dresser. What I'm describing are the warmth and colour Eileen brought to a home. With her strong and loving personality and her mistakes at cooking and cleaning and the humour that went alongside this, the home was always busy and exciting. Once when she answered the phone and was asked what she was doing she replied, "Polishing the lavatory seat with pride", Pride being the brand-name of a polish. We laughed about this for years.

As well as the pictures in the front room dotted about the house were prints of Van Gogh, Cezanne, Franz Marc, Gauguin, Van Dongen, Titian, Giorgione and Piero della Francesca, watercolours and charcoal sketches by Evan Walters, a prodigy of John's, including a lovely pastel portrait of Eileen that Sean hung in his room, and two drawings by John.[11] Paintings were the love of them both. Picasso and Braque were also talked about a lot. Sean and Eileen were into modernist design, modernist drama, film and even music when attached to dance. They knew about Diaghilev and had seen the ballet, *Petrushka*; we used to listen to the record they had of

---

[9] Adrian Maurice Daintrey (1902–1988) was an English portrait and landscape painter who studied at the Slade School of Fine Art and was a friend of Augustus John and Rex Whistler; he illustrated Elizabeth David's *Summer Cooking* (1955).

[10] Heal's is a British furniture store founded in 1810 by John Harris Heal.

[11] The Welsh painter Walters (1892–1951) had gained prominence during the General Strike of 1926 with a one-man exhibition in a London Gallery of industrial-themed works.

it.[12] They had seen many of Eisenstein's films and had also seen the Gorky Trilogy.[13]

In London, when Eileen was heavily pregnant with Breon, Sean had taken her over three nights to see Shaw's *Back to Methuselah* at the Royal Court,[14] and after one of the performances she had taken a long time finding her shoes that she had taken off as her feet had swollen, finally finding them near the front row as they had rolled downhill; she couldn't put them on again and walked barefooted for a while. They were both full of these new ideas on how to express art. Sean was a great admirer of James Joyce and in drama was familiar with not only Strindberg and Ibsen but Gogol, Adamov,[15] and other expressionist authors. They had both met Michel St. Denis[16] and knew some of his pupils: Peggy Ashcroft, Laurence Olivier, etc. In Dublin Sean had met Augustus John, and also Gordon Craig who had designed sets for the Abbey Theatre. Sean thought Craig a fine designer and the man who worked with Craig, the musician Martin Shaw, had arranged the Gregorian chants for C.B. Cochran's production in 1928 of Sean's *The Silver Tassie*. Added to all these great people was his love for his friends George Bernard Shaw and Eugene O'Neill, two men seeking to make theatre bolder and more imaginative. But always his bedrock was Shakespeare and the Bible.

Later at Dartington, Sean and Eileen saw performances by the Jooss Ballet and particularly reminisced about *The Green Table*.[17] Shaw had

---

[12] Stravinsky composed the music for Diaghilev's Ballets Russes Company's performance of *Petrushka* (1911).

[13] These were three biographical movies based on Maxim Gorky's three-part autobiography and directed by Mark Donskoy: *The Childhood of Maxim Gorky* (1938), *My Apprenticeship* and *My Universities* (both 1939).

[14] *Back to Methuselah* played at the Royal Court Theatre, London in March 1928; the cast included Ralph Richardson, Edith Evans, Cedric Hardwicke and Laurence Olivier.

[15] Arthur Adamov (1908–1970) was a Russian playwright. Already French-speaking, he moved to Paris at the age of sixteen. As an avant-garde dramatist he was influenced by the work of Strindberg and Kafka and became associated with surrealism and the Theatre of the Absurd.

[16] Michel Saint-Denis (1897–1971), French actor, director and theorist of the drama, arrived in London in 1935 where he started an acting school, the London Theatre Studio. In 1947 he founded the Old Vic Theatre School.

[17] Kurt Jooss (1901–1979) was a German dancer and choreographer whose best-known ballet is *The Green Table* (1932), anti-war in theme, and which premiered in Paris in 1932, The next year Jooss left Germany rather than dismiss the Jewish members of his company. He settled in England where he and Sigurd Leeder opened a dance school at Dartington Hall.

hoped that Sean would get work with Michael Chekhov who had a Drama School at Dartington Hall, mainly there for Beatrice Straight, the daughter of Dorothy Elmhirst (née Whitney) by her first marriage to Willard Straight. "Biddy" Straight became a well known actress in the States and won an Academy Award as best supporting actress for her brief role in *Network* (1976). It didn't take Sean long to realise that it would be impossible to work with Michael Chekhov as his method was to build a play with improvisational work by his students, directed by him, the playwright writing down what they devised: not Sean's idea at all.[18] The Chekhov group sounded as if they were very serious indeed and a little up their own arses. Eileen told me that when they came into Totnes the women wore long practice-skirts and moved in a rather unnatural way. She describes them going into ecstasies over an orange at Mrs Lamson's dairy shop, as she watched in disbelief.

From the beginning of Sean and Eileen's friendship with the Elmhirsts, a dignified distance was forged between Sean's ideas and those of Michael Chekhov. Sean was not in love with Dorothy's philosophy of the drama although he admired and was grateful for the School and was fond of her kindness. He had an attachment to Leonard and his vast knowledge of trees and nature, and they often spoke about this and Sean would send him leaves to identify.

Eileen had always had help of one kind or another. At first in London her theatrical dresser Mrs Earle looked after her; she was like a surrogate mother to Eileen and they were very fond of each other. Eileen was very generous and would give whatever she could to people. Sean said she would give the coat off her back if someone needed it; and sometimes did. She had a large flowing Donegal tweed coat that was made for her when she was pregnant with me. It was her warmest coat for the winter but

---

[18] Beatrice lived in the United States until her mother remarried and established Dartington Hall with her English husband Leonard. From New York she told her mother about Michael Chekhov (1891–1955) whom she saw performing with Russian actors. Chekhov, nephew of the famous Russian playwright, was an actor, theatre director and author. He studied under Stanislavski in Russia before moving to Lithuania and then to England when Dorothy invited him to Dartington Hall in 1935 where he established the Chekhov Theatre School. He moved to the United States four years later and became an influential drama teacher; Beatrice worked with him when she returned to the United States and achieved her popular success; Chekhov, too, found popular success and received an Oscar nomination for his acting in Hitchcock's *Spellbound* (1945). "Beatrice Straight", Dartington Trust October 15, 2019; "Michael Chekhov", Wikipedia.

THE WAR YEARS 1938–1941

anyone she knew who was pregnant ended up in this coat until the baby was born. When the family came to Devon, Helen came down to look after Niall. She had been living with the family in Battersea for about three years and had turned out to be one of the family. She had trained at the Melchett Day Nursery, Chelsea, founded by Lady Violet Melchett, where working-class mothers could leave their babies and toddlers while they went to work. But the cook Ruth also came down; Ruth had arrived when they were at Battersea. She was desperate for work after she had been asked to leave her previous post as she was "getting on". Eileen and Sean felt sorry for her and took her on. She was a stickler for formality, having morning and afternoon uniforms that she insisted on wearing. I think Eileen was a bit afraid of her and so when she insisted on coming down to Devon, down she came, even after Eileen said they really couldn't afford to pay her. She stayed for a while but the "bohemian" informality of this new place was too much, and she missed London, so she left in a bit of a huff.

The furniture arrived from Battersea in a Harrod's van, and a home was made. There was a rough routine in our family. Even during the war, my father provided the steady dignity of an orderly worker's life while my mother disrupted this structure, giving it an uncertainty and passion. But by the time the family had truly settled in and were getting to know their new surroundings, the threat of war stuck its head over the Devon hills.

THE WAR STARTS FOR REAL

On September 1, 1939, Germany had invaded Poland. On September 3, Britain declared war on Germany. The blackout started two days before war began. Children were evacuated on December 3, 1939. A terrible danger was sweeping everyone up in a whirlwind of activity, changing lives and altering the ordered way of things. After I was born in late September, a letter came to my parents from Shaw.

4th October 1939

My dear Eileen,
It is important for the boys to have a sister. Sisterless men are always afraid of women.

    I enclose a birthday present for her. The next one will only be half-a-crown. The budget, oh, the budget. The end of the year will clean me out.

We take it you are doing as well as can be expected.
G. Bernard Shaw[19]

Another letter came from Sean's publisher.

October 5th 1939

Dear Eileen,

I was so glad to get your letter and its very exciting news. I congratulate you – If your daughter is born into a temporarily unhappy time, I am confident that she will grow up in a better age, which I believe will succeed these horrors and follies which now seem terrible.

I am so glad to hear that you are both well. I am sure Sean will be delighted with his baby.

I wonder whether any time you will be coming to London. Do let me know if you do; and tell Sean to let me know if he is ever to be up and come and see me.

We have handed over our house at Birch Grove for a nursery school. We already have 40 children and are expecting 60 more. We shall move into one of the cottages ourselves. My daughters are at school and my Sarah at home. Maurice is in the Field Artillery to which the Sussex Yeomanry have been converted – and is stationed at Brighton. This is quite nice for us, for he can get home alternate Sundays to see us. I hope they will be there for some time yet before going to France.[20]

For myself, I am at present looking after the business, as well as going to the H of C. [House of Commons.] I am trying to get back to the Grenadiers, but am not wanted at present.

Well – this is a boring letter, all about ourselves – so I will end as I began, with all familiar good wishes to you and your family, with a special extra blessing for the baby.

Yours
Harold Macmillan[21]

---

[19] Eileen O'Casey, *Cheerio, Titan: The Friendship between George Bernard Shaw, Sean O'Casey and Eileen O'Casey* (1989; New York: Scribner, 1989), p. 105.

[20] Harold Macmillan's only son Maurice served in the Second World War; after the war he was a Conservative MP and chairman of Macmillan Publishers.

[21] This letter is with Eileen's letters in the National Library of Ireland; her daughter Shivaun has a copy.

Sean replied:

22 Oct 1939

Dear Mr. Harold,

... Yes, we have another member of the family, a girl this time, – another blessing, yes; but another burden too.

I am buried down here, and I'm afraid I must remain buried, for it takes a lot of money to be able to go from place to place. Willy nilly, we must stay here till our lease is up, and then, well one place seems as good as another. Anyway, with six kids in the house, now, one has a lot to do for oneself.

But the war wont last as long as the lease. It darent. Neither side can win. They can only hope to destroy each other. The thing is futile. The young will be destroyed again. But they are asking questions at last. Three of them from Exeter college were with me yesterday – one, just joined the army, from Clonakilty, in Cork. I tried to tell them what I thought of everything. If the damned fools that rule only planned in peace as they try to plan in war, things would be better, for sooner or later the fools would be thrown out – liquidated, if you like –, and the able would take their place. And it is far more important to plan in peace than it is to plan in war.

I'm sure you and Lady Dorothy will be happy in a cottage. You and she, I think, are Communists in heart. She and you must be anxious about your son. Sons, sons, sons of guns, literally. The young, the young, if England can spare them, life can't.

With sincere affectionate regards to you and all
Sean O'Casey[22]

On Eileen's arrival back home with me bundled in her arms, she found Breon and Niall and three evacuees, Doris, Zoe and Bobby, all spruced up. Although Breon told me that he and Niall weren't very interested in babies then, they were curious to see what I was like. Helen was making a fresh pot of tea; a spread was laid out on the kitchen table to celebrate Eileen's return with her curly-headed baby. Sean joined us all and I,

[22] *The Letters of Sean O'Casey, Volume I:1910–1941*, ed. David Krause (London: Cassell, 1975), pp. 819–820.

bundled up, was passed around or deposited like a parcel to different arms, different faces.

The three evacuees billeted on Sean and Eileen were of the children moved from East Anglia and the Home Counties on September 3. Doris at twelve years old helped to look after her little sister Zoe, aged five, and Bobby who was only three. They were from a poor family as many of the evacuees were and were "riddled with lice" according to Eileen. But Helen was well able to cope with this, as at the Melchett Nursery she had looked after children from poor and sometimes disturbed families, some of whom had been physically abused, and lice were no strangers to her. Sean was unruffled as he had seen it all before among the poor of Dublin.

In the recording I made with him in 2009 Breon said, "Bobby was a little simple, poor thing. He used to wet his bed every night. Eileen used to have to help him, wake him up and make him go to the lavatory and then tuck him up in bed again. ... When he arrived he had a suppurating sore in his ear that Dr. Varian, our friend and doctor, said was most likely damage due to a hefty thump – several thumps."

Eileen's mother, Kathleen Reynolds – Grannie – had wangled her way down to Torquay to convalesce just before I was born and was a hefty burden on Eileen. She was full of exaggerated ailments most likely made worse by the drink. Once down in Devon, and near Eileen, she decided to stay, especially when war was declared. Eileen wrote in a letter to her friend Mina: "Am having a little bother just now to find a suitable place for my mother, she will have to come here Sat for a few days while I search around Paignton or Torquay. I dread her staying as she and Sean don't hit it off at all."[23]

The bombing in Plymouth started on July 6, 1940 and ended April 30, 1944. As the bombing stopped in the south-east (mainly raids on RAF airfields and radar stations), the evacuees went back home. But Hitler hadn't given up on his Blitzkrieg and in the early part of June 1940, prior to The Battle of Britain, a second evacuation took place and over 160,000 school children were sent from London and south-east England to the "safe" areas in the south-west, the Midlands and Wales. Eileen pleaded

[23] Mina Schoeneman (1892–1974), born in Chicago, was a socialist. She met and married Jack Carney in the United States to where Carney had emigrated in 1916. Mina became politically active alongside her husband and was secretary of the James Larkin defence committee after Larkin was indicted and imprisoned in the U.S. on charges of criminal anarchy. See the Royal Irish Academy's online Dictionary of Irish Biography, s.v. "Carney, John ('Jack')".

that Sean had to work in order to bring in some money, and so they were given only one evacuee, this time called Peter Doughty who was the same age as Breon.

I don't remember the first three evacuees and I only remember Peter vaguely, but after the war he visited Totnes and we used to see him on the local bus. He had big blue eyes and curly blond hair. Eileen explained that he had lived with us for a while and she felt sorry for him as his mother had wanted a girl and dressed him in dresses and bows until he went to school and was evidently very protective of him and frequently rang to find out how he was. Breon didn't care for Peter: "He was billeted on us because he liked the theatre and they thought it would be good for him to be with a theatrical family."

Living in digs and convents as a child, Eileen's main meal had been provided, the washing done and rooms cleaned. This hadn't spoiled her and she didn't mind laying grates and scrubbing floors if she had to. Sean was a better cook than her, being able to boil an egg and cook a reasonable stew, but they both had a disaster the first time they roasted a chicken: it got bigger and bigger and looked wonderful but when they cut into it the smell was terrible: they hadn't known to clean out the innards before cooking it. After that all the chickens tasted and smelled good.

My early memories are like snapshots that you find in a muddle in a box and you have no idea what went before or came after, but the incident remains fixed and vivid in your mind. One is of being bundled in a dark pink eiderdown held close in my mum's arms: being squeezed under the kitchen table together with I presume Niall, Breon, the evacuee Peter and Helen: crouched and huddled. I remember panicked voices and my mum and dad speaking steadily, soothingly, and being hugged close by my mum's protective arms. I remember from under the table seeing my dad's legs walking up and down and then his smiling face bending in and smiling – "Peek-a-boo". Another memory is of a mad rush down the stairs with the screech of the siren going, I was in someone's arms, and we all dashed as one, sliding and jumping to get to the cellar: noise, lots of noise.

I understand that the kitchen table was deemed not strong enough to protect a fly. Sean and Eileen decided to try the cellar below the kitchen. The outside granite steps that led down to it were a death trap at the best of times and so they had a trapdoor made in the kitchen floor that pulled up to reveal some newly made wooden steps; the last down would pull the hatch closed. Breon remembered the first time we all clambered down into the damp black space: very damp and also cold. Eileen had tried to make it comfortable with a bit of carpet and some chairs but it was all mouldy. Breon remembered: "We heard these footsteps in the house and we all froze thinking it was a German, a spy maybe, and we all kept terribly quite. Then the trap door opened slowly – Cor! We all gasped; but it was Lesley Ramsden [a neighbour] doing his round as one of the Home-guard, saying 'Are you all right down there?'"

Letters were returned to me in the early 2000s that Eileen and Breon (and occasionally Niall) had written to Mina and Jack Carney. Jack met Sean during the Dublin Lockout 1913–1914. He was thin and alert, clever and amusing with a nervous side to him. Jack had come to London and was now a freelance journalist and he and Sean had remained in close touch.[24] Mina was a sculptress. We had her bronze bust of Jim Larkin for a while but Sean didn't feel it did him justice.[25] Mina was a small stout, upright lady, who walked with her head aloft and chest out; an open inquiring face with her hair scraped severely back into a tight bun. She had a soft brown-coloured skin.

I have chosen some of the letters to give an idea of what Eileen had to do to keep the household going, also Breon's letters that give his take on our family during that time. Mina and Jack were called uncle and auntie by me, and Mina made clothes for my doll Daffodil Rose and made a toy for me, Dumbo the elephant. Once when we visited them after the war, when she brought in my doll all newly dressed, mummy and I were sitting having tea on a divan when they let out their canary, Mickey. Mickey was like their child, they adored him; he came on to my head and started pecking it. "Isn't he sweet?" cried Mina. I didn't think so and had a hard time, with Eileen looking knowingly at me, urging me to pretend I loved

---

[24] Jack Carney (1887–1956) was born in Dublin but raised in Liverpool after being orphaned. He became a socialist after hearing Larkin and moved to Dublin to join the Irish Transport and General Workers' Union. In the U.S. he worked with Larkin and his radicalism brought him a prison sentence for criminal syndicalism, though he was pardoned after ten days. When Larkin, too, was pardoned and returned to Dublin, Carney followed. He broke with Larkin when the Workers' Union of Ireland, of which Jack was an official, forbade him to denounce General Franco on its public platforms, allegedly under the influence of the Irish Catholic Church. Carney then moved to London from where he maintained his friendship with Sean.

[25] Mina Carney's bronze bust of James Larkin is in the Hugh Lane Municipal Gallery of Modern Art in Dublin; Christopher Murray includes a photograph of the bust in his biography, *Seán O'Casey: Writer at Work* (Dublin: Gill & Macmillan, 2004).

being pecked. I was also made to hold him on my hand and he pecked that as well. I never wanted a tame bird after that.

Eileen started her wartime letters to Mina just before Christmas 1939. I would have been three months old and she was still breast-feeding me, something she did until I was six months. Mina was a brilliant seamstress and when rationing kicked in and money became short she offered to make clothes for me and some for the boys. Jack and Mina also sent sweets and jellies and tobacco for Sean. In return, Eileen sent them chickens, ducks, "breakables" (eggs), fresh vegetables and sometimes "smokes" (cigarettes). Eileen didn't save any of Mina or Jack's letters to her so I don't know exactly what they said but it is a common theme in Eileen's letters to apologise for not replying sooner; Mina and Jack seemed to expect a speedy response. Mina most likely couldn't comprehend the amount of work children and particularly a baby entailed. For one thing the washing of the nappies. In those days terry-towel nappies were used with sometimes a muslin nappy inside, both held together with a large safety pin. No washing machines, no dryers – just a soaking and a washing by hand in a large metal tub and a washboard to rub the clothes against to get rid of the stains, then the rinsing and the wringing. Standing near the back-door was a hefty mangle and the wet washing was fed through, coming out the other side flat and almost dry. Then it all had to be hung on the clothesline to flap in the breeze or madly dance in the wind, all the colours looking like gay flags. There was a lot for Eileen to do even with help. Sean was good at tirelessly holding me and lulling me, especially at night. In the winter the fire had to be kept going in the kitchen, shopping and cooking done for the family and evacuees. On top of this, Eileen was involved with the evacuees at Dartington and helped Sean with his letters and work.

November 1939

My dearest Mina,

Please forgive us all at Tingrith. The dress was so lovely it really was beautiful. I have meant to write last evening; but Nannie was still away, and I have been on the go all day and Shivaun is cutting a tooth & I had some bad nights … Sean has had a nasty cold as well. Dear Mina always please know I am deeply grateful for anything you do, I am anything but careless in my thoughts and feelings, but my letter writing has always been my weakness … Well we have had rain rain and more rain, but now lovely sun. L.K. [Leonard Elmhirst] is back. ... Nannie returns on Weds. I shall really hate giving Shivaun back, it's just the time; but I do love to be with her and of course I don't do much for Sean when I have her. ... Breon wrote enclosed days & days ago & I was supposed to post it. He is thrilled to death with the plane.

Now I'll write next week with news this is just to say Thanks again and again.

My love Eileen

Just before this, Jack gave Breon a small film projector and some short clips of film.

The projector came out at every party and celebration. At birthday parties it caused huge excitement: laughter and screams of delight as we watched Charlie Chaplin eat his boot or best of all, the mayhem of the Keystone Cops.

There was a small picturehouse, "the Cinema", in Totnes. When they had newly moved into Tingrith Eileen sent Breon off to the pictures. He was used to London cinemas and so when he was lined up along a wall with the other children hoping to get in he got very apprehensive, and when the owner of the cinema then proceeded to check each child's set of teeth he thought about going home. One of the kids told him that the owner could tell your age from your teeth and see if you were allowed to see the film on show without an adult. Then he went to pay at the little kiosk and bought the pricier ticket in the balcony. There was a hush and then a great commotion. He was asked to wait and then was ushered up to find that he was the only person up there and his seat was right next to the projector. The balcony was very dusty except for the seat dusted for him that was obviously never used and the whirr from the projector was deafening.

Summer 1940

Mina dearest,

How are you? Are you well? I have meant to write but I seem on the go all the time & the children are home now. I am going to go and live in a tent with Breon & Niall for a week on Tues. week. Bardie [Bardi Tyrrell, a friend] has a caravan, & it will be a change from this for

them. Hope it doesn't rain. I expect I'll look like Mrs Rip Van Winkle.
...
I sold my coat & was diddled, still it's done now to hell! My God I wish I kept money when I have it, but I never think until it's dwindled!!
Sean's book 'Pictures In the Hallway' to follow 'I Knock at the Door' is great & goes into his early manhood. You'll love it. ...[26]
Eileen

Mina Dearest,

We didn't go yet as the weather delayed Bardie; so we hope to go someday soon. ...
The children had good reports from school, Breon is working harder & Niall's was fine. I am sending one of Shaw [signed postcard] if you can sell it. I don't like to worry you with two; but I'd be glad if you sold it. Things will straighten out in a few months I am sure; so long as Sean doesn't really worry; he is writing again actually & his proofs are coming in, so we are busy. ...
Bless you & love to Jack.
Love from Sean & the children
Eileen

My dear Mina,

We have been here nearly a week, the weather was wet and we had sea fogs the first two days. But now its glorious. Breon, Niall and I share a tent and do all our own cooking, its grand fun: we have the two Meths stoves. I have a camp bed and the boys sleep on the ground. They are out all day from after breakfast and eat like hunters and sleep like logs. ... Sean is at home with Nannie and Shivaun and Peter [Doughty] is home again he went to London for a holiday. Sean's proofs are in now, and I like to be home to help him, but it was now or never to give the children the holiday. ... I do miss Shivaun. Now Mina maybe we will see you sometime. The war news isn't too good do you think? I think the R's [Russians] will end up on the right side, but the awful loss of life & crops. ... My love to Jack. Breon is so thrilled and excited over the planes.

[26] *I Knock at the Door* (1939) was Sean's first volume of autobiography; *Pictures in the Hallway* followed in 1942.

My love dear
Eileen.

The War went on overhead. "I can remember looking out of the window one morning," Breon said, "You know getting up early and a beautiful sun-rise. As I was leaning, you know how there was a ledge as you leant out of the window, there was an exercise and there was a Lysander flying across. A Lysander was a smallish kind of plane, they used to call them the conservatories because they had quite a big cock-pit on top.[27] They were used for carrying really; officers and things. And then a Hurricane coming alongside it, and somehow they had got too near and slipped into each other – and just their wings tipped and the whole top of the Lysander just came off and went phumff down. The Hurricane limped along with one wing and then it went down – and there were two of these great plumes of black smoke - and no sound. Not a sound. … But it was so surreal you know. It was so quick. Phaff."

By the end of 1940 Hitler decided to bomb the population of England into fear-stricken submission. The siren meant panic, the all-clear meant relief. Breon chuckles at the memory – "At the start of the war the chap designated to blow the Totnes siren had a wooden leg. The first call came to sound the siren and he answered the phone that lived downstairs and the Siren was fixed onto his roof. 'Blow the siren!' they commanded, 'Right you are!' he replied. But he had to screw on his leg before he could climb the stairs to set it off. So by the time he got to the handle all the other towns were sounding the All Clear. So off our Siren went as everyone was climbing out of their dugouts. Unbelievable! But the war was comically mad as well as horrific."

Tingrith fronted on to the main road from Totnes to Plymouth. The big double deckers passed by our gate and now they were joined by British army vehicles speeding by full of supplies and men. Eileen told me they were billeted everywhere, in tents on the Totnes playing fields, up the drive to the Hall and many fields around and about. Sean often walked about the camp in the Totnes Park talking to the squaddies and later Sean was to walk among the tents of the GIs talking to them about their faraway homes. They were all very nervous and anxious of what lay ahead of them.

[27] The Westland Lysander entered service in 1938 and was used as a spotter and light bomber; it was also useful in rescue missions to retrieve downed air crew in enemy territory.

1941

For all their friends in London it was a terror time, from September 1940 to May 1941, more than eight long months. Hitler pummelled and shattered London. On December 29 Hitler hit St. Paul's and Jack and Mina were bombed out of their home. Sean in writing to Harold Macmillan's brother Daniel on January 12 told him: "Two of my friends had an extraordinary escape. They live (or lived) in St Paul's Churchyard, and had to pass through miles of flame before they reached safe standing. ..."²⁸ Jack and Mina found a flat on Finchley Road, London NW3.

Eileen's letter to Mina and Jack:

7 January 1941

Mina and Jack,

Please forgive me for not writing sooner. ... Niall had his party on Saturday ... and was there some <u>row</u> and some fun! Your cake had seven candles, and we made the jellies & the choc. biscuits & before they went I produced the large bottle of sweets. ... [Shivaun] loved the balloons we blew them all up & made a great enormous bunch in the centre of the room, & each had one when they went; but of course the ones with the pictures on were in demand. Niall said in bed, "I've had a really lovely birthday"; and of course he was delighted with the golden envelope the telegram arrived in.

Now for news Sean is writing the article on Lady Gregory for the Times man,²⁹ and the P[lough] & Stars is to go on in the Abbey they haven't done a play of Sean's for ages.³⁰ Harry Pollitt spoke in Newton [Abbot] & came & had tea here first, he's nice and direct I like him; he got an enormous crowd for Newton, he got £30 my little effort made £11.3.0, not too bad for such a small place, mostly small ones like 3d

---

²⁸ *The Letters of Sean O'Casey, Volume I*, p. 875.
²⁹ See footnote 7 in Chapter 2.
³⁰ The response to the first production of *The Plough and the Stars* may have been famously riotous, but the Abbey Theatre re-staged the play every year from 1926 to 1939. In all, there were more than twenty-five separate Abbey productions, on site or on tour, between 1926 and 1964, the year of Sean's death. See: https://www.abbeytheatre.ie/archives/play_detail/11029/

and 1d's.³¹ Well Jack & Min I don't seem to have really seen much of you, still when you come next it will be nice weather & we'll go to the sea; & do some grand trips. Peter our evac. has gone to London for good now, he came back & then he didn't seem able to face Grammar School again & he wanted to study Drama and Education, so after two days of worrying himself silly as to whether to go or stay, he has gone.³² He'll be happier really he's not a country boy at all & time hangs so if you don't like the country; and there is no hope of studying drama down here. It's a relief really. …
I do hope you both come again as soon as you can.
My love to you both Eileen

Something Eileen said or did upset Jack; it can't just be that she didn't send his hanky back quickly enough (see below). Maybe it was the workload she was giving Mina. I think he felt she was spoiling us children sending us to an expensive school they could little afford. Eileen was beautiful, carefree and also a caring mother, who fought her corner when she had to as her letter to Jack Carney shows.³³

31 Born in Lancashire, Harry Pollitt (1890–1960), a boilermaker by trade, joined the Communist Party of Great Britain, rising to become General Secretary, 1929–1956, and Chairman, 1956 until his death. He was a convinced Stalinist to the end; the Soviet Navy named a ship after him. In 1936 Pollitt's visit to Dublin provoked a riot after members of the Catholic Young Men's Society protested and fighting broke out in Rathmines Town Hall. Pollitt defiantly spoke, as did Jim Larkin Jr. See Donal, "Flying fists, pokers and chairs. Harry Pollitt's visit to Rathmines", Come here to me! Dublin Life & Culture January 6, 2016: https://comeheretome.com/2016/01/06/flying-fists-pokers-and-chairs-harry-pollitts-visit-to-rathmines/ Also: "Harry Pollitt", Wikipedia. Thirteen years later at Dartmouth in Devon during the Cold War, Pollitt was given a welcome of hurled fruit and eggs and retreated to Totnes where he was to talk at Dartington Village Hall; in the local newspaper, Sean, reported to be too ill to be interviewed, is identified as being on the Editorial Board of the *Daily Worker*: see *Torbay Express and South Devon Echo*, April 23, 1949. Before Pollitt's 1940 visit with him, Sean had published a review of Pollitt's *Serving My Time: An Apprenticeship to Politics* in *Labour Monthly*, May 1940. See Ronald Ayling and Michael J. Durkan, *Sean O'Casey: A Bibliography* (London: Macmillan, 1978), p. 216.
32 It is possible that this is Peter Doughty the actor who acted in the BBC TV series *Now Barabbas* (1949), *Robin Hood* (1953) and BBC Sunday Night Theatre (1958) and appeared at the Theatre Royal, Stratford in *Macbeth* in 1957; see "Peter Doughty" IMDb.
33 It was said of Carney that he was "a born rebel … who seeks instinctively the center of every row" (Quoted by Lawrence White in his entry for Carney in the online Dictionary of Irish Biography: https://www.dib.ie/biography/carney-john-jack-a1487)

THE WAR YEARS 1938–1941

July 1941

My Dear Jack,
Now please what do you mean by your attack of sarcasm on me. Please spill the beans if you're feeling sore about me, I did say I was busy when Nannie was away, I was; and to hell with who makes fun, I did say Sean had a cold and if I choose to wipe his nose for him as you so kindly suggested well that's my business, not knowing Sean he is hard to keep in one room with a temperature much else attend much on him. So if you have any ill feelings over my not writing to you let's have it out & we might as well fight and be friends. ... Now Jack for news, thank Mina for the sweets they were lovely & I will send the money in my letter to Mina, also your hanky with the initial I have and will not dream of using I'll post it, God you've really got a knife ready for me – hate me like poison! The dresses are really lovely & Shivaun is getting nicer than ever. Jack we are now in rather a thin patch I knew it was coming. ... Breon is sending you the Shaw picture, he'll have to sell them to buy a winter outfit!!* Niall & Breon & Shivaun are so well & the weather's grand I wish you were here.

I am writing to Mina & whether I write or not I love you just the same. All the best. Don't work too hard. ...
Give my love to Mina. Eileen

* Shaw sent Breon a bunch of photo-cards of himself, signed, for Breon to sell.

Things must have resolved themselves because they all remained friends. That is, until long after the war when Sean upset Jack saying he couldn't sign a book for a friend of his who had done something he considered unforgivable.

Things were hotting up down our way, too, as the Nazi planes flew in their masses to bomb the hell out of Plymouth. In the same letter to Daniel Macmillan on January 12, Sean wrote: "Last night we were shaken to a degree by a great explosion caused (it is said) by a land mine dropped in the Town." [34]

[34] *The Letters of Sean O'Casey, Volume I*, p. 875.

Spring of 1941 was very busy for the family. At last they decided to get a Morrison Shelter and put it in the downstairs room,[35] empty now their evacuee Peter Doughty had decided to go back to London to study drama. Sean had always thought the cellar a death trap for all of us, not only because of the cold and damp but also the precarious steps down and the floor would have most likely fallen in with the house on top of us. The Morrison Shelter arrived; a steel cage was erected it was about as high as a table and it was put in the small room off the Hall and it took up practically the whole room. It could only hold Niall, Eileen and me as the area inside if covered in rubble would only hold enough oxygen for three, so Breon and Sean had to stay outside sitting on stairs near us or walking about, depending how long the raid took. If no aircraft was heard Breon often went back to bed before the All Clear sounded and later often slept through raids, only leaping out of bed and down the stairs if a bomb landed close by and shook the house.

I loved being woken up in the night to play in the shelter. "Houses" was the favoured game, also played during the day. Niall was petrified, imagining all sorts of horrors, while I was unaware of any danger at all. The boys and Sean could tell the different type of aeroplanes overhead by the sound of their engines; when it was a German plane all became quiet, and if I chatted during this intense listening Mummy would hush me up as all eyes looked upward as they listened, as if they could see through the ceiling to the sky with the planes flying overhead and the spotlights following them. When the All Clear sounded Sean went immediately to boil the kettle to make a pot of tea and all the family sat around the kitchen table sipping the sweet tea, comforting and calming themselves with each sip and recovering their ragged nerves.

Many nights were spent snuggled amongst the pillows and blankets in our steel house. I tried to play games with Niall but Niall couldn't relax, he was rigid with anxiety telling me gently but firmly to be quiet and stay still and asking Eileen to shut me up. So Eileen would tell stories and sing songs until (for Niall's sake) I hope I often fell to sleep. I am sure Niall never fell asleep until he was back safe in his bed.

During these times, local people were being bombed and slaughtered a few miles away in Plymouth, and many made homeless and orphaned,

---

[35] The air-raid shelter, introduced in March 1941 and named after the Home Secretary Herbert Morrison, was a wire-sided, steel indoor cage (6'6"x4'x2'6") for sleeping or crouching in and meant to offer safety from bomb debris.

filling hospital wards. To Breon "Plymouth was like a firework display. And the search lights – and they'd catch a German plane in their beam and it would be dodging about and the other searchlight would go on it. They must have been so scared inside that plane of course. I remember going to Plymouth and seeing all these burnt out buses on the way in and lorries, parked on the sides of the road. – Funny enough when I came back from school, I used to cycle back, you heard the German planes, they had a different sound to the English planes, 'Errrr', and if you were cycling back in the countryside you felt no fear because it was most unlikely of a bomb dropping on you. But, as soon as you were in the house you felt frightened, as if it was all going to come in on top of you. Strange that."

In Torquay and Paignton you saw the wounded soldiers and RAF pilots wheeled about or being helped to walk. I played on regardless, thinking all the worry and anxiety and the scrambles to our shelter were normal. Sean was preparing for an invasion by Hitler and had it all planned out. He knew he stood little chance if he was caught, in his mind he would be shot or imprisoned, because of his far left views, and us alongside him. So, we were to fill my grand pram with what we needed and push it, alongside others, carrying what we all could on our backs all the way to the moors, wet and windy and unrelenting Dartmoor. In the wilderness with the Dartmoor ponies and sturdy little cows and sometimes sheep.

Eileen's letter to Mina:

April 25 [1941]

Dear Mina,

The trousers are lovely, the blue ones are right the green long but otherwise O.K. The blue are cute & will be lovely with just nothing else on her in the summer. Both garments are lovely; You really are clever. …

Things look rather grim I think, don't you feel somehow the G's [Germans] are getting up steam again. Wouldn't it be grand if it were over & we could start rebuilding a new type of life & not this dreadful bloodshed & disfigurement of men & youths. I hate seeing these young airforce boys in Torquay who are wounded; they look such boys.

Well dear only five weeks now until we see you both.

My love as ever

Eileen.

Breon recalled the ridiculous side of war: "Lesley Ramsden had this little factory where he mended car radiators and such like; he had welding gear and all that. The Home-guards had this little Austin they wanted to make into an armoured car to protect them if they had to fight the Germans when they invaded. You'd see pictures of this armoured car in the *Totnes Times*, Mr Ramsden standing there beside it with his torch – GETTING ON WITH THE ARMOURED CAR. Then suddenly there was silence. Well, you know what Sean was like he was curious about most things but he was intensely interested in this. 'Mr Ramsden what's going on with your armoured car? Come tell me.' Eventually he got it out of him that they had taken the completed armoured car to the firing range and fired a rifle at it and the bullet had gone in one side and out the other. So that was a disappointment."

Eileen's letters to Mina:

[Spring 1941]

My dear Mina,

Please can you lend me £5. I can promise to return it middle of Sept. I have to pay for my caravan hire in advance & Sean really had better not be bothered. I am going to take Niall & Shivaun & Breon is coming on when he finishes his work for a bit & help me. We go next Friday for 2 or 3 weeks. I am sure its better to get the children away for a short time, the rush & the noise are rather a lot all the time & Sean must work. I have arranged for his meals & Breon will be with him half of the time. If you can't manage the money don't worry send a note & say so & I'll borrow it somehow. I'll write from the caravan. The children are very good really. Shivaun is getting to help with the dishes (slow motion) now, she lays the table very well: she is really very sweet & worth it all. Nannie is to learn to drive, she will love it.

My love dear. Love to Jack
Eileen

Mina dear,

I have worried over the letter I wrote & really must be crazy to ask you such a thing, when I think it over how can you more than I afford or manage to ask friends of ours for loans for me. It will all straighten out don't worry. Actually I worry too much in case Sean knows we are in a muddle, & exaggerate in panic when I get the demands for bills I owe; but dearest I'll ward them off & please forget it. Bless you both you will think I am really quite beyond all to ask such a thing. If I am really jammed I'll pluck up courage & ask a person I know for some. Well dear we are all very well. Sean is better, and his neck dried up I am going to try to persuade him to have treatment in a week or so.

Much love to you both Eileen.

Sean's neck had been operated on to remove tubercular glands in Dublin during the time the wounded soldiers from the First World War were being treated. Big Jim Larkin had got him into a Catholic hospital that held beds for the General Workers' Trade Union: an experience he used for his anti-war play *The Silver Tassie*. Now and again his neck wounds suppurated.

Mina dearest,

Thank you very much not only for the loan, but for the very kind and lovely way it was lent. I have taken it, as I feel it better to try & ward off trouble for the moment. I will see you have it without fail before Jan 1st I hope sooner. Should you need it though do tell me. It won't mean you can't come & stay with us will it, because I should hate that. I know Sean would be quite upset if he knew I had asked you such a thing, still let's hope one day I'll be able to do the same for you. ...

I send Shivaun's [coupon] book & also some Viyella for a winter dress, & also an old evening slip of mine which may save buying lining. I have also sent you the empty tin for sweets. But I feel you are really very kind over it all and don't really know how to thank you.

Our love to you & Jack. Sean is writing to Jack.

Best love Eileen

We had our holiday in a little caravan in a field of long grass on Dartmoor. There was rather a nervous drive up to the field with Eileen getting hopelessly lost as all the signposts were taken down for fear of a German invasion. We finally got there with the help of the locals. I loved the little house on wheels, the fresh smelling grass as it waved about in the wind, going for eggs and milk every morning from the farm house and sometimes a little bacon – no coupons needed. Feeding the chickens – cluck, cluck, cluck. Playing soldiers with Niall in the long jungle grass.

Summer also meant swimming at Goodrington beach, considered reasonably safe from mines and strafing from German planes. I loved the sea and Breon had taught me to swim under water, so I could swim when I could toddle. Then the leaves began to fall. Breon came back from a holiday with Jack and Mina with presents for Niall as well as me, and the school term was to begin.

Eileen's letter to Jack and Mina:

My dear Jack & Min,

Breon had a lovely time, & loved Mickey [The Canary] and Oscar [Kokoschka]!![36]

Shivaun's sweets & pinafore were lovely, the cake we had a birthday tea yesterday & it looked glorious, all lit up, we drew the curtains & Shivaun was absolutely delighted with the birthday cake. Breon really didn't want us to blow the candles out, but he didn't let on; it all tasted good – it was a grand present. ...

Totnes had a small raid on Thurs last, the noise was terrific & it really was lucky it wasn't us, the block of houses by Shinners Bridge got it badly, no one was hurt badly. Niall & Shivaun were very good; Niall was chatting away in a very quivering voice. Shivaun just said not to go out, and was very quiet and good. ... When are you coming down to us?

Mina I send a coat; do you think anyone would buy it; its rather a nice one – its in a separate parcel? I leave the price to you do you think £2 too much?

... I enclose a note from Breon Sean is writing.

Well my love to you both, and thank you so much.
Eileen

In October of 1940 Sean had signed a contract for *Purple Dust* to be staged in New York and also signed the English rights. So now it was going ahead or so they thought.

---

[36] Mina Carney hosted a salon in London attended by leftist artists and writers. These included Oskar Kokoschka (1886–1980) who had fled Austria in 1934, having been denounced as a degenerate by the Nazis. He settled in Cornwall and during the war produced anti-fascist paintings.

THE WAR YEARS 1938-1941

Eileen's letter to Mina and Jack:

September 28 1941.

My dear Mina & Jack,

Have meant to write earlier on in the week, we have heard the play [*Purple Dust*] is to go on & it is pre advertised in New York papers, so we are pleased. Sean has had Flu, he has been in bed all week, but is up & better today. I think he wrote Jack today, he likes to get letters from Jack he always has something to say original. Nathan has written Sean in great hopes over the play, all the letters we should have got must have gone down.[37] The children return to school to-morrow, Niall goes up a class also Breon. ... Breon has gone off to meet the train with the boarders & go on up with them all to-night & have a chat. I met Kay again & she seems very cheery, I was with Shivaun & Niall.[38] Shivaun is learning Jack & Jill & I said to her the other morning, do you remember Jack & Mina? & she said "poor Jack & Min all fall down the hill." Niall laughed & said no Jack & Jill; & Shivaun said "Yes, Shivaun knows they all fall down." She's sweet now. Well there isn't much news, my love to Jack. The war news doesn't sound too good but of course we don't get it all, oh I do hope the Russians pull through, but they have a tough job, & seem to be pushed back so latterly.

Bless you. My love to you both.
Eileen

---

[37] Presumably Eileen means that the letters were lost when a mail steamer was sunk on its voyage to Britain. The distinguished American critic and editor George Jean Nathan (1882–1958) wrote Sean on September 9, 1940 about the plan to produce *Purple Dust* in New York after *The Time of Your Life*, a play by William Saroyan, ended its run. On August 25, 1941 Nathan wrote Sean that production plans were proceeding and Nathan had already published testimonials to the play: *My Very Dear Sean: George Jean Nathan to Sean O'Casey, Letters and Articles*, eds. Robert G. Lowery and Patricia Angelin (Rutherford et al.,: Associated University Presses, 1985), pp. 56, 57.

[38] Kay Starr, Leonard Elmhirst's secretary and Mina's close friend. She worked for the Labour Party before being appointed at Dartington Hall in 1928. She was active in the art scene; Oskar Kokoschka painted her portrait. She died in 1976. See: https://www.dartington.org/kay-starr/

But in February of 1942, the producer/director, Eddie Dowling had to give up all thoughts of doing *Purple Dust*. This was a blow to them both as by then things were getting very tight indeed.[39]

---

[39] Eddie Dowling (1894–1976) was an actor, author and producer. Nathan spoke with him while production plans were afoot. Nathan in a letter to Sean of April 3, 1942 reports Dowling's "serious illness": *My Very Dear Sean*, p.58.

2
The War Years
1942–1945

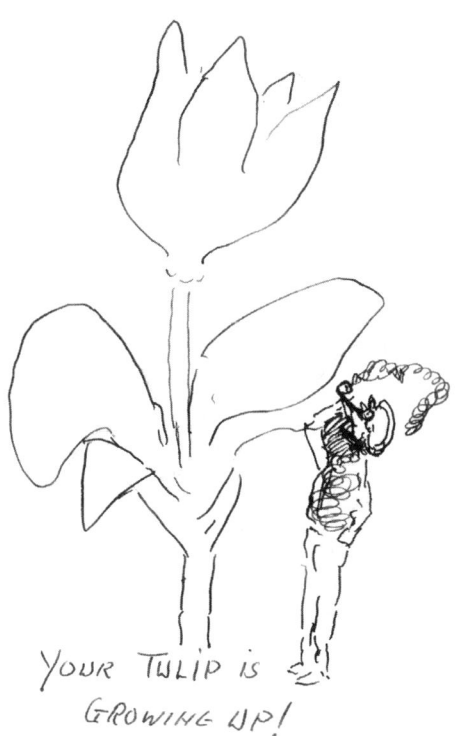

THE WAR GETS CLOSER TO HOME

Niall's birthday on January 15, 1942. He is seven. Each of his birthdays heralded a New Year for us. Sean had helped Eileen start a Committee of the Anglo-Soviet Alliance in Totnes as he thought there was still a lot of half-hidden, quiet enmity to the USSR. Part of its function was to send books to Russia. A shop was planned and Eileen began to collect things for sale: profits from The Russian Shop were to go to the USSR Medical Fund.[1]

Eileen's letter to Jack:

My dear Jack,

… We are having our ceilings done just now, we had a near raid on Sunday & the houses had another shake & it did the trick to the ceilings. It was a good way off really, but several houses had the shake. …

The children are fine. Shivaun sends a kiss for Jack. Niall's party was fine. I had a nice cake and jellies (yours) and Breon showed the films, 6 boys Niall's age – Niall was so pleased. The films really are a Godsend at parties….

I am so sorry about M Londonderry its very sad she is very young to be so ill & I think a nice girl. Sean always liked her very much.[2] Saw Fr Russell the other day he was at the play at Dartington. Breon is working in a play these days the scenery and is very pleased.

[1] In the face of the Nazi threat, the UK and USSR became allies formally with the Anglo-Soviet Agreement of July 12, 1941. It was replaced by the Anglo-Soviet Treaty of 1942. On October 7, 1941 Churchill's wife Clementine started a campaign to raise funds for medical aid and clothing for the USSR and Sean remarks on support for "Mrs Churchill's Russian Red Cross Fund" in Totnes: "Red Laugh of War" in his autobiographical volume, *Sunset and Evening Star* (1954).

[2] Mary Vane-Tempest-Stewart (1921–2009), later Lady Mairi Bury, was the daughter of Charles and Edith, Marquis and Marchioness of Londonderry, whose second home was Mount Stewart, County Down. Sean was a friend of Edith, Lady Londonderry and attended her house parties in Londonderry House in London. Anne de Courcy claims that Lady Londonderry introduced Sean to Harold Macmillan who later published Sean's plays: *Society's Queen: The Life of Edith, Marchioness of Londonderry* (London: Phoenix, 1992), pp. 143–44, 287.

Well Jack and Mina there is no great news. I have sent by this post tea, apples are off for us all we were too late in the year.

I am sending this in a hurry so excuse the scribble.

My love to you both always, Eileen

Eileen must have been very tired indeed and I had woken up very early, cried & cried, climbed out of my cot and toddled into her room to play. She must have told me "No", and I had begun to cry again. This tipped her balance & she grabbed me up and went to the window – by now I was screaming – Breon rushed in and took me from her and into his room, saving me from a possible flight out of the said window. Eileen says that an hour or so later she woke to silence, and wondering what had happened opened Breon's door and looked in. I put my finger to my lips and said, "Shush – Bre sleep." I was sitting quietly "looking after him". That was one of his tricks, to make me look after him, later as a nurse, and not to let anyone wake him. I could tuck him in, very gently brush his hair, but protect him from waking up.

To help Eileen Sean took me off her hands a bit more. We played proper games together, my favourite we called Little Boys. He was my little boy and he was inclined to be quite a nuisance at times. I did all the things children have done for centuries: I cooked him food made from my wooden bricks and other things collected from the garden that he pretended to eat with me; I put him to bed and sang him songs. We walked around the garden shopping and I put things like stones, leaves and flowers in my little basket for the house. Often we went for longer walks along the back lane and down to a field that bordered the River Dart. One day on the way home I saw a blackbird lying on its side and I picked it up, only to drop it in horror as its other side was full of crawling maggots. "What's the matter with the blackbird?" I gasped. Sean explained that after a wild thing dies it is eaten by maggots and that helps to keep the countryside clean. "That's why you very rarely find a dead bird," he said. I was glad to get home that day.

When Eileen and Sean came to Totnes it was a quiet market town that sat along the banks of the River Dart. The High Street or Fore Street ran up a steep hill from the flat area of The Plains. The Plains was a busy area where the only bridge crossed the Dart to a part of Totnes called Bridgetown and took you to Newton Abbot and Exeter sharp left or straight on to Paignton and Torquay and the sea. On the corner before you crossed the bridge was Totnes's main garage called Baldwin's. It was Mr Baldwin who found Eileen her old Morris car that broke down a lot; the water tank had to be stopped with chewing gum when it sprang leaks. On another corner was The Milkbar, an art deco American-like soda bar, where Breon, when they first moved, went with money from Eileen. He ordered a Knickerbocker Glory and he said the whole place went quiet and they all looked at him. No one had ever ordered one before. On the river banks were warehouses, one being Reeves the timber merchant's. The produce for these warehouses came upriver on fairly large boats taken from even bigger ships. After the war Sean told me that wood came from all over the world, even Russia. He uses this in *The Drums of Father Ned*.

The Fore Street was narrow and got narrower the higher up you went until it took a sharp turn to the left and became the appropriately named The Narrows. On the corner on the right was the butcher that Eileen used, and just around the bend on the other side of the road stood the shop Eileen set up during the war to help raise money for Stalingrad Hospital and the Russians who suffered so many deaths during the winter of the German invasion.[3] This was after they became our Allies. The little shop sold all sorts of things, a bit like an Oxfam shop today only more cheerful: a lot of home-made toys and clothes, also books and maps and posters. On this corner stood a traffic policeman to direct the traffic, as it was a two-way street and this part was only wide enough for one vehicle. This policeman was also the outlet for any racing bets put on with the chemist Mr Bennett. If he had any money for her he stopped Eileen and held up the traffic while he carefully counted out the winnings into her hand. Years after the war I won a raffle and also put a pound each way on the horse I drew called Arctic Prince; we were stopped and Eileen was given £25, a fortune with two large white ten-pound notes and a large five-pound note.[4] Eileen gave me some of it and I bought two fans, as I collected them, but the rest was needed by Eileen. I was then thought to be lucky and with a

---

[3] In 1943, there was a nationwide campaign in the United Kingdom to provide £75,000 (£1,250,000 in today's currency) for a new wing for the Stalingrad Hospital, locally administered by motivated individuals and civil groups, including women's organisations. See, for example, the North Lanarkshire Council website: https://www.culturenlmuseums.co.uk/blog/russian-solidarity-in-airdrie-and-coatbridge-during-the-second-world-war-the-leningrad-album-in-context/ In addition, the Communist Party of Great Britain-inspired Anglo-Soviet Friendship Committee raised funds for food and medical supplies.

[4] The Irish-bred Arctic Prince won the Derby at 28/1 by six lengths in 1951.

pin I must have lost Totnes people a lot of money as I don't think I ever picked a winner again.

When the war started Sean and Eileen found out, with the early bombing of Plymouth and the Docks, that Totnes, along with other places, was on the main escape route taken by the German planes when the British artillery and aircraft attacked them; as they fled they dropped any bombs they had left, willy nilly, to lighten their load so they could fly quicker. Hence the odd farm house and home were shaken. Local bombs during the war hit a military hospital in Torquay, a church full of children at St. Marychurch, buses etc; people on beaches were strafed. All this apart from Plymouth's continual pulverization and the Exeter bombing.[5] The threat of danger was sweeping over everyone in the land and there seemed nowhere to hide.

In early 1942, after the Pearl Harbor onslaught on December 7 1941, American GIs had started to arrive in their hundreds, speeding past the house in their jeeps and lorries with the star sign on the side. Sometimes they would stop and all the kids around would rush and gather round as they chucked us sweets, Hershey bars and Double Bubble gum. Bliss. Once a convoy went speeding past as I was standing by our gate and a sailor's hat blew off his head and landed at my feet. They didn't stop, I picked it up and waved it and they all laughed. I kept it for years until it was lost by someone who borrowed it.

The Americans didn't realise the strength of the local cider, Scrumpy: it had the habit of attacking the legs, so that when they got up to leave their legs fell from under them. Many were so far gone at closing time that if the weather was good they were laid outside the Seven Stars Hotel to sleep it off. Sometimes in the mornings Eileen found a few asleep in our hall. Helen gave them cups of tea before they left, heavy-headed, for their billets. Breon played baseball with them on the playing fields outside the Senior School. It started as they joined in to play cricket and held the bat like a baseball bat and gave the hard cricket balls terrible swipes. Evidently the GIs always won.

Breon, being that bit older, eleven when the war started, was co-opted by the Home Guard to help with minor tasks. He wasn't pleased: "I had

---

[5] Plymouth suffered fifty-nine air raids between early July 1940 and May 1944. Exeter was first bombed in August 1940; there were particularly intense air-raids in April and May 1942. Fifteen hundred houses were destroyed by enemy action.

to paint this fucking hut. There was a little hut, not much bigger than a phone box, where the Home-Guard kept their equipment. Charles Inman who lived behind our house and as you know taught bookbinding at the school.[6] Well he, being serious and dedicated to the cause of protecting the local citizens, ordered me to paint this hut over the weekend. I was told I had to camouflage this stupid little hut: as if a plane going overhead would see this little white hut and think, 'Oh, that must be where the Home-Guard keep all their equipment'. They would be more likely to bomb it if it was camouflaged. Bloody weekend lost."

Breon wasn't the only one to witness some of the Home Guards' activities as several times they crossed our back garden on practice, sometimes late into the night. They clambered up on to the roof of our outdoor loo to haul themselves over our 12 foot wall and drop with excruciating thuds and curses into next-door's garden, the garden of Mr. Roper, the bank manager, who was also a Home Guard. They must have done themselves many an injury.

So Breon "did his bit"; all Sean could do was write to keep all our bodies and souls together. Luckily the American sales of Sean's autobiographies, *I Knock at the Door* and *Pictures in the Hallway*, were good so far. Both Sean and Eileen said the Americans kept the O'Caseys' heads above the water during the war – just.

Eileen's letter to Mina:

Friday February 1942

Mina dear,

... The time seems so long since you were here. I have had a real brute of a cold for the past two weeks ears throat & just felt miserable – all better now, as the children say. Yes it sounds as good arrangement over the coat, I wish I had let you sell my fur coat for me; I'm hopeless it was a good coat & the woman beat me to £10. I did better over the bits of jewellery; still it's all gone now. Well dearest I feel yards cheerier since my cold it gave me time to think as I had to get to bed early at night, & somehow I know in my heart all will be better for all humans

---

[6] Bookbinding workshops have been part of the "Craft Revolution programme" at Dartington Hall since the school's inception in 1926. Charles Inman oversaw the installation of a press in 1935 and taught printing as well; he retired in 1947.

eventually. The Plough has run a week at the Abbey, Dublin & is running a 2nd week & that means we can pay some off the school bill. Sean has written such a nice article on Lady Gregory for the "Saturday Book", for which they are to pay him £25.[7] He is writing hard at a new play now [*Red Roses for Me*]; I don't think the other will go on [*Purple Dust*] in the States now. ...

My love to Jack & dear for yourself a large share.
Eileen

Before the war Eileen had helped Sean with his work by reading his proofs and some letters with him, but with all the extra work the war crowded into her life, her help was far less. It still fell to Eileen to continue to look after Sean. He was muscularly strong because of the many years he worked as a navvy on the Northern Railway and on the roads, but hardship had taken its toll; his digestion was poor due to past malnutrition, the doctor said. He had smoked cheap cigarettes from an early age; they all did in the poorer districts as it helped the empty feeling in the stomach. When Breon started to smoke Sean let him buy better cigarettes while he continued to smoke his cheap ones. Breon tried one of Sean's and said it was lethal. Sean later was told to stop the chain smoking of cigarettes and smoke a pipe instead, which he did, but he still inhaled the smoke. So, he very often got chest infections and bronchitis. Niall and I used to laugh and imitate his hacking as he coughed up the phlegm every morning. But his biggest hurdle was his poor eyes. Every morning he had to fetch hot water to bathe his eyes open as they were encrusted by pus from his type of conjunctivitis. He rarely talked to us children about his ailments except later asking us to pull the ingrown eyelashes out of his eyes for him. Eileen had to find the food and clothe us. Sean himself had very little requirements apart from his books, pen and paper: he had a suit jacket, felt hat, and saffron scarf he had bought in better days, flush from his early success in London; apart from that all he had were two pairs of trousers, about three shirts, a few socks, one pair of boots and a pair of slippers for the house. He never wore vest or pants; until the very end of his life, the long-tailed shirts kept his bum warm and comfortable and in his day only toffs or old men wore underwear.

[7] This appeared as "The Lady of Coole" in *The Saturday Book 1943*, ed. Leonard Russell (London: Hutchinson, 1942). See Ayling and Durkan, *Sean O'Casey: A Bibliography*, p. 153.

Eileen loved clothes and had many of her old Twenties dresses and camiknickers and lovely silk shoes. Great for me and my friends to dress up in. She looked good in anything but always managed to look neat and "smart", even in dungarees with her scarf tied like the stereotype of a southern black woman, a style often used by women then.

As the war progressed, even with rations divvied out, things became scarcer, not only food but clothes and shoes and household things such as sheets, etc. The best thing was to buy material with the coupons and make clothes, or make them from old clothes. Eileen wasn't any good at sewing although she was a good mender so Mina had become the seamstress and Eileen the supplier of "under the counter" or black-market goods from the country. Living down in Devon and by having good friends, we had access to things that would perish if not eaten immediately: rabbits, ducks, pheasants, chickens and eggs. Tobacco was sometimes sent to Sean by Jack as his sort of moist tobacco was scarce. Jack was able to get books for Sean and lend him some of his own as he had an extensive library. It went up in smoke when Jack and Mina were bombed out in 1940 but as soon as they had found new accommodation at Clifford's Inn he started to build a new one.[8] Mina and Jack also supplied us with extra sweets, sugar, biscuits and jelly packs as often as they could, usually near birthdays and Xmas.

Then for Eileen came a blow. Helen was told that she would have to take on war work. For the present it was decided that she could help at the Dartington Nursery School, as they needed extra help, and she was a trained nurse. I was to go with her between 9 am and 3.30 pm, the toddlers' school hours. I was three. I remember arriving at the little school on the ground floor of a white house. The excitement of it all. I was given a hook for my coat all of my own; each hook had a painted tile above with a different animal on each of them: mine was an owl. Everything was toddler height, hooks, chairs & tables, lavatories, basins: everything. After our lunch at our tables we all had to lie down for Rest Time. Little camp beds were set out at one end of the room with screens, with an embroidered square of our animals on them, put between each bed to cut us off from the other children so we could calm down and stop chattering. We were covered up with a blanket, had a small pillow for our heads and

---

[8] Clifford's Inn, a former Inn of Chancery off Fleet Street, founded in 1344, was dissolved in 1903; some of the undemolished buildings then housed apartments, in one of which Virginia Woolf once lived.

THE WAR YEARS 1942–1945

were told firmly "not to talk until the bell rings". We didn't have to sleep but we had to be quiet. We usually did all fall asleep.

At first Eileen thought it would be too much for me, as I was rather little. Eileen was a worrier. She worried about her children's safety, especially the boys, only relaxing when they arrived back through the door from school. Niall always seemed to be hungry but never put on any weight. The first thing he shouted through the hall door, as he laid his bike on its side in the conservatory, was, "Where are my extras?" Bread and dripping, anything – fuel was needed.

Eileen didn't have any security of knowing where the money would be coming from or when, from year to year, even week to week. She was married to a self-employed artist and so it was a continual worry for her. No matter how hard Sean wrote no money came in unless his published work sold or someone put on one of his plays, except for a small amount from articles that he hated to write. Sean worried, too, and this sometimes made him silent and brooding; he wrote about this to her in a last love letter, a poetic will and testament where he apologised for his lack of understanding for her feelings when he became morose and described the debts they had to meet like a necklace tightening around her beautiful neck. I can't say I ever noticed this awkward feeling but Breon said he did. For me it was Sean who always managed to get me out of a stubborn mood after Eileen and Breon had failed.

When things became really bad financially (the school was very expensive and they had three children there now), Eileen was driven to ask friends or old boyfriends for loans to tide them over. She did this when she felt she couldn't ask Daniel Macmillan for any more help. Dan Macmillan ran the Macmillan publishing house with his brother Harold, but when Harold became an MP Daniel took over the practicalities of the business. The money from Dan was a loan and not an advance, for Sean could never know about it as he was too proud to take any money on loan. After Sean died Eileen paid back whatever was owing. Pleased with herself she told her then admirer, Harold Macmillan, that she had paid Dan all she owed; "That was very foolish, Eileen," replied Harold, "you do realise that Daniel is a multi-millionaire and wouldn't be expecting its return." Dan and Harold had tried to help openly, too, offering to buy Tingrith for them when the owner wanted the house free of us, his tenants, in order to sell. But, of course, Sean wouldn't hear of it, although he was touched by the offer. (Much later he refused the CBE that Harold had offered during one of his terms of office as Prime Minister. He also told the Ulster Group Theatre and others, who were campaigning for him to be nominated for a Nobel Prize, not to waste their time as he wouldn't accept it even if, which was very unlikely, he was offered it. James Joyce hadn't been offered it, he said, by way of explanation.)

While the war was in full swing Jim Larkin visited Sean several times. I was there and evidently we did meet, so to speak as a man might take note of a little girl. His real desire was to talk with Sean about the old times and about what may happen in Ireland in the future, immediately after the war, and the fear of a boycott by England as Ireland had remained neutral.

The first time Jim came to visit Sean in Devon was in June 1942. Eileen was away in London. Sean felt they needed some rations to feed Jim with. Breon recalled the visit for me. "You know Sean would never go into the shops, or very rarely, and we ran out of butter. So he said, 'Oh, we ought to get some butter 'cause Jim's coming'. He went over the road to Mr. Boas's little corner shop. They were all amazed to see him, and Mr. Boas said, 'Yes, Mr. O'Casey' to all he asked; and Sean said , 'Is there any butter?', and Mr. Boas said, 'Yes, yes, how much would you like?'; and Sean said, 'Oh, about half a pound.' 'Yes, yes, yes', said Mr. Boas as he cut it and weighed it and wrapped it up carefully in greaseproof paper. And when my Mum came back she was amazed and said we weren't even rationed there [Mr Boas's] for butter, we were rationed with Mrs. Lamson. We went to the station to meet Jim Larkin and this big man got out of the train, you know, in a Fedora hat kind of thing and a black suit that was a bit tight for him. 'Halloo, Jim,' said Sean. 'Halloo, Sean.' And all this – 'How's the strike going?' 'Oh, it's going very well', and all this sort of stuff. 'Like your suit.' 'Oh' he said. 'This undertaker died and I felt sorry for the widow so I bought the suit off her.' He was a lovely man." Breon went on: "Jim was talking of old times, and he started to thunder out, and crikey the hairs on the back of your head stood up, you know. He was obviously very very good at stirring a crowd. And he introduced my father to Eugene O'Neill you know. He had come back from his stretch in Sing Sing and Sean was digging in a ditch & he threw Sean a book saying, 'I think you'll enjoy this Sean'. It was O'Neill's plays." Later Sean met Eugene in New York; they both admired each other's work and kept in touch via George Jean Nathan.

Eileen longed for London but the war made getting to London more

THE WAR YEARS 1942-1945

difficult and dangerous. When she did sometimes manage to get up to London, Sean hated her absence, as even after the Blitz London was often bombed, if not every night. He was petrified she would get hurt while away. A few times during the war Breon persuaded Eileen to let him go and stay with Mina and Jack, if he had saved enough for the fare, and when this happened it made Eileen as well as Sean nervous. When Eileen got away she usually stayed with Zoe and Sidney Bernstein in their flat near Whitehall or with her friend Helen Elliot who lived just outside London.[9] Strangely, Eileen said it was the war that saved her marriage. "I so wanted London and the bright lights until the war broke, and then I became completely busy and occupied and worked so hard. And the friendship between people during the war, all working for survival. By the end of the war I had grown up a little bit." But she still had a yen for London and the excitement it held for her. Yet she stayed with Sean and with us; the main glue to their companionship I think was not only a fond love but their great sense of humour.

In one visit to London, Eileen took Breon and Niall to stay with Mina and Jack and later wrote to thank her friend.

Mina dearest,

... Thank you Mina so much for having us all ... Shivaun had her birthday and I made a cake & found some icing sugar & iced it and put her name on in silver sweets, 3 candles, she had some little girls to tea & wore her blue silk dress & looked sweet & was absolutely thrilled & full up. Con sent a doll it didn't open its eyes, but was very pretty & Shivaun was so pleased; we didn't have her party until last

---

[9] Sidney Bernstein (1899–1993; created Baron Bernstein in 1969), founder of Granada Television, also owned a string of theatres and cinemas; he co-founded the London Film Society in 1925 and in the 1940s briefly formed a production company, Transatlantic Pictures, with Alfred Hitchcock. Sidney and Zoe (née Farmer) married in 1936 and divorced ten years later. Eileen met Helen Seldon (who married Yule Elliott in 1926) early in her theatrical career in London. According to Eileen, Helen was an orphan who was in the guardianship of the Napier-Clavering family of Cavendish Square. Helen was rich and travelled around London in a chauffeur-driven Daimler; she was immensely generous to Eileen, taking her to New York and Monte Carlo. See Eileen O'Casey, *Eileen* (London: Macmillan, 1976), pp. 54–55, 69, 71, 96, 103.

Saturday, as school was enough for her for a bit. ...[10]

Macmillan's didn't send on our money yet, as soon as they do I'll post some for shirt & coupons; also I must not let you bear Breon's dentist or my telephone bill, so say no more dearest. I'll send the money in bits for the dentist as I suppose its about £6 or 7 he went so often & its either a guinea or ½ a visit. Really we had a grand time, I feel so much better & dear you were so marvellous in doing all the cooking & feeding us all. Breon also as you know had a grand time. Niall still talks of it all – The parcel arrived, the dress is lovely. Thanks for the prunes and the currents. Sean is smokin me out with the tobacco he likes it. ...

Our British Soviet is having a dance by the soldiers on Oct 17th & Film 18th, our shop opens November 1st. Really this Stalingrad is beyond any comment, it is so tremendous

Please give Jack my love & Breon's & Niall's, and to yourself dearest my love and many many thanks.

Eileen X

Before Christmas 1942, Eileen told Mina the shop run by the Committee of the Anglo-Soviet Alliance in Totnes was doing quite well. "Macmillan is oversubscribed for their edition of "War & Peace" Tolstoy, but Daniel Macmillan is letting me have 6 for our shop."[11]

The German planes used to fly low to avoid the radar. Totnes Station was bombed during the daytime in 1942, on October 21. Two people were killed and two injured. One of those killed was a young air force man on leave, just changing trains and had nothing to do with Totnes. Not a mark on him, he was killed by the blast. One of life's little ironies. Breon

---

[10] Cornelius McElroy, the son of the wealthy coal-merchant William McElroy who Sean in 1926 heard singing the Robbie Burns song, "My Bonie Mary" – "Go, fetch to me a pint o' wine,/And fill it in a silver tassie." In "The Silver Tassie," *Rose and Crown* (1952), Sean doesn't identify the singer beyond his being a coal merchant sitting "idly" (the miners then being on strike) in a London office, but a sharp-eyed reader two chapters further on might identify the singer by virtue of the "big-brimmed black hat" shared by the singing merchant and "Billy McElroy, roguish, bombastic, laughable, and a wonderful personality." Eileen remembered the occasion in the London coal office in her autobiography, *Eileen*, pp. 93–94. When he heard the song, Sean decided to give its name to his next play. McElroy was best man at the wedding of Sean and Eileen on September 23, 1927.

[11] Macmillan published Tolstoy's *War and Peace* in Louise and Aylmer Maude's translation in 1942.

THE WAR YEARS 1942–1945

immediately pedalled back from school to see how they were at the house. He found Sean and Eileen covered with dust from the ceilings falling down and a window blown in. The walls had shaken and the door buckled in to an alarming degree. They were in one piece. The cracks were taped and checked to see if they got bigger.

Breon remembered the repairs to our roof: "These men, this Irish group that came round to mend our roofs which the tiles had been knocked off. Not by the bombs but by the Spitfires coming up and firing on them you know. Dropping all their empty shell cases clattering on our roofs. They had this group of Irish labourers that sort of went around repairing bomb damage. And they'd been to Coventry and they said that Plymouth was worse than Coventry. Plymouth was absolutely flattened, and, I don't know, two or three places left standing. Just the roads between them."

Eileen worried about Sean and her being killed during this war. She wrote to Jack and Mina to ask them if they would look after the three of us if anything should happen to them both. She later wrote them: "I will never forget your answer over the children & it may have seemed rather foolish to you but I have friends who might mind them under such circumstances; but the heart of the persons for the children can't be found often. You understand without words what I mean".

1943: ON AND ON IT GOES

Sean often played with me inside the house and outside to give Eileen some relief and he enjoyed entering my world. The older I got, the games I played with Sean became more uprooting – that is, the upsetting of the furniture. My favourite was sailing the high seas in the upturned kitchen table with a tablecloth as a sail tied to a broom that was tied to one of the table legs. We sailed through storms and calm seas and were pulled to shore by dolphins and seagulls. The other game played with Sean consisted of turning over the sofa in my nursery and making a dark hole I could make into a castle or a palace. This sofa had been made for Sean by a carpenter friend in Dublin, made after he made some money from *Juno* (I wonder if this carpenter made up part of Fluther's character in *The Plough And the Stars?*)

By now I could now die very effectively when playing with guns with Niall. One day Breon and Niall were playing hide and seek with me. I hid behind the door in the front room and shut my eyes very tight. "We're coming" they shouted. I remained stock still. Then I heard them laughing at me – "We can see you with your eyes closed". I opened them "No you can't!" It was around this time they made a drink of whisky and a lot of orange squash. They sipped at it and said "Ugh". Then they gave it to me to try and were taken aback when I gulped it down. Eileen was alerted by their laughter and shocked to see me slightly drunk. She was very angry and I was carried up to bed where I slept for a very long time. The boys were sorry and very attentive for a time. I now realised you could be seen with your eyes shut tight. Sean played with us all: with Breon and Niall playing handball against the side wall of the house; on the lawn playing cricket with a tennis racquet and ball; "Grandmother's Footsteps", a game I was included in; also "Gathering Gold on Tom-Tiddler's Land", "Statues", etc. Inside we all played Monopoly and card games. Sean read Dickens and other novels to Breon and maybe Niall listened in. By the time I was old enough, Sean's eyes were too bad to use for this and had to be reserved for his work.

I liked to go shopping with Eileen, I liked to walk beside her as she pushed the big pram up the steep hill that took us up to the top of Totnes High Street. When we came to the railway bridge over the main-line track that took you to London, we always stopped to look out for trains and waited to see if any came and if one did we screamed with delight at being covered in the coal-smelling smoke. I think Eileen would have leapt on to a London train if she didn't have us all there to look after.

Warm, kind and funny are three words that describe my mother, but add sometimes outrageous to this. She was also vulnerable to criticism as she had been pulled to bits by her mother since a child, telling her that she was not "a lady" and plain because of her snub nose. Nonsense, her nose was lovely but not long thin and straight like Grannie's: not an aristocratic nose. Her mother was a snob and wanted Eileen to be part of the higher society so she could be there too. As a child Eileen had been told to always look respectable. They were related to the MacDonalds on Grannie's side, a wealthy Catholic family. Grannie wrote to them begging their help and Mrs MacDonald put Eileen through a strict Ursuline convent in London. Later Eileen sang at their parties when she was starting out as a young girl first as an architectural drawer and then leaving that and joining the D'Oyly Carte as a young soubrette, much to Grannie's horror.

Summer was a lovely time even in the war. Some people still managed to go on picnics and to the sea-side. Barbed-wire barriers stood in readiness by the beaches; these were rolled out if it was forbidden to go on to a beach, mainly for fear of invasion but also because of washed-up landmines or those floating not far out and likely to come in. Sean and Breon tended the crops, for everyone grew vegetables wherever they could during these times of rationing. Summer was the busiest season in the garden. They had planted cabbages on the shady north-side of the house and by mid-summer we all dashed about with butterfly nets to catch the cabbagewhites; a bit late really, as their caterpillars had already eaten their fill; I suppose it helped lessen the next generation. I helped wielding a large net and was being continually told not to bash into the cabbages or slam down the net too hard. At the back of the house a big patch of earth had been dug up and there they had planted potatoes, carrots, onions, and rows of runner-beans, peas and sweet peas to pick and smell the house. The back garden also had three apple trees but it was the big tree, a Bramley cooking apple tree, that produced the most. The plums trained against the wall never produced anything. Coming home and into the conservatory you were greeted by the smell of growing tomatoes. I loved walking down the lines of beans and peas picking and eating them, and pulling up a young carrot to munch: bliss. Sean loved the birds and would sit for hours in an old deck chair with his old felt hat on watching them eat the food he put out for them. He trained a blackbird, whom he called "Charlie", to hop right into the scullery for treats.

One day Sean and Breon killed a snake: they thought it was an adder but it was a beautiful harmless grass snake and they felt terrible about it. We all stood round looking at the poor thing and then Breon buried it.

The winter months were long and made life a little more difficult. Not only was it dark now for longer but it was very cold in Tingrith: the kitchen was always warm but not the scullery where Eileen cooked and Sean washed up – that was freezing. Winter meant a lot more work for Eileen as coal and logs had to be carried in and fires lit. Winter and summer we had to save all our food waste and carry it over the road to a big steel bin that stank to the heavens; this was to be pig swill.

Sean felt the cold when he was sitting to write but his room was warmed by a gas fire and he typed at the end of his table that was pulled up near to it and sat in his arm-chair as close to the fire as was safe. He did sometimes smell of singeing.

Helen finally left us in July 1943 to do war work in nurseries, the forces or in munitions. Eileen and Niall missed her a lot. Eileen hated thinking of her up in London where she was in more danger than down here. Eileen worried about Jack and Mina and the Bernsteins and all her friends. I loved Eileen and now I had more of her time; this meant I went with her wherever she went if I was not at school; that's how I remember the Russian shop so well. Eileen checked in most days and spent time there on Saturdays and I went with her. I played on the floor and to get me out of the way I was put on the flat ledge for display along the window that had lots of home-made toys, games and a few children's books. The atmosphere was always friendly and I loved sitting in a wicker "cradle" chair just looking and listening to the talk. In the winter it always felt snug and in the summer light and breezy. We weren't to see Helen again except during her leaves and of course when the war stopped.

CHRISTMAS TO CHRISTMAS

I am four, Niall 8 and Breon 15. By Christmas of 1943 people were tired and although most of the bombing had stopped down in Devon, the threat still lingered; the black-out still kept the windows dark, rationing was tight, and the thoughts of sons and daughters in the thick of the horror showed on people's faces. Eileen usually made our Christmas fun. Sean dressed up as Father Christmas in the dark pink eiderdown wrapped around him and a funny hat on his head. After Christmas, usually into the New Year we went to a pantomime.

Breon's letter to Jack and Mina:

January 1944

Dear Jack and Mina,

A line to thank you for your lovely Xmas present. I now have such a collection of art books – as would make Mr. Elmhirst jealous, & he has enough god knows.

Niall and Shivaun have both asked me to thank you both from them both. Shivaun thinks she is a real lady now, & as for Niall, when he saw the name Los Angeles on his tie, well he wouldn't take it off, not even in the bath; so help me for I'm [not] telling a lie. Anyhow they were both very pleased – It was some morning I can tell you; there I was at about 9 o'clock, trying to stay asleep, & there they were across the hallway unwrapping parcels – there would suddenly be a great "Ooh mummy, look what I've got," and then there would be silence, – & then an even bigger Ooh, – & so it went on – & of course I had to listen, & of course I soon gave up, the idea of 'sweet slumber' & went & sat in the nursery to avoid the suspense before the Oohs.

... Once again thank you for the two fine books, and in the words of the great newspaper man, "Love to all of you there, from all of us here." – and that includes Mickey, & Shivaun says that includes Dumbo & Daffodil Rose, & Mary & Rose-bud, & etc: she says they all send you their love, believe it or not.

Yours Breon

With Helen gone when I was 5 or thereabouts, I moved from the nursery school at Dartington to the kindergarten, called the Children's Cottage, in a little grey granite house with clapboard on the upper floors, and leaded windows. They were a new build made to look like old artisan cottages, rather in the style of the Craft Movement, and in keeping with the Estate. The house was on a corner where a road to the right ran downhill to the Middle School, Aller Park (ages 8 to 12 or 13) which was still commandeered for the use of evacuees. All the Junior School children (5 to 8) in the Old Postern now shared Foxhole with the Seniors (12 or 13 to 18). This was possible as many of the elder pupils had been sent to the US and Canada for the duration of the war. But Breon remembers it being very crushed. Breon told me: "We had very odd and interesting teachers because a lot of them had been called up and some were interned. Others, like David Lack took up war duties. Mr Lack went to work in the Ministry for Health. He told me later that they were terrified there would be a pandemic during the war & that was one reason they were so keen on everyone having a good diet. David Lack was a biologist who was a specialist in birds, he wrote a famous book about the Robin. He taught me to call a bird down to your hands and mesmerise it."[12] This was very useful when we found an injured blackbird; Breon mesmerised it while we found a box for it to live in in the conservatory, and I was able to feed it without panicking it. The bird mended and flew away. I wondered if it was the same one that came into the scullery to visit Sean.

The teachers who had come from Spain to escape from Franco during the Spanish Civil war stayed. Margalida Comas Camps, known to us as Dr Margarita Camps, taught biology. She was the first Spanish woman to be awarded a research degree in the natural sciences at a Spanish

---

[12] David Lack, a prominent English ornithologist, published *The Life of the Robin* in 1943.

university, and taught at the University of Barcelona. She left Spain in 1937 and in England worked for the Peace Pledge Union.[13] In that capacity, she spotted, among the 4000 Basque children sent as refuges to the UK, the teenage sisters, Marina and Carita Rodriquez. She mentioned them to Dr Curry who took them on as teachers at Dartington after they passed the necessary exams. Marina was a lovely biology teacher in the Junior School and Carita taught at The Old Postern. Then there was the energetic Federico de la Iglesia who taught geography and Spanish, and his gentle wife Laura who gave us treats sometimes when I was at the Children's Cottage as the De la Iglesias lived in the house next door.[14]

I loved going to school and by now it was like a second home. Being with all my friends, playing in the sand pit, climbing the Jungle Gym, painting, sticking and pasting, & singing and dancing about. The little drive from the road to the school had a flower bed on each side that was full of sweet williams in the summer and their smell greeted us all in the morning. We ate lunch at school and we all had to have a glass of milk and a spoonful of malt every day as part of the war food programme. We were issued with vitamin C tablets that we were told made you see in the dark. Mine never worked. I believe families were issued with tins of blackcurrant puree and powdered eggs as well as the fresh rationed food; anyway we had them in the larder: rations of milk, butter, margarine, eggs, sugar, meat, tea, Camp coffee, etc. We had a lot of spam and corned beef. To make the precious butter go further, we always had a jug of boiling water on the table to dip our knives in to make the butter easier to spread very thinly. It worked very well.

Soon after my start at the Children's Cottage I was reprimanded. The school had a cloakroom where we all took off our boots and shoes and coats before school started. On a rainy day I remember being told to go into the cloakroom as I was distracting the other children. I can't

---

[13] See Núria Radó-Trilla, "Margalida Comas Camps (1892–1972): A Woman for all Seasons", *Contributions to Science* 10:107–110 (2014), available online. This pioneering scientist and activist taught at Dartington between 1942 and 1959.

[14] Federico de la Iglesia (c1902–1958) was a professor at the General Military Academy before fighting in the Spanish Civil War on the side of the Republican government; he became a Major in the 43rd Mixed Brigade and secretary general of the Central General Staff. At the end of the Civil War after Franco's victory he went into exile in the United Kingdom. He took an external degree at Exeter University while teaching at Dartington. He wrote to his friend, the poet Robert Graves, that "There is no country like England, the cream of this otherwise uncivilised world": his daughter Leina Schiffrin, personal communication to the author (October 26, 2020).

THE WAR YEARS 1942–1945

remember what they were doing or how I distracted them. I refused and Nora our teacher got very frustrated. She tried to grab me but I avoided her, laughing, thinking it was like a game. She must have got hold of me as I remember being pushed into the cloakroom and told to stay there and be quiet. She shut the door. When I went to open it she said not to, that I must stay there alone until she said I can come out. By this time some of my friends were crying. Nothing like this had ever happened to me before and I burst into uncontrollable tears, followed by the most frightening gasps for air. I couldn't stop. I suppose she had to come and comfort me, it being that sort of caring school, but all I remember was a group of rather worried friends and my little friend Carole consoling me. But these horrid sobs went on for what seemed like ages.

The next day I definitely never wanted to go to school ever again. My demonstrating made me miss the bus so Breon had to take me on the crossbar of his bike. But, poor Breon, when I got to the gate of the school no way would I go in. I remember my terror: whatever it was, feeling humiliated or afraid I don't know. I caused an enormous scene and Bre, at a loss as what to do took me home and he was late for school. And not pleased. I calmed down eventually and through Eileen's gentle persuasion managed to go back to the camaraderie of my little friends.

A letter from Nora to Sean and Eileen, her report on the incident, was forwarded, with comments, by the headmaster W.B. Curry to Eileen.

Nora Grout's letter to Eileen:

March 1944

Dear Sean and Eileen,

Shivaun had quite a happy Christmas term at school, in spite of the numerous emotional scenes connected with her strong will and desire for preferential treatment, and more than her share of things.

Somehow, she came back after the holidays on the wrong foot, and there was little right with the day. Whether this was because her return was a week or so after the others had settled in, or that she was upset at home while you were away, I don't know. Then I was in bed for a week and the routine here a little changed, and the balloon went up! I have talked with you and Eileen so recently about Shivaun and her difficulties and how I feel that at home, in the past, she has got away with more than is helpful to her development. I'm sure it is right at the moment for her to stay at home with you if she so wishes, and perhaps next term she will feel more like coming. As I told you Eileen, the only reason I attacked the difficulty in the first place from a different angle was because you were so indefinite with her, and led me to believe that you could not have Shivaun at home each day. Whatever our differences are towards this educational problem, I feel that it is important, if we are going to help Shivaun, to work home and school together and try to have a common plan of thought and action. I shall be seeing you soon, I hope, and we can discuss anything further.

>Yours sincerely
>Nora Grout
>Group Teacher

This provoked Sean, who saw educational principles at stake, to write to the headmaster.

Sean's letter to W.B. Curry:

22 April 1944

Dear Mr. Curry,

Thanks for your kind letter. In some respects, you have either misunderstood me, or I have failed to make myself clear. I didnt mean to attach the Shivaun incident to any general or particular principle; to me it seemed too simple for that. In some way or another, the teacher's attitude to the will and egotism of Shivaun – common to all youngsters – was a wrong one. That is my main point. Whatever it was it terrorised the child. That is quite clear to me. It gave the child a psychological shock from which, regarding the school, she hasn't recovered; and, I'm afraid, it will extend to future school connections, because whatever it may have been couldn't have happened here, and so, for the time being at any rate, naturally fixed a preference in the child's mind for (to her) a safer life at home. My letter meant nothing about preferential treatment for one child, or for all – it was the teacher who brought this to the front in her report. She, not I, harped on that string. To connect the tears and terror of the child about going to school with the commonplace one of wanting her own way is just nonsense. The claim for "preferential treatment" (Latin, I suppose for wanting her own way) evinced by Shivaun was clumsily tackled, both when the first incident occurred, and afterwards during the attempt to humour the child back to a normal feeling for the school again. My letter does not "disapprove of Nora's unwillingness to accord preferential treatment," but it does disapprove of something done to frighten the child – a very different thing. There can be no excuse even in an overcrowded school (though we may understand it there) for frightening a child into meek obedience; and least of all is there an excuse for the school of Dartington Hall.

I hope what I have said above is clear now.

Now, I'd like to say a few words on the general remarks in your letter. First, I'm a Communist, not a Socialist – a very different thing. This isn't said in any arrogance of spirit, for many Socialists are finer fellows, personally, than many Communists, as indeed are many Tories, for that matter. But the ideal aimed at by Communists is, in my opinion, a much higher one, and it is this which counts in the end. I don't agree that the youngest member of a household "usually gets preferential treatment". Certainly not in working-class families. They are often thought of as a nuisance, always in the way. As a Communist, I am in favour of preferential treatment to all in all schools – that is the adapting of educational methods to each child according to its needs. Oddly enough (not oddly, really, but naturally) you are out for that too. Each particular, or peculiar gift in every individual child should be fostered in its own peculiar way so that each can enjoy life in its fullest, and give of his best to itself and community companions. Many would be inclined to call this preferential treatment, but I don't think you would.

Let me say, too, that this is no sudden Shivaun interest in these things. I have been staring into them for over 35 years, since Padruig [sic] Pearse founded St Enda's School in Dublin. which would "teach modern languages orally; which should be bilingual in method; which should aim at a wider and humaner culture than other Irish Secondary Schools; which should set its face like iron against 'cramming' and against all the evils of the competitive examination system, which should work at fostering the growth of the personality of each of its pupils rather than at forcing all into a predetermined groove."

Indeed, I am at the moment, writing, or rather, referring, to this great man, Pearse, who, unfortunately, was executed as a "rebel" by the

British Authorities in 1916, in the next volume I hope to have published.[15]

Finally, a strong will and a desire to have one's own way are not necessarily evil things, you will agree, I think provided they are linked with a sane humility, and an intense feeling towards all men of goodwill, a proper respect for human life, and an intelligent realization that no-one is infallible. So they should be encouraged and guided, rather than suppressed in the young by either psychological or physical intimidation, if we are to have the enlightened leaders humanity will always need.

Well, there you are, now; and let me end up with my warm regards to you, and my best wishes with you in your work.

Yours sincerely
Sean O'Casey[16]

Another event that sticks in my mind was when I was taken into a little separate shed, a shed built to keep in with the style of the house design: it was built in stone and wood with a slate roof with little windows, about the size of a small garage. A lady called Mrs Isherwood was the teacher inside, someone we didn't know very well as she wasn't permanent at the Cottage. It was furnished with a low table and chairs and had a carpet on the floor. I was given a puzzle to do and asked some questions. I remember doing more puzzles and rather enjoying it although it was a strange feeling to be in there alone without any of my friends. We were taken in one by one and when I came out was asked a little anxiously, "What was it like? What do you do?". I said it was quite fun.

Sean came along with Eileen to pick me up on that day; he sometimes did this as he liked to see the children and the drive to the school was beautiful, even on a miserable rainy day. While I was running up to him as he stood at the gate, Mrs Isherwood rushed out of her little shed and exclaimed something like: "I have been testing your daughter and she is very intelligent". Sean wasn't expecting this and possibly thought he should have been asked if he had wanted this to happen, but whatever went through his mind he wasn't too pleased: "I never gave any permission

---

[15] *Drums Under the Windows* appeared in 1945. Pearse was executed for his prominent role in the Easter rebellion of 1916.

[16] *The Letters of Sean O'Casey, Volume II: 1942–54*, ed. David Krause (New York: Macmillan, 1980), pp. 165–66.

THE WAR YEARS 1942–1945

for an Intelligence Test – I don't believe in them. I don't need you to tell me she's intelligent or any other of the children here. I don't think children or anyone else for that matter should be tested for their intelligence. Intelligence in what? People have all sorts of different talents that your tests could or would not understand." I rather shrunk behind his legs as Eileen with laughing diplomacy covered it all over and Mrs Isherwood didn't seem too cross as she sailed down the little drive and back to her nest.

The big push called D-Day was to take place in seven months and troops were building up in the camps everywhere all around us, making ready to embark from Plymouth. All very hush-hush. No-one knew why so many were rushing around in Jeeps. Some more bombs were to fall; it wasn't quite over yet. We were very lucky on that score on one occasion.

Eileen had taken Niall, with myself in tow, to see a film in Torquay at the big cinema with the organ that rose up from the floor to play, changing colours that reflected on the little man madly playing the keyboard. He crashed away, making loud mingled mangled sounds that deafened us all. There were the ladies in their pretty uniforms and trays of ice creams held by straps around their necks, and then the Pathe News. If GBS was on it, Eileen would whisper that we must tell Sean we saw Shaw. The film ran a little late and we had to run like mad to catch the bus for Totnes. Sean hated us being out after dark. The bus was still there and about to go, but it was chock-a-block full. Eileen pleaded with the conductress but there was simply no room; everybody was in a hurry to get safely home so no-one took sympathy and offered to get off for us. We could do nothing but wait for the next bus. It was cold and began to rain and the next bus was very late in coming. "Sean will be very cross", Eileen kept muttering. By the time the bus pulled in it was very late and dark, and the rain was falling in gusts. But we were the first on and went and sat on the seat in the front, me on Eileen's knee and Niall beside us at the window. Eileen wondered why we were going the long way round, through the smaller roads and lanes but no-one could give an answer. Safe and warm at home we were to learn that the main road had been strafed. A very sombre evening.

Sometimes I would wander into the front-room to find Sean sitting by our large radio – as large as a small bureau, about three feet high and two feet wide, with a walnut veneer and a pretty fretted pattern cut out of the wood, backed with black fine net. This is where the magic sound came out and if you peered in you could see the valve lights when it was turned on. Sean's right arm rested on the top of the radio, his head bent, his left hand holding his pipe. He was listening to the news or to the rantings of Lord Haw Haw. Sometimes Father Russell, whom he called Father Ned, would stop by to listen with him. You heard this creepy voice drawl – "Germany calling, Germany calling, Germany calling". At these times everything was tight and tense, as if a football match was coming to its conclusion and your breath was held until the final whistle blew and hopefully it was victory. I had to be very quiet or go and play somewhere else; this was serious and I understood.

Sean's letter to Jack:

29 May 1944

... News-Chronicle has asked me to write an article 700 words on Eire's Neutrality. I'll try anyhow...[17] They say there's a wall of thick prejudice rising up against Eire. That wall was always there.

I seem to have no time to spare these days. Something to do all day. I can't begin any work until nine at the earliest. However, I've finished 18 chapters of the next biography volume, & about two more should be enough & to spare for a thick volume. I have got up to Easter week.[18]

We had a nasty raid here – too near – last night. I really thought things were going to happen. The children (Niall and Shivaun), & Eileen stretched themselves into the Morrison Shelter; Brian & I stood or sat in the Hall – our hall, not Dartington. At each explosion I could see the door bending its belly inwards, while the house shook like a thing infirm; and Sean O'Casey felt that heroism was a thing of naught; a bubble. Then our guns spat out at the planes, & made things livelier. The youngsters took it splendidly, & Breon as usual, acted as if he was just waiting for his pretty girl to come as per appointment. The old man wasn't a bit perturbed, not a bit. But he was damned glad when the "All Clear" sounded. Life was worth living again. ...

---

[17] *Time and Tide* had already published two letters by Sean on "Eire's Neutrality", April 22 and May 20, 1944. See Ayling and Durkan, *Sean O'Casey: A Bibliography*, p. 224. No article by Sean on that subject in the London newspaper *News Chronicle* (1930-1960) is listed in Ayling and Durkan.

[18] *Drums Under the Windows* appeared in 1945.

THE WAR YEARS 1942–1945

Your ever
Sean[19]

In London during the last summer of the war Hitler, desperate and furious, in his effort to turn the war back to his favour, sent the people the first unmanned bombs, the dreaded Doodle-bugs – they were uncontrolled killing machines – first the V1 and then the even more terrifying V2. The V1 you could hear up in the sky and knew it was dropping to explode when their deadly engines cut out – that was that if you were under it. The V2 arrived in September 1944, five years after Hitler started this bloodbath. These flew higher, silently, and you couldn't tell when the engines stopped, no warning at all – just Boom!! Evelyn Waugh said they "were as impersonal as the plague, as though the city was infested with enormous venomous insects."[20]

Eileen's letter to Jack and Mina:

December 1944 [Christmas]

My dear Mina & Jack,
Thank you so much for the children's presents. Shivaun loves Dumbo, he went to the Torquay panto & Daffodile Rose went to Plymouth. The records are very precious & Breon and Sean equally like it. Breon's book he will write about also and Niall will when he settles down but he's just one bold wild soldier these days & is off with guns each morning. I think the mood is waning.

We had a good Xmas, we had to bear my Ma for a week & had no help so I really had an orgy of cooking. We had good eats & made the best of it. Nannie as you know by now is going abroad so my & Breon's trip was nipped she wanted to come for a few days but her mother wouldn't let her come unless she came too & I really thought Helen was better to have a rest & enjoy her leave in one place, also I was worried over her travelling to me overnight & overtiring herself. So I won't see her before she goes.

Shivaun of course I didn't mention it to at all yet, she's such a girlie

---

[19] *The Letters of Sean O'Casey, Volume II*, pp. 175–76.
[20] For Waugh, see Steven McKenzie, "World War II's Doodlebug hunters' 'lost story' told": BBC News: https://www.bbc.co.uk/news/uk-scotland-highlands-islands-22767210

now she is not difficult but great company & a very happy person always singing. ...
All sorts of good wishes
Xxxxx Eileen

I recall sitting on the propped-up seat at "Babes in the Wood" in Torquay, with Eileen's coat on top to make me even taller. I remember the Babes covered with leaves, and the nasty men, and the aerial ballet of birds that swung out over our heads in the front stalls, where we sat: they saved the babes. I remember vividly my first taste of the magic of the theatre. It was always an anxious travelling back at night with no headlights on the buses or anything else. But we were so full of the panto, we sang some of the songs we liked to sing, especially when we drove our car. When we got home Sean was bombarded with all we had seen and Breon sat on Sean's bed and joined in. No siren that night.

Events in 1945 moved quickly. On April 12, Franklin D. Roosevelt died and it hit Sean hard. He wrote to Jack on April 14: "A big blow to us all, the sudden death of F.D.R. Feels like one of the family has gone; or so it does to me. I hope Truman will be worth his name. Churchill and Stalin must be feeling it badly. He was badly needed for another few years."[21] Finally, all his selfish efforts dashed, Hitler killed himself and his wife underground in his bunker on April 30. Goebbels and his wife, after murdering all their children, did the same – all "honourable" to the end. Sean wrote to Sgt Peter Newmark of the British Army on April 23: "Well, Hitler is caput. Fascism is destroyed everywhere, save at home by our ain fireside. Here's to seeing you soon on the Plains of Totnes".[22]

VE DAY: OPEN ALL THE WINDOWS

All over England preparations were made for VE day on May 8. The blackout was taken down from my window, and at last the window could be opened easily to let in the Spring air, and at nightfall for the first time I could look out at night and see the stars and the moon – and Totnes was lit up. I went with Eileen to a field with a huge bonfire burning in the dark. The smell of the trodden grass and the burning wood filled the air. People were hugging and crying and long candles spiralled around with red were being handed out; even I was given one to hold with both hands. So many

[21] *The Letters of Sean O'Casey, Volume II*, p. 229.
[22] *The Letters of Sean O'Casey, Volume II*, p. 231.

people were there and as one by one the candles were lit we were surrounded by this glorious light that fell on their faces, turning them a glowing yellow - on this clear brisk night. I asked Eileen why so many people had tears running down their cheeks and she said, "although it was a good time and we were all happy it was also very sad as many people weren't here to share it with us as they had been killed in the war. But that we could rejoice that it was all over now". Not quite, of course. Not yet in the Far East. Slowly the procession started, silent and slow, down the hill it went. We were in the middle and could see the long path of lights snaking down the hill to The Plains. We walked along the road that led to our house. It was sombre and triumphant: I held my candle firmly with both hands, watched by Eileen. As we passed near our house there Sean stood with Father Ned, watching us turn left, standing at one of our yellow brick gate-posts (the gate was gone, taken for its metal near the beginning of the war), Sean watching and waving to us, and we waved to him as we marched past in solemn silence back around and down the hill again to end at The Plains. There may have been a band at front playing slow sad music. It was a beautiful torch-light procession, torches for as far as you could see in – front of me and behind – a glorious triumphant serpent.

We reached Totnes Plains and the band struck up. Different sounds now: old marching songs and dance music. "Run Rabbit Run Rabbit run run run". ... Eileen said she would take me home but I begged her to let me stay for a little, and she did. Up struck "Hands Knees and Bumps a Daisy" and off we went dancing together; huge bottoms came hurtling towards me and sent me flying; it was great fun. People were happy now and started to sing to the music. Finally back to Sean and to bed and a different life to come. Eileen went back to the Plains and danced till sun-rise. Sean stayed with me. I was tucked up in bed in "my Nursery upstairs".

Breon's letter to Jack and Mina:

Dear Jack & Mina,

Just a line to thank you for remembering my birthday [April 30], my collection of art-books is really beginning to make people who see it quite jealous. Thank you very much.

Well Totnes is covered with Union Jacks & we have one, on the command of Niall and Shivaun, flying out the nursery window: the old house don't seem the same.²³ The Victory Holiday was very pleasant down here, everyone was in very good spirits, singing & bidding everyone else good-night. The school had an enormous bonfire a-top of a hill – & we cooked sausages, drank cocoa & sang until about 3 in the morning, all round other bonfires could be seen, it was a beautiful night, a wonderful fire, and a marvellous feeling – at 12 O'clock the last all-clear was sounded, & Lucas, a trumpet player blew the last-post, and then cease-fire, and then we all sang very sentimentally "When they sound the last all-clear" – and everything was wonderful.

Eileen took Shivaun to the Totnes Bonfire & Shivaun was thrilled beyond words. Well it is all over now – classes have started again & one is supposed to go to bed at night again; most people are tired, & quiet, but the feeling still persists. I will never forget the sound of that bugle in the dark, it brought tears to one's eyes. The country is able to celebrate so simply – no one seemed to get hopelessly drunk, although the Mayor managed to fall in the river – I am gradually growing to prefer the quiet & simplicity of the country to the noise and life of the city – well I must leave off before I send you to sleep. Once again thank you & Mina for the art book.

Yours Breon

Breon later told me – "Niall was up there with me. I wish I knew what he had been thinking – I do know he quietly took it all in with his clear and funny sense of irony. We listened to Pop [A teacher Breon liked], it was quite a solemn occasion in a way; he was saying this is a historic day and you will always remember, and so on: he spoke as a historian. But a lot of people were in tears because although it was VE Day it wasn't the end of the war; there were a lot of people still fighting, in Burma for example. It was a victory over Europe, Germany, Africa but not the Far East." "They hadn't dropped the two atom bombs yet", I said. "No", he replied.

It was one day around that time, when we were shopping up the top-end of the High Street, that Eileen stopped to comfort a lady – trying to get on with her shopping but who had broken down in tears. Eileen explained as we wandered home that her son had been killed on the day of the cease-fire. The war had been officially over and he was shot. Breon

---

²³ I am pretty sure we also had the USSR hammer and sickle flying – the author.

recalled: "When the Americans left, they left suddenly. They went to D Day: and Bill Elmhirst, who lived up at the Hall came and told us that they'd gone and we went and broke into the Officers Mess; and I got an enormous tin of grapefruit juice and this vast box full of books they were supposed to have been distributed to the troops but they hadn't. They were all little paperbacks, they were quite small but they were complete, they weren't cut at all. And so I read all these American books, all these American authors."

3
Back to Peace
1945–1948

THE WAR YEARS 1945-1948

TURN ON THE LIGHTS

Our war had finished but the war in the East with Japan didn't end until Sept 2, 1945. In Devon by September 1945 the evacuees had all gone back to their homes. Most were delighted but some hated to leave their war-homes and their kind minders. An old couple down the road were devastated to see their two go and the children cried and clung on to the old couple. I hope they came back and visited them.

Breon knew what "back to normal" meant; I really didn't, as normal for me had been the war years. And things didn't get back to normal at the flick of a switch; it took years to rebuild the country after such devastation. Rationing went on and got even worse. Food was very scarce: bread was even added to the rationing as the wheat harvest had been bad. This lasted a few years till 1948. Clothes came off the ration books in 1949; petrol rationing didn't stop till 1950; sweets rationing was halved and ended in 1953; meat rationing stopped only in 1954.

Never having lived in peace-time conditions I noticed only that things changed to something new, and that the fear and the bombing had stopped. No more German aeroplanes overhead; everyone was exhausted but more relaxed. The most noticeable change was the lights shining at night and the blackout curtains having been pulled down, and the windows washed on the inside; the windows could be opened and the breeze could now blow the curtains; I could lie in bed and see the stars and the moon and the sun rising. During dusk and the night you could also see through the windows into the lighted rooms of our next-door neighbours: Niall and I liked to watch Mr and Mrs Fletcher take their baths with Eileen protesting as we laughed at what we saw. We could see the police station opposite lit up, with its blue light by the door shining, and over all this the glow from the lights of Totnes. The streetlights were all switched on and the buses and trains that passed were lit up inside. The buses no longer needed torches to show people to their seats as though by cinema usherettes. We no longer had to shield our torches but could flash them up to the sky. And we could look forward to November the 5th and the fireworks and to more bonfires like those we had on VE Day.

There had been a rough routine in the family during the war, often interrupted, but now it became easier to stick to it. During term-time the morning was always a difficulty for Eileen and it turned into a rush. Eileen usually stayed up late with Sean, helping by reading things out for him: also staying up late was a habit for her as well as Sean, as that's what her life had been as a young woman in the theatre. Sean described theatre people as "artists of the night" and Eileen's clock was set by that, so getting up early to see us off to school was a nightmare for her. She shouted at the boys to get out of bed helped by me jumping on them. She made me air my clothes by her gas fire in her bed-room; in the winter the amount of steam that rose up from them was alarming; the house was damp with no proper heat. It really needed all the fires lit and blazing to keep it warm but all the upstairs fireplaces were blocked off and Eileen and Sean, Breon and Niall (who shared a room), had small gas fires. The bathroom had no heater but when we had our weekly baths an electric fire, also very small, was connected by a long flex from the upstairs landing and left on for half an hour before we started to run the water. I used to like flicking water on to it and see it spark but was frequently told off as it was considered dangerous. Our loo on the half-way landing had a paraffin burner, one of those old black ones with a little red glass window in the front and a lever on the top to open and close the holes that let the heat out: they made very pretty patterns on the ceiling. This was mainly there to stop the pipes bursting but it was lovely and warm to sit there.

Once up we sometimes had time for a piece of toast and a glass of milk: if not I would take my toast to the bus stop and eat it on my way to school. If I missed the bus, Eileen would have to coax the car to start and drive me there, often still in her night-dress with a coat pulled over it. By then the boys both cycled to school and shot off quickly to avoid having to take me on the cross-bars.

As he worked until 2 or 4 in the morning most days, Sean usually slept through the pandemonium, or pretended to, always getting himself up by 9am. He slept in his long-tailed shirt so that made getting dressed quite easy. After pulling on his trousers and the braces, he pulled on his socks and slipped into his zip-up boot-like slippers. The first thing he had to do was to go down stairs to the stove and boil a kettle of water to bring up to his room to bathe his eyes with; they had to be soothed to unstick completely. After all the bathing of his eyes he shaved with the water that was left. Putting a towel over his lap he did it by touch as it was no good looking in a glass as he couldn't see well enough. His room then smelt of pleasant soap. Then in the peaceful house he went down to make his breakfast, gather his post and the papers from the door mat. He got *The Times* and *The Daily Worker* and sometimes *The News Chronicle*. He had *The Irish Times* sent to him. He also got weekly papers and other periodicals.

At bed-time after washing my face and teeth, I was put into my dressing gown that was getting rather small for me (the one made by Mina out of Eileen's wedding coat) then my slippers, and I would go and sit in Sean's comfy arm-chair by his gas fire. The chair seemed very big then, although looking at it now it is just of ordinary size. We would chat, and he would let me make people and animals out of his pipe-cleaners, or draw on a piece of paper. Into bed and a story had to be read to me by Breon, Eileen or Sean. Sean often decided to tell me stories about Ireland where he said he had come from, where they had banshees and a white horse. There were also Irish heroes who seemed to do a lot of killing but one had a dog that was very faithful and died when he came back from somewhere. He read me Rupert Bear and Toby Twirl; he insisted on calling him Toby Twirrril as he rolled his r's so much. He sang a bit but I preferred Eileen singing as she had such a lovely voice and sang her old popular songs that were funny, "All Alone by the Telephone", "Oh What a Surprise", "Two Lovely Black Eyes" and her version of "After the Ball was Over":

> After the ball was over,
> After the guests had gone,
> She hung her false wig in the corner,
> Put her false leg on the floor
> Put her false teeth in the basin
> Popped her false eye in the drawer
> The remainders went to by-bys -
> After the ball.

When I was in bed Eileen sometimes drew for me pictures like comics of two families called the Fatifers and the Thinifers. The Fatifers were lovely and warm and kind, they had a lovely nice round cat that purred and a round dog that liked you. The Thinifers on the other hand were mean and cold and cruel, with a thin cat that scratched and a skinny dog that barked and snapped.

Soon after peace was declared, Sean and I swapped rooms.

The adjoining door to Sean's new room was left ajar and then the "good-nights" again - and Eileen's good-night word "Goblessu"; that I much later realised meant "God bless you" - then the typing started.

THE GREAT ROOM MOVE

The move happened because Dr Varian said that my upstairs nursery was lighter than Sean's downstairs room and better for his eyes. His left eye had been dark for a very long time and his right one was now at one third capacity, and his eye-doctor was worried that his right retina would detach, meaning he would be totally blind. So it was up to Breon to take over the wood chopping duties, helped by Niall, who was reluctant, and myself, who was over eager but useless. The wood was supplied from the Estate; Dorothy and Leonard Elmhirst kindly arranged for it to be given to us free, saying it would only go to waste if not used. It was delivered by a small lorry that backed up the drive then tipped it out at the top outside the garage door. Then we all wheeled and carried it to the old stable behind the garage and stored it where a horse once stood. It was a sweet little stable with a wooden ladder leading to a hay-loft that had a double door that opened to reveal a lovely view over rooftops to the trees that lined the river Dart. It had a hoist to winch the hay up. Later I cleaned the loft out and used it as a hide-out. Eileen stored our apples there, carefully laid out on newspaper, not touching so if one went rotten it didn't taint the others. Breon told me that Mr Boas, the man who ran the little shop opposite, was in charge of all the "point stuff" during rationing, and he didn't have anywhere to store it, so he asked Eileen if he could store it in our loft. So she said yes, which was very nice because he used to give us the odd tins of things.

Sean made a terrible fuss about the move of rooms. Any movement of his books or writing things on his table, or on the shelves, meant he had great difficulty finding them again – and he hated to have to ask for help. Normally everything he used was in the "right" place – pen and pencils, papers, envelopes, sealing wax, string, notebooks, tobacco, tape-lighters, pipe-cleaners, pipe-tool, slippers, shoes, hankies, clothes – everything he used. That's why we all learned not to move anything, not to leave toys scattered about that he could trip on or worse for us, break, to push back chairs pulled out from tables so that he wouldn't bump into them, anything he could knock or fall over. He worked out every inch of the house, how many stairs on the staircase, for example.

There were rows and shouts of despair as he saw Eileen and Joy, a young girl who worked for us, carefully packing in a box what was on each shelf and transferring it to the same position upstairs. Eventually Eileen burst into tears. Dr Varian arrived and told Sean in so many words to pull himself together and to think of Eileen. Which he did. Fully admonished, he became very quiet, just hovering in the background.

I liked the move. I got to sleep in a tiny "dressing-room" off Sean's room with a connecting door. At night, after being tucked up and all the kisses received and goodnights said, the light clicked off and, at my insistence, the adjoining door was left half open for the light to slant in. I could hear Sean at work, scribbling with his scratchy pen or typing on his old typewriter – clicketty, clank – trrrrr , as he pushed the bar across that raised the paper to the next line and to the left-hand side of the paper. It sent me to sleep with a feeling of companionship. I need a recording of that sound now; maybe it would help with sleepless nights.

Sean's downstairs room was now replicated on the top floor; his room always stayed the same, a copy of his first room in Dublin. A mahogany oval dining table with thin legs, most likely a copy of Georgian furniture, sat in the middle of the room with one of the matching Carver chairs, also thin-legged, set sideways-on at one end of the oval near the fire. These were part of the furniture from Eileen's London flat that a friend of hers called Stella Greer, had furnished for her when they were young women in London. (Stella was a Canadian heiress, a relative of the actor Raymond Massey, and very generous; Eileen wrote about her in her autobiography, *Eileen*, in the chapter called "On My Own".) One of Sean's two typewriters sat in front of the chair, or pushed back a bit if he was writing by hand. A thick heavy green glass ashtray with high sides was where he beat out the tobacco ash and rested his pipe when it wasn't in his mouth. A box with pencils (lead, red and blue for marking his writing), his fountain pen, his pen knife to sharpen his pencils, and some other writing tools. There was a blue and white pottery container with a lid that held his tobacco with a cabbage leaf on-top of the 'baccy to keep it moist. This was given to him by Jack Carney during the war. There were ordered piles of papers and piles of books, and only he knew exactly where each thing was. Sitting somewhere among all this was a pile of unanswered post and also two spikes on wooden bases, one holding answered post and the other bills. His writing paper was kept in one of four filing drawers that stood on top of a long bookcase. He had about ten of these file-drawers all along the top of his long bookcase that stretched along one wall. In one drawer typing paper, in another thinner paper for copy, and in another the carbon paper that was placed carefully between the two sheets. In other drawers were envelopes, sealing wax, stamps, etc. All the drawers were carefully labelled. On the top of a roll-top filing cabinet behind the door were two more of these shelf-files standing on top of each other, and in one of them he kept some cash that Eileen would draw from the bank for him, in a little pink cardboard box, an old face-powder box with a flap lid that fastened with a popper, kept there for tips and small payments. Many times Eileen would get me to distract Sean outside his room and take some change out of the little box to help with the food shopping or for some treat. As we were going out the door sometimes Sean would call me back and go to this box to give me a sixpence or a shilling, saying, "I am sure I had more money than this, it must have flown away".

Over his mantelpiece he had a print of Gauguin's Tahitian ladies sitting on a bench, one with a bright orange dress, and full of colour. On the mantel-shelf he had a photo of George Jean Nathan, later joined by a picture of me holding a baby rabbit, a copy of Picasso's drawing of Stalin and a picture of Niall and Breon in a little motor boat on the pond at Goodrington beach. Other pictures in his room were a print of *The Sleeping Venus* by Titian, a print of an angel by Piero della Francesca, and a framed photo of him standing next to Augustus John at the opening of one of John's exhibitions. This hung on the wall alongside his bed: at the end of his life this had snaps of babies and children stuck all around the frame, sent to him by women who were moved by his work, especially the autobiographies.

He kept many of his daily papers and these were piled in a corner or on his Dublin sofa placed in front of the bay-window. This was the sofa made in Dublin by a carpenter friend when he had got his payment for *Juno and the Paycock*, and it was covered in a black satiny kind of material. Very important was his arm chair set to the other side at the end of his table and near the fire. This is where he sat to read and to think, and sometimes to worry about where the money was to come from.[1]

By a wall was his single bed at the top of which was a screen to stop some of the draught. Every afternoon that I can remember he'd tie a handkerchief around his eyes and take a rest after lunch and before tea. He often fell asleep. A doctor had advised him to do this after he had a blackout from stress. Working in the night was an old habit from his days as a workman in his one room in Dublin, as the night was the only time

---

[1] After his death when Eileen returned to Ireland, she took Sean's sofa and chair with her: *Eileen* (1976), p. 94.

THE WAR YEARS 1945–1948

he had then, and it was quiet; then he would work into the morning and then get up very early, possibly 6am in those days to get to work on time. At another wall stood a desk, made out of the same wood that they use for making cigar boxes, and it had that same lovely smell. This he also brought from Dublin, but he didn't write at it, he just piled more books and papers on the top and used the drawers to store his things. He hung his jacket and his heavy coat on a hook behind the door, and his cap also. His other large brimmed felt hat sat on top of the filing cabinet behind the door and another straw one on top of the bookcase. He didn't have many clothes, ever. Two or three shirts with long old-fashioned tails, two or three pairs of socks, and a couple of jumpers, hankies and much later-on, underpants. In the top left-hand drawer of this desk he kept some sweets, as he had a very sweet tooth, often putting six spoonfuls of sugar in his tea. The great treat was for him to offer you a Turkish Delight or some fudge when you were sitting in his room – that was after the war and sweet rationing ended. There was a 1930s art deco rug in front of his fire.

THE AMERICANS LEAVE

Our American wartime visitors now went back to the States and only visited now and again over the years, usually during the spring and summer months. Now that travel was safer they were joined by many more including Sean's American agent Richard Madden and his wife.[2] They must have visited us early after the war as food was still scarce. Eileen was worried whether we would have enough food for everyone and whispered to me not to ask for more: Dick heard and laughingly said – "Oh, a case of FHB – that's what we say in the States -Family Hold Back". I missed the excitement the Americans brought with them. One wartime visitor had been Professor David Greene and a fellow American GI, arriving in a Jeep from their billet near Plymouth.[3] Mainly I remember the

[2] Richard J. (Dick) Madden (1880–1951) was a New York-based "international play broker and authors' representative" whose Richard Madden Play Company's clients included T.S. Eliot, Eugene O'Neill, Somerset Maugham and Cole Porter. His obituary appeared in the *New York Times*, May 10, 1951. See *The Letters of Sean O'Casey, Volume II*, p. 808.

[3] David H. (Dave) Greene (1913–2008) was a professor at Harvard University, then New York University, who taught Irish literature. He was the co-author of *J.M. Synge, 1871–1909* (1959). He escorted Sean when the playwright spoke on American campuses in the 1930s. In 1966 he arranged for NYU library to buy 126 letters that Sean had written to Jack Carney. In the Second World War, he served as a U.S. Navy intelligence office in the UK. 2 See Greene's *New York Times* obituary, July 17, 2008.

big army men getting out of this jeep and his friend, the driver, taking Niall and me for a spin while Sean talked to Dave. They came quite often until the Normandy Landing. It was Dave who was sitting with Sean in the front room at Tingrith when Sean got the first phone call from Hollywood asking him to write the screenplay for Look Homeward, Angel. After Eileen refused on the phone for Sean, saying he couldn't possible do such a thing, he wouldn't know how, Dave said, "You sure turned down a load of hay."

But the person I most remember with most excitement was a young uniformed American who arrived and left by train, called Thomas Quinn Curtiss, or Tom. I liked him from day one – he was fond of children and great fun and he actually listened to what I said and chatted to me.[4] He laughed a lot and was always telling hilarious anecdotes. He was working in Intelligence in a London Office as he spoke many languages, including Russian and Japanese. He was a close friend and prodigy of Sean's old friend George Jean Nathan, and so a strong link to Sean's beloved New York and the best time of his life that he spent there with George and all his friends: O'Neill, Lillian Gish, Maxwell Anderson, Elmer Rice, Brooks Atkinson and his agent Richard Madden. Not forgetting Tallulah Bankhead. America and Americans suited Sean. Tom was very generous. I understand that he came from a wealthy family; maybe he did, but he gave easily and with thought – Christmas boxes during the war with Hershey chocolate bars, sweets, Double Bubble Gum with the little comics wrapping them and beautiful chocolate Father Christmases. I can still recall the particular vanilla smell of this American confectionery.

After Sean died Tom remained a friend to Eileen until she died and a friend to me until he died in 2000. But I let him down at the end. After a lot of effort I managed to get from the manager of the Tour D'Argent restaurant in Paris the phone number of the home Tom had gone to. Tom

---

[4] Thomas (Tom) Quinn Curtiss (1915–2000) had served with the Allied Expeditionary Force in Europe in 1944. He was a New York drama critic whose letters to Sean kept the latter apprised of the New York theatre scene and who occasionally visited Sean in England. Another visiting American theatre critic was Richard (Dick) Watts Jr. (1898–1981) who was the theatre critic for the *New York Herald Tribune* and *New York Post* and one of Sean's correspondents. There was an American College Drama Summer School at Dartington Hall which attracted American scholars. See *The Letters of Sean O'Casey*, Volume II, pp. 745, 834, 1087; Garry O'Connor, *Sean O'Casey: A Life* (London: Paladin, 1989), p. 343.

lived in this building, a great honour as only one other person did.[5] He ate there or out at a local cafe. His kitchen looked as if he never even boiled a kettle there: preserved in aspic. His main room was just piles of books, books and more books; a table and chairs all covered in books. A view of Notre Dame. But now Tom had dementia. Finally I managed to speak to him by phone and he was obviously distressed and not quite with it. He begged me to come and take him away. I said I had no way of doing that, that I was very hard up. I said I would do my best to get over there. But the next time I rang he was dead, and I could find out nothing more about him. I hope a part of him understood. I can feel myself sitting on his shoulders as Eileen walked him to the Totnes Station to catch his London train. His khaki wool rubbed my fat legs.

The Forces were kept to help in the huge clear-up abroad and at home. It took a while for the horrors of the concentration camps to creep out from the dreadful fog that covered them: horrors worse than anyone could have dreamt of. All were discussed in murmurs that we the children weren't meant to hear. Sean and Eileen's close friend Sidney Bernstein was one of the people chosen to enter Bergen-Belsen to be a witness of what was there. He made a documentary about it with Alfred Hitchcock.[6] Sean said he could hardly bring himself to speak about it.

Here, locally, there were families without mothers, without fathers, with children killed, and with homes blown to smithereens by the bombs dropped from the skies. New homes had to be built. Prefabricated homes ("pre-fabs") went up and in Totnes we had several railway carriages on the sidings that were lived in, and slowly the families planted flowers and vegetables along the side-banks. Plymouth was to be re-built – a Phoenix rising out of the ashes, and Nancy Astor and her husband were on the

---

[5] La Tour d'Argent on the Quai de la Tournelle is claimed variously to have opened in 1582 and 1650, though it doesn't appear in Baedeker until 1860. Marcel Proust mentions the restaurant three times in his famous novel, and in 1908 a dinner was given there for the Wright Brothers. "La Tour d'Argent", Wikipedia.

[6] This project, with a working title of "German Concentration Camps Factual Survey", was shelved in July 1945 for diplomatic reasons. The film using Allied and captured German footage was shown on the BBC in 1985 as *Memory of the Camps*: "Sidney Bernstein, Baron Bernstein", Wikipedia; "Bernstein, Sidney (1899-1993)", screenonline.org.uk.

Committee that made the plans, though not very good ones at that.[7] Exeter, though less so, needed patching together. Everywhere needed some repairs to bring life back to normal.

Eileen said that as soon as peace was declared people drew back into themselves and all the camaraderie between people fighting a common enemy went. I can't know – but maybe she felt a bit bereft. Suddenly all the good work she had being doing was ended: she didn't manage to continue with the Russian Shop or other work outside the house, partly because there was always so much to do for and with Sean that pulled her back, not forgetting us, the children.

It was around this time that my first big row with Eileen happened – not like the little rows over tidying up toys or not flooding the bathroom, but a heavy scary row. She had been to see Dr Varian, up the hill at Bridgetown. I waited in the car. We set off home a long way round making a circle behind the main road into Totnes. Suddenly she said, "Would you like me to have a baby?" A feeling of utter panic hit me: the same feeling I had when Eileen left for London without me in tow. "NO, no no!" I shot back. I actually couldn't think of anything worse. "It would be good for you and you love babies." "No I don't, I hate babies". Then it started: "It would stop you being so selfish and spoiled." I remember something like that being said. I was spoiled and did so often get my own way with Eileen, but not with Sean and the boys. I broke into uncontrollable sobs. Eileen had to stop the car. Finally she assured me she didn't want another baby. But for the first time I didn't really believe her. I still remember the shame I felt after saying "No", like it was a weakness on my part, a childish response because I liked to be the youngest. And the worst of it was that I had to pretend for a long time that I hated babies. "Come and look at the lovely new baby," Eileen would say when we were out shopping and a pram went by. "No thanks," I would have to mumble, or look and say nothing. "I don't know what's wrong with you, I thought you loved babies."

NEW SCHOOLS FOR NIALL AND ME

Niall now went to the Middle School, Aller Park, reopened after the evacuees left, and I went to the Junior School, the Old Postern. This

[7] Nancy, Lady Astor (1879–1964), although born in the United States, was the first woman to sit in the British House of Commons. She and her husband Waldorf lived in Cliveden, a large estate in Buckinghamshire. She and Sean corresponded over the decades.

THE WAR YEARS 1945-1948

September I was to be six years old and felt quite grown up. All my friends from the Children's Cottage were moving to the new building as well, so it was not such a big deal – or so I thought – but when Eileen left me at the gate I walked up a long drive with bushes each side that gave way on the left to a large open field of grass with an enormous conker tree standing tall with its golden leaves beginning to fall and conkers all over the place; and from one large branch a long swing hung, with children already sitting on it. You could get four on at once at a pinch. One or two of the younger children were crying. We were what were called "the day pupils" – we went home after school but now here were children called "boarders" whose parents lived a long way away and who didn't go home again until the holidays. Some were feeling very homesick. I understood what that felt like because I felt it when Eileen went away to London. The only person who I could stay with and not feel too bad was lovely Trudl, a gentle Austrian who had looked after me in the Nursery School after teacher Nora left, and her jolly and pretty daughter, Christl. Christl was full of laughter and stories. She was already at the Junior School, being a little older than I was, in the group below Niall. Niall was now ten and would have been at Aller Park a couple of years already if the war hadn't happened.

The Postern was so much larger than the Children's Cottage. There was a big open lawn to its front where the conker tree stood; to the right of the building two small wings stuck out and in-between was a paved area where we lay on our towels to get dry after swimming in the small pool. In the summer we all swam in the nude and this continued throughout the school. Along the bottom of an inset wall was a flower bed where we were each given an area to plant-up, and over the other side of the pool were enormous, to us, rhododendron bushes we used to climb and hide in. One of the wings was our classroom and the other was a woodworking room and art room. A man called Wincey taught woodwork, though I much preferred painting and drawing.

If you entered the building through the main entrance at the front, you went through a medieval stone arch to a large porch with stone benches on either side and opened a heavy medieval oak door with difficulty. An arched door on the left went into a small music room with a piano, but if you went straight on you entered a grand main hall that rose up two stories with a gallery along the front-side and to the left. The stairs to this gallery and the second floor that flowed from it were through an arch to the left rising up from a small second hallway, where we left our hats and coats. The stair rail was great to slide down. Straight ahead were the wings with the classrooms. Through an archway to the right was the dining room, and at the back of the building was a huge kitchen.

The boarders had their rooms upstairs along two corridors, one running off the gallery on the right, the other on the left. Down one step and into a snug there was the welcoming housemother's sitting-room with a bedroom and bathroom off it. In the winter there was a wood fire in the grate. This room was for the boarders to come to in their pyjamas and dressing-gowns after baths to hear a bedtime story and have a mug of milk or other warm drink. The housemother was called Toe Ogilvy and there was also a "house father" called Anne Grant. Toe had a little boy called Oliver. When I asked Toe who his daddy was she said he didn't have one and that he was born in a bottle.[8] This was surprising to me as I hadn't heard of that before and I thought he must have been very special. Whenever I hear the character of Mr Grigson, an alcoholic, in my father's play *The Shadow of a Gunman* say, as he raises a bottle to drink from, "Here's to Adolphus Grigson, who was born in a bottle!", I always think of little Ollie.

It didn't take long for us all to make friends with the new day pupils and the boarders. There was a little boy from Holland who had horrible nightmares and we were told he had gone through a lot of bad things. He was often visited by his older brothers who were at the Middle School; they seemed a very close-knit family and were very kind. I made new friends with Jane Phibbs and Ann Stott. Jane was very pretty and had an older brother called Giles who became a close friend of Niall's. Her uncle was a writer, I think.[9] Ann had an older sister called Rosemary who was as musical as Ann was, who I thought was brilliant at the piano. They also used very long words and Ann told me that her parents encouraged this and that they read plays in the holiday. Imagine!

Another friend of Niall's was Marcus Tyrrell, called Marky. He became very interested in trees and became a forester. His mother Bardie who we

[8] Mary (Toe) Ogilvy and Ann Grant, both unmarried, together adopted Oliver. Ogilvy continued to be involved in Oliver's life after Grant married. Toe Ogilvy, born in 1908, died in 1983. See The Dartington School magazine, *The Voice*, for 1983/84.

[9] London-born Giles Phibbs (1934–2014) became a TV actor and appeared in *Doctor Who* and *Z Cars*. Jane and Giles' uncle was the Norfolk-born Anglo-Irish writer and editor from a Sligo Big House, Geoffrey Phibbs (later Geoffrey Taylor), 1900–1956, friend of Robert Graves and Laura Riding.

went camping with was the member of the local Communist society. Bardie and her husband wanted Sean to be a member but he never was or wanted to be a member of anything anymore. This didn't alter his opinions but made it easier for him to disagree from outside with things the Party did. Sean didn't like the Totnes Party; he had been used to working with Jim Larkin as a member of his Union in Dublin, the Transport and General Workers' Union, involved with his fellow workmen; here was a group of middle-class people who he felt were dogmatic about their beliefs. It caused some bad feelings but Sean kept to himself and life went on. Most people in the rural parts of Devon, away from Plymouth, were Conservative or Liberal; I think it is fair to say that many of the Dartington teachers and people who ran the estate were Liberal. Many farm workers voted Conservative, a thing that bewildered Sean. Fred Seyd, the French teacher at Dartington, was a Communist along with his wife Juliet. She was one of the people Sean avoided as he thought her too dogmatic, which was a shame as he liked Fred. Niall had French lessons with Fred at the Middle School and I was longing to try them. When I finally got there I only had Fred for a few lessons as he was asked to leave the school and Dorothy and Leonard didn't stop the sacking. His lessons were full of fun: you spoke French as soon as you entered the classroom and then you made up scenes with puppets, speaking French. None of the other French teachers was nearly as good as him. The result was that Niall had a good start with the language and spoke it well but I never managed to get over the first hurdle. Why was Fred asked to go? Sean thought that his wife going on about Communism didn't help but if that was the case it doesn't excuse virtually blacklisting a teacher because he belonged to a party you didn't like and whose wife was bit of a nuisance.[10]

We were taught by our teacher "Goofy" and also the young Spanish girl, Carita. We loved Carita and Goofy (named after the Disney character who we thought she looked a bit like): they were both kind and funny but Carita was more fun. We learnt letters and numbers, were read to every day, and I tried to learn to read but preferred being read to. We played outside and went on nature walks. In our free time we played many different games outside: Kick-the Can, Chain-Hee, Cock-an-olly that was a version of Cops and Robbers, Statues or Freeze Tag and Kiss Chase.

[10] The answer is presumably to be found in the correspondence between Curry and Seyd held in the Devon Heritage Centre in Exeter as part of Fred Seyd's personal correspondence, 1942–1986.

Smaller groups skipped, played Ring-o-Roses, The Mulberry Bush, The Farmer in the Dell, London Bridge and What's the Time Mr Wolf?, Inside and Outside, Sardines and Truth or Dare. My favourites were Kick-the Can, Chain Hee and Cock-an-Olly. The last was the hunting game; one player had to find the others and bring them back to "home" while also guarding the home, as the ones already caught could be released by someone running up and touching them, saying "cock-an-olly".

By the time summer came, my friends and I had become more adventurous and wandered farther afield. First we discovered the Farm – and the cows being milked. We became friendly with the farm-hands and "helped" them bring the cows from the field for milking; actually all the cows knew exactly where to go, each finding her own milking-stall with her name on it. Once I rode Jill for a moment; I was held on by the farmer, but she didn't like it much so we gave up. Jill was our favourite cow as she had a "crooked horn" and was very gentle. You could stroke them all and let them suck your hands – what strong sucks they had with their raspy tongues. This farm was "advanced" as it was part of Dartington and the cows were all milked by machine. We watched them all being hooked up as they munched their feed laid out in their troughs as their hot breath steamed out of their mouths and vanished amongst the smell of warm milk.

It was on one of these visits to the farm with a friend that we heard a little desperate mewing in a barn from the top of some bales of hay. I clambered up and found a dead black cat, with dead kittens, except for one little scraggy Tabby that was mewing. I took the kitten, that smelt dreadful, and tucked it up my jumper and we ran to find someone to tell. "Looks like the mother was killed by a rat. Shame. Nothing to be done now." "Can I keep the kitten?" "If yous want, we'd drown she otherwise. Doubt if she will live."

I couldn't wait to get home. Keeping my kitten in my jumper on the back seat of the car, luckily the windows of cars were kept open in those days as the driver had to make hand-signals so Eileen didn't smell anything foul. As soon as we got home I rushed up to the bathroom and gave my kitten a scrub with Persil. Eileen came in as I was drying her. "What is that?" "A poor little kitten that I found next to its dead mother and I want to keep her." "My dear, how can we possibly keep her? You know Sean doesn't want a cat or dog in case he treads on them because of his bad sight." "Please, please, please!" I took her into Sean and begged him as well.

THE WAR YEARS 1945–1948

"Well, I suppose we can see if the poor thing survives and then think again."

And so Dr Varian was called who prescribed warm milk every hour, given from a doll's bottle I luckily had. So every hour Eileen, not me, had to feed Kitty, that is what I called her. Sean sometimes called her Tabby. She soon opened her eyes and grew bigger until she only needed feeding every four hours or so and not so often during the night. Sean had a way with animals. I couldn't understand why she didn't sleep on my bed but always slept on Sean's and on his sofa, facing the bay window, in the sun when it shone. Once I remember finding her at the end of my bed asleep and I was so thrilled I jumped up and off she sped. I couldn't resist touching her no matter what Eileen said about leaving her alone and then she might come to you. Kitty liked to make nests in the newspapers Sean left in a pile on his sofa; tearing them up in the process. Once Sean left his first draft of an article on the sofa and Kitty tore it up and he found her sleeping on it. He was very upset, not with the cat but with himself for leaving the work there, where she so often slept. On one of our walks together I noticed dad didn't have his top-coat on. It was bitterly cold with a north-easterly blowing. "I am fine with my muffler," he said, "anyway, Kitty was lying on my coat and you should never disturb a cat". He then told me about St Francis who cut a hole out of his cloak, around a cat sleeping on it, so as not to disturb it.

Kitty loved Eileen best of all, after all she was her mother, had fed her as a kitten when her eyes were still tight shut, and still was the one that remembered to feed her. So, it was at the side of Eileen's bed where she left her gifts of dead mice and once or twice a bird. Eileen was terrified of mice, even more than thunderstorms, and we would all hear an ear-ripping scream and think, "Another mouse". Niall or Breon would pick it up by the tail and take it to the dustbin. The good thing was that once Kitty became a killing machine cat we had very few mice and no more rats. Before she came I remember Sean and Breon sitting on the back stairs, one with a hockey stick, the other a cricket bat, waiting for a rat to appear that had been spotted. Hours later we all heard crashing and cursing and silence, until a peal of uncontrollable laughter issued forth. No way had they hit the rat but had managed to hit each other.

At school Goofy lived in the room above the porch. One day her door was open at the end of the gallery overlooking the dining-room; she was tidying her room. A few of us walked up to her door and asked if we could sit and watch. She said we could and asked if we would like to see her jewels. Our eyes widened as we gasped, "Yes, please!" Goofy took out a box, rather like a shoe box, from her bottom drawer and took off the lid: there were lots of glittering jewels; necklaces, bangles, brooches. I was dazzled. I couldn't forget these gewgaws and thought how I would like to take them home to Eileen, how pleased she would be. I must have known it was wrong as I remember creeping later along the gallery, opening the door and the drawer, opening the lid of the box and taking a handful of the shiny trinkets and putting them in my pocket. When I got home that afternoon I showed them to Eileen, who, to my surprise, was horrified. "You shouldn't have taken these darling, they don't belong to you and we have to take them back right now." I thought they were ours now as we had them but Eileen said a firm "No". She rang immediately to tell Goofy what I had done and she hadn't even noticed, then we got in the car with the jewels and drove back to the Old Postern. I had to hand them back and say how sorry I was and I would never do it again. It was all very amicable – they seemed to be smiling rather than scowling, and Goofy didn't take it out on me – ever.

Eileen was up in London again and I was staying with Trudl and my friend Christl at the Children's Cottage. Eileen was up to watch rehearsals for *Red Roses for Me*.[11]

I had an old bike, one of Breon and Niall's, a boy's bike with faulty brakes. To stop quickly you had to jump off the back and then run and rescue the bike. One day while staying with Trudl I decided to bike down the hill to Aller Park and see if I could find Niall. I was haring down the little hill and suddenly a little child ran out in front of me. I automatically pulled as hard as I could on both brakes, the front ones being the only ones that worked I went flying over the handlebars, landing on my head and face. I remember flying through the air and then nothing until I came round in a big man's arms going through the back gate of the Kindergarten and then fell back to sleep. Later I came to in bed with the school doctor and Trudl looking at me. I was violently sick several times. He looked in my eyes with a torch and asked me to count his fingers. He told Trudl not to move me and not to feed me but to try and keep me awake. I couldn't

---

[11] Sean signed a contract in late 1944 with Bronson Albery for *Red Roses for Me*, manager of the New Theatre in St Martin's Lane. Sean thought the play would be staged after Christmas, but it was February 26, 1946 before it opened. The New Theatre became the Albery Theatre in 1973 and was renamed the Noel Coward Theatre in 2006.

THE WAR YEARS 1945–1948

have eaten anything if I had tried as I felt so sick, and I kept being horrid sick.

The next day Dr Varian came to see me and said that when Eileen came back she would take me home and he would look after me. The following day Eileen arrived and drove me home all wrapped up in a blanket and Niall holding my hand in the back. Eileen was rather worried that I would never look the same again as the whole of my face was grazed raw with lots of little bits of grit embedded in it. But the valiant Dr Varian came to the rescue with a special ointment used during the First World War made from comfrey. He smeared it all over my face and the next morning Eileen was overjoyed to see my pillow covered in bits of grit; and eventually it all came out and only a few stubborn ones had to be helped. I thought he was a very clever doctor. Sean's Notebook reads: "Shivaun fell off her bike & got slight concussion, & a torn-up face: she's all right again – a narrow escape."

BREON IS CALLED UP

Not long after this Breon passed his army medical. Sean was pleased but Breon was in two minds. The last thing he wanted to do was his National Service. The day came for Breon on November 5; he told me he remembered bonfires and fireworks – the first time for six years the day was celebrated. Eileen had arranged for him to spend the night at the Connaught Hotel, London with his girlfriend from school, Sophie. Breon loved Sophie too much and was devastated when she went and married a Guardsman. Her family wouldn't have wanted Breon as a son-in-law – no money and not much social standing. Her family, I was told, were very well-off. I liked her sister, Stella, very much. She was older than me but we had something in common as our siblings loved each other. I wasn't very aware of this but Stella pointed it out to me. I remember once when I was at the gate of the Middle School waiting for Eileen to pick me up – she was always late – Stella came up and chatted to me. She had a black and white tooth-check kilt on and I asked her where she got it, as I rather fancied it. "Our kilt-maker made it for me." she said. I think I asked if he could make me one, but that was obviously not possible – not her fault, just not easy to arrange.

On November 8 Breon travelled down to Farnborough by train and started his stint in khaki.

Tingrith with Breon gone felt empty; we had all been together for seven years or so and his quiet, sometimes sulky, presence and funny humour were missed. Breon had taken a major part in bringing Niall and me up. He had taught me to swim and to ride a bike; Sean and Niall taught me to catch a ball and not to be such a cry-baby; he and Niall had both helped to toughen me up a bit. Niall was also there to protect me. One day a friend of mine, Caroline, who lived two doors away, and I wandered a little further than usual into a field that sloped down to the train track. The end of a large concrete pipe sticking out from a mound took my interest: a stream ran into it maybe to eventually trickle into the River Dart. Suddenly a gang from the street along the track appeared at the top of the slope and started to throw stones at us as we sat on a rock at the entrance. We darted into the large pipe and were trapped inside. Caroline who didn't have two big brothers started to cry and that delighted them all. They continued to shout abuse – "Cry-babies. Mummies favourites." "I am not crying" I said, "I think you are all mean." "The big one is brave," mumbled their leader, "I'll give her that." "I'll get my big brother on to you! He'll tell you what for!" "Ohhh, aren't we scared. I don't think!" Then, what luck, Breon was there as if by magic calling out for me and Caroline as he couldn't see us. I came out and shouted, "I'm here Bre and we are surrounded." To them I said "That's my big brother." And he was big, very tall and broad. "Ho-we!" he shouted, "What's up." And started running down the slope. All our tormentors ran like the clappers. "Cowardy custards" I shouted, rather feebly. "Go after them Bre." "No, thanks. We'll leave it for now. Dinner's ready and Mrs Niche is wondering where Caroline is". Caroline had stopped crying and Breon gave her a piggyback to cheer her up. I ran along beside them feeling very relieved. We never went back to the concrete pipe. Niall was amused to hear the tale of adventure, laughing into his tea-cup as usual. He was growing up fast, still in short trousers but tall like Breon. Very soon he would don long trousers, grey flannels like they all wore then, and suddenly turn from a boy to a man.

In his barracks and missing us, Breon had asked for a photo of us all to have, so when we were all in Torquay walking along the promenade, Eileen got one of the photographers (there to take photos of the holidaymakers) to take a snap of us all. A few days later she went to get it and sent it off to Bre. "Thanks!" he said later, "for sending me such a dreadful photo; you all looked so bloody miserable, except you Shivy." Sean had his cap pulled over his bad-eye and was grimacing because of the light, Niall in summer short trousers looked fed up and Eileen grim and determined, and me smiling in my jodhpurs, as I did a little riding at the behest of Eileen who told me that she lost a job for a film part when she was an actress because she couldn't ride a horse. So I was being groomed not to lose a job in a film I might one day be offered if I could ride, even though it didn't matter a damn, as I learned they had doubles to do that sort of thing. Sean missed Breon helping him to do the heavy tasks about the house and garden. Niall helped a bit but was very good at avoiding work like that.

TRIPS TO LONDON

Now the war was over we used the car a bit more. It was an old Austin; it had not been in very good nick before the war but now after years of being used very little indeed and not being able to be properly repaired, it was always breaking down. We had a very good local garage, Baldwins. Mr Baldwin was kind and a good mechanic, and kept the old girl going. We never used the car for local shopping, only to pick me up from school after the buses had stopped and before I could ride a bike safely, my brakes being still ropey. The car was used for trips to the sea-side at Goodrington, our summer holiday resort. It also took us to the pictures at Paignton and Torquay. We often took several of my friends along and we sang the songs from the film all the way home, especially if it had been a musical like *Annie Get Your Gun*. My friend Christl remembers singing all the songs again to Sean when we got back. I know he liked "Oh, What a beautiful morning" from *Oklahoma* as he sang it a lot with me and it is sung by the Codger in his play *The Bishop's Bonfire*.

Then my trips to London started: another world. Up by train, usually an hour late. Some joker wrote on the top of the ticket booth, "This week's train has gone." The compartments were comfortable with padded seats like benches facing each other, with racks for luggage overhead made from string netting – on night journeys people stretched themselves out in them and went to sleep. Running alongside the compartments was a corridor from which you could reach all the compartments in the carriage and look into them if the curtains weren't drawn. I liked to run up and down the corridor as the train was going and stick my head out of the window to see the long snaking train turn bends. I was told, "Don't put your head out too far or it may be knocked off by a signal-pole or something". Eileen always got tickets for the second sittings of lunch or tea in the dining car,

"It helps to pass the time," she always said, and being the last sitting we could sit on longer at the table. The Great Western trains had lovely dining cars then; each table had banquette seats, wooden frames extended to hold etched glass above the backs of the seats, making each table feel private. The cabinet work was beautiful and the etched scenes were different on each train: birds and fishes, exciting things to do when on holiday in the English Riviera. The tables were laid with crisp laundered white cloths and big napkins, china and silverware. As if on cue from the waiters, the train always speeded up just as the food came and Eileen and Niall showed me how to drink while the train was speeding along, or how to eat soup; "Move with the train, that's how to do it," Eileen said. Lunch was a three-course meal.

In those days after the war it took five hours to get from Totnes to Paddington Station in London (it takes just over three hours now): but there were very often stops on the line and being two hours late was quite usual. Then, if that happened, we sometimes had tea as well as lunch! Tea consisted of bread and butter and jam, cucumber sandwiches and cakes, with a pot of tea, of course. Eileen poured it with great ease.

Eileen had a nasty habit of popping out at stations to buy magazines. The train normally stopped for ten minutes at each station to unload and load goods, especially afternoon papers if it was going homeward. Niall and I and Breon if he was with us would be on tenterhooks until she got back on, leaving it to the last minute and sometimes even hopping on the train as it was starting. Once or twice we thought we had lost her as she had hopped on at another carriage. I was very upset and angry; after all she had the tickets and any money we had.

Arriving at Paddington, the train would stand heaving out its steam and blowing its whistle, shunting to a stop, often making people fall on to people's laps as they reached for their luggage; it would creep a bit and shunt to a stop again, with everyone holding on tight and eager to get out. The drivers must have enjoyed all that. Eileen would declare to Niall, and later to me, "Go and find a porter, dear." We stood looking helpless until one appeared with his trolley to lift the cases down off the racks (yes, we didn't even do that and we were in second class), stack them on his trolley in order of size and wheel it quickly along with us all half-running behind him through the thick throng of people arriving and those intent on finding their friends or families they had come to meet. Arriving at the taxi rank the porter would wait until we got our taxi; they came into the station

THE WAR YEARS 1945–1948

from around a sharp corner and straight on to a very steep incline that landed them on to the last platform. Eileen always tipped the porter well after he had stacked the luggage in the front-space beside the driver, held on by a strap, as it was open to the elements. "The Regent Palace Hotel, please," she said to the driver and with a "Right you are" in reply, off we sped. Down Bayswater Road past Regent's Park and along its railings, even in the daytime there were some very dressed-up ladies walking up and down waiting for customers; they hadn't been herded indoors then and could seek their customers openly, gaily coloured and with an air of defiance. At the Marble Arch entrance we turned right and went down Park Lane, all names familiar from Monopoly, then we swung left past the Ritz, where Eileen used to meet Harold Macmillan after Lady Dorothy and Sean had died, and down Piccadilly past Fortnum's and the Royal Academy into Piccadilly Circus, turning off just after Regent Street and stopping at the Regent Palace Hotel. The doorman took our luggage and we went with Eileen to reception where, after we had been given our key, she asked if there were any messages for Mrs O'Casey and there usually were. Eileen loved London and her excitement infected me as I loved being up in London with her.

It seemed to me a huge hotel, with an elaborate patterned wooden floor black and white marble pillars with fancy tops, booths and desks each side before you got to reception and a circular hall with a big glass dome above: dining rooms and lounges all in an art deco style. It was rather crude art deco, though, as it was owned by Lyons and definitely had its rather showy imprint. It had three electric lifts. We got into a waiting lift with our key with a heavy brass tag attached with the room number etched on it. The lift-man asked the floor, we told him the room number, and he would tell you the floor you were on, usually four or five; there were nine floors in all. The lift-man was trained to stop the lift exactly at the right point and if he didn't he would tease it up and down until it lined up with the floor; he pulled down on the lever to open the doors and there would be the hall porter waiting with our luggage to take us to our room. All the staff wore very smart uniforms.

The rooms were spacious with a big window. Ours was a double room with two beds. Eileen and I slept in one and Niall in the other. Wardrobe, dressing table and a bedside cabinets with a chamber pots inside. "What's this for?" I exclaimed. "It's very useful if you want to wee in the night. It's best for ladies if they don't want to wander around in their dressing-gown in the night," Mum said. The loos and bathrooms were shared and you had to ask for a bath, and then it would be drawn for you and cleaned after you had finished. Very grand, I thought.[12]

Downstairs, if someone phoned or came to meet Eileen, a page-boy would page her: "Mrs O'Casey. Telephone call for Mrs O'Casey" or "Someone to see Mrs O'Casey." You could hear it coming from the desk, increasing in volume as he got nearer. Often there were two or more messages being shouted at the same time by different boys with their pillbox hats. Great excitement. When we came back from being out, Eileen always went to the front desk to ask for messages. Sean wrote to Eileen, Niall and me when we were away and his letters came the next day, sometimes on the same day. Sadly, all Niall's letters were lost but I have most of mine.

Directly outside the hotel was Piccadilly Circus and at night all its lights were a magic sight. Piccadilly Circus lights were turned on again in 1949 after the war and the blackout. There were neon lights that moved, as well as pretty single lights that made pictures. BOVRIL with arcs of white lights lighting one by one and then all together, SCHWEPPES TONIC WATER. Not as many as now but amazing to see. The Regent Palace had its name up in lights. Up Shaftesbury Avenue all the theatre fronts were lit up with the names of the Stars. Eileen said she was starved of theatre and managed to go most every night, and took us to matinees.

Niall looked after me when Eileen was out but once an old Irish friend took us both out while Eileen went to see a show. George Gilmore had been active in the IRA and he and his brother were renowned for escaping from prison.[13] He liked "adventures" which consisted of my walking around London with him until I was exhausted and longing to get to bed.

[12] The large Regent Palace hotel near Piccadilly Circus opened in May 1915 and closed its doors in 2006. Its three lifts and marble stairways were among its distinctive features. In its heyday it employed over 1000 staff. In the Second World War it was a favourite haunt of airmen, particularly Canadian airmen: "Regent Palace Hotel", Wikipedia.

[13] George Gilmore (1898–1985) was, like Sean, a Dublin-born Protestant who became a committed left-winger. He joined the IRA and led the South County Dublin Battalion between 1925 and 1926. He was one of those Irish republicans who rejected the Anglo-Irish Treaty of 1921 and fought on the anti-Treaty side during the Irish Civil War. In 1926 and 1931 he was arrested by the pro-Treaty Irish Free State authorities and twice released. In the late 1920s, he sought training for IRA members from the Soviet Union. In August 1932 he was shot and wounded by the Free State police, the Garda Síochána. He was a friend of Sean's and there is a letter to him of November 7, 1951 in which Sean thanks him for befriending Niall when his son visited Dublin: *The Letters of Sean O'Casey*, Volume II, p. 836.

THE WAR YEARS 1945-1948

This night George, in his usual trench-coat, buttoned and buckled, Niall and I went from the hotel to the entrance to the Piccadilly tube train – past the newspaper sellers crying out the evening news, adding "Read All About It!" They shouted the names of their papers so quickly it was a chant: in unison their different cries at once were a chorus. We went past the man who sold his papers on the corner and had no nose. (When I asked Eileen, "Why hasn't he got a nose?" she said: "He has syphilis, dear, it eats up your nose and then your brain, so you often go mad. Don't worry it's not catching, normally". There was also a man who moved around on a board with four little wheels, using his knuckles, bound with cloth, to move him along; he had no legs. "It's the result of the terrible war", Eileen sighed.)

The best thing George ever did was to take us to one of the longest wooden escalators in the Underground and run up the down escalators with us and down the up ones. At that time of night there weren't many people and we stopped or went around surprised travellers, some frowning and tutting but many smiling. Another time with George, this time during the day, he took Niall and me to boat on the Serpentine to teach us how to row properly. George lived high up on the Howth Hill in Dublin, at somewhere called The Slads. He had a rowing boat and rowed out to Ireland's Eye where he swam with the seals. Niall later did this with him when he biked around Ireland with a school friend. So we hired the boat on the Serpentine and off we set. I kept standing up and wobbling the boat to George's disgust; not heeding his warnings I fell overboard and was amazed that I could actually stand up with my head above that water. They hauled me in and we had to row the boat back. George lent me his coat and I had a very humiliating ride back on the bus to the hotel and warm clothes and a hot bath. Niall was concerned but also displeased as we had to stop the rowing: George was none too pleased either and thought it all my own fault.

But the most surprising visit to London was almost immediately after the war. Soldiers, airmen and sailors were everywhere. The bomb damage was awful – great gaps in the streets where a building had once stood, some cleared but others still full of rubble, the imprint of the house on the walls left standing; paint, wallpaper, wooden floor supports set into the brick showed where the floors used to be; the oddest thing were the fireplaces one on top of each other following the chimney, suspended, empty. Spivs with suitcases appeared mysteriously offering "smokes" or "nylons". Eileen usually bought a pair of nylons, sometimes a little short but wearable.

This time Trudl had come as we were to meet a young Irish girl who was coming to "help Eileen manage". This meant that Christl came too which was great as she was so much fun. Christl and I had a room of our own with an adjoining door to the room where Eileen and Trudl slept. Left to our own devices if they went down for a drink, Christl and I dressed up in Eileen's posh clothes, underwear and high heels and made up with her rouge and lipstick. Then we walked up and down the corridors, then up and down in the lifts with our new friend, the lift-man; he even let us have goes at working the lift when no one was about. We talked with grand accents and pretended to be very upper-class ladies – then Eileen and Trudl appeared and we burst out in giggles and were mildly reprimanded and told to take it all off and get into bed, as it was very late.

The next morning Eileen went out to do some shopping and left us behind presumably with Trudl. She came back in a very long royal blue woollen tweed coat; she said it was called the New Look. "I think it's horrible," I said. "Well, I love it, and it feels great. It's got lots of material in it and swings as you walk." In the late afternoon Eileen went to meet the boat train and came back with a pale, dark curly-haired young woman, Kathleen Peavoy from Phibsboro, Dublin. She actually looked green and as she was very fat her head looked very small. Eileen took her directly to her room so she could undress and lie down; she said she wasn't hungry and just wanted to sleep. The next morning a knock at the door and in walked a slim pretty girl. "What on earth!" Eileen gasped. Then Kathleen explained that her sister had made her wrap a pair of sheets around her under her clothes to avoid them being confiscated by the customs. She also had some bacon that she had also concealed somehow. We all thought it was hilarious and got dressed quickly to go down to breakfast. I liked Kathy a lot.

Kathy was to live with us for two years; it kept stretching out as it was difficult for her to save enough to take her to Pennsylvania, her determined desire. I didn't want her to go at all. She was liked by everyone and a local farmer, Farmer Tucker, had a "graw" for her, or a soft-spot,[14] although he was married. When he came to the house, always by the open back-door, he would call out, "Kathleen, where be you?" Sometimes she would hide, other times Eileen went down with her. Kathy was very prudish, brought up to be ashamed of showing too much of her body. Dr

[14] "Graw" was a word Sean used – the pronunciation of the Irish *grá*, meaning "love".

THE WAR YEARS 1945–1948

Varian was very cross once when he had to check her chest for infection and she screamed when he approached her; Eileen took ages to persuade her to let him go ahead. "Good God, what does she think I'd do, silly woman."

Eventually she bought her one-way ticket to the States. Before she left she went on a shopping spree with Eileen to buy some new clothes for her new life, with a little of what she had saved; clothes rationing stopped in 1949. Sean and Eileen bought her a warm and smart coat. Eileen thought coats were essential: "You are all right if you have a good coat and boots". It was even better if some gentleman would buy them for you.

Soon after Kathy had sailed away and had arrived in Philadelphia, she sent us a photo of herself surrounded by at least four hunky men: all in bathing costumes and laughing and waving. So her puritanical streak had certainly lessened. She married over there and had several children. Eileen visited her once in the 1980s but I never managed to get down to see her from New York when I lived there.

BREON AS A SOLDIER, 1947

Breon sometimes stayed with Jack and Mina if he was on short leave. They remained close for many more years.

19098225 Pte O'Casey
13 pln 13p.i.n.
Middleway Camp, Taunton, Somerset.

Dear Jack and Mina,

Thank you for writing. The first six weeks, they say, is the worst; certainly the first week is bad enough. No time to read, or even think. No room to put anything, papers or food. The only way out is to get as many laughs as possible & hang on. I met a friend of mine, Neville, who got the sword of honour at Sandhurst for his year & is now an officer, and today we were allowed out of camp for the first time & could see a picture & ring up home. It is such small things one has to cling on to. One misses one's leisure, & the colour of civilian life, & it is hell to be ordered around & have someone think for you instead of regulating your own life, but it gets easier day by day & it is surprising how decent all these various – & believe me they are various, they range from fair men & farm workers to public school boys – fellows are, &

how one can be friendly with them, although at first the only common subject seemed to be sex, but now it is more varied. If I ever get posted to London you must let me come and see you & get in touch with the outside world, but that won't be till after Christmas for certain, perhaps never. In a few minutes now its lights out, so all my love

– Breon.

Jack and Mina were extra fond of Breon. Jack sent him many art books over the years that were important to Breon who wished to become a painter. I think they looked on him as a son. They were aunty Mina and Uncle Jack to us all.

Sean's letter to Breon:

Jan 23rd 1947.
My very Dear Breon,

A line or two to show we remember you, & often think about you. We haven't heard now for some days, but take it you are fit and well. ... The house is very silent & lonely, now that you and Niall are away; but Shivaun is left anyway, & that's something. ...

You've heard Bill Elmhirst is thinking of going down into the mines. I wonder what's the real reason. He says he wants to get in touch with the workers.[15] As if the army was an army of dukes and earls, & propertied gentlemen. I hope you got the sweets & h'kerchiefs all right.

All the Best. Our love Sean

That month, Breon applied to become an officer, partly because the pay was better. But he failed his interview and was pretty cut up about it.[16]

[15] William (Bill), 1929–2016, son of Dorothy and Leonard Elmhirst, was described on his death as "a sensitive and spiritual millionaire". He was educated at Dartington Hall. Towards the end of the war he was conscripted as a miner at Betteshanger colliery in Kent, so the degree of choice and the motive in the matter are unclear. He became a spiritualist and was estranged from his father when he and his second wife started a movement called Solar Quest to balance the Earth with divine help. He was a philanthropist who among other generosities funded a residency for the famous musician Ravi Shankar at Dartington. He also became an actor. See Dartington Trust: dartington.org/william-elmhirst-dies-aged-87/

[16] Breon had applied to a War Office Selection Board to become an officer but was turned down. WOSBs were psychiatric-based attempts, after British military setbacks, to find officer material. The procedure involved written self-descriptions by the candidate, an interview, an intelligence test, a choice-reaction test and a performance under stress test.

THE WAR YEARS 1945–1948

In February Totnes was practically snow bound.[17] Eileen and Sean had to plod through deep snow to get necessities like milk, bread and spuds as nobody could deliver. After a couple of days the milk was delivered on a big sledge pulled by a cart horse; he looked magnificent, his nose breathing mist. It was magic to me, the soft sound and the whiteness of everything, the sparkle when the sun came through: ice to slide on and the snow to chuck and to build snowmen, women, cats and dogs. Trudl skied down from Dartington and left her skis in our garage then walked to the shops. After having a cup of tea she would ski back with all her shopping in a rucksack strung to her back.

During this time Sean had bad influenza that always lasted a long time with him, and while he was ill Eileen had a very bad fall in early February.

Sean's Notebook:
Eileen slipped on a patch of ice on the old bridge and came down on the back of her head, giving herself concussion, a bad bruise & a nasty cut. She lay unconscious for a long time, but the cold awoke her, and she managed to totter home, dazed, & bleeding (before coming in to me, she took off her rubber boots at the door, for fear of spoiling the hall – Oh, these women!) Fortunately our doctor very generously braved the snowy night and the icy roads to come to us. He dressed the wound and stitched it and after some days in bed she got better and went about with a bandage. There wasn't a soul about, when she came out of the black-out, so there was nothing to do, but pick herself up and stagger home.

The bandage covered her whole head. Eileen being ill and looking so odd with her head all bandaged up was upsetting. Sean being ill was one thing, he just vanished into his room and Eileen kept us away from him as best she could, but Eileen stricken was another thing altogether: the person who ordered the day, from breakfast to bedtime, and in bed. Breon was away serving king and country, so Sean, Niall and I had to muddle through until Eileen gained her feet again.

In this freeze school friends and I went with teachers along the banks of the River Dart. We all ran down the side of the field that stretched from the edge of a small wood to the gate that stopped the cows walking along the banks of the river. We vaulted the gate and looked for minnows in the

---

[17] The notorious winter of 1946–1947 was one of the coldest and harshest on record, with snow and plunging temperatures causing massive disruption to manufacturing, energy supply and travel.

little stream that ran along beside an electricity substation that supplied the Estate. We fished with jam jars with string around the rims to form a handle. As we walked we cracked the ice that covered the puddles and made the cow-dung crisp. There was a very large puddle all covered in ice. Someone slid on it and it looked like great fun so I followed; I was heavier and the ice cracked and I fell in, only up to my waist but as I sat back I was wet all over. I laughed it off – everybody laughed, except the teachers who were annoyed at our stupidity. I began to shiver so one of the teachers insisted she take me back and dry me off. We set out back across the little stream over the gate and up the hill, with all the cows looking at us as their hot breath made mist from their mouths. By the time we got to Aller Park I was shivering more and more and feeling rather sick. They took off all my wet things, found things to put me in and wrapped me in a blanket. I was given a hot sweet cup of tea to drink but all I wanted to do was to lie down. They had rung home and I lay on the back seat as Eileen drove back home. By the time we got there I felt very hot, my temperature had risen and I had a fever. I was put into Eileen's bed and I can't remember anything much after that only voices and cold water on my forehead. Dr Varian had taken my temperature that was dangerously high, and I became delirious. He rushed back to his surgery to get a new wonder drug that he had never used before called penicillin.

Breon, home on leave at the time, remembered Dr Varian coming back with the penicillin. He stopped to prepare the dose in our hall; I was upstairs in Eileen's room. Breon said he was all nervous getting it ready and then he gathered himself together, climbed the stairs and went into where I was lying with his bedside manner. "Halloo, Shivaun, I'm giving you an injection in your right thigh – right here". He patted it and according to Breon, "he took from behind his back a bloody great syringe and in it went". Breon added, "You didn't utter a sound". He then told Eileen that someone should watch me all the time, night and day, and if I get any worse to ring him immediately. The next morning he rushed up the stairs; I remember him rushing up the stairs and seeing the effect, you know, and seeing you jumping about on the bed: extraordinary. But you were very, very ill."[18]

[18] Penicillin, discovered in 1928, was not widely administered until the Second World War. It became available for civilian application in March 1945 in the United States; it was not until June 1, 1946 that the antibiotic became a prescription drug in the UK, less than a year before Shivaun's mishap and illness.

THE WAR YEARS 1945–1948

Before Dr. Varian had injected me I was having a wonderful euphoric dream. I was floating down a long, long tunnel with a light at the end, a beautiful yellow and blue light; and that's where my body wanted to go. I wanted to give in to the gentle pull, but then I felt as if I was being dragged back – but I didn't want to wake up – the dragging became faster and stronger and I opened my eyes. There was Eileen and she hugged and kissed me. It was the very early morning. I could sit up and I could eat a little and evidently jump about on the bed. But I couldn't walk properly for a few days and I was sat in a chair in her bay-window, wrapped up like an old lady, to look out on the world.

I loved the dog next door, Tray, a brown Spaniel. He was owned by Mr. Spiller, another bank manager, and his wife who now lived next door, and Tray was completely untrained. Once we saw Mr Spiller tempting him indoors with the Sunday joint. "Can Tray visit me? Please, please". I can still hear him rushing up the stairs bursting through the door and jumping on to the bed and licking me all over.

Breon's leave was over a few days later. I hated him going, he made me laugh, and Niall and he could so often be heard screaming with laughter in the room they shared together.

Breon's letter to Jack and Mina:

June 9, 1947.
(Woolwich Barracks, London)

Dear Jack and Mina,

How goes your holiday? I won't be able to come down for a week-end because, now, on a new job, I get every second day off, on the strength of getting up at 3.30 on the day on. Still it's well worth it. There's a very fine exhibition on at the moment with Bonnard as the centre of attraction, it's well worth seeing.[19] One of O'Neill's plays is coming on, Eileen is coming up for a day soon, life is really pretty wonderful. I hope the rainy spell didn't hit you too hard, – & this day off is marvellous. 24 hours on, 24 off, who could ask for more? No bull, no parades, no boss but yourself … I'm getting known at the camp now

---

[19] The French painter Pierre Bonnard died on January 23, 1947. Breon is presumably referring to the 179th exhibition of the Royal Academy which ran from May 3 to August 10, 1947. There were two paintings by "The late Pierre Bonnard Hon. R.A."

as the son of Sean O'Casey which is bloody, so I started the story that he's taken up ballet dancing & and is writing an opera, anything to pass away the 2 years.

Love Breon

They believe anything.

With "No bull", Breon is recalling the time a bull ran into the army barracks in the country. All the soldiers ran inside, looking out of the windows in terror. The farmer was called to come down and fetch it back. Into the barracks walked a little girl, about nine years old, who went up to the bull, stroked his neck and put a rope through his nose-ring, and led him quietly away.

EILEEN AND LONDON AGAIN

Eileen and I would row and then have the joy of making up. I was stubborn and I suppose as the youngest, spoilt, or put another way I did get my own way a lot, particularly from Eileen who took the easiest route; Sean was sterner and saw no problem in saying "No" and sticking to it. Eileen was inclined suddenly to lose her temper; she never struck me, but would raise her voice in frustrated anger. Once she said with icy determination, "I'm fed up with you and everything, I'm going to leave this house for good!" After she had swept out and I heard the front door slam, I broke into hysterics. Sean came rushing in and calmed me down saying, "Don't worry, she didn't mean it. Look, she wouldn't go forever without a suitcase. She just needs to let off steam. Come on, let's sit down in my room for a while. Now," he said, "I challenge you to look me straight in the eyes and not to laugh." I did this with a very sad look, "Now, don't laugh", he said. And I couldn't help but laugh, try as I may not to. And she did come back and we all hugged and I said I would be much better.

After Kathy had left for Philadelphia I moved into her old room at the back of the house above the back stairs. It was very dark and once I woke up to very loud strange noises coming from down the corridor. I climbed out of my bed and, very scared, crept along to Eileen's room, the noises getting louder as I got nearer. I opened the door, thinking Eileen was being murdered: to my horror Sean was on top of her, looking as if he was killing her and she was making horrid moans.I screamed out "Leave Mummy alone!" and then I heard him groan: "It's the child." Eileen sort of laughed as he groaned. As I rushed out and dashed to my bed, I could hear him say. "Leave her, Eileen, leave her be." "No, I must make sure she's all right." Then she appeared in my room to say something about only having fun and Daddy wasn't hurting her at all. Fun? It was all very odd, I didn't think much of their kind of fun. I looked at Dad for a long time with a very wary eye.

It was after the war that Eileen had started to take Niall and me up to London mainly to see some shows. The first musical I remember was *Oklahoma*. I loved it all – the breathtaking sets and costumes, the singing, the dancing, the beautiful men and women, the very bad guy and the funny guys. They sounded as if they were American actors, it was one of the American musicals that hit the West End one after another. The musical form was back, but with a difference. Eileen had been in the early musicals, *Rose Marie* and *Bittersweet* among them.[20] According to her, the American chorus was always perfection as they worked so hard and were so well choreographed. The man who had directed and produced her musicals was Charles B. Cochran "He was", she said, "an English exception". He had chosen his girls and men with rigorous precision; his chosen girls were called Cochran Young Ladies, and she had been one of them. Sean had seen her in the chorus of *Rose Marie*, especially remembering the Totem Pole dance, so brilliant that it got many encores and dancers had to be replaced, slipping in and out from the wings so that no one fainted. Now the choruses went on from there, adding leaps and bounds never imagined before. Of course, now we can see how influenced it was by the amazing dancing of the (then called) negroes, the African-Americans. Over the years we saw *Annie Get Your Gun*, *South Pacific*, *Call Me Madam*, *Kiss Me Kate* and *Guys and Dolls* and then, of course, much later, *West Side Story* that was like a modern opera. *Porgy and Bess* I saw in America many years later, also like an opera to me.

Life in London was very different to home; we were taken out to lunches and after theatre dinners. Very often it was with Zoe and Sidney Bernstein to the Caprice, a small restaurant in a long narrow room with banquette seats down both sides. Zoe and Sidney had a flat in the same apartment building and it was always buzzing with conversation. Eileen was in her element, laughing and telling funny stories, topping many of those told by

---

[20] Eileen recounts her years on the stage in *Eileen* (1976), pp. 52–92.

others at the table. She usually put me on the seat next to hers so I could go asleep with my head in her lap. How I struggled to stay awake and watch the chatting faces, watch the waiters in their black and white outfits balancing trays of food and drink and never dropping them.

In the afternoon one of the things to do was to go to newsreel and cartoon cinemas, usually dingy and small. Once while watching Pathé News a man's hand crept up my thigh and between my legs – I was frozen but managed to creep closer and closer to Eileen, grabbing her hard; I couldn't utter a sound. "What on earth is the matter, Shivy?" – then she looked and let out a cry of disgust – "Oh, you dirty old man! How dare you touch my child!" "Come on Shivy," and she grabbed my arm as we moved immediately. I was mortified. We sat beside two ladies on my side and we saw this little thin man, yes, in a dirty brown mac, skulk out of the cinema and up the steps to the busy street; to be lost, I suppose, until the next time.

In order to go to London Eileen had to devise a way to save up money, a thing she was very bad at. She hit on the idea of opening a Post Office savings account in my name so that she couldn't withdraw the money without my signature. There she put any little cheques that Sean gave her that he felt weren't worth putting in a bank account.

Also before they actually married, Sean's friend, the coal-factor Billy McElroy, told him he had to buy Eileen an engagement ring. Eileen and Sean had chosen it together – a platinum ring with a modern cut Sapphire in the centre and two diamonds either side, in an Art-Deco setting. She pawned this ring every time she was in London for £30; no more, as she wanted to be able to buy it back over the months and get it back by post. I used to go along with her to a shop that had three very beautiful brass balls hanging outside. It was a strange dark place with little mahogany cubicles along a counter from behind which a man appeared with an eyepiece to value your wares. It was a very extraordinary thing but after Sean died she lost the sapphire out of the ring and later lost the whole ring down the plug-hole.

BREON'S DEMOB

This call-up by the army took Breon away for a long time. One Christmas he came home without telling us and the yells and shrieks of delight should have brought the police flying over from the station opposite. We all loved having Breon about.

THE WAR YEARS 1945–1948

In the Spring of 1948, on March 15 according to Sean's Notebook, Eileen took Niall and me to Oxford to stay with Jack and Floss Daly at the Youth Hostel they ran.

Sean's Notebook:
Niall and Shivaun went to Oxford, to be joined there on a forty-eight hours leave by Gunner Breon; so I am alone in the house. I don't like it. Strange that one has grown to be attached to Eileen & all that is hers. That to be without her is to be without everything. I've been alone before; it was never exhilarating; it was always trying; but now it needs constant and positive effort to silently bear it. Books, thoughts, nothing compensates for her absence. If not her close company then her voice speaking to the children, or her step heard going from room to room have become an essential part of [the] feeling of life.

Jack was an old and close comrade of Sean's when they both lived on the North side of Dublin in the early 1900s; both were members of the St. Laurence O'Toole Club where Sean's first play was read, called *The Harvest Festival*, though they daren't have put it on as it depicted far too accurately the two main funders of the Club. So Sean sent it to the Abbey Theatre and it was rejected. They also both fought in the 1913 Dublin Lock-Out and Strike of 1913.[21]

The Youth Hostel in Oxford, where the Dalys now lived, was on a tree-lined road, and down some steps. Floss and Jack welcomed us with such warmth that they immediately became my friends too, and were called Aunty Floss and Uncle Jack from then on. They were able to give us a room to ourselves with four bunk beds, as they weren't full; if more people turned up we would have to share with them, but we didn't mind. What fun to sleep on the top bunks and both Niall and I were able to do this. Jack and Floss continued to bubble over with talk all the time we were there, telling us what to see and how to get around. We walked all over Oxford and I was very impressed by all the bicycles and the bicycle lanes running beside the roads. Why didn't every town have these? We visited

---

[21] The Saint Laurence O'Toole Gaelic Athletic Association Club was in existence 1888–1896. It and the church it was associated with were named after the Archbishop of Dublin at the time of the Norman invasion of Ireland and who was canonised in 1225. O'Casey joined the Club as a youth; it encouraged Irish music, Irish sports, and a general Irish cultural nationalism. See Garry O'Connor, *Sean O'Casey: A Life*, pp. 51, 55, 111; *The Letters of Sean O'Casey, Volume II*, p. 61.

the Museum and walked around some of the colleges, a staid and beautiful centre of town, with a hushed air of unreachable learning going on around us.

The brief holiday was over too soon; we had really come to be with Breon for his two days but stayed for four days. I wish we had seen more of Jack and Floss over the years. Floss used to send us a cake every Christmas, always covered with lashings of icing, usually pink; Eileen said they were sometimes a bit heavy inside but I loved them, and Sean gobbled them up as well.

Breon was at last demobbed! It took a while, it was postponed but then suddenly he was out! On the train back home he went into the toilet and changed from his army uniform into his demob suit: shirt, tie, etc. He wanted to surprise us when he opened the door, as we had never seen him in a suit. Sidney Bernstein did send his old suits for the boys, now and again, and Breon wore them while in the army when he was allowed to go out in civvies, but we never saw him in them. So he did give us all a shock when he entered Tingrith – we were all overjoyed – and laughed at his very uncomfortable look, as he stood grinning at us.

4
A Few Trying Things
1948–1952

GRANNIE

Grannie was Mrs. Kathleen Reynolds from Belmullet, Blacksod Bay, Mayo, Ireland. She was Eileen's widowed mother and a very different kettle of fish to Sean's mother. Now there was someone I would have loved to have known: I do, in a certain connected way, feel I know her, even though she died in 1918 from the Asian 'flu twenty years before I was born. But we had Grannie Reynolds née Carey and not Sean's mother, Grannie Casey, née Archer, to deal with.

I found Grannie's "A Nuptial Contract" drawn up by a John Andrew Reid of Cape Sorrow, Cape of Good Hope, in which she was written down as Kattie Carey. On her certificate of marriage she is Kathleen Carey; the name Kattie Carey sums up for me a very different person to the Grannie I knew; it paints a picture of a pretty and more carefree young lass. Maybe she was then.

Eileen's father had died when she was a teenager. He had, Eileen said, gambled away the little he and Grannie had, and then went back to South Africa to try to get back to his old work as an accountant for a mining company. This didn't work out for him and so he travelled back to live with Grannie, Kathleen (or Kattie) Carey. While he was away their little boy died of bronchitis. Grannie was so ill at the time with rheumatic fever that she was unable to nurse her little boy. Grannie had been trained as a nurse, and believed she could have saved him. It must have been unbearable for her to see her tiny son not being nursed properly, trying to help, but too weak to stand. Possibly things weren't too good between husband and wife before he left but they were very bad when he came back. Eileen remembers Grannie nagging him a lot and her father getting more and more inward. He eventually had a nervous breakdown and was hospitalised in a place for mental patients. Eileen adored her handsome and, yes, she said, funny father, and remembers visiting him at the home and their holding hands together on a bench. That was the last time she was to be with him, as he died soon after.

In 1928 Eileen married Sean, much to Grannie's disgust and huge disappointment. She had wanted Eileen to marry one of her wealthy boyfriends so that she could be looked after, and also so she herself could boast about her connections. A while back she had decided that she was too ill and weak to work any longer, and had for a long time relied on Eily, as she called her, to look after her. This was always a drain on Eileen as she didn't earn that much from her chorus, and acting work. Before she met Sean, Eileen was being "kept" by a wealthy impresario called Lee Ephraim, and, although he was married to a sickly wife and would never divorce, he did buy Eileen lots of things and arranged an account for her at Harrods and some other posh stores.[1] But Grannie was only thinking of herself and didn't notice that Eileen was actually lonely and longing for a home and a family. Sean filled her mind and truly gave her affection and notice; he was smitten with her from the first and then grew to love and admire this kind-hearted girl with a golden laugh.

Grannie so objected to Eileen's marriage to Sean (she was by then pregnant with Breon: maybe Grannie hadn't noticed this) that she arrived at the wedding at the Church of the Holy Redeemer in Chelsea in widow's weeds, clad in black from head to foot with a large brimmed black hat bearing a black veil that fell to her ankles. She tried to stop the ceremony but the priest, a friend of Eileen's, took her aside and told her not to be so foolish. After the marriage, and forgetting this, she installed herself on the O'Casey's bankroll and was kept as best Sean and Eileen could manage, until she died in 1962, two years before Sean.

When my parents moved down to Devon from London, it didn't take long before Grannie followed and was a constant annoyance, mainly to Eileen. She lived at Tingrith but Sean soon realised the continual strain she put on Eileen and after a few arguments it was decided that they would find her a suitable room in a respectable house and, of course, pay for it. At that time many people kept boarding houses where old ladies and gentlemen had a room and were fed, their rooms tidied and bed linen changed once a week. Grannie liked to stay exclusively among women. This would have been all right except that she was a snob and considered everyone else at these establishments beneath her. No one was good enough for her, not even a woman who had looked after a duchess, so Grannie never made friends and eventually would become so difficult to cope with that the landlady would beg Eileen to find somewhere else that

---

[1] Lee Ephraim was born in Kentucky in 1877. Among the shows he produced on Broadway were *Theatre Parade* (1936), *Spring Meeting* (1938, co-written by the Irish novelist and playwright M.J. Farrell, aka Molly Keane), and *Under Your Hat* (1940). He died in London in 1953. He features in Eileen's eponymous autobiography.

would take her in. By the time she died, twenty-three years later, she had stayed in every boarding house in Torquay and Paignton that was suitable. Eileen had to plead with the nicer of the landladies to take her back for a while to give her time to find somewhere else.

Grannie was what was known as a secret drinker who attempted to hide her addiction. She was also a devout Catholic, so after a bout of the drink she would become very holy, confessing her sins daily, but ready to start again after a week or so. Eileen used to say she didn't know which was worse – to put up with her drunken periods or her holier-than-thou ones. During both, she pulled Eileen to pieces. Grannie had only negative interests: what life had brought her, her ungrateful daughter, and her terrible suffering. Eileen had been brought up "in the faith" by Grannie and enforced at the convents that schooled her. Sean had no problem with Eileen "practising" as long as she didn't bother him with it. Breon was taken to church with Eileen until he was twelve or so; we were all baptised, but Breon also took his First Communion with Father Russell when we lived in Totnes. One day on the way to the little Catholic church in Totnes, Eileen asked Breon if he liked going to church; "No, I don't," was his reply. "Well, then we won't go any more darling." And with that they turned on their heels and walked back home. The decision she reached was entirely her own – and Breon's. I wondered if, nearing her death, she would go back to her faith like George Jean Nathan and others. When this time came and she was having very disturbed nights, I arranged for a rather bohemian priest to visit her, in case being absolved of things would help her to sleep at night. He came, and was very presentable, so she immediately enjoyed his male presence; but when he asked if she would like to confess she said, "Darling, if you don't mind I would rather not." The priest said he thoroughly understood and said, "I absolve you from all sins anyway". She never asked for a priest or said any prayer but died quietly and peacefully, drifting into that oblivion, with, I am sure, thoughts of Niall and Sean and maybe even Ephraim.

Religion was Grannie's crutch and a crutch to knock everybody's head with. She kept going on at Eileen for not bringing us up in The Faith. She had learnt that Breon no longer went to mass but Eileen pretended she still went in order to stop the nagging. Niall and I were never taken to church. I was too young but I often wondered how Niall avoided it. At some point Grannie taught me the Lord's Prayer and for one week I was very holy indeed and built a pretty altar in front of my books on my little bookcase.

Sean and Eileen would look at me praying with a bemused look and Sean told Eileen not to worry, as I would soon get tired of it. He was right, I very soon lapsed and never took it up again, and try as she did, Grannie never managed to make a nun, nurse or lady out of me.

The one thing Dartington children did with the best of them was swear; it was second nature to us. Grannie did have one person she admired who taught hockey at a local girls' school. If we passed by the park and the girls were playing hockey on the green, she would make Eileen stop and point out her friend, Miss McDuckham, a rather mannish sporty woman with a large posterior and this very unfortunate name; "Oh," said Niall, "What an embarrassing name. Miss McFuckham". At this Niall and I collapsed in a heap of giggles as Eileen and Grannie remonstrated with us. Sometimes he would say to Grannie with his polite voice on, "And how is your friend, Miss McFuck – Oh, I am so sorry, I mean Miss McDuckham. Is she well I hope?"

Before Breon was born, Sean sat down and wrote a letter to Grannie.

Dear Mrs Reynolds,

I have opened & read the letter you sent yesterday to Eileen, & I am writing now, as I intended to do many times, to tell you we are tired of your wailing letters bursting with their everlasting whimperings and complaints. You are ever wanting something and are ever complaining about something. You are never content for a moment: your room is too large or too small: too hot or too cold: too high up or too low down. Since I have known you you have changed to more places than a bird hopping about for berries. You think that Eileen has nothing to do but to be running about after you, but this will have to stop now. I don't forget the night on which I came home, I found you had been with her, & found the pregnant woman in a bout of hysterics. I remember the Christmas you were here sick from having drunk too much or eaten too much, & you expected this girl to stop awake all night listening to you & attending you. When we were shortly married I noticed whenever she had seen you, or got a letter from you she was upset and agitated. ... You try to interfere with the conduct of the house, but Eileen is boss here & you must recognise that. You have suggested that Eileen missed her 'gayer' life that she had before she married, and this is hardly a good (Catholic) thing to do - to insinuate anything that might breed dissatisfaction in a wife's mind for her home.

You are always preaching an invalid's body but you can't be too delicate, nor your heart too bad when you are able on a blazing day to go gadding about all day about Hampton Court. ...

I'll give your letter to Eileen, & tomorrow we'll talk about what will be the best & final way to arrange with you.

Eileen must have persuaded Sean not to send this letter and so the cat-and-mouse situation existed throughout their marriage, Sean protecting Eileen as well as he could from this woman. Breon, being the eldest, and living at home a lot of the time, bore the reality of looking after Grannie. It was to him Eileen turned when she was rung up of an evening from a pub requesting someone to pick up Mrs Reynolds. Breon described her as often being completely drunk and having peed herself. He was very shy and sensitive and it must have been completely humiliating steering her out and helping to clear up her mess, especially someone you didn't even like or respect.

NEW SCHOOLS FOR BREON AND ME

Breon got an army grant to study art. He went for an interview at the school he wanted to attend, the Anglo-French Art School, in St. John's Wood. The man who interviewed him was looking through his work, turning each drawing or painting over and giving little grimaces. Then Breon told him, "I have a government grant." The man's eyes lit up and suddenly Breon became a budding genius. "These drawings are really very interesting indeed." And he was quickly accepted. Breon had to go to London to start at the school – now a freer and happier soul. Eileen went to London with him to help him settle in. Breon's letters from London showed an excitement not seen while he was doing his National Service. He sent back a laundry list of immediate needs.

55 Greencroft Gardens NW6 1948

Dear Sean & Eileen,

That little French Dictionary.
Haldane's – 'Keeping Cool'[2]

---

[2] *Keeping Cool and Other Essays* (1940) by J.B.S. Haldane, the eminent geneticist, Marxist and "perhaps the most brilliant science populariser of his generation" (Arthur C. Clarke), was published in a Services Edition in 1944.

Shirts, shirts, shirts.
one or two little jars to put turpentine etc.
Have you, among the many coverings for the tea-pot one to spare?
Can you get one of those wire racks to make toast on. – I have the tin, but can't get the wire piece to go in it.

I have to describe the evolution of Egyptian architecture from the 1st Dynasty to Greek conquest, and show how climate, geology, religion & politics affected the style & construction. – What a dim and dusty task! – I wonder have you any entertaining books on the subject? – so far I can only think of, what I consider a fine opening sentence. "Egypt (exclamation mark), land of bronze skins, golden corn, & waving reeds." I have found some books in the public library, but they all seem to be only vague outlines, gloomy & un-instructive. If you have none, don't bother trying to get any, it's not that important, but if you have some at hand, I would be glad of them.

Nathan's book turned out to be a lot better than I had hoped – a bloody fine piece about the different methods of hack writing – I seem to be the quotation type – great on Shaw, laughing the pants off the "turkeys".[3] – I liked the play Uranium 235, too.[4] He seems to have picked on a very difficult subject – dramatising the atom & all that – but I thought it was a very fine play – with Marlowe standing in the wings.

So everyone is coming up for half-term. – as long as you don't invade the Anglo French place. I don't mind, but for God's sake don't come there in bulk, that would be too much. ...

I can't think of anything else.
Love Breon

The year before, Niall had moved up to Foxhole, the senior school where you started to study for O levels and then went on to do A levels. So he wasn't at Aller Park as I had hoped when I started there. Aller Park was

---

[3] Breon took to London with him George Jean Nathan's book *The Theatre Book of the Year, 1947–1948* (1948): *Letters of Sean O'Casey, Volume II*, p. 564. Sean told Nathan he read the book only after Breon had.

[4] *Uranium 235* (1946) is a documentary play by the left-wing Anglo-Scottish folksinger and playwright Ewan MacColl (James Henry Miller, 1915-1989); its subject is the nuclear age and was set to music when performed; it involves a scientist explaining the history of the atomic bomb. Sean recommended the play to Nathan in November 1948 and remarked: "A 'documentary play', but written, I think, by a poet": *Letters of Sean O'Casey, Volume II*, pp. 565, 771.

thus another experience on my own. I knew the building as we had picked Niall up from there and it was just down the road from our Children's Cottage. Upstairs in a lovely room with a bay window was the music room with a grand piano. Downstairs opposite the Biology room there was the Art room, divided into two separate spaces – one for painting and the other for pottery. Bernie Forrester taught there. He was a potter with an electric wheel and a kick-wheel, a small electric kiln and a brick kiln built outside in one of the garages opposite.[5] There was one more classroom and this was in one of the boarding houses called Blacklers; there were three boarding houses; Orchards, Chimmels and Blacklers, each holding about 13 boarders, both boys and girls, and each child had a separate study-bedroom; They were a modern design by William Lescaze who also designed the headmaster's house at High Cross.[6]

At Orchards we had a house mother and a house father living together; they were two ladies called Winnie and Aileen who were, we thought, lovers, or partners as we would say today.[7] They had a bedroom and a sitting room where children went for night-caps or if they felt sad or ill. If they were really ill they went to the sick-bay that was in the main building. These were the days of measles, chickenpox, whooping cough, mumps, etc. Mrs Dodi Kabraji served the whole school, looking after the sick-wing. In the winter all the house mothers and house fathers had log fires burning.

Downstairs was the kitchen with the warmth of an AGA stove, a dining-room and a common room with a little platform at one end used to

[5] Bernard Forrester (1908–1990) was a well-known English potter specialising in bowls, jugs, trivets and dishes; he taught at Dartington for thirty years. See the Dartington Trust website: https://www.dartington.org/bernard-forrester/
[6] William Lescaze (1896–1969) was a Swiss-American, New York-based architect and pioneer of Modernism; he designed the Philadelphia Savings Fund Society Building (completed in 1932), "the first International Modernist skyscraper": William Lescaze: Wikipedia. See also "1930s William Lescaze Modernist Houses in Dartington Hall, Totnes, Devon": WowHaus: https://www.wowhaus.co.uk/2019/12/13/william-lescaze-modern-houses-dartington-hall/ (posted 13 December 2019); "High Cross House: Modernist Icon": Dartington Trust: https://www.dartington.org/wp-content/uploads/2018/12/Open-House-02-HXH.pdf
[7] Winifred (Winnie) Norris was housemother at Dartington Hall and Aileen a cook. Winnie received correspondence from both Barbara Hepworth the English sculptor and her husband Ben Nicholson the English painter. Nicholson sent a copy of John Summerson's *Ben Nicholson (The Penguin Modern Painters)*, West Drayton, 1948 with the inscription "For Winifred and Aileen from Ben, Dartington July 1948".
https://archive.dartington.org/calmview/Record.aspx?src=CalmView.Catalog &id=DWE%2FA%2F1%2FA1%2F41

perform small plays, etc. This is where my friends and I performed the first witch scene from *Macbeth* to a small but appreciative audience. From the classrooms at the front of the main grey building called Aller Park, you looked out over gently dipping fields; some on the left dropped down to the River Dart while those in front rose up again to the Dartington Hall buildings, where Dorothy and Leonard Elmhirst lived surrounded by a courtyard full of music students and their teachers and also some of the staff that ran the Estate.

I soon made friends with a dark-haired Yorkshire boarding lass from Doncaster, with a great spirit and sense of fun, and a good inquiring mind. She gave me an idea of what it was like to be a boarder and away from home. At the start of their first term many of the new boarders felt very homesick, missing their family and home. She missed her home a lot, she was very close to her mum and dad and her younger brother, Eddie, who came to board later. So Jane Pearce sometimes came home with me for the weekend where Eileen and Sean spoilt us both. One of the things they did, and something we enjoyed most, was egg and chips in bed. This was also a way of getting us both undressed and into bed. Sean used to bring them up with a dish-towel folded neatly over one arm like a posh waiter and say, "Here you are ladies, your dinner is served".

A few years later I was asked by Mrs Pearce if I could come to stay with Jane up in Yorkshire for a week over the holidays. Eileen took me up on the train to meet Jane and her mother at Doncaster station. It was a long and exciting journey through open countryside and many towns and stations I had never heard of. The only journey I had taken by train was from Totnes to Paddington and I knew most of those landscapes.

Doncaster Station was large like Paddington, with engines letting off steam in a hissing chorus. We walked through the steam and saw Mrs Pearce and Jane walking towards us. I was thrilled to see Jane but when Eileen said, "Well darling, have a lovely time. I'll see you here in a week's time. Now, I must dash to get my train back to London", I felt a terrible pang in my stomach, and began to feel for myself the miserable sickness Jane had suffered at the beginning of each term. I was not as brave as Jane. Their house seemed very different to ours. I thought how odd Jane must have felt with us in our muddled house. Theirs was neat and tidy and compared to ours sparse and perfect. I was shown a huge American-style fridge, and a delicate bone china tea set that lived in a glass cabinet, similar to the cabinet we had in our front-room. They were all very kind to me and I met Eddie who was a few years younger than Jane but with blond hair, not dark like Jane's. Even the sight of Jane's bedroom made to look like Princess Margaret's didn't cheer me up. Come the night-time the dreaded homesickness struck. We had twin beds in the guest room so we could be together, as Jane's bedroom was too small for both of us. I sobbed myself to sleep. One day we went to see a pantomime with George Formby in it, as Buttons I believe. I was used to sitting in the best seats, the house seats that Eileen was usually given by Sidney Bernstein, so I was a little amazed to find us sitting quite far back in the balcony: only amazed because Jane's parents were much better off than us, also I was a theatre snob I suppose. When we got home there was a card for me from Eileen saying "Hope you are well and having a lovely time. Niall and I are seeing lots of shows. Lots of love Eileen. Niall sends love too."

What a spoilt old thing I must have been because that night it was no good; I was inconsolable and couldn't stop crying. Poor Jane crept into her parents' bedroom with me in tow, and they looked at us from their bed. Mrs Pearce came and comforted me in such a lovely way; she said she thought I should go home a few days early and she would ring my mother the next day to suggest it. As she tucked us up in bed she said, "Now, try and get a little sleep" and we did. She was so understanding it must have been difficult for them to send their children away; they must have really liked Dartington's unusual progressive and modern educational methods to do so.

A school treat every weekend were the films for children at the Barn Theatre.[8] Niall would take me in and sit me near his friends. I had to sit next to him because *The Clutching Hand* was very scary and I did clutch his hand in terror. This was a series with a different episode every week ending with a terrible cliff-hanger and then the clutching hand would come on from left-screen and "clutch" and the words – "What will happen to ...? Continued next week."[9] *The Scorpion* was another children's horror movie series with a man in a cape and a big hat.[10]

Luckily there were also the cowboy movies: Tom Mix with his huge white cowboy hat, Roy Rogers with his neat little scarf tied around his

[8] The Barn theatre and cinema at Dartington Hall is in a converted 14th century barn in a medieval courtyard; it is still in operation.
[9] *The Clutching Hand* was a 15-episode serial produced in 1936, based on the 1934 novel by Craig Kennedy.
[10] *The Adventures of Captain Marvel* was a 12-episode movie serial of 1941 in which the caped superhero faces a criminal mastermind called The Scorpion.

A FEW TRYING THINGS 1948–1952

neck; but my favourite by far was Hopalong Cassidy, all dressed in black but more casual and with a proper cowboy hat, with his funny sidekick Gabby Hayes and the young romantic sidekick, Johnny. Finding out that Sean had made up his surname, O'Casey, and that he was called Johnny Cassidy in his books, I ran up to him and said "We must be related to Hopalong Cassidy as our names are really the same". He said he was very sorry to disappoint me but his name was originally Casey and we weren't any relation. I was mortified as I had already mentioned it to some of my chums and would have to disappoint them. A group of us played cowboys a lot: I was usually the lead, that is Hopalong Cassidy, while Jane was Johnny, my friend Sim Rushton was Gabby and her pretty twin-sister Carole the lady in Johnny's life. We wore gumboots all day as cowboys do; a lot of us wore them anyway as shoes were still scarce and expensive. Classes interrupted our play but I can't recall people playing truant; anyway there wouldn't have been anyone to play with. Bridget Edwards taught us maths and needlework and also took eurythmics in the Assembly area, where we all ended up as a Greek frieze.[11] Toddy, or Walter Todds, was our handsome English teacher, until he was whisked away by the BBC as he had a beautiful voice for transmitting. He later became their Head of Music.[12] We also had music appreciation with him, sitting and listening to records. Toddy would say: "Imagine scenes that the music suggests to you", but I never could; I just liked to listen and feel the music. I mean, obviously you could imagine a trout jumping during Schubert's "The Trout". Songs had words but complicated orchestral harmonies? It was mainly the sounds and rhythms I could grasp. In an English class I remember reading with great feeling Shakespeare's lines from *A Midsummer's Night's Dream* about sweeping the dust behind the door and being praised for it. I liked being praised.

[11] Bridget Edwards was also an actress and was in a 1949 Dartington Playgoers Society production of *The House of Bernarda Alba*: https://archive.dartington.org/calmview/Record.aspx?src=CalmView.Catalog&id=T%2FADR%2F7%2F003%2F005. In her review of William Feaver's biography of the artist, *The Lives of Lucian Freud: Youth, 1922–1968* (2019), Fiona Green, the former art student, participant and hostess in London's bohemian scene, recalls that she and the artist (who later became lovers) attended Dartington Hall school and remarks that "We also shared a love for a little old lady called Bridget Edwards, a house parent, who seemed to understand how troubled we each were, and cared": *Islington Tribune* and *Camden New Journal*, both March 12, 2022.
[12] London-born Walter Todds (1920–1983) went to work in the BBC TV Music Department where he co-founded the BBC Young Musician of the Year Award.

EILEEN ON THE ROAD TO LONDON, 1949

Niall was a keen reader of the newspapers at home and at school. At the Senior School, Foxhole, there was a long high table at the top of a flight of stairs in the main clock-tower building, where the daily papers were displayed for all who wanted to read them: the *Times, Manchester Guardian, News Chronicle*, the *Daily Telegraph*, even the *Daily Worker*. One year Curry, affectionately called Beaky, decided that too much was being spent on the papers and one would have to go and that this would be discussed and voted on at the next Moot, the school meeting of elected members of the students and presided over by Curry. Niall was a member. It was decided that either the *Times* or *The Daily Worker* would have to go and this was to go to the vote. Just before the vote was to take place Niall said "I propose that we drop the *Daily Telegraph* and keep both the *Times* and the *Worker*". His proposal was carried unanimously, possibly to Curry's annoyance who may have wanted the *Worker* to go since I understand he wasn't keen on the Communists.[13]

In the spring of 1949, a new adventure took place: Eileen was to drive Niall and me up to London for a holiday to stay near Breon. He was to have two wisdom teeth out and Eileen wanted to be up there with him. By then Breon was a confident driver but he was in London waiting for us, and Eileen was a very nervous driver who really couldn't reverse properly. Niall was to navigate and Eileen had written to the AA, of which she was member, for a route map. This was a great little book made up for each journey you asked for; each page flipped over from stage to stage, usually from one major town to another. The route was laid out very clearly and all the directions written by the side; on the back was a list of interesting landmarks.

So we packed up the car, including bottles of water to fill up the water-tank. Sean hugged us all, making a very good job of hiding his apprehension; we had all been talking about it for weeks and Eileen was very nervous about the trip but determined to make London at any cost.

---

[13] In his autobiography, *Geography of a Life* (Xlibris, 2012), p. 51, the distinguished Sinologist, Martin Bernal, author of *Black Athena* (1991), recalled that it was he and Niall who challenged Curry on his proposal, and were joined by Nicola Seyd, daughter of the French teacher, Fred. This is confirmed by the author of Nicola's *Guardian* obituary (Dec 7, 2015), Bruni de la Motte. Nicola was a committed Communist and went to Cuba in 1960 where she met Che Guevara; her life of political activism was spent mostly in Camden.

A FEW TRYING THINGS 1948–1952

Niall sat in the front beside Eileen; I sat in the back with a full breeze blowing as both windows remained open for the whole journey. Of course Eileen had to signal with her hands in those days and it was easier if she didn't have to wind down the window before doing this.

By then we had our little black Ford Popular, licence number GUO 423, bought soon after the war ended; it was the car manufactured for the people as its name implied. It managed 40 miles per hour, with tops of 60 mph for overtaking. Lorries had a speed limit of 12 mph on a disc at their rear where we could see it; there were none of the container-like vehicles on the roads like today. When we were stuck behind a lorry there were minutes of agony, wondering if and when to overtake, and then very often halfway past the lorry we would see a car approach and have to ease back behind again, Eileen getting more and more panicked. The only time I saw her drive brilliantly was up Totnes High Street on a market day when we were having a row; she got so annoyed she put her foot on the pedal and wove in and out of the traffic at an alarming rate without even a scratch by the time we got to The Narrows at the top of the town: by then she and I had calmed down, and she broke into her hilarious laugh and said she must try being in a temper more often while driving.

Not in a temper now, Eileen was in a state of controlled nerves. Niall was a good navigator; he didn't get muddled with his left and right like Eileen and me; and with his sense of humour he was able to see the amusing side of it all. All I did was pass him a sweet now and again and sometimes to Eileen – this was all we had to eat in the car. We stopped at towns on the way to rest the car and let it cool down and rest ourselves. There were no motorways then and the A30 was the most direct route. It was a pretty journey on the whole that took us past Stonehenge when we were nearing London. Our first stopping place was Honiton, and we found a nice old-fashioned cafe that did snacks and delicious cakes. This was a town that made the famous lace and we stopped to look at a couple of the lace-makers sitting in their windows working.

We had to stop every now and again even before we got to the next town as the steam would start to rise from under the bonnet and Eileen's feet would be getting very hot. We usually gave the car ten minutes before Niall carefully unscrewed the cap of the water tank with a cloth to let the steam out, keeping his face well back. Then we waited another few minutes before adding cold water from one of our bottles. Whenever we stopped for petrol, and we had to do this several times during the journey, they would also top it up with oil and water, after waiting for the engine to cool again.

As we got to the large artery roads going into London, Eileen became more nervous. At Sean's insistence, Eileen had arranged to be met by an AA man who would drive her into central London. The thing was finding the place where he would be standing waiting for our little car to arrive. We were on time and she pulled off the main road where Niall indicated. We had to wait for a few minutes and then he appeared, all dressed up in his AA uniform. What a relief! Niall clambered into the back and Eileen collapsed into the front seat next to the AA man. We were all very jolly as he drove us to a little hotel called the Pig and Whistle in Gloucester Place that ran parallel to Baker Street. It was near to Breon's digs and cheaper than the Regent's Palace. We had a room all together and the room had a bath in it, screened off from the room by a faded cotton flower-print curtain: what fun! We did laugh about it though; luckily the loo was separate and on the landing. We stayed there for a long time as Breon was not very well and didn't go home until the end of May.

Sean wrote to me from home:

7th April 1949

Dear Shivaun,

Thanks dear for your letter. It was good of you to remember me. The house is very quiet and lonely now. I am glad you like where you are, and that your bed is comfortable.

Mind yourself. I hope you will enjoy yourself in London. Mammy must be a grand driver. Such a journey to go in a small car.
Love to youngsters
Love to Niall
Love to Breon
Love to Mammy.
xxxooo Sean

Breon was living in a room in the house of one of his teachers, called Leslie. He had a delectable little baby that was put out in the shade in a big pram with nothing on; he looked adorable; the pram was in a magical overgrown garden. Breon had a big room and had just had his wisdom tooth removed. It hadn't gone very well and he was in agony. He had a fever and Eileen was busy looking after him. Niall took me about to see Madame Tussauds, London Zoo, the Changing of the Guard, etc. In the evenings we left Breon in agony and Eileen took us out to eat, mainly at a Lyons Corner House, as they were "clean and reasonable", according to Eileen. The girls serving had pretty black dresses and little lacy aprons and hats like cake frills around their heads; they were called Nippies, most likely because they served and cleared so quickly. Breon later told me that Leslie had committed suicide; I couldn't believe it as to me it looked like an idyllic family. This scared me.

THE BOYS TO AUSTRIA

In the summer of 1950 Breon and Niall both went on separate holidays to Austria. In those days foreign travel was rare and expensive and visas were not easily had. Our family never had holidays abroad but this was Niall's second trip out of England. He had missed a school outing to Paris as Sean couldn't afford it; he was very upset about that and moped about for days. Eventually Eileen bought him an electric gramophone player to replace the wind-up one he had and he was in his element playing his traditional jazz records and the few classical records he had. It was mainly his jazz that resounded round the house, and it never bothered Sean who liked to hear the activities of life around him. Sean often went into Niall's room and listened with him, loving Bessie Smith singing "Muddy Water", and Big Bill Broonzy singing "Goodnight Irene", and Louis Armstrong and Sidney Bechet blowing sweet jazzy music. Later Niall was asked to France by a Dartington school friend called Jeremy Wiseman who Niall said had this fantastic mother who if she felt the meal they had eaten was not worth the money that was charged, would surreptitiously take the difference in crockery or silverware, sliding it into her very large bag. He described their kitchen as being full of all this interesting different china and tableware.[14]

Breon had been to Holland with the school, and talked about it all his life; he particularly loved The Hague and always wanted to go again. He described the cheese markets and the canals and bicycles along the towpaths with all the tulips either side stretching on for miles. Apart from

---

[14] Jeremy Wiseman and his three brothers attended Dartington while their father Dr Wiseman worked in Totnes and the family lived in a house on the Estate; Mrs Wiseman lived separately from her husband after 1942 and later in the 1940s lived in France; see "Wiseman v Wiseman", vlex.co.uk (report of a divorce case in 1953).

these adventures and later visits to Ireland our family spent the summer holidays by the local seaside, hiring a hut at Goodrington.

However, during my childhood I went up and down to London a great deal, like a yo-yo between two very different environments. Up for a week of theatres and this time staying with Sidney and Zoe Bernstein, and dining at the Caprice. We went to see a Tyrone Guthrie production of *Top of the Ladder*, with John Mills in the lead. Of course we went backstage to see the actor. It was a great production and my first experience of a truly modern approach to drama.[15] It was my treat with Eileen before the boys went off abroad to Austria.

Niall was going to Austria with his school-friend, Giles Phibbs. It was a big event in our household and he was busy packing all he needed into his rucksack. They were to be looked after by Trudl and Christl. Austria was Trudl's home and her husband, Christl's father, Heinz Beran, had been a famous Austrian radio personality before the war broke out.[16] Packing and counting out the money needed and checking that he had all the papers Niall required to get there took some organising. Breon on his separate holiday to Austria found he could go with more ease when he discovered he could travel on his Allied Forces Permit and left before Niall. The boys intended to meet up at some point and come home together.

Niall came back bristling with stories about the beauty of the mountains, which he walked on with a long stick with Giles; and a lot about a farm he stayed in up in the mountains, where you had to climb some long and rickety steps up to the outside loo. When you did your business on this high platform, you could count to five before you heard the plop. All this excrement was used to fertilise the soil and was very precious. He had these vivid thoughts of what would happen if the platform gave way and you plummeted; you would have a cushioned landing, as it was really like a manure heap with straw scattered over it now and then.

[15] *Top of the Ladder* was the only staged play written by Tyrone Guthrie (1900–1971), the English actor and director of Irish extraction. Its premiere was at the St James Theatre in London in 1950 with John Mills as the ruthless businessman who confronts his past while on his death-bed. Regarded as "a prestigious flop", it was nevertheless revived as a TV play in 1967: http://wymark.org.uk/ladder.html

[16] Heinz Beran later became the London correspondent of the Austrian Radio Corporation. He had been a student of the philosopher Rudolf Carnap and a student friend of Karl Popper. See:
https://link.springer.com/chapter/10.1007/978-1-4684-8830-2_38?noAccess=true. See also
https://genome.ch.bbc.co.uk/979e2ff07d25409f80f1039f2875bab2

Back they came, first Breon and then Niall. I was very pleased to have Niall back; I missed him when he was away more than I did Breon, most likely because Niall was more gregarious and outgoing and we talked a lot together. Breon had become more solitary, and liked to shut himself in his room and paint or read or think. Niall had brought back a present from Austria for me, a skull-cap: white felt embroidered with edelweiss and other mountain flowers, with a hem made of green ribbon, or bias-binding, and stitched with yellow. As soon as Sean spotted the white cap or beanie as the Americans call them, he put it on and it took a lot of persuasion to get it back. He said it kept his head warm where he had no hair. One day I couldn't find it and there he was wearing it again. "Give it back." "I'll give it back if you will make me one but can I use it until then?" I had to let him. That Saturday Eileen and I went and bought some felt and silk thread and I set to work copying the Austrian favourite. The one I made was out of navy blue but I sewed on bright coloured pieces of felt to make a pattern and the border was red bias-binding. Sean loved it and I got my cap back immediately. He wore it for years, his indoor cap, all the time. When he went out he wore his workman's cap with a peak to protect his eyes from the light or a felt broad brimmed hat he had bought when he had money during his early times in London, now nicely worn. Slowly Americans who visited him asked him about his beanie and all sorts of hats started to arrive with them, bought when they were abroad in exotic places: he had two or three from Tashkent. Dr Doran bought him a very elaborate affair from Lapland. Some didn't fit him but he liked to look at them all, and had them dotted about his room, showing off their colourful embroidery. He always went back to mine when the visitors had gone; for them he had donned yet another one reserved for "company". They all sit now at the National Library of Ireland, along with his pipes, jumper, red-coat, and whole library. The cap lies in a box keeping no-one's head warm, its past usefulness over – no longer covering my Dad's clever head.

VISITS AND VISITORS

On September 25, 1950, Sean told his Dublin friend Seamus Scully in a letter: "I and the family were wandering through the wind-swept Plain of Salisbury, lingering long to look at the massive monoliths or trilithons of Stonehenge; & then strolling through the Cathedrals of Winchester &

Salisbury – Old & New Sarum, & many other places."[17] I remember Banbury Cross where we all sang in the car, "Ride-a-Cock Horse to Banbury Cross/To see a fine lady upon a white horse". We all stayed at the Red Lion Hotel, covered at that time with hanging red Virginia creeper – it had an old courtyard where the stage coaches would have once pulled up.

Niall and I loved it there and it was so great to have Dad with us. We travelled all over in our little Ford car – and walked all over the majestic city of Salisbury; I went a couple of times with them all to discover the cathedral. I had never been in such an overpowering space – it did seem as if it lifted you up into the sky – maybe to the heavens. The tall many-coloured windows, the grace of its height. Then we walked to the river's edge to look back at the cathedral in its beautiful setting. We walked the enclosed Cathedral Close. We even climbed up Glastonbury Hill and saw the ruins of the old church. Then Stonehenge – I had read *Tess of the D'Urbervilles* so it was very sad indeed to see where she had been caught. We had an old Brownie camera and I took some photos although it was very overcast and dull. They didn't come out very well but Sean used one in a book of his because it had our Niall standing there between Sean and Eileen.

We had tea as often as we could in the tea-room at the hotel. There was a very lovely lady who was la patronne and showed us to our table. She took a shine to Sean and he to her and she served us herself. – I think Eileen was a little jealous while Sean was all smiles and sweet chatter. Niall and I loved it and teased Sean a little. Eileen said Sean liked "a good pair of legs".

Sean's letter to Robert Lewis:

17 April 1951

Dear Mr. Lewis,

Miss [Jane] Rubin, Secretary to The Richard Madden Play Co., has written to say you'd be in London next month, and that you would like to have a talk with me there.

---

[17] *The Letters of Sean O'Casey, Volume II*, p. 743 (where he is Seumas rather than Seamus Scully). Seamus Scully (1910–1994), a frequent correspondent of Sean's, was an enthusiastic theatregoer by night, a clerk by day; his book, *The Dublin Rover*, was published in 1991: see his obituary in *Dublin Historical Record*, 47:1 (1994): 122–23; *The Letters of Sean O'Casey, Volume II*, p. 636.

Indeed, I'd like to have a talk with you, but I'm afraid I couldn't go to London to have it. I rarely go there now, for I am an old codger now of 71, unable to do a highland fling or take part in a four-hand reel as I used to in the days that are gone, boys, gone. ... I have been chatting with my elder boy, an art student in London now, about COCKADOODLE DANDY when he was here on holiday, and he had to pass the time, did a scene and put down some ideas for costuming and characters. Maybe, you'd be able to take a day or two off out of London and drop down here. We could put you up for a night or two, and give you the best of what we have, and show you Totnes, the oldest Borough – bar London – in England; founded it is said by one Brutus who fled from Troy while it was burning. The residents point to the stone in the sidewalk, and say, There it is, Brutus's stone, the one he planted his foot on thousands and thousands of years ago. ...[18]

Bobby Lewis arrived in May 1951. I was excited as he was such a renowned director. When I met him I saw a strange looking man, small, with a large head supported on square shoulders; he shaved his skull close so he appeared bald. He wore big thick-rimmed glasses and had an air of self-importance married with a great sense of humour: the quick witty humour of America and the theatre. He brought with him a very beautiful young man, with dark glossy hair and big eyes with the longest eyelashes in a grown man I had ever seen. I spent a lot of time with this young man looking through a fashion magazine Eileen had just bought: she liked to keep up with the fashion.

Sean and Bobby talked about *Cock-a-doodle Dandy* and Bobby explained to Sean how he envisaged the production. In the evening we all went to the Cott Inn for dinner. The Cott was an old inn dating from 1630.[19] I remember Bobby saying as we entered that we were all VIPs, and everyone laughed. I had to ask what on earth that meant; Very Important People I was told. It was a jolly evening and Sean shone and talked and told great stories of Dublin. Eileen and Sean were very excited about the

---

[18] *The Letters of Sean O'Casey, Volume II*, p. 786. Robert (Bobby) Lewis (1909–1997) was a theatre director and actor who founded the Actors Studio in New York and wrote to Sean in the summer of 1950 proposing to mount *Cock-a-Doodle Dandy*.

[19] The Wikipedia entry for "Cott Inn" offers the even earlier date of 1307 as the founding date of this, the second oldest inn in Britain. "The inn served travellers, including those carrying wool or tin, on the packhorse road between Ashburton and Totnes."

possible production, very hopeful. But it never happened as Bobby couldn't get the financial backing he needed.

When he taught at Yale University Bobby did direct it with his students and some professional actors from the Actors Studio. The young student who played the leading character, Loreleen, was Meryl Streep; in the programme she called herself Meryl O'Streep. Bobby said she was wonderful. Breon did some designs for the sets but I don't think these were used. I wonder where Breon's designs are, as Bobby took them with him for his dream production.

Bobby sent us food parcels after he visited. Sean enjoyed watching us enjoy them and swallowed his pride. There was a particular smell that came from the American food parcels and presents: Hershey's chocolate, double bubble gum mixed with sweet vanilla. The shredded paper to keep the goods safe – it all smelt delicious.

In 1951 on September 28 I turned twelve. Sean sent me a drawing of him and I pointing at a clock with both hands at twelve o'clock. He wrote underneath "Hurrah! I'm twelve today; a round of the clock!"

The Great Exhibition opened in May and was not to be missed.[20] Eileen, Niall and I duly went up to enjoy the Festival of Britain, and could stay at Breon's pad at 28 Abbey Gardens, as Breon was looking after Sean for us and Breon's flat-mate Anthony was away for a while. We didn't use Anthony's room, a room on its own with a door, but we all slept in Breon's room that was the communal room used for sitting and eating as well as sleeping.

The next day, off we went full of excitement to the Festival site, on a bus to the Strand and then a walk over Waterloo Bridge, joining the stream of people heading there. As we rounded the corner to the bridge, we could see the new Festival buildings on the South Bank, especially the cigar-shaped Skylon, the Dome of Discovery and the Festival Hall, modern and fresh, rising up like the phoenix from the war-ashes. We bought our tickets for the day at one of the kiosks. I told Eileen in a loud voice that it was my friend Jane Pearce's father's company that had made the ropes that supported the Skylon: British Ropes; I felt proud about that. At night the Skylon lit up from inside; with lights looped from the trees and the lampposts it looked glorious. The site ran along beside the Thames with

---

[20] The Festival of Britain began as a centenary commemoration of the Great Exhibition of 1851. It expanded to become a post-war recovery celebration of science, culture and the arts and involved travelling exhibitions and local celebrations around the kingdom.

jetties where you could take river trips. There was a tree-walk where you walked among the branches and the leaves; there were patios all about with new brightly coloured bent steel and plywood chairs surrounding light modern tables; newfangled large cement pots holding plants. The grand Festival Hall housed some of the concerts; the Dome of Discovery was a smaller version of London's Millennium Dome, and much more pleasing, full of depictions of discoveries. My friend and I ran out of the lavatories holding some of the toilet-paper for Eileen to see: it was made from soft absorbent tissue and you didn't have to rub it together to try and make it soft like the Jeyes paper we were used to. Later we would discover the American tissue-paper handkerchiefs! There were many places to eat and in the evening there was dancing and even some singing. Fireworks as well. It was the lightness and the colour that lifted the spirits after the greys and duns of the war. There was hope.

Sean wrote to me:

31st July 1951

My very dear Shivaun,

Thank you, sweetheart, for the lovely card of Constable's picture of 'The Bridge over the Stour.'
I am very glad you like the Exhibition & the Festival so much; and I hope Niall will like it, too. The lights and the fireworks must be grand.
I hope you won't lose the 5/- bit, so that I may see it when you come back, I am very busy.
I send you a dear kiss – give one to mammy from me; & one for Niall.
    My love
    DAD.

FEASTS OF OPERA AND PLAYS – 1952

At Aller Park, a brisk lady with short thick hair called Tan Tivy taught us music and gave piano lessons.[21] She adapted operas for us, greatly simplifying them: *Hugh the Drover* by Vaughan Williams was the first I

---

[21] May (Tan) Tivy trained as a piano teacher at the Royal College of Music and taught music in Wales, Sussex and Africa where she lived before coming to Dartington. She answered a newspaper advertisement and went to teach *Contd.*

saw, done by the older groups. Then when we moved up we did *The Bartered Bride* by Smetana in which I played the Showman; then came Gluck's *Iphigenia in Aulis* in which I found it very tricky to sing the aria of Agamemnon's, being as grand and serious as I could manage. Then *Il Trovatore* by Verdi in which I played the evil Conte di Luna. Of course I had wanted to sing Leonora or Manrico's mother but as most of the boys avoided singing and performing in operas the tall alto girls were given the men's roles. It was a meaty part, though, and I loved the Count's treachery, anger and remorse. We all sang our hearts out – Libby Cope whose father was a singer was a very accomplished Leonora while Miriam May sang Manrico with Theo Parfitt[22] as his mum – the part I wanted. When I sang the songs from this opera at home, Sean started singing along with me to "Home to Our Mountains", then he told me that he had put this song into his play *Juno and the Paycock*, sung by Juno and Mary in the second act. He told me how he used to go and see the touring companies at the Olympia Theatre when his older brother Archie was the property master there. They would have had a small orchestra while we only had Tan on

[21] *Contd.* music at the Middle School. This information comes in an email to the author from Leina Schiffrin who remembers meeting May Tivy much later "walking by the Dart when both she and my father had cancer and having a serious conversation in which she said she believed that everything always turned out for the best. I think she called people who could sing in tune nightingales and people who couldn't owls. This shocks people and it might be that sopranos were nightingales and altos were owls. I remember the little Mozart operas she crafted, I was fire in the *Magic Flute*."

[22] Libby (Elizabeth) Cope is the daughter of the English composer Cecil Cope (1909–2003). She attended ballet school and later sang in classical musical performances arranged by her father; she lived for a while in the United States where she taught spinning and other handiwork in a Waldorf school. Miriam May was born in Jerusalem in 1939 to German Jewish parents who fled Nazi Germany. They returned in 1947 but without Miriam who was enrolled at Dartington Hall. She later married John Gross, the literary historian, and as Miriam Gross was a literary journalist, editor and writer. She became Lady Owen in 1993 when she married Sir Geoffrey Owen, theatrical and literary critic. In her memoir, *An Almost English Life* (2012), she had some harsh words for Dartington pedagogy despite its progressiveness. See the review of her memoir by William Skidelsky in *The Guardian* of September 8, 2012; her article, "Living in England as an Outsider", *The Guardian*, September 7, 2012; and "Miriam Gross", Wikipedia. Theodora Parfit (b. 1939) was like her younger brother Derek born in China where their parents were medical teachers in missionary hospitals. The English family left China for the U.S. in 1944 and the following year moved to the U.K. Theo later lived for a time in New York with Derek who was to become a distinguished moral philosopher. For some information on Theo, see Larissa MacFarquhar's substantial bio-philosophical article on Derek, "How to be Good", *New Yorker*, April 29, 2011.

A FEW TRYING THINGS 1948–1952

the piano. He also described seeing Henry Irving acting there, playing shortened versions of Shakespeare and that in one production they had real rabbits jumping about on what seemed like real grass.

Once when Eileen and I were on one of our sojourns to London, I noticed Covent Garden was staging *Il Trovatore*. I really wanted to experience a full-blown, professional production and persuaded Eileen to get us tickets. The music and singing were brilliant but the main singers were all very fat and when they finished singing an aria, the audience broke out in applause and all the action stopped while they bowed and bowed; I thought that was very unprofessional. They even got up again to bow after they had died! It was as if it was expected of the audience to break the flow of the music in order to praise the singers' egos. I also hated it in theatre when a lead actor got a round of applause on his or her first entrance.

Our first visit to Stratford-upon-Avon was without Sean. Eileen took Breon and me and we drove again in the little car but with Breon driving this time, thank God. The reason we went was that Eileen's great friend and one-time admirer, was now the Artistic Director of the Shakespeare Memorial Theatre. She had known Glen Byam Shaw (another GBS!) from *The Miracle* at the Lyceum in London when they used to hold hands in the stalls while watching rehearsals and waiting to go on.[23] Eileen was for sure a terrible flirt, but we did get complimentary tickets and good house seats for the plays. I never sat in a bad seat when I went to see plays with Eileen; it was later as a student in London that I queued for seats in the gods. You put your little fold-up stools out in rows, that were provided by the theatre, and you sat on them chatting to your fellow theatre buffs. You could even leave your stool to go and get a cup of tea and it would never be moved.

We stayed at a lovely hotel, called, I think, The Shakespeare Hotel where all the rooms were named after a Shakespearean character. One reason we had come to Stratford was to see Siobhan McKenna as Celia in *As You Like It*; Margaret Leighton played Rosalind and Laurence Harvey was the leading man. Siobhan also played Volumnia in *Coriolanus* opposite

---

[23] Glen Byam Shaw (1904–1986) was an actor who later became primarily a director. He was director of the Shakespeare Memorial Theatre, Stratford from 1952–1959 and later held important posts at the Old Vic Theatre School and Sadler's Wells Opera.

Anthony Quayle. We all thought she was very good in both parts. I remember her Celia as being light and funny.[24]

One afternoon Breon took us all out on the Avon in a boat and taught me how to row and how to "feather" the oars on the returning stroke. I felt very good at it. We pulled into the side by a field, tied it off, and had a picnic. It was a beautiful day and peaceful: green trees, willows seeping into the water – you could drag yourself along in the boat by pulling on the low branches. I was old enough not to want to run around and so we all sat quietly knitted together. It was unusual to have Breon with us and this was a real treat. Someone had to stay with Sean, and Niall had opted for this.

It was on this holiday that I remember the first of our daily trips to the Post Office, where Eileen had set up an account in my name, to prevent her from taking out the savings so that they would lie undisturbed for our holidays. Breon and Eileen would accompany me to the PO and ask for a withdrawal form; we would all then sidle to a high-up ledge for filling in forms, where they would instruct me what to do and where to sign, rather like the two men in Sean's one-act play, *A Pound On Demand*. Then they would tell me to go to the counter to get the money; I think you were allowed about £5 a day. We did get funny looks, and as we all went off to have a treat we would laugh about how the lady at the counter must think they were taking Shivaun's money. We went every day until we weren't allowed any more and the book had to be sent off; this happened when one had withdrawn a certain amount.

We went several times to Stratford while Glen Byam Shaw was there and saw many of his productions with Motley's sets and costumes.[25] I started to collect autographs and joined the crush by the stage door. I was left to my own devices while the others went off for a drink, they wanting nothing to do with my hobby. We seemed to be standing for hours before anyone appeared. The techies came out first, rushing to the Dirty Duck

---

[24] Profiles and photographs of the chief actors in *Coriolanus*, *The Tempest*, *As You Like It*, *Macbeth*, and Ben Jonson's *Volpone*, all staged during the 93rd season, can be found in the richly illustrated *Shakespeare Memorial Theatre 1952* (Stratford-upon-Avon).

[25] The Motley Theatre Design Group was started and run by Margaret and Sophie Harris and Elizabeth Montgomery. After the war, following a stint on Broadway (where Montgomery stayed), the sisters Harris taught design at the Old Vic Theatre School, 1947–1953 and the Group was also closely associated with the Shakespeare Memorial Theatre Company, 1948–1959. See "Motley Theatre Design Group", Wikipedia.

pub, then the quick changers with no one visiting them backstage, finally the leading actors, often accompanied by their visitors (often famous in their own right). Some of the leading actors were not very polite, signing without looking at you, some swept past as if in a tremendous hurry; but the smaller parts were usually lovely and I especially remember Michael Hordern and the lady who played the nurse in *Romeo and Juliet*. They came out together and talked to us all for a long time about what we thought of the production. I loved their work from then on, especially his. Michael Hordern had been a perfect Caliban in my eyes – to Gielgud's Prospero and Margaret Leighton's Ariel; I can still see Ariel and Prospero plotting together in their battle against evil.

WOMEN THINGS

When I wrote to my old friend Christl (now called Christa), she described the difference between our two mothers. I told her what an important part of my early childhood her mother Trudl was, and how much I loved her: how I wouldn't stay with anyone else for many years when Eileen went on one of her sojourns to London, when Eileen thought I was too young for Sean to look after with his very bad eyesight.

Christa said she didn't remember that much but did remember Eileen taking us to the movies and taking in one show and if I asked if we could see another one over the road, she took us straight right over and in. Christa said her mother thought pantos were crude but let Christa come with us – "Then after the Panto Eileen would take us to a cafe for tea and we sang the numbers and Niall would be begging us to stop and being terribly embarrassed. Then we'd go back to your house and do it all over again for Sean. And then we'd sit in our nighties in front of a fire in the bedroom and I'd ask Eileen for cocoa and chips and she'd go down and make it and bring it up and while we were chewing it she'd tell us stories about when she was living in a hostel for girls and a man walked by waving his penis and all the girls were watching from the windows in amazement; and also when she was a chorus girl she didn't wear knickers. I think my Mum was your safety net and your Mum was my window to the world. She was the one who bought me my first scent, that would never occur to my Mum, who never wore makeup of any kind except for once a year for the Christmas party she'd take out this little silver box; it contained a tiny powder puff and generic coloured face powder which she'd dab on to the tip of her nose."

Often when I was an older teenager Eileen did embarrass me. But she was the warmest, kindest Mum you could wish for: slightly naive at times for someone who had lived such a vibrant, active life in the Twenties and Thirties.

Sometime during the year when I was ten I heard Dr Varian say to Eileen – "Shivaun should soon get her curse". What an earth did he mean? If it was what I thought it was I was only ten and it was for much older girls. Not long after I was horrified to bleed when I had a pee. "Eileen!" I screamed and up she ran to assure me it was fine, shooing away Sean who had run out of his room to see what an earth had happened. He went dutifully back into his room to wait for Eileen to come and explain the situation. We sat in her room as she lent me her sanitary belt saying she would buy me one tomorrow. She showed me how to attach the two hoops at either end of this large cotton-wool pad, covered in a net material to the two hooks hanging each end of the elastic belt. And there it was, this uncomfortable wad dangling like a hammock between my legs. I was mortified. Why me? Why now?

"Now don't worry darling, I'll let the school know. You'll most likely start losing some of your puppy-fat". I did lose weight very quickly and it left horrid stretch marks on the side of my thighs and stomach – another mark against any hope of good looks, I agonised. I was glad to hear that another girl in my group, a boarder, had started her "curse". So Naomi and I had a secret in common and I clung to her for assurance. She was more mature than me and very clever. Not swimming during the bleeding week was really a curse for me. Neither Sean nor Eileen told me much, if anything, about sex and what was happening to my body and my young friends' bodies. Sean must have known something but Eileen only knew what happened to her, but not why or how it happened. She was clueless about the inside workings of the human body, or any other creature's innards. She had never been taught these things at the Catholic Convent school save possibly a rudimentary lesson about blood circulation, the nervous system and skeleton. I don't imagine the nuns taught the digestive system or the renal system as they had a lot to do with lavatories. In fact, when her periods started it was covered up and hidden. So Eileen left school and went out into the world, full of life but ignorant of many important things life was going to chuck at her. When a few years later I had a bout of bad nose bleeds, Dr. Varian told her he had no idea why they occurred, except that it did often happen at this age with boys as well

A FEW TRYING THINGS 1948–1952

as girls. At home Eileen told me, "It's probably your curse coming out another way".

Unluckily for me and Naomi the school didn't teach the reproductive system until we were at the senior school at 13. Then it was taught well: all sorts of systems relating to earthworms, fish, various mammals and finally our own. Our teacher, Dr Margarita Camps, was very thorough and scientific. So Margarita explained ovulation, why and how our reproduction system works: the eggs, the sperm, how the sperm was deposited in the "virgina" (a few giggles here), how masses of sperms swam to the egg and one entered the ovum and then fertilisation took place and the baby started to develop. We drew all the different phases of the egg dividing, etc. I liked drawing illustrations. We thought nothing of the fact that we were boys and girls together being taught the facts of life; we thought it fascinating and very important. I don't remember being taught about contraception but I was aware that if you had proper sex with a boy you could become pregnant. This made me very careful and frankly terrified, as I definitely didn't want a baby. We were told there was a cycle in the woman and there was a time when they were more fertile, when they ovulated, but one could conceive at any time. Interestingly there were very few pregnancies at the school, unlike the girls' school in Totnes; I only knew of one.

When I was ten I was beginning to look at myself and want to be beautiful. My mother was very beautiful, and she was well aware of it, but along with this beauty and sexiness came a strange lack of confidence and her fear when going out that she wouldn't look absolutely lovely. She had the gentlest touch when you were sad or ill and the warmest softest breast to lay your head on and so her beauty was not something I thought about until one day, sitting next to her on the upright sofa, as a visitor chatted while Sean left the room, I heard him say to Eileen, "It's a pity the little girl has inherited her father's looks and not those of her beautiful mother". This could have been not so bad but I happened to look at Eileen and see a brief smile as she absorbed this compliment, but she quickly replied saying, "What a foolish thing to say, everyone is different and have their own beauty". It struck me as very worrying indeed. I started to look at myself in detail in mirrors and decided I had a huge nose that I hated. I started to draw pictures of myself with pigtails, cross-eyes under my eyebrows that stretched across as one, as mine did, and an elephant trunk as a nose.

Luckily I was too busy with life to brood about my lot too much, but I remember another surprise during an art class with Bernie Forrester. A group of the pretty girls were pestering him to say who he thought was the prettiest. I wasn't a part of this and was smoothing some rolled out clay onto a mould so I was shocked to hear him say, "Shivaun will grow up to be the most beautiful". "Don't be daft", they all said, and so did I. "No. Tell us, tell us, really". He replied, "I told you, Shivaun". Everyone went back to what they were doing and no doubt forgot what was said, except for me. It was nice to have this to remember no matter what, even though he most likely said it to stop all their foolishness.

BECOMING AN ACTRESS

Slowly I was beginning to see the difference between a good professional production of a play or opera and not such a good one. I started to open my eyes a little more one summer when a young American director called Alan Schneider brought over a group of students to work at Dartington.[26] With the pupils gone they lived at Foxhole and at the end of their stay they performed a play by Thornton Wilder set on a New York-Chicago train in December 1930 called *Pullman Car Hiawatha*. They had no scenery, just chairs that they turned into a Pullman car, miming hanging on the straps, the movement, etc. ... It was brilliant – a lesson for me of what you could achieve with little money but with a great deal of imagination and talent.

Alan visited Sean while he was there and a friendship was built between Alan and the family. Part of his brief while there was to direct a play with the Playgoers Society, using its members. He chose the play *My Heart's in the Highlands* by the American playwright William Saroyan. I wasn't a member of the Dartington Playgoers Society but my friends Sim, Carole and Ita were, and they were in it and I was very envious of them.

In our last year at the Middle School our group got to work with Bridget Edwards on a play to be performed at the Barn Theatre up at the Hall: this was a step up and one I had been looking forward to. Every year Bridget put on a play with the group that would be going up to Foxhole,

[26] Born in Russia and emigrating to the U.S. with his family, Alan Schneider (1917–1984) became a theatre director who directed the U.S. premieres of Beckett's *Waiting for Godot*, Albee's *Who's Afraid of Virginia Woolf*, Orton's *Entertaining Mr Sloane* and Pinter's *The Birthday Party*. He was a member of the Actors Studio. He died when struck by a motor-cycle in London. See his *New York Times* obituary, May 4, 1984 and "Alan Schneider," Wikipedia.

A FEW TRYING THINGS 1948–1952

the Senior School. I had seen two productions that she had done and was enthralled by both of them: adaptations from the book *Alice in Wonderland* and *Emil and the Detectives*: and now it was our turn.[27] What's more, the Barn Theatre was a real theatre with wings and a heavy curtain. I loved the theatre that Biddy (or Beatrice) Straight had built; it was also where the children's films were shown at the weekend and where the Playgoers put their productions on. Eileen was delighted when a repertory company was housed there for a while, with Margaret Leighton and Yvonne Mitchell among its actors. Another group came some years later with James Grout, who I fell madly in love with, and Charles West.[28] Interesting people were involved in these events, such as Riette Sturge Moore, the daughter of the poet Thomas Sturge Moore. Joan Cross directed Benjamin Britten's opera *Billy Budd* with Peter Pears singing the lead.[29] So with all the other music that came to the Hall, I inhaled a lot of good work and strange sounds.

Bridget decided to adapt Thackeray's *The Rose and the Ring* for our year and we were to make the costumes and sets ourselves.[30] She cast me as Countess Gruffanuff, Lady of Honour – heaven to me. During the holidays before the summer term began, Eileen would take me up to Aller Park where we worked on my costume with Bridget. I painted sheets with bold red stripes with purple roses between them This was the bodice and panniers – added by lace cuffs and a red underskirt; I had a lace handkerchief to faint with. During the performance I caught sight of Sean in the audience next to Eileen, his glasses catching the light, keenly upright

---

[27] *Emil and the Detectives* is a 1929 novel by Erich Kästner, first published in English in 1931.
[28] Charles West (1927–2021) studied singing at Dartington Hall Music School and acting at RADA. He was a member of the Old Vic Company, 1958–1962. He later appeared in musicals, including *Annie* in the West End and *Man of La Mancha* on Broadway. Later still, he became a successful writer of crime novels. James Grout (1927–2012) acted with the Royal Shakespeare Company, 1950–1955. He was in the original cast of *Half a Sixpence* (Cambridge, 1964, Broadway, 1965). He later acted in films and on television, most notably as Chief Inspector Strange in the ITV *Inspector Morse* series.
[29] The half-French, half-English Riette Sturge Moore (1907–1995) was an interior and stage designer who designed *Dr Faustus* for the 1947 production by the Shakespeare Memorial Theatre. Joan Cross (1900–1993) was an English soprano who often sang in the operas of Benjamin Britten. She also directed operas in London and abroad.
[30] This same year, there was an American CBS-TV dramatisation of Thackeray's 1854 satirical novel.

and leaning forward with a delighted animated look on his face. He loved it and thought that Bridget should run a Children's Theatre similar to the one in Moscow. In her production he loved the armies at war: the opposing armies, one in red the other in blue, marching towards each other, falling back, getting quicker and quicker to a beat of a drum until they all fell down dead.

I am afraid it was this production that put the idea of becoming an actress seriously into my head; I saw that it was a possibility: you didn't have to be beautiful and could be funny instead. This urge didn't budge until I had given it a go years later. Meanwhile, a week-long school camp at Blackpool Sands ended our years at Aller Park. Next year we would enter the Big School as teenagers.

5
Foxhole and *Purple Dust*
1952–1953

FOXHOLE

Now for the first time at school I was to be in the same buildings as Niall. He was now studying for his A-levels. All the sciences fascinated him and he had decided he wanted to be a geologist. But his first love was traditional or New Orleans jazz.[1] The day before school started I went with Niall to meet the school train at Totnes Station. Niall met his schoolfellows and I met mine and we went with them to see their new rooms at Foxhole. The building was a modern craft-cum-Art-Deco structure. There was a central courtyard with a lawn divided neatly into four with paths dissecting it and surrounding it. Around this courtyard most things existed: bedrooms, classrooms, the assembly hall, the dining room and the offices. Most of the children's bedrooms on two floors looked out on to the courtyard. The bedrooms were divided into "houses": red, yellow, blue and green, and the yearly groups were called X, A, B and C. C Group came first and X group was the last while you were working for your A-levels over two years.

The new arrivals were us, C Group, and most if not all were given rooms on the upper floor. My friend Jane was upstairs in the Blue House. The boarders were allowed to decorate their rooms pretty much how they wished though not painting them; anyway, paint was still difficult to find and expensive, so it didn't cross anyone's mind.

On the first day of term Eileen dropped me off at the main entrance. I gathered up what I needed from the car and went up the low broad steps and through the open half of the oak doors, waved good-bye to Mum, and there was a throng of all ages looking at the time-table and copying down their lessons. There was a smell of bleach mingled with the stronger smell of floor polish. We discovered that a thing called Useful Work was to start any moment now, before lessons, so we went to another list to see what tasks we had been allotted. I was cleaning the bedrooms in the Blue House! The cleaning ladies were all local and very nice and helpful as I

[1] Twentieth-century New Orleans jazz music, played primarily by black American musicians, steadily gained an audience in the United Kingdom after the Second World War (stimulated in the beginning by the wartime presence of American GIs) and what began as start-up local tribute bands became a serious British variant of the genre; by the late 1950s jazz even broke into the pop charts as "Trad" before declining with the arrival of the Beatles. Niall was a very early British aficionado and exponent of this jazz tradition.

wasn't very good at cleaning sinks and brushing floors and once a week polishing the parquet floors. Before we polished the corridors and rooms, they sprinkled tea-leaves on the floor to help gather the dust and stop it flying in the air when the floor was swept. Useful work lasted an hour and then it was a dash to the first lesson of the day. Two lesson periods before Break, when we went to the houses we were assigned to as day-pupils for milk or water. You could make toast or just have bread with margarine or dripping; sometimes there was curd cheese that the house-mother made from the sour milk; she hung it over the Butler sink in white gauze, a dripping sour-smelling white ball.

I soon grew to love English with a teacher named Bosence, whom we called Bo[2] and biology with Margarita Camps, art with Joy,[3] and music, including piano lessons, with Timothy Moore.[4] (Niall was a major part of the School jazz band called The Stomping Scholars, and it was headed by Timmy Moore, a kind, rotund, jolly-faced man, always smiling; he was also a composer and I tried to play some of his compositions at my piano lessons with him.) Lots of pupils loved history with Ted, and had crushes on him as he had big eyes with long lashes and was very energetic.[5] Kings and queens didn't interest me at all but for O-Levels we opted to study the

[2] In 1942, Wilfred (Bo) Bosence married Susan Bosence, the textile blockprinter, then secretary to W.B. Curry; Susan was inspired by the pottery of Bernard Forrester. She was the author of *Handblock Printing and Resist-dyeing* (1985). See https://www.independent.co.uk/news/people/obituaries/susan-bosence-1320127.html.

[3] Joy Abrams (1929–2017) began teaching art at Dartington in 1950 but left because she felt the school was a kind of lotus land and she needed a bigger reality. On a kibbutz in Israel she met and married Ed Mickelson from Edmonton, Alberta where they went to live. She switched from art to social work and at the age of 65 earned a PhD in educational psychology from the University of Alberta. Her first book was *Our Sons Were Labeled Behavior Disordered* (2000) over the name Joy Ruth. Her second was *Facing the Shards* (2017), a coming-of-age memoir over the name of Joy Ruth Mickelson recalling her evacuation as a Jewish child from London on the eve of Hitler's Blitz. See https://illuminate.ualberta.ca/content/joy-ruth-mickelson-wonderful-example-us-all

[4] Timothy Moore (1922–2003), an old boy of Dartington Hall, was director of music there from 1950 to 1982. He was a son of the philosopher G.E. Moore. His CV combined studying classical music with (Sir) Michael Tippett and playing piano in Humphrey Lyttleton's jazz band. One obituary called him a "composer and eccentric, his influences included madrigals and jazz": *The Guardian*, March 10, 2003.

[5] In *Geography of a Life* (2012), p. 54, Martin Bernal, who attended Dartington 1947–1954, identified the history teacher as Ted Fitch and gives a thumbnail sketch of a lively and inspiring teacher.

American Civil War and that I did find interesting. Geography was fun because the Spanish teacher, Federico, was so lovable and passionate, and I liked drawing maps. Maths was another matter; it had left my consciousness years ago soon after I had my bout of pneumonia. I had been sent to a maths tutor during the holidays – a dull dusty man in a dull dusty house, who droned on about numbers and solutions and I understood absolutely nothing of what he said. I liked chemistry until I came to realise measurements and maths played a part, and I decided I didn't need it as I was going into the Arts. Before I left the class I managed to make an explosion that burnt a hole in my skirt, and nearly in me. Physics was a write off: I went into both these subjects knowing I wouldn't understand them, that I didn't have that sort of brain.

Now Niall *had* the right kind of brain; he was good at both chemistry and physics, and so was my friend Jane, who had by now decided that she wanted to be a doctor. This meant she had to take Latin. Now that was an extraordinary class taken mainly by those who wanted to go to Oxford or Cambridge as you had to have Latin or Greek to get in. I think I managed about four lessons before quitting. It was in a small upstairs room and taken by a larger than life German who had fled Germany with his family before the war as they were Jewish. He had three children who came to the school: Michael who was in Niall's class, who became a painter, Gabriel who played the cello beautifully and babysat me, and Andy who was a year below me. Rosie, as he was called, was I believe interned during the war for a while, a thing that was quite unnecessary and brutal.[6] Christl's Dad, Trudl's husband Heinz, was also interned. Fear makes people do foolish and often dangerous things. Anyway, Rosie was a handsome robust man who entered the room like a dishevelled cannon shot, gesticulating with his arms when explaining the meaning of the Latin. He jumped on a chair to demonstrate the word "across" and proceeded to step "across" to another chair when he fell thump on the floor. He was up like a flash and went on with the lesson ... he didn't miss a beat. In spite of this magic energy I was completely at sea; never bothering to try and work it out or learn the endings, I lazily gave it up. French was taught by a highly-strung thin man, as small and spiky as Rosie was large and

---

[6] Bernal also recalled Ludwig Rosenberg (always called "Rosie"), who with his family had sought refuge from the Nazis. Bernal remembers him as a deeply cultured man and was told that the Amadeus Quartet was formed in the small living room of the Rosenberg house in Totnes: *Geography of a Life*, p. 54.

imposing; he often made fun and had an ironic grin on him. I stuck to French, although I was terrible at it, as I thought it would be useful. Sean and Eileen both kept telling me how important languages were. Tom Curtiss, our old friend and then the theatre critic for the *Herald Tribune*, who lived in Paris, said he would finance me to study at the Sorbonne after I left – but I was to turn this down as all I wanted at the time was to be an actress.

So, after the first year I gave up Chemistry, Physics, Latin and Geography, leaving me with English Literature and Language, History, Maths (!), Biology, Art and History of Art, and French (I gave up French before O-levels). The other sex was of great interest and daydreaming about it did occupy a lot of my time. We had to discuss the dropping of the subjects, of course, with our parents (and with me that included my brothers), but also with our tutors. I had chosen Margarita to be my tutor, as she was also Niall's tutor. It was decided as Jane and I were friends we would share the sessions together. Margarita's husband was Guillermo, an artist who wore a Basque beret and spoke no English to speak of. He would bring us in something to drink and some biscuits. He was a jolly man and when he came in Margarita always smiled and became soft with a glint in her eyes, not like she was in class. They loved each other. He painted small landscapes. Carrying his equipment on his back, he looked from a distance like a very amiable Van Gogh. There are still many of his paintings around Dartington and in the Elmhirst Collection. We had one but Eileen and Sean didn't like it much, so it was only brought out when they visited us for tea.[7]

My main interests were Art with Joy and English with Bo. My main interest in English was drama. Bo always swept into class with his head held high and books under his arm. He had a kind open face and not much hair. He spoke with enthusiasm as if performing. If the class got distributive and we wouldn't shut up talking he would lob the odd book at us till silence fell. English Language grammar – verbs, nouns, adverbs, pronouns – went over my head. I had learned to read pretty well by now, not having mastered it until I was eight. Dad with his bad eyes hadn't learned to read until he was twelve, so there was hope for me, as now Dad read all the time even with his sore eyes. I loved reading and hearing grand

[7] The photographer and oil painter Guillem (or Guillermo) Bestard (1881–1969) was born in Mallorca, whose island life he pioneeringly captured through his lenses.

language, especially in novels where you could lose yourself in other times and worlds. Just before coming to Foxhole I had read *War and Peace*, and this majestic novel came into my life. The romance touched me but it was the vivid descriptions of the battlefield and the carnage, the smells and sounds Tolstoy described, that hit my guts. Then Sean introduced me to Dickens, and then to Thomas Hardy: two "friends" I read over and over again. Shakespeare was already there: I had seen the productions at Stratford and was familiar with his words, as Sean quoted him so often. Sean also quoted from the Bible but it was Shakespeare that stuck. As I was growing more and more away from home Sean would hold my arms, look me in the eye and say:

> This above all: to thine own self be true,
> And it must follow, as the night the day,
> You canst not then be false to any man.

The next term I tried to change my Useful Work to the Art Room: cleaning it and setting out the paper and paints. I always liked working rooms or studios, Sean's room with its old typewriter and Breon's room full of paints and canvases. Sitting in these rooms was peaceful to me, I felt important and easy at the same time. The Art Room at school reminded me of a studio – pictures on the walls, paint splattered tables and the sink full of brushes to clean – heaven. I finally wangled it the following term and this was my job until I left. Joy taught us Art, an ebullient, jolly person, with a great joyful laugh and twinkles in her eyes. She loved her subject and we loved her. She was a friend of the theatre director, Frank Dunlop.[8]

Early on, I was asked to be in a play directed by an older girl called Elspeth MacDougall. Her father, Roger MacDougall, had recently written the Oscar-nominated film *Man in the White Suit* (he was also known in the theatre for the hit *To Dorothy, A Son*).[9] Sean had helped us out on the choice of play and we decided on Synge's *Riders to the Sea* in which I was

---

[8] Frank Dunlop CBE, Chevalier of the Order of Arts and Literature, 98 at this time of writing, studied with Michael Saint-Denis at the Old Vic School. He joined the National Theatre in 1967 as Associate Director and was the founding director of the Young Vic in 1969, and director of the Edinburgh Festival, 1984–1991.

[9] Besides co-screenwriting *The Man in the White Suit* (1951), Elspeth's father, Roger also co-wrote *The Mouse that Roared* (1959); his play *To Dorothy, A Son* (1950) was a West End success and was adapted as a film in 1954. Elspeth after Dartington lived in New York and then Los Angeles.

cast as the Mother. I designed the set with a flat proscenium made with canvas, flats, decorated with abstract painting of the sea, but it had to be modified and we ended up with just flats making a small dwelling. I couldn't begin to get the pain of the mother – "They have all gone now and there's nothing left the sea can do to me. ..." It was very dramatic and we all took it extremely seriously.

I never saw Breon perform in anything, although he was remembered at the school for playing Prospero in *The Tempest*. Breon was a great mimic and often had us in stitches imitating people. I did, however, see Niall as Captain Burgoyne in *The Devil's Disciple* and was very proud to be his sister. He had a good baritone singing voice, like Sean, and I remember a group of them performing, as if in a pub, "The Foggy Foggy Dew". Shaw, the family friend, who was such a large part of the dining-table conversation that I felt I knew him intimately, was coming into view for me. I had read at Sean's suggestion *Fanny's First Play*, and then I read *Pygmalion*; now *there* was a part for me, I thought. Sean gave me a copy of *The Intelligent Woman's Guide to Socialism and Capitalism* as a present, and I read parts of it. It was very funny and also made absolute sense.

My friend Jane became a very hard-working scholar with a group of other girls who seemed to turn their backs on boys, and set their minds to study of another sort. Not openly looking for a boyfriend, I pretended I was utterly uninterested. This was due to my embarrassment when my brothers ridiculed me while I was still at the Middle School: I blurted out that I was in love with Niall's friend Alister Shakeston, thinking it as a normal thing to do. Niall did one of his splutters-into-the-tea-cup, and laughed with Breon: even Eileen laughed. Sean didn't – a pal for life. I wasn't going to let that happen again if I could help it. Anyway, no one fancied me and so the odd crush was all that happened in that line. I did like being amongst a group chatting and gossiping, and although I did work it wasn't my prime objective. So, Elspeth Edwards (or Speth), who wrote very good essays and had been in [Christopher Fry's] *The Lady's Not For Burning*, became one of my friends.

My nose was put out of joint when a new girl called Kate Duckham (of Duckhams Oil) arrived; she was good at acting and had great sex appeal.[10] She was also very good at art. She became the girlfriend of Martin Bernal who I secretly fancied. His father was very famous and had won the Nobel Prize for physics, his mother one of the professor's partners called Margaret Gardiner.[11] Speth and I remained without a sweetheart, so we decided to set our caps at Nicholas, a boarder from London, a kind, clever boy who was amusing. We saved up and bought him some Sobranie cigarettes, and although he accepted them gratefully that was that, so to speak. He was usually clad in a beige duffle coat and was friends with a boy from Scotland, Charlie Allan, who was as extrovert and funny as the other was quietly sardonic. Their party piece was singing "Dear Old London Town" and "I Remember Glasgow".[12]

I enjoyed seeing Niall hanging out with his classmates. He had a couple of girls he was interested in; one was very aware of herself and swung her hips as she walked, as did the other older girl he fancied but never got very far with. I would tease Niall about them but unlike me he was always sure of himself and didn't need to apologise for anything he thought or did. Once Alister had come to stay for a while and when he arrived the first thing Niall said was, "Have you brought your whites, old boy?" Breon and I fell about, and we taunted Niall with it for ages but he never minded. He had a way of often sounding upper class and had no problem mixing with anyone. Asked to play tennis at the Hall, he didn't miss a beat but went up there and joined in with ease. He was actually very left wing politically, even at that age, and followed politics in the papers and talked about it all with Sean. A friend of his, Lot, told me recently that he would go with Niall to the Tory meetings in Totnes and Niall would question the Tory MP and tie him up in knots. Both Sean and Niall were mad about football and cricket. There was not much hurley or Gaelic football about

---

[10] Duckham's oil firm, still in operation, was founded in 1899. Martin Bernal confirms that at Foxhole pupils were now more interested in each other than in the outside world, including nature, and above all courted popularity rather than academic or sporting prowess, and that ranking was established by the status of boyfriends and girlfriends: *Geography of a Life*, p. 50.

[11] J.D. Bernal (1901–1971) was a distinguished Irish-born physicist whose career was in England; he became an active member of the Communist Party of Great Britain. Margaret Gardiner (1904–2005), his partner, was an art collector and patron.

[12] After Dartington, the versatile Charlie Allan (1939–2023) became a university lecturer in economics-turned-farmer, all-round athlete – rugby, football, cricket, athletics, caber tossing (world champion, 1972) – ballad singer and publisher.

for Sean, although it is said that years ago Cornwall played Cork at hurley. Sean was very proud that he had played hurley when he was young. He was terrifying when he played hitting the ball against the wall; he whacked it with such mighty strength that even the boys declined to play with him. I am told when he was young he mistook a bird for the hurley ball and killed it. Breon played hockey at school but never had much interest in teams or scores. I never saw him listen to a match on the radio, although he may have when he was younger, whereas Niall and Sean glued themselves to the radio listening to the football matches unfold. They supported different teams: Sean supported Tottenham Hotspur and Niall Charlton Athletic.

Niall took his A-levels in the summer of 1953. He did very well and was accepted by London University, which is where he wanted to go, and what's more they would hold his place until he finished his National Service.

PURPLE DUST

Another exciting thing happened in 1952: the production of *Purple Dust* directed by Sam Wanamaker. Not only was the idea of a production exciting but it was the beginning of a close friendship with the Wanamaker family. Sam had contacted Sean in 1952 with the proposal. In a letter to Sean, Sam said that a Mr Henry Sherek was to put up the money.[13] Now, almost a month later, Sam Wanamaker was about to arrive at Totnes Station for a visit to talk about his ideas for his production. Breon went to meet him at the Station. "A handsome man stepped down from the train, in a brightly checked bespoke wool suit with a Stetson hat on his head," Breon said. As he walked up the platform, Breon said to him, "You must be Mr. Wanamaker." "How did you know it was me?" he replied. Breon just said intuition; he could hardly say: "No one else down here wears Stetson hats or bright checked suits". "Call me Sam," Sam said as they chatted on their way to Tingrith. Tingrith was a five-minute walk from the station. For Sean this was the start of an interesting and stimulating rehearsal period and production and our friendship with the Wanamakers.

[13] Sam Wanamaker (1919–1993) was an American actor and director. Concerned that he might be blacklisted in the United States for his Communist views, he decided in 1952 to reside permanently in the UK where he was a visiting actor. His wife Charlotte Holland (1915–1997) was a Canadian actress. Henry Sherek (1900–1967) was a prominent English theatrical agent and producer.

Sam had an idea that *Purple Dust* should have more songs, so Sean wrote more for the production. Sam wanted Sean at rehearsals. It was a credit to Sam that Sean agreed; he must have liked him a lot, for travelling and staying away from home was a difficulty for Sean. Sean travelled to London with Eileen; they both stayed with the Wanamakers. Here Sean met and loved Charlotte, Sam's gloriously warm, kind sparkling wife. It was Charlotte who looked after Sean and he was entertained by their two children Abby and Zoe. The family was then living in Albert Mansions, near the later built mosque, on the West side of Regent's Park, in a large flat that had once belonged to Glynis Johns.[14]

The first time I met Charlotte was on a visit to London before that. I came up with Eileen, staying again at The Pig and Whistle. Charlotte was downstairs waiting for us with Sam; she was wearing a red swing coat with a neat matching pillbox hat on her head and a neat little fur muff. Out of the fur collar beamed the prettiest, most pleasing face imaginable. The next day Eileen and I journeyed to Hampstead to see her at home. They were renting a house before moving to Albert Mansions. It was a beautiful Regency "cottage" behind a tall wall; through the gate in the wall was a pretty walled-in garden. Charlotte asked if we would mind going downstairs to see her little girl Zoe who had been waiting for us. We found her sitting on a decorated puff with her arms in the air and outstretched legs, in a ballet pose; she was in a blue fairy tutu, pink tights and little satin ballet shoes. She captivated Eileen and me immediately. She was, of course, going to be a ballet dancer. Their older daughter, Abby, was at school and on that day we missed seeing her. I got to know Abby well during the following days and when I almost lived permanently in Albert Mansions while I attended RADA. Then she helped me babysit her siblings and put them to bed. Abby was another gem, with a great sense of the strange ways of life; she still has an open laugh that draws you in.[15]

Sean was excited by this production and by the work he was doing directly with Sam and the actors; this is what he needed so badly for his later plays, to work on them in action so to speak, but it also gave him a contact as an artist. He told Sam he thought *Purple Dust* could be a

[14] Although South African-born, British raised and educated, and the daughter of the well-known Welsh actor Mervyn Johns (who died at 93 in 1992), the actress, dancer and singer Glynis Johns, who died in 2024 aged 100, found fame in Hollywood as well as in British film productions.

[15] Abby Wanamaker helps administer the Shakespeare's Globe Theatre; her sister Zoe became a well-known stage and television actress.

commercial success now that he was better known. The dress rehearsal was set for April 21, 1953. Sean and Eileen and myself went up for the final week of rehearsals. Sean stayed at the Wanamakers by himself. Eileen and I stayed later with Don and Ella[16] nearer the Wanamakers but first with Sir Hardman (Harvey) Earle (5th baronet), but really with his wife, Maie Drage, who had been a friend of Eileen's in the chorus and who had married into the aristocracy. Staying there was a strange interlude. Hardman and Maie had a pile in the country that Eileen told me they were letting while they lived in the Gatehouse: but in London they had this very little house in SW London. Eileen's friend Maie was a slim dark pretty lady who we often met for tea when we were in London. She had a handsome young son called George, I think, who was starting out in the city, and a daughter called, maybe, Belinda. The house seemed dark and Harvey was not overjoyed to have us as guests, especially me. On the first night we were to have dinner there and as we were getting dressed Eileen was told that I had better have mine in my room, I thought because their dining room was so tiny; but no, it was because Harvey insisted that they all dress in formal attire every night at dinner and young people never attended these meals. Eileen had to put on her theatre regalia and attend a very stiff meal. I now understood why the wife wasn't happy in her relationship; it must have been unbearable trying to keep up appearances with the money scarce.

During our stay we went to see Ella and the next day Eileen said that Ella had recommended me for a part in Joe Losey's new film: this was to be *The Father* by Strindberg, starring Wendy Hiller and Trevor Howard. Joe came to the little London house and interviewed me in the bedroom: we talked and I read for him from the play: this was my first audition and what a strange one it was. When we got back to Devon a salary was discussed with Sean and Eileen (I was to get £2000!) who wondered what

---

[16] Donald Ogden Stewart (1894–1980) was an American playwright, satirist and screenwriter. He adapted the play *The Philadelphia Story* for the screen in 1940, for which he won an Oscar. He was blacklisted in 1950 for his membership of the Communist Party USA and emigrated to Britain with his second wife Ella Winter. The last four pages of Stewart's memoir *By a Stroke of Luck* (1975) are a summary of his life in Hampstead in London. The Australian-born Winter (1898–1980) was like her first husband, Lincoln Steffens, a campaigning journalist. Converted to socialism by reading Oscar Wilde's The *Soul of Man Under Socialism* (1891), she published an account of her visit to the Soviet Union in 1930. See: "Ella Winter", Spartacus Educational: https://spartacus-educational.com/Aella_winter.htm. There is a portrait of Don and Ella in Mary Gilliatt's *Fabulous Food and Friends* (Barnsley: Pen & Sword Books, 2008).

on earth to do with it and if I should actually do the part. I wanted to, so it was decided I could. But I never did as Joe never managed to get the funding.

The rehearsals for *Purple Dust* were in full swing at the Princess Theatre in Lower Shaftesbury Avenue and there was a buzz around them. After moving to Don and Ella's at 103 Frognal, Hampstead,[17] in the evenings Eileen and I would join Sean at the Wanamakers. Zoe and Abby loved Sean and hugged him and sat next to him, till, I have to confess, I felt slightly jealous. One evening Gerard Hoffnung and his wife joined us all – soon we were all rolling about on the floor listening to Gerard's stories.[18] The one I liked best was his description of a family picnic. They all gathered together in the large kitchen, packed the food and drink into rucksacks, put on their walking gear and started to walk around the table hundreds of times; finally stopping and laying out the cloth and unpacking the food. Then, he said, his grandfather exclaimed, "We've forgotten the bottle opener!" "I'll get it", the young Gerard replied and went to grab it from the drawer. "No. Stop!" they all yelled, "You have to walk back around the table to get it and then back again to us here." Which he said he proceeded to do. It was the way he told it, and described his family, in his excited and emotional way – on the cusp of hysterics – that made us all roll on the floor.

Gerard designed the Curtain for *Purple Dust* – one of his cartoons with all the characters exaggerated. The dress rehearsal was wonderful. The music was written and arranged by Malcolm Arnold and dances choreographed by John Cranko; the cast included Liam Redmond as the 1st workman, Joseph O'Connor as 2nd workman and the storm, Miles Malleson as Cyril Poges, Walter Hudd as Basil Stoke, Siobhan McKenna as Avril, Eithne Dunne as Souhan, Doreen Keogh as Cloyne, Sheamus Locke as O'Killigain. I don't know who designed the sets and costumes. I sat in the stalls filled with excitement to be allowed in to watch with a small invited audience. Sam explained that they may have to stop if things

---

[17] In his memoir, Stewart tells us the house had belonged to the politician Ramsay MacDonald.

[18] Gerard Hoffnung (1925–1959) was a German-born artist and musician brought to London as a boy in late 1938 to escape the Nazis. He excelled as a music-themed cartoonist and comic anecdotalist. In 1996 Humphrey Lyttelton recorded a portrait of him for BBC Audiobooks: see "Gerard Hoffnung", Wikipedia. Also: *Gerard Hoffnung (1925-1959)*: https://gerardhoffnung.com/biography/

went too wrong but hopefully they would sail through to the end. It was colourful and funny. All the cast were terrific and Miles Malleson and Walter Hudd were hilarious. What could go wrong? So off the show went, to receive an unfavourable review in the *Glasgow Evening Press*, April 28 by W.C.G. who attacked the production and the playwright. A blow for Sean and Sam. Sean, however, reminded Sam that he, Sean, had mentioned doubts about Glasgow that had a powerful Roman Catholic church presence as in Liverpool. "I imagine Edinburgh will be very different. ... So don't let Glasgow frighten us, Sam".[19]

Sean was now determined to go up to Edinburgh to see the play open there and support Sam. Eileen went by the sleeper and Sean followed during the day, arriving on May 4. In *Sean*, Eileen later wrote: "The change in the play at the Lyceum Theatre was startling: we were utterly mystified by the half-hearted manner in which Miles was acting, a style that meant trouble for Walter Hudd who relied upon every line of Miles to hold up his own part. As they had to be the life and soul, it was simply was not the same play we had enjoyed in London rehearsals. ... because of Miles much of the life had ebbed. ... in the end, though nobody could have tried harder than Sam to do it worthily, a fine play got little further. Terribly worried - not least about finance - Sam could not understand what had happened, and we could get no explanation from Miles; when he came to lunch with us the warmth between us had disappeared and it was merely an ordinary polite meal. Possibly Coronation year was bad for a piece that might have been mistaken for a skit on English life and a laugh at the system as it was. I think myself that it could be called a prophetic play in the mood of *The Cherry Orchard*" (p. 215).[20]

Sean and Eileen had a great time in Edinburgh despite the bad things happening to his play. Sean met up with his old friends, among them the poet Hugh MacDiarmid.

This was the first professional production I was a peripheral part of. I was allowed to watch some of the rehearsals. I remember an incident at the technical rehearsal when Miles came on stage angry about his wig. Sam took him off to talk about it quietly in his dressing room. He then

---

[19] *The Letters of Sean O'Casey, Volume II*, p. 365.

[20] Although he was a pacifist, socialist and during the Great War a conscientious objector, the English actor and playwright Miles Malleson (1888–1969) might well have taken umbrage at the depiction of the English in *Purple Dust*. Or perhaps he came to think that the play was not going to achieve a West End stage and thus lost interest.

came back to the stalls where we were sitting: "I can't understand why he doesn't just take off his toupee and use his own bald hair. He insists he doesn't wear a toupee. Anyway his wig has to fit over it – as he won't take it off." Malleson also didn't get on with "Dicky" Hudd; there was a coolness between them off stage.[21] Did this conceited man, after receiving bad reviews in Glasgow, decide he didn't want the production to go to London where he might get further bad reviews? Who knows. It seemed like sabotage of the production to me. I saw him a couple of times at my school. He had a son called Nicky at Dartington; he entered the dining room as if he was a VIP and found me out to send his admiration to Sean.

Sean had been positive about this production and liked Sam very much, so I write about this to show the heartbreak Sean so often went through. This *Purple Dust* was in truth a good, exciting and colourful production and I am very glad I saw it in rehearsals in London. Charlie Chaplin came to see a rehearsal and met with Sean. There was a rumour in the newspapers that he would be making it into a film.

Ella and Don knew Charlie from their Hollywood days. While Don wrote many famous scripts, some for Katharine Hepburn and Spencer Tracy, Charlie was busy making his films that we all saw and loved. Ella told Eileen and me that Charlie did seriously consider using *Purple Dust* for a film but, as Sean said, nothing came of it. I imagine backing would have been difficult for such a work at such a time.

AN UNWANTED VISITOR, JUNE 1953

A strange thing happened on June 12, 1953 (I know the date as Sean wrote about it in his Notebook). Eileen and I were shopping in Totnes Fore Street when our help Winnie Garside came flying up to us: "Mrs O'Casey, come quick, Sean's chucking a great big man down the stairs". "What on earth do you mean, Winnie?" "It's a bailiff!" she panted. "Hurry or he may murder him". We all rushed back like maniacs to find Sean collapsed in a chair. Breon had cycled down from school. Sean had evidently done his best to throw one of the bailiffs down the stairs; he was strong from the physical work on the railways and the roads. Faced with his force and strength the bailiffs decided to come back another day. Eileen was worried

---

[21] Walter (Dicky) Hudd (1897–1963) was a London-born actor and director; he appeared on stage in Stratford and the West End and in movies, including *Look Back in Anger* (1959) and *Sink the Bismarck!* (1960). He later became Head of Drama at the Central School of Speech and Drama. From the 1930s to the 1950s he was a member of the Hampstead Communist Party.

about Sean as he had years of intermittent silicosis that had pulled his heart about, and he was not meant to exert himself.

Sean's Notebook:
Unannounced, in walked Mr. Mason, an Income Tax Collector, with a bailiff at his arse – second time of meeting a bailiff; came some months before. This time £99 pounds owing. On the first occasion ... asked what I had to sell. I said all I have is here in this room. ... The stout, consequential bailiff went round the room, bringing his snout close to the books, sniffing at them as he went along; but learning little about them by a look. Asked me if I had any rare books. Told him most of them were rare, & most of them lovely. He wrote something on a slip of paper in his hand. Some more chat, & then, he extended the slip of paper to me asking me to sign it. His companion, The Collector, – a civil courteous gentleman – murmured that it was a mere formality. I signed it, accepting the murmur. When they had gone discovered the slip on the table shoved in between other papers which declared that if the money wasn't paid within a certain date, my two typewriters – the old and the second hand, in use for 40 years, & another never; second-hand one, used for final drafts of work; original manuscripts, rare books. Kind of them. The money wasn't paid before the date specified, part of it was, the rest later.

So, here they were again on the prowl, for typewriters, manuscripts, rare books; the fat, smug faced bailiff flatulent with an air of important authority. Well, he heard some elegant opinions from an Irishman who was for years and years a worker among men. He didn't like it. Said he wasn't used to it: told him if he visited me regularly he'd soon get used to it. Pay Taxes for 27 years, & yet England, true to type, sends her bailiff in on top of an Irishman – £49 owing out of £174, and yet this flat-faced, ignorant bum of a bailiff, came to take two typewriters away – the one means by which the amount due could be paid. Was unaffected by loveliness, saw nothing in the grandeur that was Greece save wretchedness, weariness, & woe.

Sean wrote a long letter to the Chancellor of the Exchequer, R.A. Butler, recounting the visit in careful order and denying any attempt to evade taxes.[22]

[22] The letter (and a reply to it) is reproduced in *The Letters of Sean O'Casey, Volume II*, pp. 976–979.

Eileen later told us that as a result of the letter a telephone message from Whitehall informed Sean that the Chancellor was sending a high official from the income-tax world to sort things out. He was evidently charming and asked Sean if he could go through his accounts. When he had finished he said he had found several uncashed War Bonds (money collected by the Government to help it get through the war and repayable now). At last the official said: "Well, you may owe the revenue £47 but the Revenue owes you £100." He asked if Sean and Eileen would dine with him in the Totnes Hotel. Sean explained that he really didn't eat out but Eileen had a lovely meal and says they noticed all later tax demands were signed by somebody with a different name. So that turned out well and we could all breath again in relative peace.

A VISIT TO STRATFORD

After the summer of 1953 Niall was due for National Service. At that time all healthy males of 18 or over had to do a military service of two years, or, if they were conscientious objectors, serve in the mines or, if they were lucky, on a farm. (When Breon was called up to do National Service it lasted 18 months; it was the Korean War that made the government extend the time to two years). Sean didn't approve of conscientious objectors, although he hated war or violence of any kind; he believed, though, that sometimes we literally had to fight for our lives. Both Breon and Niall thought the same; after all, we had just come through a horrible war against the Fascist dictator Hitler and his gang.

While waiting for Niall's call up date and after the disappointment of *Purple Dust*, Eileen, Sean, Niall and myself all went for a week to Stratford – the time we saw Peggy Ashcroft. In 1953 she was playing Cleopatra to Michael Redgrave's Anthony. I believe this was directed by Glen Byam Shaw with Motley sets; I think Peggy may have also played Juliet during this season, as I know I saw her play the role that everyone said she was too old to play. If so I thought she was wonderful in it and captured the essence of youth, the innocence and the first love. Her nurse was wonderful too. There seems to be no record of this performance but I surely didn't dream it. Did Laurence Harvey play Romeo?[23]

---

[23] Peggy Ashcroft famously played Juliet in John Gielgud's production at the New Theatre in 1935; Laurence Harvey did play Romeo in a Royal Shakespeare Theatre production in 1954, but Juliet was played by Zena Walker. Shaw played Benvolio in the 1935 *Romeo and Juliet*.

During this season Michael Redgrave was also playing King Lear. A friend of Niall's, Charlie Howard, was in the company and so Niall stayed with him and spent most of his time with him. Charlie told Niall that one night during *King Lear* when there was royalty in the audience, Michael Redgrave entered and sat on his throne and looking down realised he had forgotten to put on his full costume and was in his underpants. He ordered everybody to follow him off the stage in character, and the curtain came down leaving Charlie and another young lad standing in front of the red velvet curtains holding their spears. "Ho! Let us follow" says Charlie and marches to a door in the proscenium that unhappily didn't open. They then sheepishly walked across the stage to the other door, which opened. In a few moments the show went on with a fully clad Lear.

I remember being fascinated by a brooding man who stood in the foyer of the theatre, leaning against the wall, romantically observing or thinking. I was told he was Robert Colquhoun, a Scottish painter who designed the sets for *Lear*. The sets were different from the Motley sets that were usually beautifully evocative and very much of the place. These sets by Colquhoun were made from huge monumental stones like the ancient stones of Avebury and nothing much else, a simplicity that also had great atmosphere, and against the monochrome of the sets the costumes were bright and colourful. Marius Goring played the fool and Yvonne Mitchell Cordelia.[24]

Sean came with us because he was tempted to see where Shakespeare had lived, the streets he had walked, the Avon River he had pondered by. He knew Shakespeare's walks in London but not where he was formed and where he went back to spend his last days. Shakespeare was always very close to Sean's heart: he signed a set of Shakespeare plays he bought for me from Macmillan's when I went to Drama School: "Hoping Shakespeare becomes as great a friend to you as he is to me." This book was stolen but I remember the inscription. I had told Sean all about these houses with their low ceilings and doors and short beds, where the smaller Elizabethans had lived, and about a clever metal device that they believed his children (maybe even he) had learnt to walk in. It was a pole that went from floor to ceiling with a little metal seat fastened around the pole so that when the child was fastened in and its little feet were touching the

---

[24] There is a review of this *King Lear* by Philip Hope-Wallace in the *Guardian* of July 16, 1953 which mentions Colquhoun's "near-abstract sets". : https://www.theguardian.com/theguardian/1953/jul/16/1

floor it could use its feet to walk around and around the pole. We stayed again at the Shakespeare Hotel, Sean and Eileen in a room together and me on my own; by then I was more used to being on my own in hotels and anyway, Eileen had to help Sean find his way in new surroundings and sort out his eye drops, etc. It was here my gold charm bracelet was stolen, given to me first with one charm and added to every Christmas and birthday. I was gutted by my first experience of theft.

Sean didn't want to come to any of the plays as he had a persistent cough and couldn't bear the thought of coughing during a performance, but we did all go to visit Peggy Ashcroft at the house where some of the leading players were staying. Sean and Peggy were delighted to see each other again and talked about the early days of Michel St Denis and about her husband Tomas Komisarjevsky.[25] We had a jovial and busy-with-talk tea and then we all took a stroll around the garden; suddenly Sean tripped down a flight of steps he hadn't seen; we all gasped as we watched him do a most miraculous quick-step down the steps, landing like Fred Astaire at the bottom with a bend of the knees standing upright with his arms upheld. We clapped and cheered and found his cap that had flown off. He was remarkably well balanced and agile for his 72 years. Peggy thought I would like to meet Vanessa and Lynn Redgrave; I can't remember if Corin the brother was there, maybe he was there, in the background. It was the last thing I wanted to do as I was extremely and painfully shy and I knew I would have nothing to say. But they were fetched, most likely against their wills. But we didn't play together as we were all too old for that. Vanessa was very grown-up, two years older than me, which is a lot at that age, and Lynn four years younger. Their mother Rachel Kempson came down to meet Sean and we luckily all joined the grown-ups again and the pressure was off.

By then Vanessa had decided she wanted to act and spent most nights at the theatre watching the performances. We saw her standing at the back that evening and Glen told us she came nearly every night to watch her father and the other actors. What a great way to learn your craft and how lucky she was! I was very envious. In the intervals we were always called into the VIP Lounge where Glen would be hosting the complimentary

---

[25] Peggy Ashcroft (1907–1991) was married to Theodore Komisarjevsky from 1934 to 1936. The Venice-born Komisarjevsky (1882–1954) was a Russian stage director and designer but worked later in England and became a British citizen; he directed plays at the Shakespeare Memorial Theatre.

ticket holders and other dignitaries of the evening. The only person I remember, apart from Glen, is Robert Morley who was so much bigger than life, and very amusing, that one could never forget his booming voice and raised eyebrows. An upper-class Falstaff.

We did visit all Shakespeare's houses with Sean and the one he was most interested in was the last one he lived in and had bought, with the large mulberry tree in the garden. It had a display with pictures of all the flowers the playwright mentioned in his plays and the extracts where they were mentioned – and histories of the flowers. Sean loved the way Shakespeare was so in touch with nature, so in touch with life: he thought that any writer worth his salt should include the flowers and the bees in their writing. It was fun going with Sean; he engaged in talk with those showing us around, and I learnt far more than I had learnt the first time we visited: they knew far more than they normally were obliged to say and were animated while talking with Sean.

Niall said goodbye to Charlie Howard and we all said goodbye to Shakespeare's birthplace and Eileen drove us, yes drove us home, with Sean sitting in front fiddling with his pipe.

6
Bivouacs, beaches and bonfires
1953–1955

Shivaun and Sean, "Tingrith", 1945
PHOTOGRAPH: Alfred Eris

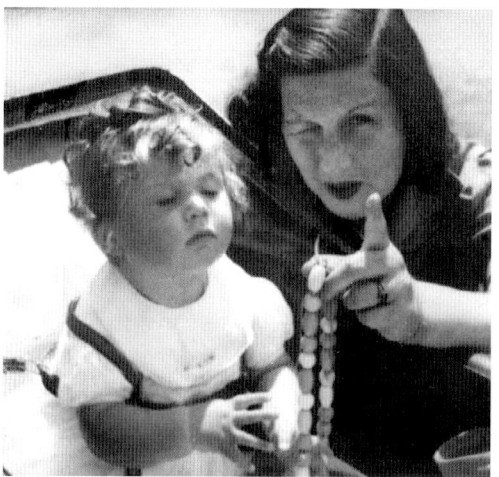

Eileen tries to make me open my eyes, 1940
TOP RIGHT: Me, Eileen and Niall, Goodrington, 1946
LOWER LEFT: Niall and me, Paignton Front, 1942
Breon and Sean playing draughts, Goodrington, 1940

Sean and Eileen, "Tingrith", Totnes, 1954. PHOTOGRAPH: Gjon Mili, Shutterstock

Niall, me, Breon, Eileen and Sean, "Tingrith", 1943

TOP: Pupils in front of Dartington School, I am standing to the right, *c.* 1945
LOWER LEFT: Breon and Sean, "Tingrith", 1945. PHOTOGRAPH: Alfred Eris
RIGHT: George Bernard Shaw. Postcards GBS gave Breon to sell

The Stomping Scholars, Niall on trombone, *c.* 1951

LEFT: Niall and friend at the crease, school playing fields
ABOVE: Me, Eileen, Niall and Sean, Paignton Front, 1947 or 1948

Niall, me, Sean and Eileen having tea in "Tingrith",
1953. PHOTOGRAPH: Gjon Mili

Sean washes up in the scullery, "Tingrith", 1953
PHOTOGRAPH: Gjon Mili

Niall, me with Kitty, Eileen, Sean and Breon outside the garage, "Tingrith", 1950. GBS kept this photo on his desk in Ayot St Lawrence.

I watch Breon painting in his room, 1945

Sean, Eileen, Niall, me and Breon on the steps of "Vil Rosa", St Marychurch, 19
PHOTOGRAPH: Wolfgang Suschitzky

Filming for the NBC documentary *The Exile*, 1

POST-WAR VISITORS

Before Christmas 1953, we had a visit from Gjon Mili, an Albanian living in New York. Gjon, a photographer with *LIFE* magazine, came with a young assistant called Robert Emmett Ginna, who we very quickly called Bob. Their assignment was a photo essay on Sean.

Gjon and Bob brought a lot of energy to the O'Casey household. Sean and Gjon talked endlessly about their remarkable mothers. Both their mothers worked hard to keep their families fed and clothed as best they could, to prevent them from dying. Neither woman seemed to complain but "got on with it", bearing their hardship in silence but always ready to rush to help others; both died quietly and with dignity. Gjon told Sean about his family's exit from Albania as refugees, of mothers giving birth by the side of the road, and of his final home in New York where he kept in touch with his family. He was now a famous photographer who among other things liked making the little cine-camera he filmed Sean with. He was the photographer who invented the shutter strobe effect – where he photographed the series of a movement on one plate. He used it a lot for dance.[1]

While he was with us he made a film on his home-made camera. In Paris they had overrun their expenses and Bob pawned his camera. It was on one sunny afternoon that Gjon asked Bob for his camera to take pictures of Sean; when he found out what Bob had done he was furious with Bob; Sean had to point out that it was Bob's own camera, even if Gjon liked to use it, and he was driven to pawn it to keep them going. That evening we all went out to eat, on the *LIFE* money, at the local Cott Inn. We had many jovial and hilarious meals while they were with us. All of us appeared in Gjon's home movie, but the star was Sean. We were filmed around the kitchen table having a meal – that is, all of us except Breon who was away at Sidney Bernstein's farm working to make some money: Gjon went there and filmed Breon leading a bull into a field. I wished at the time both Gjon and Bob lived down the road so we could be with them both much of the

---

[1] Gjon Mili (1904–1984) was also a film director and in 1944 directed the jazz film, *Jammin' the Blues*. See "Gjon Mili", Wikipedia.

time. They stayed for two weeks, and became a welcome part of our life.[2] Gjon Mili looked like a taller and thinner Einstein; Sean called him "The genial Albanian friend". Later when I met him in New York he had become unhappier. A terrible thing happened to him; the building where his studio was burned down and many of his negatives were destroyed (I think his black cat survived). He had been given a studio in the Time/Life building. This studio was now a smallish room with full glass windows – and made interesting only by the photos hanging up to dry on a clothesline. But only when we left this room and we all went to eat at an Albanian restaurant that he frequented did he blossom again into the Mili I had known for a while back in Devon.

Sean was relaxed with Bob and Gjon and enjoyed being photographed by them both: the excitement, the talk, the songs. I sat watching Bob sketch Sean as he sat in a deck-chair among our three apple trees in our walled back garden, and Gjon moving around with his camera, bending his long legs, and squinting with his left eye; Sean fiddling with his pipe; lighting it, putting it out, lighting it again; contented. The sun shining through the trees, the leaves dappling the light. I felt I would like to draw like Bob, and for this scene to go on for a long time, for the curtain to be delayed coming down. But after two weeks of filming off they both went to Ireland to take more pictures for the *LIFE* photo essay. We were sorry to see them go.

A young American academic called David Krause had started to write to Sean in 1949 when he sent his MA thesis about Sean's work.[3] In his reply, Sean wrote that he hoped "the knock you give to the door of life will sound good in the hearts of others, and echo soundly in your own" and added in a postscript: "Don't be discouraged if your knock doesn't sound clear and loud at first – knock again; and again".[4] In David came,

---

[2] This was Bob's first visit to Ireland. Robert Emmet Ginna became an editor (with LIFE magazine and *Scientific American*), writer (a travel chronicle, *The Irish Way*, 2003), teacher (Harvard) and filmmaker. His filmography includes the dramatisation of Sean's early life, *Young Cassidy* (1965), and the documentary, *Sean O'Casey: The Spirit of Ireland* (1965). See Scott Hauser, "A Walk Through Eire," *Rochester Review* 66.2 (2003–04). He died in March 2025 at the age of 99. His papers are at the Harry Ransom Center.

[3] David Krause (1917–2011) had begun his M.A. research on Sean at the University of Minnesota when he first wrote to Sean. Krause later became an O'Casey authority while he taught for years at Brown University, Rhode Island. He first met the playwright when he travelled to England in 1954. See Professor Krause's obituary in the *Providence Journal* of August 29, 2011.

all smiles: a short, well-built man with masses of dark hair and bundles of energy. Did he have a beard then or was that grown later on? We were to discover that he was a searching machine, finding out things for Sean such as manuscripts and past printed material and talking to Sean's old friends and enemies. When he started on collecting all of Sean's letters he was accompanied by his lovely Irish wife Anne; they were to have four children, all as loving and talkative as their parents. While he was with us Dave stayed with Clare and her husband not far from our home: Clare had taken on Winnie's role as a help for Eileen. Sean liked Dave at once and they talked and laughed for hours. The continuation of a friendship started by letters that lasted until Sean's death.

NIALL'S CALL UP

Niall applied in July, 1953 for the Royal Air Force, and sat and waited; after several false alarms he was finally called up for the Army and on October 15, or thereabouts, he left with two other lads from Totnes, climbing with them on to the train that would take them to the Royal Artillery Base in Oswestry. Eileen describes watching them from the railway bridge and her blood chilling.

Here I was, the last of the Mohicans at home; and I missed my two brothers' presence even though I was busy enough at school and at what I wanted to do. I was a dreamer of the future and what it could bring. I wanted to act but knew Sean was worried by this, although Eileen would have liked a personal contact with the theatre.

Niall's letter to me (December 10):

2293297 O'Casey N
D.1 Sub Section
172/64TH Ty Regt RA

Dear Shivaun,

I'm writing from the guard-house – no, I'm not in prison merely on guard – at present we have a four hours trek it's now nine-o'clock at ten I must away with my rifle and pace up & down for two solid hours in a drizzling rain then in again at twelve & its bed – well, on the bed, for four hours until 4am then out again until 6am. You are dolled up

[4] *The Letters of Sean O'Casey, Volume II*, p. 628.

to the nines for guard & really even I felt quite proud at first, you look so very smart – you wear your best B.D. [battle dress?] with a lanyard as white as snow a great coat – pressed immaculately – your braces, belt & boots shining out like beacon lamps & rifle with stock & barrel somewhat like the top of a marvellous walnut table – your straps should be perfectly matched & Blancoed evenly all over – you get four days notice for guard, that is four days to get ready & prepared & when you actually go on guard you undergo a most rigorous inspection first by the Orderly Sergeant & then by the Orderly Officer - the best turned out man is called "Stickman" & he is off guard that means he can go back to the billet & is free to do whatever he likes; the worst is called "attending man" he goes back, changes into overalls gets the mugs, knives, forks, etc of the guards, reports to the guard-house & is then the general odd-job-man cum errand boy for the guard. ...

Yesterday we travelled 100 miles to a place called Traunosfinnid (Trosfinny) to fire off our guns.[5] We started at 5.30am arrived at 11am fired at 2.00 left at 2.30. We froze to death on top of the Welsh mountains, fired off two shells, and got thoroughly soaked – the whole thing was a complete farce, the journey to and from Traunosfinnid was quite pleasant & we travelled through some beautiful scenery.

Today I had an awful moment – we were told three people had to stay here over Xmas – well, to decide who the unlucky three were we drew lots, for a minute I thought I had drawn the unlucky slip but thank heavens it was OK. So, now, I think I'm finally certain to be trotting home sometime Wednesday fortnight ... Well it seems that I must now depart with my rifle to my duty.

So cheerio for now
All my love as ever Niall

Niall's letter to Sean:

D.I. SuB-Section
172/64th Training Regt. R.A.
Milne Lane
Park Hall Camp Oswestry
Salop

---

[5] Trawsfynydd ("across the mountain" in the native tongue) is a small village in Wales near which the War Office opened an artillery range before the war.

Dear Daddy,

Yesterday morning we had our first T.A.B. injections (Anti-Typhoid Bacillus) the fool of an M.O. gave us a double dose – 50% instead of 25%. Today everyone is feeling bloody, it effects some worse than others – I'm just about average. You get all shivery & your arm goes as stiff as a ramrod, in a way it's a relief as your given 36 hours leave and can lie in as late as you like. (That's 8.00 instead of 6.00 am). ... We're in a split up barrack room, that is one side are all O.R.I.'s (officer ratings) & the other side are more Tech assistants. Our side consists mainly of a lot of ex-public-schoolboys – who aren't bad but one couldn't call them exactly pleasant – all of them have a curious vicious & callous side which is shown surprisingly enough when things are not going too well for them. They hold themselves very much aloof – down at 6th where there weren't many of them to a squad they had a rather awkward time. But here there are enough of them to band together & so protect themselves by numbers. My best friends are a chap from the opposite side who used to play a tuba in a jazz band in Brighton & a Scotch chap in the bed next to mine – actually a good fellow. If the above mentioned are to be my colleagues if I became an officer, I really don't much care if I don't make the grade. (I mean of course the public-school chaps). Apart from this I've found out that if you pass W.O.S.B. you then have to undergo 3 months training at the O.C.S. school at Mons – Mons is really just a physical endurance test – whether it's worth undergoing it or not I'm not quite sure. If I pass W.O.S.B. I think I shall but I shan't be all that disappointed if I fail. How they decide who is designated to become an O.R.I. I just don't know ...I would be quite satisfied to end up as a Bombardier - I'd almost prefer it to a 2nd Lt. I've long ago given trying to fathom out what useful purpose the actions the army have, you have to take most everything with a pinch of salt & if you didn't laugh at some of the most ridiculous things you'd rapidly go cracked. Luckily you always laugh and remain sane.

Up to now time has gone really quickly. Extraordinarily so, it won't be long now before I shall be home for Xmas. ...

All my love Niall

And home he was and also Breon: we were all together again for Christmas 1953. These were the times I loved the most when we were all together –

just us. Niall was in the kitchen making the rum butter bread sauce and a punch from white wine and generally cooking with Eileen, playing his records and his trombone and, along with me, the piano.

The day before Niall was due back we all helped to polish his buttons and Blanco his webbing. He was very particular about it, saying that "if you played the game" of looking smart you could get away with other things.

Niall's letter to me:

21 January 1954

Dear Shivaun,

Well, after having a lovely rest & relaxation in London last weekend, I'm now back in the old routine. I'm still waiting to be interviewed by a bloody man who calls himself the SPSO (Staff Personnel Selection Officer) – I want to see him but it seemed he's in no hurry to see me. ... While I write this you'll never guess what I'm doing, I'm invigilating an exam or test of our 3rd class pupils; I thought it would look more efficient if I did something so I decided to write a letter. I have also started teaching & you can't imagine how dense the people I have to teach are - it's quite extraordinary. If in one 45 minute period you've got them to write one sentence you've done well – it's completely hopeless hardly any of them have the least idea of anything at all. For instance one of the questions set on the paper I'm now invigilating is write what you know about the Mau Mau (you'd better ask Daddy what the Mau Mau are) & the answers you get are quite extraordinary. – One chap said the Mau Mau was "The Emperor of India". Another said they were a tribe of "Chinese in Africa who had been fighting us for a long time: and another said they were the "cause of strikes!"[6] I ask you. ...

Love Niall

Niall passed his WOSB examination!

---

[6] The Mau Mau (the Kenya Land and Freedom Army) was an insurgent force that waged war on the British authorities from 1952 to 1960 in the colony of Kenya; their campaign dominated British newspapers of the mid-1950s.

WE MOVE TO ST MARYCHURCH

In June 1954 we moved to St Marychurch.[7] I took photos of every room in Tingrith – I was the only person sorry to leave the old house. Of course, Sean didn't want to move at all because he would have to move his books and his work, and learn again where everything was. Now his eyes were too bad to read the spine of a book on a shelf, until it was taken out and he could hold it close to his good eye. So he had learnt where his favourite books and the books he often referred to lived and could tell one from the other by touch. For weeks the question asked was "Do you need this anymore?" We were moving into Flat 4, Villa Rosa. It was a two-bedroom flat with a small entrance hall leading into another hallway that all the doors to the rooms opened on to. There was a good-sized sitting-room and dining room, that became Sean's room, both looking out to the front of the house. The main bedroom was going to be for the two boys. There was a smaller bedroom which Eileen and I would share: that is, it was hers, but when I was home I would sleep there and she would make up a bed on the sofa/bed in the sitting room. This was because I was inclined to sleep longer than her, even though she wasn't an early riser: she also kept it tidy. I was disappointed by the arrangement with Eileen and myself – it was, of course, really her room and meant I didn't have a room of my own. It was difficult for her too. There was a table where I could work and she was kind and accommodating, but we had many tense moments.

The kitchen was very small but serviceable with a built-in sink unit in front of a window that looked out over the back-side of St Marychurch from up high as we were at the top of a built-up hill. Lit up at night it reminded Sean of his time in New York.

Eileen and Breon had painted the flat white – except Sean's room as they ran out of time. In the entrance hall they painted one wall a vivid orange at which the landlord, Mr Norman, screamed in horror: "Oh, My lord! What have you done! I thought you were only going to paint the front room white. Oh, its frightful, frightful – all that lovely wallpaper covered up! – Don't do anymore. You've only a three-year lease and you must not spoil the flat." He did have a point – he wasn't to know we were going to stay put for ten years.

[7] Nine miles from Totnes, St Marychurch as a settlement dates back to Saxon days; in 1900 it became a ward in the borough of Torquay; Philip Henry Gosse the popular Victorian naturalist and father of Edmund Gosse the writer, was a resident.

The orange wall looked lovely with the old oak chest in front of it; always flowers in the green or orange glass vases or a cyclamen plant. On the other long wall were Sean's bookcases with the glass fronts, pegs for coats and the small umbrella stand. The front room had, of course, the upright Bechstein, and the sofas and armchairs at the fireside end, with the bed-sofa at the other end in front of a large modern bookcase Breon made for Eileen. Above the Heals sideboard on the wall was the pride and joy, the Augustus John portrait of Sean. (It is now where he wanted it to end up – in the National Gallery of Ireland). Sean had a basin in his room with hot and cold water, so he could bathe his eyes with no trouble: no more boiling kettles downstairs and carrying them up to his room. Sean's room was nearly the same as it had been at Tingrith, also Chelsea, Woronzow Road and 422 North Circular Road in Dublin – always the same.

All in all we were in a sturdy Edwardian villa, built when Torquay was a fashionable watering hole and trips to Europe considered dangerous. It had parquet floors throughout and well maintained roof, windows and doors.

I left my chestnut tree that Sean remembered as "planted by Shivaun as a conker when she was six, and now full twenty feet and more high". Goodbye to all that.

DANGER AND SUN IN TREYARNON

During the summer holidays, my friend Speth came along with us for a week at Treyarnon in Cornwall. Niall was still in the army; Breon decided to come and camp while Eileen and us girls stayed at a little hotel.

I reported back to Sean:

Waterbeach Hotel
Treyarnon Bay
Nr. Padstow
N. Cornwall

Dear Daddy,

After the intense excitement and talk of Ireland and the Irish at first this seemed a bit flat. It is full of retired ex-servicemen, people who seem to have pushed the Cornish locals back far into the background. In every little tea shop & post office you are greeted by the fla-de-la (except for a family called the Olds – who have a few shops in St. Merwyn). So with depressing weather and stuck in the quiet hotel where it really does become embarrassing if you talk above a whisper – if you aren't talking about cars or the 'latest'. On the first day. You can't imagine a summer day being much worse, Mummy was asked, "What ho, are you braving the brink.[8] Holiday spirit and all that!" So we did our best and all four of us went for a walk that evening. (My pen has run out) Breon has gone healthy though, camping and surfing as much as the rest; although he doesn't quite manage the morning walks and has been set back just now by some bites [Breon was allergic to horse-fly bites] . ...

We have been into Padstow quite a lot, which is nicer than Brixham. There really isn't really much more to say except surfing is lovely & we are having a nice time.

> I will write you again.
> Lots of love Shivy xxx

It was during this holiday that Speth and I were caught in a rip-tide. Breon had painted three surf boards with lovely patterns and we were using two of them. We were swept out to sea just beyond the beach headland and tried very hard to swim back. Breon saw us and ran, dived in and swam out to where we were; he told us to let go of the surf boards. "No, they are so beautiful!" we cried. " Let go! Fuck the surf boards", he shouted. I let go first and swam with all the strength I had to the rocks; which I could just about do. Speth wouldn't let go until Breon demanded it saying, "Do you want us both to drown?" Speth wasn't such a strong swimmer but had a lot of determination and sense; Breon helped her along with a great effort and they finally made it to the rocks, and scrambled up to meet me. We had all been cut on the rocks, as the waves hitting at us made us stumble, and our wet legs and hands were streaming with blood. All we could think of was the loss of the two surfboards. Breon said he would decorate some more ... maybe he did. Later when it sank in how dangerous it had been for all of us, I felt a fear of the sea I had never had before. In those days there were no life-guards posted on the beaches, just warnings about not swimming too near the edges of the beaches, or other local information. If anything happened, you had to run to the nearest

---

[8] The sea, or strictly the edge of the sea, or else he or Shivaun meant "drink", slang for the sea.

phone and ring the lifeboat station; it often took a while but many people were saved by the boat, mainly if they stayed calm, trod water, and went with the current.

We left for Devon and home and left Cornwall behind. Niall was to arrive on embarkation leave. He was being posted to Germany, British Army of the Rhine for his last 14 months. While he was in Germany he was to hear the Ken Colyer Jazz Band play at Dusseldorf, as Breon relayed to me in a letter: "I have just started to learn sculpture at the St Martin's School.[9]

I'm working on a head at the moment and after that I am to design a couple of statues for Torquay High Street. ... I had a long letter from Niall, all about a jazz club he's been to in Dusseldorf where Ken Collier's [sic] playing."

LONDON IN SEPTEMBER

Eileen and I went to London and stayed with Don and Ella at their house in Hampstead that had been Ramsay MacDonald's house. Sean met MacDonald a couple of times and tried to warn him against the way the Conservatives were undermining him. Don seemed to live by a cupboard set in a small recess, possibly for the butler years ago, where he made his famous martinis – and also drank them. He was hilarious, quipping sardonic American dialogue as dry as his martinis – dialogue of the kind he used in the films he wrote. He was even funnier in real life. Ella buzzed around with biscuits and all kinds of nuts in bowls – she served the tea and coffee and soft-drinks, pouring any of the dregs from the cups or pots on to her indoor plants; as some were enormous, it must have done them a lot of good. Guests at these events were many and varied, but mainly left-wing: Simone Signoret, Katharine Hepburn (a regular who liked to spend all her time in the garden tending the roses), Jean Seberg, Joe Losey, David Lean (very serious and dull); students from China, Alan Lomax (who collected folk-music across America and the UK), Ingrid Bergman (who in comparing me to her daughter made me feel very inadequate).

On this visit Eileen and I had been invited up by Robert Lewis (Bobby) to see his production of *The Teahouse of the August Moon* at Her

---

[9] Saint Martin's School of Art, a college established in London in 1854, merged in 1989 with the Central School of Art and Design to become the Central Saint Martins College of Art and Design. Ken Colyer (1928–1988) was an immensely influential English trumpeter, a seminal figure in the post-war British New Orleans jazz revival.

Majesty's Theatre, Haymarket. It wasn't the first night; it was doing very well and its star, Eli Wallach was highly praised.[10] He was such a good actor and the evening was exciting for me – the setting, and the rest of the cast too, as well as the production. Bobby's handsome young man (a different one than had come down to Devon with him who looked at the fashion magazines with me) met us and took us backstage where Eileen hugged Bobby and we said how much we loved it: we were taken to see the cast, all sitting and taking off their makeup. In those days the lighting for shows was harsher and not so clear so you needed much more makeup, particularly around the eyes so that they weren't "lost". Bobby took us off to a restaurant where Eli and his lovely wife, Annie Jackson, would meet us.[11] An evening full of theatre gossip and serious dreams; I loved it and listened as they all held forth – mainly Bobby, with Eileen taking part more and more as the evening went on and her confidence grew.

The first thing Eileen did the morning before the *Tea House* was to take me with her to Bourne and Hollingsworth, a department store where Eileen had a thing called a budget account. It meant you could buy things and pay a little bit off each month or pay into it and build it up. Now we have credit cards instead. We bought a Horrocks dress each, cotton dresses with large gathered skirts. Eileen's was dark blue and black patterned with a V neck; mine was more demure: light blue and white checks, with cap sleeves and a higher square neck.

Another amazing thing happened during this visit. Marlene Dietrich was singing and Eileen was determined I see her, as she thought this might be the singer's last visit to London. Sidney Bernstein must have got us tickets. We were to meet Sam and Charlotte at the table that had been booked. For some reason Eileen went into a panic and couldn't decide what to wear. Finally, after taking things off and putting things on many times, and trying various combinations, she decided to put on the dress she had bought at B & H, and wrapped her Chinese embroidered shawl around her shoulders. I had on my dress, a white cardigan, white ankle socks and pumps. Eileen's stockings, of course. I thought Eileen looked lovely but she always felt she looked bad, with her clothes now very different from the ones she had as a young bride, and the silk dresses and underwear;

---

[10] *The Teahouse of the August Moon* is a 1953 comic play written by John Patrick adapted from a 1951 novel by Vern Sneider. It ran in Her Majesty's Theatre from 22 April 1954 to 11 August 1956.

[11] The actress Anne Jackson (1925–2016) often shared the stage or television screen with her husband Eli Wallach, and occasionally the movie screen.

slips and cami-knickers, outdated by now, that I dressed up in with my friends when I was little.

We were very late and ended up getting a taxi for the last leg of the journey. There it was in glittering lights: The Cafe de Paris. We started down the long flight of steps that led into the large restaurant, a balcony that looked over another floor where the stage was and some other tables. On the way down I stood on the trailing edge of Eileen's shawl – "Look where you're going!" she spat out at me, and heaved it from under my foot. She was in a right tiz woz. The maitre d' welcomed us and pointed out Sam and Charlotte sitting at a table in the distance. As she swept through the tables with me creeping behind to our destination, the fringe of her shawl got stuck on the back of a chair – as she pulled it off she said "Fuck the bloody thing", and rolled it up under her arm like a swimming towel.

At last we reached the table; everything was forgotten as we talked and joked. We apologised for being so late and ordered some food as Charlotte and Sam had started to eat as they thought we might never appear; we hadn't eaten all day and were very hungry. After I had stuffed one bite into my hungry mouth the lights went out and the show began. We looked down from the balcony to the small stage and the grand piano. The lights changed to pink and on she came in her famous dress: clinging all-covering lace that showed her body (or the colour of flesh) beneath. She was charming and funny and sang in her rich sultry voice. Then the interval. The lights went up and we looked down at our plates and they had gone. Sam called the waiter – "Sorry sir, the kitchen's now closed". We had eaten practically nothing and I suspect had paid a fortune for it. The lights dimmed again and this time Marlene was in a top hat and tails; she was as mesmerising as before, very intelligent and knowing and funny.

After the show I implored Eileen to take me to get her autograph, a thing I still did. Although I was shy I was also determined, with an ambition to do what I wanted but in a fright at how to achieve it, these two things always tussling within me. Eileen begrudgingly agreed. We went down the stairs and saw a long line of old men in Dicky suits, like a row of creaky penguins, waiting in adoration to shake her hand. We joined the end of the queue. Eileen was getting hot and bothered until finally the last old man was gone and we stood before her. I looked at Eileen as she said, pointing at me, "This is Mrs Sean O'Casey and I'm his daughter". As quick as a flash Marlene responded, "What a fascinating man – I should love to meet him". Then we all fell about laughing. She signed a picture of herself and the programme, and back we went to Sam and Charlotte and got some drinks to help Eileen calm down.

Christmas came and Niall came back to Villa Rosa for our first Xmas there; he showed us his lance-bombardier stripe on his arm, a single chevron. He brought with him a couple of cigars for Breon and a pretty white cotton traditional German blouse for me with a gathered lace collar. I loved it. Sean gave me a manicure set, in a green leather case zipped around. Eileen must have told him it was time I started to look after my hands. There was no liquid nail polish in those days; you polished your nails with a buffer. My thoughts were always against "looking after your hands". Grannie believed it was part of being a lady, so that was a good reason to do the opposite. Sean always wanted Eileen's hands to remain beautiful and not red and chapped like his mother's often were. By now I wanted to be like his mother, Susan, and felt affiliated to people who used their hands and didn't want to protect them over much.

SEAN'S NEW PLAY IN DUBLIN

This year was full of the upcoming production in Dublin of Sean's new play, *The Bishop's Bonfire*. In April 1954, Cyril Cusack had written to Sean inquiring after the play and Sean agreed to send him a copy for a week to be read only by him and his wife Maureen. Sean also made it clear that he never now sends new plays to The Abbey. That theatre had lost its heart for Sean since Lady Gregory and Yeats had gone. Cyril liked the play and wanted to produce it at the Gaiety Theatre in Dublin. Cyril visited Sean to clinch a deal and by October they were discussing the cast. Breon was setting his hand at doing the scenic design, encouraged by Sean. In the end they didn't use Breon's designs but went for more conventional settings. Tyrone Guthrie later wrote to Sean saying that he thought he had made a mistake and should have used Breon's designs.

All was excitement in Flat 4, Villa Rosa. Eileen and I had been invited over by Sidney Bernstein; he paid for our fares and put us up in a room at the Shelbourne hotel where he and his new wife Sandra would also stay. Eileen's new friend in St Marychurch, Madeleine Solomon, was to join us for the first night. Madeleine and her husband Louis were paediatricians working in Torquay, both from Dublin, both Jewish.[12] Sean wouldn't consider going to the first night with all that that meant but thought he might go later on to see it and some of his old friends, Barney Conway in particular and Dr Cummins.[13] I was going and was brimming over with excitement; not just because of the world premiere of Sean's play but I would be seeing Ireland for myself.

Tyrone Guthrie's letter to Sean:

February 26th 1955

... Cyril and I are differing – but very amiably, no squeals or pouts - about the style of the production. He wants it quieter, more sentimental and Tchekhovy than I do. He thinks I'm making it both too farcical and too melodramatic. Well, God knows he may be right, but I'm sticking to my guns. I think the theatre in general, and your work in particular, must be high-coloured, larger, louder, funnier, more rambunctious and disastrous than 'Life'. ... I don't think there will be much fuss – a hiss or two and maybe a flutter of scurrility in The Standard, perhaps even a vote of protest from the Sewage Disposal Committee of the Letterkenny Urban Council. ...[14]

We flew over to Dublin and as the plane landed we saw a band at the end of the runway. Dublin Airport was tiny then – just one building not unlike my local Exeter airport nowadays. As we came to the plane's door to climb down the steps the band struck up and we were greeted by an ebullient smiling man, with curly white hair – the Chairman of Aer Lingus on whose flight we were on, called J.J. O'Leary. He had a wheelchair for Eileen, just in case; our luggage was promptly put in it and off we went to his big car to be driven by him to the Shelbourne. J.J. was a great friend

---

[12] Madeleine Solomon is quoted by Christopher Murray as Dr Madeleine Epstein when he gives his lively account of the stormy reaction in the theatre to Sean's play: *Sean O'Casey: Writer at Work* (Montreal, Ithaca: McGill-Queen's University Press, 2004), pp. 359–362. She died in Paignton in January 2022 at the age of 103.

[13] Barney Conway (1882–1965) was Jim Larkin's assistant; Krause tells us he was the model for Brannigan in *The Star Turns Red* (1940). Dr Joseph Cummins (1882–1959) was a distinguished ophthalmic surgeon in Dublin. He first treated Sean in 1923 and they became friends; Sean dedicated the published version of *Red Roses for Me* to his eye doctor. *The Letters of Sean O'Casey, Volume II*, pp. 217, 96.

[14] Guthrie's letter to Sean like Cyril's to him, is in the O'Casey archive in the National Library, Dublin.

of Sean's old butty, Barry Fitzgerald, and was fast becoming a close friend of Eileen's and mine.[15]

Our room was on the first floor up; we opened the heavy door with our big key and there we were in a large room overlooking Kildare Street. It had two lovely comfortable beds with bedside tables, a dressing-table for Eileen's make-up, a couple of chairs and also a fireplace with a fire burning in it! The bathrooms were shared and the baths run by your chambermaid. After Eileen and I had washed and straightened up a bit we went downstairs to be with J.J., as he wanted to be called. The evening of the next day was the opening of the play but he booked us for a drive with him through Wicklow the following day.[16]

That evening Eileen and I went to the dress rehearsal, the final runthrough before they opened (no previews in those days). I loved the Gaiety theatre – red plush and a horseshoe-shaped auditorium, Victorian and decorated as such. Stalls, dress-circle & upper circle (reached as always by a separate entrance – for the more unwashed of society). The air in the auditorium was full of energy and anticipation. When the run was over, after a few stops for corrections, Tyrone Guthrie thanked the cast and told them after a break to gather onstage for notes after they had changed and taken off their makeup. This very tall man with a military moustache came up to where we were sitting and spoke to Eileen about what she had seen. Then we left him to it, after meeting his equally tall wife. Sidney and Sandra had come to see the dress rehearsal with us and Sidney was worried about the play's ending. Eileen was sure it was the correct ending, although very shocking.

Sidney took us all for a late meal together at Jammet's, the famous restaurant; it had murals all around the walls – and it was French cooking. Mr Jammet came over to talk to Sidney and Eileen. It was a lovely restaurant and like The Ivy, full of chatter and laughter. During the meal Sandra asked what we would be wearing; when I said a jumper and straight skirt it was arranged that we would go to Sybil Connolly's the next day to fit me out.[17] I must say I wasn't at all sure about it. I was put

[15] John Joseph O'Leary (1890–1978), co-founder of Aer Lingus, was a member of the Dublin Theatre Festival Committee. He is said to have subsidised the famous literary magazine *The Bell*, edited by Seán Ó'Faoláin. See: https://durrushistory.com/2011/10/28/j-j-oleary-businessman-dublin/

[16] *The Bishop's Bonfire* opened on February 28, 1955 in the Gaiety Theatre, produced by Cyril Cusack Productions.

[17] Sybil Connolly (1921–1998) was a Welsh-born, Dublin-based fashion designer who used Irish textiles. Her customers included Julie Andrews, Elizabeth Taylor and Jacqueline Kennedy. See "Sybil Connolly", Wikipedia.

into a circular skirt, made of padded scarlet wool – the same that was used for the Irish petticoats that even Sean wore as a little boy. Then they introduced a very fancy top made from finely pleated muslin, with stripes of white crochet work threaded with a satin ribbon; it had elbow-length pleated muslin sleeves. It was very beautiful but much too fancy for me; and to top it all, or cover it all, a large black genuine Irish shawl ... the real McCoy.

I very definitely decided not to wear the blouse; I never have, even after cutting off the flappy sleeves, though my grandchild looks sumptuous in it. I really wanted to wear the plain skirt I had brought over, but Eileen persuaded me to at least wear the skirt and shawl with my black jumper and pearl Poppet necklace. I did feel a bit of a Charlie at first, dressed like an Irish colleen, à la Sybil Connolly. I soon forgot myself in the surge of the evening. Both Eileen and I were nervous about how the play would be greeted. We well knew the flak Sean got from the Irish press and his sometime friend Gabriel Fallon, who wrote for the *Catholic Standard*, the *Irish Monthly* and the *Evening Press*. Most of the Irish critics repeated their song – Sean never wrote a play worth its salt after *The Plough and the Stars*; some even said *Juno and the Paycock* was the only play worth anything and this was practically written by Lennox Robinson anyway, and all Sean did was put the people he had known in the Dublin north side on the stage. Sean always responded to this nonsense by saying about Shakespeare and Falstaff: "God, if you like, created Shakespeare but it was Shakespeare who created Falstaff".

Eileen's friend Madeleine was waiting for us in the packed foyer, and we were all taken up to our seats in the balcony, about five rows back. Wouldn't you know it, right behind a row of – the Irish critics and Gabriel Fallon among them. He turned to Eileen and they exchanged "Hellos". Eileen whispered to me, "I'll tell you later, dear".[18] There were hundreds of people in the street outside who couldn't get seats, mainly young people, and you could hear them protesting outside: during the show they lit bonfires as a witty kind of protest about lack of seats. You could hear the sound of the fire brigade sirens above the singing. The play was going

[18] Gabriel Fallon (1898–1980) was, like Sean, a Dubliner. Fallon was a civil servant, actor, director (of the Abbey theatre) and theatre critic. He and Sean were close friends between 1923 and 1946; Fallon later critically assailed Sean's plays and autobiographies. Sean discusses the former friendship with Fallon in a letter of 27 October 1952 to Shaemas O'Sheel, an Irish poet and writer living in New York: *The Letters of Sean O'Casey, Volume II*, pp. 913–915.

really well; a lot of laughs – even from Gaby, who was in hysterics during the bit we call the "jeep scene". At one point a couple of people in the gods stood up and said something while chucking down leaflets; this caused such a response from the audience – a furore – that the play had to be stopped. "They want it to be like the riots at the *Plough*", Eileen said to me and Madeleine.

Cyril stepped forward and spoke in Gaelic, repeating Yeats at the time of the *Plough and the Stars* riot, I understand, in telling them "You are making fools of yourselves yet again". ... The protesters – Legion of Mary people, I believe – were finally removed and the show could wend its merry way.[19] In her book *Sean*, Eileen recalls that she was so upset that her neighbour kindly whispered, "They are just saying what a marvellous man Sean O'Casey is".

During the interval Madeleine had gone to visit friends and Sidney and Sandra were in the stalls, so Eileen and I were ushered to a corner of the Balconies Bar – and then this tall thin man with glasses precariously holding a drink in each hand, so doubled over with the drink he became a walking arch, found his way to Eileen, straightened himself up with a great effort leaning against the wall and spoke fluently, welcoming her and asking about Sean. Eileen took the drink offered to her. She obviously liked him and felt concerned about him. He told her he had a copy of Sean's play *A Crimson in the Tricolour*, the play that Sean had sent to the Abbey before he wrote *Shadow of a Gunman* and had supposedly been lost. He said he would seek it out and send it to Sean. This was the remains of Lennox Robinson, now a very sad and mournful man but part of the original youthful Abbey Theatre: also one of the people who objected to Sean's Great War play, *The Silver Tassie*, when Sean presented it to the Abbey from his home in London; the rejection of this play and the argument that followed badly affected Sean's standing and his writing life; being rejected by the Nobel Prizewinner Yeats was a serious blow. Later, Sean wrote and asked Lennox if he had found his play, but no response came. Over the years, before Lennox's death, Eileen wrote again but presumably it could not be found. She asked his executor if it happened to be among his papers and the reply was "No". He had been instrumental with Yeats in rejecting it. Maybe he had found it and then lost it again or in his drunkenness had fantasised it back.

[19] The Legion of Mary is an active Catholic association of pious volunteers, founded in 1921 in Dublin by Frank Duff.

After the interval and when the theatre went quiet there was no further interference from the audience. At the end of the play the frustrated lover of the young girl who had been forced to take a vow of chastity, shot her: the house was visibly shocked. No one had expected that! I loved it. The actress Sheila Brennan said that Tyrone Guthrie ran into her dressing room just before the curtain went up saying – "There's going to be a riot. What fun!"[20]

By now I wanted to be a part of the theatre life. I was lucky in that I had seen some great productions – and a few bad ones. I had no idea that if you wanted to be an actor, director, designer, etc., and you didn't have money behind you, you could be forced into a lot of poor productions, in TV and films in particular. That wasn't a part of my thoughts at that time! Mine were about acting in the great dramas, with great actors, directors and designers, and about the prospects that drama held for the future – like the modern fantasy, Sean's *Cock-a-Doodle Dandy*. Ah well.

Coming down the stairs at the Shelbourne for breakfast, the atmosphere that greeted us was different: people were busy talking among themselves and, I would say, ignoring Eileen and me. Not Sidney and Sandra; as we sat down to breakfast together he told Eileen about the terrible reviews in the Irish papers; including from Sean's old "friend", Gabriel Fallon.[21] The next day the English reviews were good, good enough for talk by Oscar Lewenstein of taking the play to the Royal Court Theatre.[22] The transfer to London was all go until it was discovered that one of the main actors refused to travel and no one thought of replacing him.

Imagine if Sean had been living in Dublin among these "admiring critics", a small town compared with London with fewer papers and

---

[20] According to Dr Madeleine Epstein (Solomon), she, Eileen and Shivaun at the end of the play were escorted out of the theatre for their own safety: Murray, *Sean O'Casey: Writer at Work*, p. 361. Sheila Brennan, b. 1931 in Dublin, became a busy supporting actress in BBC and ITV dramas of the 1960s and 1970s; she had several film credits, including *The Spiral Staircase* (1975). She played Foorawn in the *The Bishop's Bonfire*.

[21] A play the theme of which, according to the author, was "the ferocious chastity of the Irish", was more than likely to antagonise Irish critics, most of whom were fervent Irish nationalists and many of them, like many of the actors, faithful Catholics.

[22] Oscar Lewenstein (1917–1997) was a British theatre and film producer. Among his stage productions were Bertolt Brecht's *The Threepenny Opera* (1956), Brendan Behan's *The Hostage* (1958) and Shelagh Delaney's *A Taste of Honey* (1958). Lewenstein was a youthful member of the Communist Party of Great Britain and though he left it in 1956, the year of the crushing of the Hungarian uprising by the Soviet Union, he remained a lifelong socialist.

critics! How offensive and crippling it would have been for him – and all of us! Where we lived now in Devon these sort of things didn't matter so much; they were more distant. And Sean was used by now to the rumbles from Christian Ireland. He always hoped for some support but was not reliant on it to keep writing. He hoped too that the critics would become more literate and sensible for the good of the public of Ireland

Sidney and Sandra flew back to London; Madeleine came for coffee and then left to go back to Torquay, and J.J. arrived, beaming and full of joy to take us in his car to see the glories of Wicklow. Our saviour. He drove us to the Sugar Loaf Mountain, through a cleft called The Scalp – Was it cut by one of Ireland's mighty giants? We drove up high and looked out over the most beautiful sweeping green valleys and hilly mountains I had ever seen: even more beautiful than my home county of Devon. I would love to have lived there, where my grandmother, Sean's mother Susan, had grown up and left to marry her Michael. We lunched at a friendly pub and off we went back to Dublin's squabbling and for more talk about *The Bishop's Bonfire*.

Mrs Pandit Nehru (Vijaya Lakshmi Pandit) was in Dublin – she then held the Presidency of the United Nations General Assembly and was the first woman to do so. We learned she had wanted to see the play and there were no tickets for her on the first night so she came with the American Ambassador on the second night. Eileen and I were brought in to meet her during the interval: what a warm charming lady she seemed to me. Dignified and kind in her beautiful silk sari. She was sitting in the boxes at the rear of the stalls, good seats if you want to be away from the public but actually at the back of the dress circle. She said she could have been in better seats as she was having difficulty with the Irish accents. She said she would read the play. Eileen said she seemed to have read all of Sean's work. Sean was annoyed she had been unable to get in as, he said, Eileen and I would have willingly given her our seats. He kept Niall abreast of the play's performances.

Niall's letter to Sean:

6 March 1955

Dear Daddy,

Thanks for all your letters & the notices – its grand about the play, it sounds really good; what did the women folk think of it? I hope it comes to the West End after Dublin. I see Eddie Byrne is in the cast &

judging from the reports Cusack is excellent[23] – it seems very far away from where I am at present. Shivaun must have been thrilled; flying out like that & suddenly coming from nowhere – I bet they were flapping about the flat the night before.

I write this from a drafty nissen hut situated slap bang in the middle of the Luneberg Heide (Heath, bog, moor, & wind) the German equivalent to Salisbury Plain only much larger & without Salisbury. The regiment is up here on a six week training camp – the famed Munster Lager Ranges stretch for miles around. (Here Rommel exercised his Panzer Corps, Montgomery received the capitulation of the Wehrmacht & hundreds of thousands died in Belsen Horror Camp).[24] So you see we are not without history. ...

The weather of course is freezing cold but by putting everything imaginable on your bed & around your head you can survive a night in relative warmth – but getting up in 'the cold slow hours of the early morning' is a terrible experience. And to make it worse we are inclined to take a plunge out of camp for several nights & then all you have between you and the frost is a two foot high Bivouac. ...

I wrote to the University and they are willing to see me in April – I have almost certainly secured leave so I shall probably be back on the 13th for a week. Could you send me the fare (same address in spite of different location) £5 – you can send it in a lump sum or separately it doesn't worry me, as soon as possible. Meanwhile a place has been reserved for me to read Botany in October 55 subject to a satisfactory interview. I hope I can get home for a time – it should be possible if I can arrange the interview on the 14th [of April]. ...

Six months in Germany today & with early release now only six more to do – roll on demob. Everyone is longing the return to Osnabruck –

Maybe I will see you next month, until then
All the best
As ever love to all
Niall

[23] The actor Eddie Byrne (1911–1981) was born in Birmingham.
[24] Lüneberg Heide is an extensive heath in northern Germany. On it, Field-Marshal Montgomery accepted the surrender of the German forces in the Netherlands, Denmark and n.w. Germany. Himmler, head of the Nazi S.S.,was buried hugger mugger on the heath after he committed suicide when he was captured.

BIVOUACS, BEACHES AND BONFIRES 1953-1955

After the opening of *The Bishop's Bonfire*, Sean decided he definitely wouldn't be able to make the journey to see the show – he wasn't well and couldn't face the upheaval it would cause; he told me he would take me to Dublin quietly when nothing of his was on.

Eileen and I were taken all over Dublin City. We met up with George Gilmore for lunch and I had ice-cream with a seaweed sauce for desert; it was delicious. We met with the chattering Seamus Scully – intense with his red hair bursting out on each side of his bald patch – talking, talking, talking. We visited Ria Mooney at her home where she gave a party; I took a bit of soda bread with red berries on it and was shocked at the taste, as it was actually red caviar.[25] We had a quiet meeting with Sean's eye doctor Dr Cummins in his large apartment looking over St Stephen's Green and next door to the hotel. I liked this gentle man and felt grateful for all he had done for Sean – keeping his eyes going to write his words on paper, and also for the friendship he gave Sean and knowledge from his fine collection of art books. We spent an afternoon at Dalkey, visiting Maureen Cusack (Cyril was working) and three beautiful little blonde children, two girls and one boy: Sorcha, Sinead and Paul.[26] What an idyllic spot that was, a house set down from the road and overlooking the sea in the distance; or at least that is how I remember it: steep steps with an iron hand rail leading to the garden, Eileen and I leaning on it as we said goodbye to Maureen with her children hanging onto her.

The next day George Gilmore came to take me on my own on a sightseeing tour of Dublin's north side. We walked across O'Connell Bridge and turned right along the Quays and past Liberty Hall, the Irish Transport and General Workers Union founded by Sean's great friend Jim Larkin; turning to walk up Gardiner Street to Mountjoy Square, the site of the house where Sean stayed for a while with his Gaelic-speaking friend and is the setting for his first accepted play by the Abbey Theatre, *The Shadow of a Gunman*. I saw the families – many families it seemed – living in Georgian houses, stately once but now falling to bits, holding their dignity with great difficulty. I asked George why so many of the children didn't have shoes and he told me of the poverty they still endured. Some of the women wore patterned shawls, some black (like the one I had worn

---

[25] A stage and film actress, Ria Mooney (1903-1973) served as artistic director of the Abbey Theatre, 1948-1963. She appeared in several of Sean's plays.

[26] Maureen Cusack (née Kiely; 1920-1977) was an Irish actress from Co. Donegal. She was connected with the Gate and Abbey theatres in Dublin and appeared in the 1955 staging of *The Bishop's Bonfire*.

to the first night – I felt I shouldn't have done that). They stood erect with or without babies in the blankets. I hadn't seen poverty like this before, right in the centre of a major city. In England after the war the British socialist government started the National Health Service – and clothes and shoes could be got on rations; the war diet of vitamins continued and diseases like rickets vanished. But here, a stone's throw from O'Connell Street, there was obviously not much help from the government: the poor still had the dreaded Red Ticket, the poor ticket, for medical attention. Maybe the theocracy of the Irish government felt that suffering was good for their souls. Some years later, of course, they cleared the poor from the centre of Dublin and built some high-rise "accommodation" out by the airport. Nothing near for any of them, isolated from all they had known – Dublin city. After all, the north side belonged to them more than to the "developers". Out of sight, out of mind!

As Sean had told George Jean Nathan in a letter, the Irish critics had indeed declared against *The Bishop's Bonfire* to a man. Gabriel Fallon led the charge. He condemned the play in his review in the Dublin *Evening Press* of March 1, 1955: "'The Bonfire' Never Did Really Blaze Up At All". He followed this up with an article in the *Evening Press* of March 5, criticising the play for its didacticism: "Why Sean O'Casey Has Failed This Time". And in his Saturday column, "Theatre Notes", March 12, he attacked the English critics for liking the play![27]

Sean and Gabriel had been friends along with Barry Fitzgerald during Sean's early days at the Abbey. After Sean had gone to England to receive The Hawthornden Prize for Literature in 1926 and to give some publicity to *Juno* moving to another theatre, he decided London was a far freer place for him to live and breathe, and when he met and fell in love with my mother, Eileen Carey, the die was cast. He tried to persuade Gaby to come over and get a job in London away from the Abbey and the small clique of literary people in Dublin. Gaby came over but soon went back to Dublin. The criticisms started soon after Gaby went back. A devout Catholic, he became a member of the An Rioghacht, a conservative Catholic group in Ireland; he also became the critic for the *Catholic Standard*[28]. Sean and Gaby had remained corresponding until 1946 when

[27] *The Letters of Sean O'Casey: Volume III: 1955–58*, ed. David Krause (Washington, DC: Catholic University of American Press, 1989), p.95n.

[28] An Ríoghacht ("The Kingdom") was begun in Dublin in 1926 by Fr Edward Cahill, a professor of Church History at Milltown Park Institute and Fallon was an early member. The organisation's aims included embedding Catholic *Contd.*

Gaby wrote an open letter to Sean in the *Standard* of August 9, 1946, "Calling Mr O'Casey", repeating the accusation in his July review that Sean in his play *Red Roses for Me* was guilty of "coldly-calculated bigotry". Sean did of course reply to the paper's editor in July, how could he stop himself? The friendship waned and then stopped and Sean cut Gaby dead.[29]

Bearing all this in mind I was very puzzled by a visit to Gabriel Fallon's house with Eileen: the once best friend of Sean's and now the one who writes scathing criticisms of his plays and Sean and who had just decimated *The Bishop's Bonfire*. So why did we go and see Mr and Mrs Fallon for tea? Was it an idea of Eileen's to see what Gaby had become and face him about enjoying The Jeep scene in *The Bishop's Bonfire*? I will never know now. A taxi took us to the end of their road on the north Side, a road of red brick houses alongside a canal or small river. We were greeted by Mrs Fallon and when we had sat down in the rather stiff atmosphere Gaby came in all submissive, with smiles and a humble handshake. Uriah Heep came to my mind, "Ever so humble". Some children were there, very quiet and good. The room was dull in colours, I remember brown and beige ... the atmosphere remained tense. Eileen was withheld and so were the Fallons. I can't remember what was said; it was after Gaby's review had come out. I think Eileen said, "Why are you so against Sean, Gaby". He tried to explain and maybe he thought we would secretly agree with him that Sean's later plays were not up to scratch, that we would rush home and tell Sean to follow the wisdom of his old friend. As we left, dry-throated and stiff, Eileen said, "I will never agree with what you think and write. I am, I must say, ashamed for you". She was able to turn a screw

---

[28] *Contd.:* doctrine in the Irish Free State's educational and legal systems, promoting agrarianism, censoring unacceptable matter in the cinema, and keeping a watchful eye on Masonic, Communist and Jewish influences. "An Ríoghacht", Wikipedia.

[29] For Sean's riposte to the *Standard* of August 9, 1946 and Gabriel Fallon's open letter, see *The Letters of Sean O'Casey, Volume II*, pp. 380, 383–385. Dr Cummins wrote to Sean in a manner similar to Fallon's, objecting to a scene to which Fallon also objected; Sean replied to him and asserted in detail the non-sectarianism of the scene. The doctor, a devout Catholic, retracted his accusation of Sean's anti-Catholicism and apologised for doubting Sean's sense of justice. See O'Connor, *Sean O'Casey: A Life*, pp. 337–338.

in, my Mum, when she wanted to.[30]

While I was in Dublin I was asked to give my first ever interview, with Patricia O'Connell, for the *Evening Press*, March 3, 1955.

"It was a big week for Shivaun

For 15 year old Shivaun O'Casey, daughter of playwright Sean, this has been a memorable week of firsts – her first journey out of England, her first visit to Dublin, first world premiere, first time seeing one of her father's plays performed ... and her first interview.

Shivaun, a shy though self-possessed young lady. 'It's people who make Ireland so nice, they are so warm hearted', she said.

She likes Dublin's architecture, too, which is only natural since she is keenly interested in art. 'I'm hoping to visit the National Gallery, Trinity College to see the Book of Kells and the Museum, where I particularly want to see the Tara Brooch'.

Her Name

When I met her at her hotel she had just returned from a drive out to the Sugar Loaf and the Scalp. 'That's another thing I like about Dublin – it's so near the country'.

Where did she get the name Shivaun, with its unusual spelling? 'My grandmother was called Susan and I am named after her. Shivaun is the Irish for Susan as well as Joan, you know,' she said.

'The Bishop's Bonfire', she went on, 'is dedicated – To the Two Susans; grandmother and me. [To Susan gone and Susan here] Their spelling? Well, in all the fuss about writing down my name, after I was born, Daddy finally said: "Just spell it how it sounds". And so the phonetic spelling stuck.'

In contrast to O'Casey, the figure of controversy, it was new to hear Shivaun about Sean O'Casey, the family man.

[30] Gabriel Fallon remembered things differently. In his book *Sean O'Casey: The Man I Knew* (1965) he claimed that Eileen rang him up to complain about his review just when he and his wife Rose were about to invite Eileen and Shivaun for a meal; according to Christopher Murray, Eileen's phone call ended any further contact and no visit took place: Christopher Murray, *Sean O'Casey: Writer at Work* (2004), p. 520, endnote 104. Shivaun's distinct memory of this visit on her first time in Ireland would seem to be decisive. In "Sean O'Casey: Fact and Fancy" (*The Massachusetts Review* 7:3 [1966]), the O'Casey scholar Ronald Ayling contests several of Fallon's claims and writes: "As for veracity, it should be noted that there are in the book several errors of fact" (604), errors consistent in seriousness with the issue of Eileen and Shivaun's visit to Sean's ideological adversary.

'Daddy is a real father,' she said, 'helps with the washing up, goes [listens] to football matches with us, and brings mother and me breakfast in bed on Sunday morning.'

Mrs O'Casey and her daughter are staying in Dublin until Saturday, but Shivaun hopes to really see Dublin properly in the summer when Sean O'Casey will visit his native Dublin. He has promised to show Shivaun his town and take her to meet many of his friends.

Likes Music

What does Shivaun want to be?

... An actress, of course. 'I may go to University and do dramatics and perhaps eventually join a company.'

Music is another of her interests. The two extremes – classical music and really "hot" New Orleans jazz. 'But I hate sugary, sentimental modern hit tunes,' she said.

On this first visit I did see the Tara Brooch, the National Gallery and the Book of Kells in the grand wooden and ancient lofty Trinity College Library, and a few pages were turned for us. Sadly, Sean never made it back to Dublin with me or anyone else ... money and poor health.

I don't know if I was any the wiser after seeing Ireland for myself: so many priests in black everywhere, often relaxing at the Shelbourne hotel with their young nieces. Not wiser maybe, but a lot more aware of a seamy and narrow-minded side of life there. Religion surrounded you then, the great crossings of themselves as a bus passed a church, and the Angelus ringing out so very often and also on the wireless: all this I had never imagined.

MACBETH AT STRATFORD

Now we were home and off to see *Macbeth*, another trip with me in tow. Laurence Olivier was Macbeth and Vivien Leigh Lady Macbeth. Some years before, my friend Jane and I had performed the murder scene from *Macbeth* at school. I had to play Macbeth as I was taller and she played Lady Macbeth. It went down well at school and I had told Eileen not to come to see it, with the subtext, do come, that she didn't understand; so when she really hadn't come and people were saying they had cried I berated her for not coming: "But you told me not to come!" "Yes, but I didn't mean it!"

The Stratford production was a wonderfully dramatic production and I was dazzled by how good professional productions could be. We went backstage to see Larry, as Eileen called him, as she had known him and his first wife when their son was a baby. He took me on his knee and asked me what I thought of it. "I thought it was wonderful. I played Macbeth once." "Oh, then you can tell me how you managed his death at the end." "No", I had to mumble, "We only did the murder scene." "Well", he said, "I used to roll down the steps and do all sorts of acrobatics but I can't do that anymore, so here, as you saw, I decided to fall backwards from a high rostrum with my legs caught, so I hang there dead." I had been very excited by this ending and told him so. After we left Eileen said, "He is a brilliant mover on stage; he just uses the whole stage." And he did.

Before we left, Vivian Leigh came in through an adjoining door and draped herself on the door-frame, looking incredibly beautiful. Eileen said how wonderful she was and then they all talked for a while more about Sean and about London and Michael St Denis again. Whenever we went backstage Eileen said – "Oh! I do love the smell of the greasepaint, don't you."

My letter to Sean:

7 July 1955 (I am writing in the car)

Dear Daddy,

We are having a lovely time. Last night we went to see Olivier in 'Macbeth'; it was extremely good & I think you ought to see it & some modern acting. After the show we went behind to see The Man. He was very charming, especially to me, & is a great admirer of you & wants to see you. Miss Leigh was not too bad. Yes you definitely ought to see it. Very hot. See you on Fri.

Love Shivy xxx

7
Niall demobbed, Paris and London for me
1955–1956

DEMOB AND EXAMS

Time was pushing towards Niall finishing with his hated time in the army and we all longed for him to be home again.
Niall's letter to Eileen:

22 March 1955

Dear Eileen,

Everything arrived O.K. – P.O.'s. Choc, magazines. Thanks. Sorry for not writing but things are very busy at present.

Still, all ends in a fortnight and then we return to Osnabruck & believe me I will be very glad to see the last of this place. Grand about the play – you sound to have had a great time in Dublin. All being well I should have leave on the 13th Apr. Interview on the 14th if I can fix it, & then I hope to be able to spend a few days at home– at least a long week-end. It won't be long but its better than nothing. I'm really lucky to get it at all. Weather still vile & terribly cold, it's still snowing hard on and off, not spring by a long way, & this countrysides' enough to give anyone the pip. I've never seen anywhere so bleak. Went to Belsen a few days ago, an awful place even now ten years after, just a row of mounds – large, about the size of a nissen hut but with cold little notices – 'Here lie 20,000 Poles', and over the whole place hangs a dreadful silence.

Thank Shivaun for her letter & Breon if you speak with him - My love to everyone as ever
Yours Niall – and see you I hope on the 14th.

Niall was de-mobbed in September before my birthday and spent time at home before moving to the little flat in Abbey Gardens, NW8, to share with Breon's friend Anthony Hyman, and start at London University on October 30.

Meanwhile, I was worried, hysterical really, as this was the year of my O Level exams set by the Oxbridge universities. They took place in June and July. I hated exams; they terrified me. Breon was home and helped me with my History of Art; he told me how to remember the painter Wright of Derby: "He always painted by candlelight".[1] It was Maths that I was absolutely clueless about. Early on when I was at the middle school I hadn't been bad at it, even taking to Algebra and Geometry; it was those bloody questions where we were meant to use all our maths skills to work out a solution to the problem posed that had muddled my maths intelligence. My brain shut down; it all became gobbledegook. So Breon set me a question that he thought would lift the fog and get my mind working. It went something like this, only a bit more complicated: "A train leaves Totnes at 2.30pm for Paddington and is travelling at 40 miles an hour. Paddington is 300, say, miles away. It stops at Exeter for 10 minutes. How long does it take to get to Paddington?" I thought for a long while, and without taking into account that I knew it took 5 hours to get to Paddington from Totnes, I said a day and a half. Breon concluded that it was hopeless. I got 2% or something in the exam but passed the other five subjects, doing very well in Biology and Art, and not too bad in both English Language and Literature, despite my appalling spelling.

TO PARIS WITH EILEEN

In September at the end of my school holiday, Eileen and I went to Paris for a week, invited and paid for by Tom Curtiss. When we arrived at the Charles de Gaulle airport we felt rather lost – we both spoke extremely bad French and were unable to understand the stream of words answered back at great speed. Eileen decided we should take a taxi to our hotel. We were rather surprised at the distance of our journey. The only other place we had flown to was Dublin and the airport was comparatively near to Dublin's centre. We kept glancing at each other nervously and by the time we arrived at the hotel, very pretty and small, Eileen looked very worried: it turned out we spent nearly all the money she had had brought with her for the holiday on the taxi. Tom soon came to the rescue. He ordered champagne; I didn't drink then, but Eileen told me I drank it like lemonade, and when we got to our room I evidently told Eileen off for letting so little go to her head and be embarrassing. A bad start to the great adventure. Poor Eileen – I did cramp her style ... a shy teenager like me didn't mix well with frivolity.

The first night Tom took us to the Folies Bergère. We had a table on a raised dais around the edge of the hall-cum-restaurant. It was all very plush

[1] Joseph Wright of Derby (1734–1797) was an English portrait and landscape painter; his human subjects were painted in candle-light.

and old-fashioned, drapes and curtains and lots of waiters running about with drinks balanced on silver trays held high over their heads. I was, I thought, a highbrow, and so thought the place and the show very overblown. The long legged Bluebell Girls (started by an Irish woman who had dazzling blue eyes) rolled on – all sitting in an almost naked frieze.[2] Some others, exotically dressed, did dance and move around, I don't think the seated "nudes" were allowed to dance. I seem to remember them moving only their arms and legs. All my life at school we had all run about the splash pools and swum in the nude, from toddlers to teenagers, so the naked body in all its forms (teachers' bodies as well) was very familiar and not in the least bit shocking or titillating. I was incredulous by the activity taking place on the tables situated around the curving stage, mainly occupied by old leering men in their black tie suits; some even bothered, even that close, to look at the young girls through binoculars. The comic turns I can't remember, but I am sure there was no Josephine Baker or even Maurice Chevalier on show that night. Eileen and Tom danced after the show and I wished the floor would open and swallow me up, as I sat alone watching and, I imagined, being watched.

The next night we were taken to Tom's "local" in the same building he lived in – La Tour d'Argent. Only a few very special people were allowed by the owner to live there: Tom had the Legion d'Honneur for the work he had done in Paris during the war: he spoke perfect French and about another ten languages and was in Intelligence during the war. This was a fabulous restaurant with views on three sides from their large windows the whole width of the restaurant, curving at each end. Monsieur Curtiss's table looked straight out over and along the Seine to Notre Dame: what a view, and as the sun set and Paris lit up, it was magical. You approached the restaurant from the ground floor, through doors that opened at the rounded corner of the building. You entered a sitting area all white and gold leaf with French boudoir-like settees and chairs and a desk where you gave your name before waiting or going straight up in the lift to the very top of the building to the restaurant and the panoramic view. This was the first of several times that Tom would bring me there, every time I went to Paris, alone or with a friend. On this occasion Gore Vidal was sitting on

[2] Margaret Kelly, born in Dublin but raised in Liverpool, founded the Bluebell Girls dance troupe and was a Paris celebrity for sixty years. The name of the troupe derived from her nickname. She was awarded the Legion d'Honneur in 2000 and died in 2004, aged 94. See "high-kicking her way into a life of dance", *Irish Times*, September 18, 2004.

NIALL DEMOBBED, PARIS AND LONDON FOR ME, 1955–1956

the small two-seater with friends, with lots of satirical jokes and introductions. We left them laughing and squeezed into the lift. We were ushered to Tom's table and sat down on the blue velvet-seated golden chairs (rather delicate for anyone too heavy, I thought) amidst the rather golden decor. The pristine white tablecloths covered the round tables, and there was lots of silverware. Tom wanted us to have the speciality, "duck presse", so we did and got a card with the number of the duck that we were about to eat and the date eaten – thousands had already been eaten; we sat content at Mr Tom Curtiss's table overlooking Paris.

Tom took us to a party at a very large grand house by the Jardin des Tuileries in Avenue Gabriel and Maurice Chevalier was there. He knew Tom well; maybe they had dealt with each other in the war. He was delighted to meet Eileen. Although he was accused of collaboration during the war, it seems he was most likely playing a part to protect a Jewish family. He marched in a Communist march in 1944 and signed the Stockholm Appeal and was banned from the US during the Joseph McCarthy reign of terror.[3] The hostess was charming but I must say Eileen and I felt like the country cousins in our simple skirts and blouses as they were all in what looked like original courtier cocktail dresses: be-decked and be-jewelled and be-made-up. I only knew Chevalier as the actor who sang "Thank Heaven for Little Girls" in that weird musical, *Gigi*.

One evening when Tom was unable to be with us he told us of a restaurant to eat at just over the road from our hotel. "Don't go upstairs, eat downstairs!", he emphasised. Eileen had dressed herself up but I was embarrassed by the earrings she was putting on – another bone of contention that had bristles rising. When we got there, downstairs was full. I suppose we could have waited, but despite Tom's warning, upstairs we went. The menu up there was at least four times as dear and it was rather a quiet and stilted atmosphere unlike the buzz and camaraderie of downstairs. We didn't have the courage to leave and ordered steak and French fries: typical tourist fare. While we were chomping our way

---

[3] Although in 1942 he was accused of collaboration with the German invaders, Chevalier (1888–1972) took part in a Communist demonstration in Paris in 1944, performed for a Communist fund-raiser in Stockholm in 1949, and signed the Communist-inspired anti-nuclear Stockholm Appeal in 1950 – all further reducing his popularity in the USA (where he had performed successfully in the 1930s) while McCarthyism fingered American Communists; Chevalier was denied entry to the U.S. in 1951. He was welcomed back to the United States in 1954 when the Communist witch-hunt subsided. "Maurice Chevalier," Wikipedia.

through the meal, to my horror Eileen choked, badly, and loudly, and looked panicked, gasping for air. I got up and hit her on the back. She motioned me away with her arms and rushed to the toilet. I was mortified again and paralysed, hoping she was all right. She came back all right but was very shocked. She was cross with me and told me the attendant in the toilet had put her finger down her throat and released the offending bit of steak that was blocking her trachea. That she could have died! We both held hands, ordered some water, paid nearly all Eileen had in her purse and left. By now I had lost all sense of feeling awkward and only wanted Eileen to be safe. From then on during the holiday, we were together as usual and more forgiving of each other.

Over the road was a cinema and Eileen wanted to go and see the film - in French. We stood in line for a while then Eileen suddenly gave a little scream and pulled me away to the back of the queue, the rest of the queue looking at us in amazement. Evidently a man had rubbed himself against her and flashed his penis. I saw it briefly and it wasn't a pleasant sight. We were losing confidence at our ability to be in Paris of an evening without our protector Tom. "I don't really want to see the film, can we go back to the hotel?" I said, and Eileen agreed. Tom rang later and I heard her say the evening was "indescribable", then she burst out laughing. We went down to join Tom in a nightcap to regale him with our adventures.

The next day Tom told us of a film being made just outside Paris starring Robert Mitchum that we could all be extras in for a day. Robert Mitchum was one of Eileen's pinups and so we agreed to go – and be paid! Tom took us by train and then a local taxi. We were in a scene in a cafe-cum-bar. Tom and Eileen were chosen to sit up at the bar and actually say a line or two to R.M. I was stuck at a table with people who spoke only French, pretty difficult for a whole day. Tom and Eileen were laughing away and drinking the pretend drinks. In 1956 Niall, Breon, Eileen and I all went to see the film, *Foreign Intrigue*, in Torquay. It was pretty awful, and you couldn't blink or you missed Eileen and Tom sitting at the bar in the cafe, Tom had his back towards the camera and you saw Eileen from the side: I was non-existent. Eileen's line was cut out but Tom insisted it was in the version he saw but I don't see how.

Another fascinating visit with Tom was to the country house of Erich Von Stroheim and his beautiful redheaded partner.[4] We went on a little

[4] The Austrian-American director and actor Stroheim died less than two years after this visit; his partner was the French film actress Denise Vernac; Stroheim had never divorced his third wife.

suburban train and walked from the station. I remembered him as the evil general with an eyepatch. We had a delicious tea in the garden with their pet duck, and every time an airplane flew overhead the duck would tilt its head and look up with one eye. Erich told me the duck was house trained and lived indoors with them.

Paris. The street cafés, the silver Seine with all its aquatic traffic snaking through this grand and beautiful city; we crossed its waters every day: Tom's chuckley laugh and bursting kindness. I miss him and my old desire to go to Paris to listen to his friends talking and to be taken to his favourite restaurants.

AN NBC CREW ARRIVES

The next excitement for the family after Paris was the arrival of a film crew from NBC in early October to film Sean and include his family. Niall was back from the army and waiting to start University and Breon was here to help. The producer Robert Graff and interviewer Robert Emmett Ginna later became known as the Two Bobs. We had known Bob Ginna from his visit as Gjon Mili's assistant and loved him. The cameraman was called Wolfgang Suschitzky, who we all came to call Su, a brilliant photographer, who from that time on took many photos of Sean and later called himself the "O'Casey official photographer". With Gjon Mili, they were the only photographers that Sean got on with as friends, and later he didn't want any truck with any other photographer, or interviewer for that matter. In his later years Sean refused interviews by some of the best BBC programmes.[5]

They had wanted to hire a hotel for the shoot but Sean and Eileen knew this would make Sean less relaxed, so it was decided to set up in the flat, chiefly in Sean's room. It caused a lot of turmoil, including worries about the electric supply. But, tiring as it was for Sean, they made it as easy on him as they could, and we all enjoyed it all. One scene was around the

[5] Robert Graff (1920–2019), born in New York, had been a wartime U.S. Navy Lt-Commander. While working for NBC after his service, he produced the Wisdom Series of documentaries. In 1965 he and Robert Ginna produced *Young Cassidy*. See:
https://www.legacy.com/us/obituaries/nytimes/name/robert-graff-obituary?id=15338964. He lived until the age of 99 but Wolfgang Suschitzky (1912–2016), the British documentary photographer, lived to 104. Being a Jewish socialist he had left Austria for Britain in 1934. As a film cameraman he worked on *Ulysses* (1967), *Entertaining Mr Sloane* (1970) and *Get Carter* (1971). His biography can be found in "Wolf Suschitzky: A Life in Photography", *Visual Art 9* (Spring 1997).

dining table, the only table we had to eat on. Niall did one of his spitting into the teacup laughs as he thought it was so stilted and weird, but Sean kept the conversation going and singing "The Bard of Armagh". Everyone was happy with the result.

The evening before the first day on which he was to be interviewed by Bob Ginna in his room, Sean asked Breon to go to the hotel where the two Bobs were staying and find out what they were going to ask him. Breon came back and told Sean that Bob Ginna had said – "Oh, I'll just talk with him, and ask, for instance, 'Sean, what is life?' And he'll say something brilliant, and then. … ." Sean exclaimed, "My God! What is life?" When the question came up Sean had worked out a reply: "What is life? Ah, there's the question, Bob – What is life?'

Bob Graff was very generous and bought cakes and goodies and, on leaving, a lovely Jaeger sweater for Eileen. Then they left, the whirlwind passed over, and we relaxed into our life together again. Sean went back to his working regime; Eileen continued to shop and cook and visit her friends and help Sean; Niall (when home) played his trombone; and Breon, who now had a little room down in the town as a studio, sometimes came back to eat and sleep. One day Mr. Norman the landlord who lived below with a Mr Trip and Mr and Mrs Greenwood (she was a golf champion and practiced her swings on their front lawn) came to the door in great distress saying he couldn't bear the noise of the trombone anymore. So Niall stuffed old rags down it to muffle the noise and agreed to play at set times.

Sean told George Braziller in a letter of November 1955: "The Television I did was for NBC of Radio Center, New York; those done before included Bertrand Russell, De Valera, and Nehru; so I'm in the company of the mighty … ."[6] This episode in the NBC TV series called *Wisdom*, "A Conversation with Sean O'Casey and Robert Emmett Ginna", was shown on January 22, 1956. Stravinsky and Marcel Duchamp appeared in other episodes.

BACK TO SCHOOL IN THE X GROUP

By now I was an established weekly boarder at Dartington with a lovely big room of my very own along a small corridor with three other rooms off it. One of the other rooms was occupied by my friend Speth. She was

---

[6] *The Letters of Sean O'Casey: Volume III*, p. 200. George Braziller (1916–2017) was another long-lived acquaintance of Sean's who lived to 101; he was the founder of the eponymous publishing firm.

an excellent writer and I was convinced she would become a historical novelist. She was cleverer by far than me at English and maths - not difficult on the last one. We used to have midnight feasts in my room as it was furthest away from the house mothers and fathers. They consisted of tinned mandarin oranges, a great luxury then, with biscuits; but the whispered chatter was the best part of it.

Speth was a great knitter, and we all loved or felt protective of the French teacher, John Harris. He was always very cold during the winter and wore a hot water bottle inside his squaddies khaki battle jacket. So Speth decided to knit him an enormous mauve scarf, I think with the help of other admirers. He wrapped it around his neck several times so his head peeped out as if from a tortoise shell.[7] I had dropped French even before O Levels even if I did like John, for I was hopeless at it.

I had taken my O Levels when I was still fifteen and was starting term as an "X grouper" just before my sixteenth birthday. A Levels took two years. The big disappointment for me was that English was no longer to be taught by Bo Bosence but by Raymond O'Malley, someone I didn't warm to. O'Malley had drawn me aside after looking over my O Level papers before sending them off for marking, and with a smirk on his lips told me that I would certainly fail my "imagination", part of English Language, hence most likely English Language altogether. He said, "Your spelling and overall punctuation are appalling". But I got a good mark and I passed English Language fine. When I found out O'Malley didn't like Dickens I knew I couldn't stand him.[8] The first English class for the A Level students with O'Malley was held in his room in the clock-tower;

[7] After serving in the RAF during the war, John P. Harris (1923–2003) began teaching French, English and Latin at Dartington in 1952. French culture was the love of his life and he moved to France in 1974. His book, *Easy Living in France*, appeared in 1981. In the early 1990s he broadcast vignettes of French life on the BBC which became books, firstly with *An Englishman in the Midi* (1991). See his *Times* obituary: https://www.thetimes.co.uk/article/john-p-harris-sjd9r78x3bc

[8] O'Malley's dislike of Dickens probably derived from F.R. Leavis, the influential literary critic who inspired O'Malley when a student at Cambridge where Leavis taught. (Re his remarks to Shivaun: candour, however wounding, was held to be a virtue by Leavisite critics.) O'Malley (1909–1996) taught at Dartington from the 1930s and later at Cambridge. Leavisite thinking would have had traction at progressive Dartington, for Leavis sent his children to the school: see David Bradshaw: "Huxley and Progressive Education: Daltonism and the Dartington Hall Débâcle", *Aldous Huxley Annual* 15 (2015): 5–7. The Dartington archive records O'Malley as "An inspiring teacher of English" who was temporary Head at the School when W.B. Curry retired. *Contd.*

there were about 8 or 10 of us sitting on wooden chairs in a semi-circle around him. I thought the lesson dull and uninteresting but I didn't say anything. I did, however, start to think I had to do something with Bo to save my sanity.

Every year Raymond O'Malley directed the Shakespeare play his class was studying for A Level exams. A very good idea but the one I saw was disappointing. The acting was all right but rather static even for the standards of young students. I could do much better than that, I thought, and started to pester Bo to direct a play for us. He finally agreed if I could find a suitable one and if I could come up with other people who wanted to be in it. In B Group, that is the second year at Foxhole, he had directed some of us in John Masefield's *The Tale of Troy*, so I knew a core of willing actors. I had co-designed the costumes and co-designed and painted the set.

So back to Dad for his advice to come up with something with not too big a cast and doable for us. He first suggested *R.U.R.* by Karel Capek, a good choice. He then told me about *The Lady's Not for Burning* by Christopher Fry, and it had a great part that I hoped to do. We all agreed on it. Luckily Bo cast me as Jennet, the part I wanted. The rest of the cast included Jan Rogers (Paul Rogers' son) playing the Mayor, Speth and Kate Duckham.[9] I had looked up the period in my costume book by Millia Davenport and was fascinated by the folds the fabrics made and the shape of some of the more unusual headdresses.[10] I designed and helped paint the set and we made the costumes and headdresses with a lot of help from Bo's wife, Susan. She showed us how to dye and print the calico and heavier cotton fabrics before making up the costumes; we also block printed patterns on to the material and Sue helped us cut them out and

[8] Cond. https://archive.dartington.org/CalmView/Record.aspx?src=CalmView.Persons&id=DS%2FUK%2F1318&action=5c336bc5. O'Malley crofted as a CO during WWII and wrote an acclaimed book about it, *One-Horse Farm* (1948). He later wrote textbooks and compiled anthologies. See his obituary by the distinguished Owen Chadwick in the *Independent*, August 15, 1996.

[9] Jan Rogers' distinguished actor father, Paul (1917–2013) trained at the Michael Chekhov Theatre Studio at Dartington Hall before serving in the Royal Navy during World War Two and returning to acting in 1946; thereafter he was long associated with the Royal Shakespeare Company; he died at the age of 96.

[10] Millia Davenport (1895–1992) was an American stage designer and costumière; in 1947 she declined Orson Welles' invitation to design the costumes for his film version of *Macbeth* in order to concentrate on her scholarly book, *The Book of Costume* (1948). Like Paul Rogers, she died at the age of 96.

sew them. We made a couple of interesting medieval hats and we got tights from somewhere for the boys, possibly The Playgoers Society at the Hall. We spent a whole term at it before we finally performed it. I had seen the play at the Globe in London in 1948 with Pamela Brown as Jennet, John Gielgud as Thomas, Richard Burton as Richard. I had loved that production.

The new term started and in mid February *The Lady's Not for Burning* was performed for three nights! Frank Dunlop was visiting his friend Joy Abrams, who was about to leave. They both stayed with Riette Sturge-Moore in her house in Hampstead, where Frank told me she had hanging on the walls the original masks from Yeats's Noh plays. Years later he told me how good he thought I was as Jennet. I never really believed I was much good, although I knew I wasn't bad and I had a determination and that is why I played Jennet then.

SEAN FALLS SERIOUSLY ILL

In February, Sean had a prostate operation followed in March by a kidney stone operation, both at Torbay Hospital with a long stay at the Mountjoy Clinic afterwards The first one was bad enough and he was weakened by it. So of course he couldn't come to see the play.

14 February 1956

My very dear Shivaun.

My dear and deep wishes for success as 'Janet' [sic] in 'The Lady's Not for Burning' on Thursday, Friday and Saturday.
  With my deep love
  Daddy

In a letter of March 31, 1956 to his friend, the American theatre critic Brooks Atkinson, Sean summarised his ordeal: "I have had a rough time. I was ill for a year before my resistant will broke, and I had to yell for help. I spent fourteen weeks in hospital, underwent two major operations, & in between had to fight off (with help from doctors & nurses) a nasty bout of bronchial-pneumonia; plus inflammation of the kidney, which still is under observation – a whole anthology of ailments. ... [Eileen] came to see me three times a day; day by day, week by week month by month, & was to me what Julie was to George [Nathan] – a Godsend. Out of the misery & pain, however, I managed to pull a song for her – the only thanks I had to give." The song, "The Scents of the Blossoming May", to the tune of "The Little Red Lark", began:

> The first day I saw her,
> I stood & I wondered at loveliness
> Coming to me;
> With laughter bending and rising gayly, –
> Like Daffodils a waltzing a leas;
> And when her white hand came
> To hide deep in my hand on
> A farewell at ending of day;
> Her charm and her laughter lilt
> Around and about me,
>   The scent of the blossoming May."[11]

Once I came home I realised how serious Sean's condition was and how worried Eileen was about him. The first operation for his prostate was rather hushed up in conversation, as something very private and maybe a bit shameful. But when he was hit with the operation for the kidney stones so soon after in March, still not fully recovered from the first and having to wait for a chest infection to mend, the alarm bells rang. In those days you operated from the front to get to the kidney and remove the stones; they weren't melted as they are today.

Niall was home from London and university and with Niall I visited Sean in his hospital sick-bed with primroses and other flowers of the field to remind him what lay outdoors. Much of the three months were spent in Mountjoy Nursing Home, then situated just off the main street in Torquay, where he had a room of his own. There were one or two pretty nurses who he liked; Eileen always mentioned them with a slight ache of jealousy – no need to, though.

Slowly he got better but it had all knocked a lot out of him and he had aged in those long three months. By May he was out walking again, just around the block, with his walking stick now painted white to warn the motorists that his sight was bad. He sat in his chair on the concrete landing at the top of our steps that led to our only door and fed the birds, particularly his blackbird, Charlie, that he had enticed into the hall to eat his tit-bits.

---

[11] Although Sean mentions this song in his letter, Krause does not reproduce it in *The Letters of Sean O'Casey: Volume III*, pp. 251–252.

NIALL DEMOBBED, PARIS AND LONDON FOR ME, 1955–1956

In April of that year, his old Union friend Jack Carney died. During the war years and after, Jack and Mina called themselves Uncle and Aunt and I accepted it as a fact. After all, most people had relations and we only had Grannie.

Eileen's letter to Mina:

9 April 1956

Mina dearest,

I only heard yesterday of Jack's death & it gave Sean & I such a shock, what are you going to do & where are you going to live. Sean has been home from hospital 2 weeks, he was in hospital about 12 weeks & had two operations, he is very weak, but I hope will get strong again. Darling I do hope you are alright, I wish I had it in my power to come and see you and comfort you; because although we have not seen much of each other for many years I have always had great affection for yourself and Jack – always I shall have. I cannot write anything to help you Mina but please take the greatest sympathy from Sean & myself.
Eileen

THE CENTRAL SCHOOL OF ARTS AND CRAFTS

After my Dad was back in better health and we again went on walks along the high-up seaside walk of St Marychurch, I made up my mind that I didn't want to stay at school, being taught by two people I had no admiration for. Also, Niall was in London and I wanted badly to start facing the bigger world and to be a part of his world. Once my mind was made up I broached it with Eileen and Dad. She was almost annoyed; they had, she said, moved to be near Dartington because I was still at school and I had two more years there. But they both saw that they couldn't alter my stubborn determination. I said I wanted to study scenic design and not acting (I knew they were both opposed to acting as a career choice and so I kept that burning desire just about under my hat) and thought if I was accepted at the Central School of Arts and Crafts they would agree. As Further Education was free then, the expenses would only be living and food, and no further bills for school. Food I could share with Niall and could eat at his flat each night, so the main outlay was lodgings.

The Head of The Central School of Arts and Crafts sat behind his desk and asked me why I wanted to do theatre design now. Even after school it was usual to go to a local art college for a year or so before applying for a major college. I spoke of not wanting to waste my time where the teaching was poor and that I wanted to learn the craft of theatre design that wasn't offered elsewhere. He looked at my rather thin "folio" of drawings and paintings that I had gathered together as best I could. I mentioned that I had designed shows at school.

Eileen was asked to come up and talk to him alone, especially as I was only 16, and she did. She reported back to me: "I managed your interview and you are accepted, but the Principal said to do as much drawing as you can from now to then, just in a sketchbook and bring it with you when you go to enter yourself on September 17th as you then see the Master and I take it you go to a group suitable. The theatre design standard was quite high, they had an exhibition on of 4 of the star pupils work & it was good." What she said or did to the Principal I can't think but I did leave Dartington and go to the College thinking, as she very often said, that if it hadn't been for her I wouldn't have got in.

Sean was very pleased: I would be drawing and painting and that is what he thought I should do, and I would have done that for good if only the bloody urge to act didn't keep raising its head. Of course, Eileen had been an actress and "gave up" her career for Breon and then it was not easy to go back. It was something she regretted but knew she had to do. She really hankered after the stage all her life and loved to be with people who admired her warmth and humour and beauty. She had been in the papers as one of the young actresses to watch. She had a lovely singing voice and could dance up to a high standard; after all she had been a Cochran Young Lady and that meant a lot. Charles B. Cochran, Cocky, was renowned for his musicals and the refined and well-drilled choruses. It was very difficult to be accepted from the rigorous auditions. She had been in the chorus of *Rose Marie* and *The Miracle*, directed by Reinhart, among others. And after marrying Sean and having Breon she had gone back to be in Noel Coward's *Bitter Sweet*.[12]

Eileen came up to London with me to settle me in. She stayed with Niall at the flat.

[12] Eileen gives accounts of these stages in her theatrical career in *Eileen*, pp. 67–71, 112–115, 127–128. *The Miracle* was a wordless 1911 play by Vollmöller that was performed that year at Olympia in London with 1700 performers and a score by Engelbert Humperdinck; it was revived on Broadway in 1924 and in 1932 was staged at the Lyceum Theatre in London in which Eileen took part as one of Cochran's Young Ladies troupe.

NIALL DEMOBBED, PARIS AND LONDON FOR ME, 1955–1956

Eileen had managed to get the last room for me at a house in Abercorn Road, NW8, just around the corner from Niall and Anthony's flat. Abercorn Road had the same name as a road Sean lived on in Dublin near the East Wall. My house was owned and run by a tall, self important although kind lady called Lady Hendy. She was Toe Ogilvy's sister. My room was in the semi-basement, looking up and into the front garden and the street. It had two long windows and was decorated all round the walls with pink and white striped wallpaper; a bit like living in a hat box. Lady Hendy was separated from Sir Philip Hendy, the art specialist who then ran the National Gallery.[13] They had a very handsome son who was in the army doing his call-up and was in Aden – not a good place to be at that time.[14] There was a lovely kind girl from Dartington living upstairs, Nan Shaw, who had been two years ahead of me. She had a lovely room on the first floor with big generous windows. Living at the back of the house was a young Dutch girl – very pretty and slim – who was studying dance. There were great goings on when the son, Mark, came home and fell for her. Lady Hendy didn't like it in the least. I was grateful to have Nan to talk to and hang out with in her room when Niall was busy or needed to work after we had eaten together.

What a bonus it was for me to have Niall around the corner and to have his handsome university friends visit in the evening and some of his friends from Dartington. All the time I was there I never saw Anthony cook; it was either Niall or me. He ate all right, though. Niall showed me how to do his spaghetti sauce; with the long Italian spaghetti and grated cheddar on top; it was what we mainly lived on. It was this or beans on toast and our table cloth was the *Daily Worker*. I helped with the cooking and washing-up, also a bit of cleaning in Niall's room. For some reason I wanted to look after Niall while he worked, as he looked tired. Niall was often joined by a friend, Michael Rosenberg, a boy from Niall's class in school and now a starving artist who came once or twice a week; he had a rota of friends who regularly fed him.[15] Anthony had a pretty girlfriend

---

[13] The distinguished art historian (Sir) Kenneth Clark appointed Hendy (1900–1980) as his successor as director of the National Gallery in 1946.

[14] Aden had been in British hands since 1839 and was a British Crown Colony, 1937–1963. It was an important military base during the rise of Arab nationalism in the 1950s.

[15] David Elliott recorded a memory of Michael Rosenberg at Dartington Hall and also the death of Neal [sic] O'Casey:
http://www.dartingtonhallschool.co.uk/memories/davidelliott/davidelliott.html

called Claudia Roden, now the very famous and remarkable cook but I don't remember her ever eating with us.[16] I enjoyed talking around the fire after we had eaten and washed up.

The first few weeks at Central School were a bit of a disappointment. We drew models that were dressed in period costume and we pinned muslin and calico on tailors' dummies to make a costume. I didn't see the point in either of these activities, even when the teacher flattered me and said my drawings reminded her of Edward Gordon Craig's drawings/woodcuts. I was pleased with this as he was one of my idols, along with the Motleys and Robert Edward Jones, O'Neill's designer.[17] Because my drawing was under par I went to life drawing classes and must have drawn very badly. The teacher came and told me that my drawing was out of proportion, that the head was far too big. I muttered that the model in front of me did have a large head in proportion to her body but I have to admit not quite as large as I had made it. I should have been a caricaturist. I didn't learn from this – I wanted to act. Back at the Costume Design room, where we stayed for a year, you could hear all the fun being had next door where you designed the sets with Ralph Koltai teaching.[18] There was excitement and energy there that wasn't among the calico and muslin of the costume department.

During this time in response to the West's and Israel's threats to Egypt, Gamal Abdel Nasser decided to nationalise the Suez Canal and all hell broke loose. The students at Niall's College, the University of London, started to organise.

During all this ferment I decided, again without much warning, to try for RADA (the Royal Academy of Dramatic Art) started by Sean's old friend Bernard Shaw. It was out – I wanted to become a professional actress.

[16] Claudia Roden (née Douek; b.1936) was born in Egypt in 1936 to a Syrian-Jewish family. She went to England in 1953 to study at the Saint Martin's School of Art. Her numerous cookbooks are chiefly on Middle Eastern cuisine, including *A Book of Middle Eastern Food* (1968). She married Paul Roden in 1959.

[17] Edward Gordon Craig (1872–1966), the illegitimate son of Ellen Terry, was a theatrical set designer for the Moscow Art Theatre and Abbey Theatre of Dublin, among others. Robert Edward Jones (1878–1954) was an American stage and costume designer who worked closely with Eugene O'Neill.

[18] Ralph Koltai (1924–2018) was a British stage designer who was born in Germany and came from Brussels to England on the Kindertransport in 1939. He studied and taught at the Central School of Art and Design and was chiefly associated with the Royal Shakespeare Company.

Dear Daddy,

I know that RADA is not a good school but never the less it is a better school than Central – I know. I don't do any painting or nice things there & I never have anything to please me after my days work – just bad sketches and even worse watercolours of people in Medieval dress. That is what is so bad about it – it makes drawing, etc. a misery & not a pleasure – and that is why I want to go to RADA & quickly. RADA has many other things going on as well as acting including a course in Theatrical Design – which is not so specialised & hence much nicer. As for acting – well I don't know. But I do know that if I don't try I will begrudge myself all the rest of my life. It also has a stage of its own & you get the opportunity of acting on it but to an audience. After that I want to get into the Arts at Stratford – but we will see.

Still don't worry. If I try my audition at the end of Nov I will know whether I am accepted or not – & even if I am I needn't go. I won't say anything to the Central School & if I am not accepted I suppose I can continue my course in the dis-appreciation of Art. See?

Niall's cold has gone – almost. All the demonstrating has turned in sympathy of Hungary & people seem to have forgotten Egypt.[19] I hope everything works out in the end, I am convinced it will & that the dove will fly again whiter than ever.

Lots of love
Shivy xxx
Love to Mum and Bre
P.S. Letter is inspired by Picasso.
P.S.S. Please send & sign form for RADA.

Poor Sean and Eileen: another bolt from the blue to cope with. Sean replied:

10 November 1956

Miss Shivaun O'Casey [This meant it was serious]

---

[19] The Hungarian uprising against the Soviet-backed Hungarian government actually began a week before the Suez Crisis when Israeli, French and British forces crossed into Egypt to retrieve the Suez Canal from Egyptian nationalisation; but demonstrations against the brutal Soviet response to the Hungarian revolution took precedence over anti-war demonstrations during Suez.

My very dear Shivaun,

Oh, dear, what can the matter be? Your declaration was a little surprising to us all here. Good reasons and all as you may have, dear, I'd give the proposed change a little more thought before deciding – say after Christmas when you'll have a chance of a chat with Mam and me. Anyway, I strongly advise you not to give up Painting & design practice, Art school or no Art school. This creative work – I'm afraid acting isn't – will always be a personal pleasure, like playing the piano; & for that alone, is well worth practising. I'm afraid there's no pleasure in acting unless it is done before an audience, & that takes a long time to come about. When I was young, many a lovely hour was passed pleasantly sketching cartoons, or trying my hand at water-coloured sketches of flower, house, or country scene; and, my dear Shivaun, I hadn't even a twentieth of the talent you have for this enjoyable work. You'll find RADA just as dull as an Art School – it is an A School anyway; & no picture or coloured design to look at after the days practice. Anyway, don't give this designing up altogether, or, since we are writing of personal pleasure, your piano playing either.

I shall be delighted to see you again. Hope Niall's cold is better, or better still, gone completely. Give him my love. My love, my dear, to you, too

As ever Dad, Sean

THE NOVEMBER DEMONSTRATION

Niall helped me by hearing my lines; two pieces: the Nurse from *Romeo and Juliet* and a speech from Shaw's *Candida*. One evening he was hearing them in Anthony's room, as Anthony was sitting in front of the fire in the big room. When I asked him to hear them one more time he snapped at me, "I don't have the time, Shivy!" It was such a shock coming from Niall, who was never like that, I began to cry. He said, "I'm sorry. I didn't mean to be angry but I am so very tired. I am finding it difficult to concentrate on my study". I stopped and looked at him and noticed how pale he looked and drawn – his lips were pale. From then on I helped him as much as I could, until we were to get home where he could rest, and get better.

When Eileen came up for a weekend, she was worried and she asked him how he felt. I remember him, as we stood on the corner of his street, assuring her that he was just slightly run down and tired and he would rest when he came home for Christmas. He later told me he sometimes went dizzy when he climbed stairs too quickly and thought he might have bad anaemia.

A *Guardian* reporter claimed on July 10, 1956 that no one, including most of Prime Minister Anthony Eden's closest colleagues, knew that the French had proposed a secret Franco-Israeli plan whereby Israel would attack Egypt, giving the British and French an excuse to occupy the land on either side of the Canal under the pretext of "peacekeeping'. By October 24, Eden was covertly committed to the sham war. Niall and his friends had suspected this, maybe from reading the *Daily Worker*, and were suspicious of the Foreign Secretary Selwyn Lloyd going to Sèvres, France, where Israeli officials were spotted on October 22–24. Niall had been following the Suez Crisis since its start when the Egyptian President Nasser announced the nationalisation of the Suez Canal, a major shipping lane for us Brits. After a summit of shady diplomacy, Israel attacked Egypt; then the students and the anti-war enthusiasts organised a rally in Trafalgar Square. We now knew that Britain and France had colluded with Israel.

On the morning of October 31, we read the *Guardian* leader headed "Headlong into Disaster" that set the paper against Britain and France's threat to attack Egypt unless it withdraw its forces from the strategic Suez canal zone. "The Anglo-French ultimatum to Egypt is an act of folly, without justification in any terms but brief expediency. It pours petrol on a growing fire. ... it is far more likely to lead Britain into direct war with Egypt, and perhaps the whole Arab world – as, on the latest report, it seems to be doing. What is more, countless other nations will consider Britain and France to be in the wrong." As the leader was being written, Israel, a secret partner in the Anglo-French project to prevent Cairo nationalising the Canal, was already spearheading the attack.

A day of demonstration was called for November 4 and I was determined to go. Niall was worried as he thought it was likely to get rough but he finally agreed if I promised to stay by him. This I did readily. It was a pleasant clear Sunday and I was very excited to be with Niall and his friends and going to a demonstration. The tubes going to Trafalgar Square were packed with masses of young people. The stream of bodies emerged from the Bakerloo Line at Tottenham Court Road where we met up with two of Niall's university friends, a red-haired Scot and a Chinese student; both their names have vanished from my mind but I can see them clearly. We walked down the Charing Cross Road towards Trafalgar Square. As the crowds grew Niall grasped my hand to keep us together, as people were shoving and pushing in their haste to get a good spot near the stage for the speakers set in front of Nelson's Column. We listened and responded to the speakers. "Law not war!" was one of the cries. The speeches over, a call was made to march on Downing Street. Niall was very worried by this and held back a bit with me to the side of a building at the top of Whitehall. It was then the mounted police arrived to jeers and boos. They had long truncheons and they weren't afraid to use them. Hitting out at all and sundry, one horse stumbled and the rider nearly fell; some of the crowd tried to pull him off but two other riders came to protect him. The police started to walk up Whitehall clearing the crowds as they went. Niall's Chinese friend had climbed up on a stone balustrade and adopted the Lotus Position and when a group of police threatened him to "move on", he said peacefully, "I am Buddha, you can't move me", and they actually left him there as we were shoved about and slowly but forcefully pushed back to the Square.

The sound of the horses' hooves and the look of terror in their eyes made everyone tense and some reckless. I wanted to go and confront the police but Niall firmly shouted me down, telling me "Not to be a fool".

The very same day, according to the *Observer* columnist Lajos Lederer, the Red Army had encircled Budapest and started shelling the city "with total savagery". Like a bush telegraph, news spread among the demonstrating crowds that Russia had sent in tanks against the Hungarian citizens. Niall said we had to go home to listen to the BBC. He was very upset by the crackdown in Hungary. He rang home from the call box around the corner to talk to Sean and was shocked to hear what Sean said, so that weekend he went down to Devon to see Sean and talk with him. Sean and Niall held different views on the invasion. Sean was an old worker who had gone through the lockout and strike in Dublin in 1913 to fight for the rights of the unskilled workers against the greedy employers, and who was so hopeful and supportive of the USSR, to him the first country (and an enormous one at that) to go towards his idea of what life should be for all. He supported Marxist economics against capitalism. I find it difficult to express where he stood as it doesn't fit any convenient boxes – one reason why he never joined a party or a union since Big Jim's. He wrote about it in his letters over the years.

Niall like Sean hated any form of violence, but unlike Sean he felt the brutality against the vast demonstration for "democracy" to be absolutely wrong; and against the law of human rights. This was the Niall that Sean had often held on his knees during an air-raid, holding the shaking boy closely as he distracted him with gentle talk. Here was his beloved grown up son outraged at the Russian Army's brutality. The old Sean had not fought in the Easter Rising of 1916 but had helped his comrades in the Irish Citizen Army. During the Anglo-Irish War he had been taken to a grain store and left there until morning, the grain irritating his open sores from neck surgery for TB growths. He had seen men hung up and castor oil poured down their throat so they would hang and maybe die in their own foul smelling shit. He had been lined up to be shot only to be saved by an English officer who he had talked to about Shelley. "Old Sean" may have thought along the lines of the old boy interviewed in the *Guardian* on October 21, Arthur Merron (94 years old), a party activist from Manchester: "The CIA was a powerful organisation, the Catholic Church was a powerful organisation, so were the capitalist press and other governments and they wanted to destroy communism by fair means or foul. So I felt the Soviet Union was 100% right in going into Hungary to stop this counter-revolution".[20] The Iron Curtain had first clanked down to split Russia from the West, leaving very little room for dialogue between the people. That was one thing Sean believed in – contact – and why he belonged to the Soviet Union Friendship Society and organised books being sent to the USSR. They had helped us in the war and lost many millions and we could have remained in contact surely.

I AUDITION WITH RADA

The day of my audition with RADA came and I got off the bus in Gower Street feeling very sick indeed. I was shown into a room full of nervous young people frantically going through their lines. One by one the names were called and finally came "Shivaun O'Casey". With a deep breath and sinking feeling I followed a person down some stairs and on to the Stage L wings of the Cochran Theatre. Someone was on stage and a young man was in the wings doing exercises for his body and quietly for his voice – breathing, etc. My God, should I do this? I thought. But I had no idea

[20] Sean defended the USSR's invasion of Hungary in a letter to a Dublin friend, Mrs Kay O'Riordan on November 27, 1956; he mentioned his difference with his son in a letter to Brooks Atkinson, January 12, 1957, in which the invasion is "a sad necessity": *The Letters of Sean O'Casey: Volume III*, pp. 341–343, 371.

what to do and the young man looked decidedly foolish to me. On he went and someone else came to join me in the wings; we gave each other reassuring smiles and she said "Good luck" when my name was called.

So on I went into the middle of the stage of a real little theatre. At that point I just wanted to walk off the other side. Someone asked me if I needed any furniture for my two pieces and I managed to think and say, "A chair for my second piece, please". A chair arrived; "Where do you want it?" and I put it far, too far, up stage. I could, of course, have moved it if I wasn't paralysed rigid with fear. From the dark of the auditorium a voice resounded, "What are you giving us?" "First, the Nurse from *Romeo and Juliet* and secondly Candida's speech in Act 2 from the play *Candida* by George Bernard Shaw." "Thank you. When you are ready." I plunged into rather cold water. When the Nurse's jollying to Juliet was over there was dead silence. I went to the chair and with my courage returning brought it downstage a little, although not enough, and started. Then I heard the rattle of tea-cups and a whispered voice: "Do you take milk and sugar?" So I stopped. "Please continue and ignore what is happening in the auditorium," a voice said. So I did, and went on to the accompaniment of milk pouring and sugar stirring and the odd rather loud stage whisper. Also the chewing of biscuits. Finally the speech ended. I had moved during the speech and was so put off by all that was going on in the auditorium that I had slowly gravitated to the black velvet curtain at the back. So I stopped and took a step forward, and heard "Thank you. We will let you know." Exactly the words Eileen told us they said when she was joking about auditions and spoke of the excitement when they asked for your number and address as that meant they might call you back. The whole thing struck me as a farce and no way to find out the possible talents of a student. I thought, "Well, that's that. At least I had a go and now I will try and forget the whole thing".

Soon after this Niall was off to a party in Devon in the van with Trudi Black, who had been at school with him. She was very beautiful and they went together to a party at Dartington Village, near Totnes. I was slightly concerned as it was a long drive and Niall, I thought, was not too well. Also there was the problem of the petrol. Rationing was in force because of the Suez Crisis. This meant we had to collect more coupons to get down to Devon for Christmas. You couldn't leave any petrol in the tank overnight as it would most likely not be there in the morning, having been stolen. So we had to siphon it out by putting one end of a tube into the petrol tank and then sucking on the tube until the petrol reached your mouth and then whipping it into a petrol can until all the petrol had been drained off. The party was at Niall's friend Jill Lance's home for her 21st birthday.[21] When Niall came back he was exhausted and weak, but was also delighted, telling me he had had such a great time and all he needed was some rest before our drive back home. He was now enamoured of Trudi who had run away with me from nursery school to my home to show her my things and get some treats, all those years before.

[21] Jill Lance was an accomplished potter. She later married Ben Curry who had been a pupil at the school and was the son of Dartington headmaster W.B. Curry. Ben visited Colombia in 1957 on a Cambridge University botanical expedition and became enamoured of the country, later buying a 500-acre ranch he called Curucucu (a local songbird). Jill and Ben were there when Louis de Bernières moved to Colombia and was offered the position of tutor to Jill's children (Ben's stepchildren). Ben ("El Gringo") became the inspiration for de Bernières's story, *The War of Don Emmanuel's Nether Parts* (1990), the first novel of his Latin American trilogy; *Captain Corelli's Mandolin* (1994) is his best-known fiction. Curry published his memoir, *Curucucu: Adventures of a British Ex-Pat in Colombia*, in 2010.

8
Niall's last fight
1956

Many happy returns, Miss Seventeen.

THE LONG DRIVE HOME

We had saved up and got the petrol we needed for the journey home for Christmas 1956. The cans were sitting in a row on the stair landing: one to fill the tank before we set off and four to sit in the back of the Ford for the journey with bottles of water, also for the car. Breon had painted the van orange and we all felt proud driving in it. I hadn't learned to drive yet so Niall had to drive the whole way. That morning when I came over with my bag of stuff Niall looked awful and he said he felt slightly dizzy and nauseous. He suggested he would sit down for a moment while I packed up the van.

We left at about nine in the morning and after a couple of hours I asked if we could stop. "I don't really want to stop, Shivy. I just have to keep going." We had to pull in to a lay-by soon after to fill the tank and let the engine cool down. He looked worse and worse, almost yellow in colour but he said "We have to get on." I suggested we leave the van somewhere and take the train but he said "No, let's just keep going." By the time we got to Exeter he was so weak I was changing gears for him – "Down to second now" and I would shift it. I expected any minute he would slump over the steering wheel and I would have to pull hard on the hand-brake and steer into a hedge. He begged me to keep talking to him: "Talk about anything." I did, I even sang and he joined in and we laughed.

Finally we drove slowly down the drive to our home, the upstairs of Villa Rosa. I helped to heave him out of his seat and he held on to me as he walked to the bottom of the concrete steps. He almost crawled up them using his hands; he couldn't stand up. By then Eileen and Sean had opened the door and were shocked to see him looking so bad. We all helped him to his bed where he slumped down. "I'll be better in an hour or so, I just need to rest. It was a difficult drive, wasn't it Shivy?" How often in the past couple of months had I heard him say, "I just need to rest for a bit."

Next day was the Christmas party at the old school and friends of Niall's rang to see if he would bring his trombone and if I could bring my guitar for someone to borrow. Niall was looking forward to playing again with the school jazz band, The Stomping Scholars, and he was going to drive us both there. By the afternoon it was clear he wasn't able to make it; the tremendous effort he had made to drive first to and from the party at Jill

Lance's and then a few days later, before he had got much of his strength back, the long journey home, had taken a toll on his sick body. He insisted I should go as he would like to hear all about it. Breon drove me there and said he would pick me up at an allotted time. So many people asked where Niall was as I handed over my guitar. During most of the party I was missing him being there, but it was fun to be back with my old school pals again; and as I was leaving with Breon everyone was smiling and saying, "See you soon, and Niall, give him all the best, and tell him to hurry up and get better."

The next day Niall didn't improve and Eileen drove him to see Dr Doran who took blood samples and said it looked very like acute anaemia but evidently told Sean and Eileen it may be leukemia. Niall told me later that he had been studying this at university and all his symptoms seemed to point that way but he had hoped and wished it to be the less fatal pernicious anaemia. Dr Doran visited the next day to advise how to look after Niall and how to feed him while he waited for the test results. He had sought the advice of a specialist who said Niall should stay quiet at home and said that he would bring this specialist with him, most likely that evening. Niall played his records and then tired out again got back into bed.

That evening the specialist and Dr Doran were in Niall's room for a long time. They went to Eileen who was alone in the front room and told her Niall had acute leukemia and that he hadn't long to live. She asked if they had told Niall and the specialist said he had. The specialist asked if he should speak to Sean. "No," she said, "I will tell him myself"; she was thinking "I will tell him more gently than you told me". In her book *Sean*, Eileen remembered that she felt "utterly shocked, a dreadful feeling that returns to me sometimes when I think about Niall: I felt cold, ice-cold all over. I just left the doctors and went to Niall. There was little to say. I had not felt the full impact yet, and I could not even begin to imagine life without Niall. He was part of the family. He sat there at the side of the bed looking so young and handsome – life, I thought, must be before him. In a way he tried to help me. He actually said, 'Poor you!' I told Sean, but what do details matter? Niall had to bear the full dreadful sentence."[1]

Breon and I were sitting on the little upright sofa in Eileen's bedroom with the door shut, and had heard the doctors and Eileen in the front room, then her rushing to Niall. Then her getting rid of the doctors and

[1] *Sean* (London: Macmillan, 1971), p. 252.

going into Sean's room. Sean immediately went to Niall to hold his hand and talk. It was at this point that Eileen opened the door and said, it seemed to me too loudly, "Niall is going to die! He has leukemia and he is going to die!" I jumped up and said, "Shh, he'll hear you," and then we hugged and hugged and Breon just sat there stunned. For the first time I didn't know what to say to Niall or do for him. But I went in and just talked and talked in order not to cry - on no account did I want to upset him. A terrible heavy pall had fallen over the flat and we struggled to keep going, to keep busy, to try to help Niall.

The next day, December 18, an ambulance is to take Niall to the Royal Devon and Exeter Hospital where they have a unit that treated blood cancers. The ambulance arrives in the drive; Mr Norman wonders why it is there but doesn't interfere. The two men come into Niall's room to help support him into the ambulance. They wrap him in a red blanket. He looks so long and handsome on the stretcher being carried through the flat and down the steps to the ambulance; his lips are pursed and he just looks ahead. Eileen is close by his side and climbs into the ambulance to be with him on the start of his journey that we all hope is to recovery. She is, God knows, a great comfort to Niall. She gets a small room in the Royal Clarence Hotel so she can get to Niall quickly if needed.

Sean's Notebook:

December 19.20.21.22.

Poor Eileen the blackest blow she has ever suffered but she is there to fight off death from her handsome boy. I stay at home. The boy is never absent from my thoughts ... never, never.

Although Breon drove to the hospital each day with Eileen, only Eileen was allowed to go in to be with Niall. The hospital was trying to work out a treatment to allow him some comfort. Eileen would get Breon to buy things like small jars of chicken or beef essence to tempt him to eat something that would slide easily down his restricted throat. Breon was there to do anything he could to help. On two occasions I went with Breon in the hope I might get to see Niall.

I had come in the car with Sean and Breon to meet Eileen and to visit Niall in his hospital bed. I was determined not to cry or look sad in front of my brother and closest friend and protector. I had turned my reversible windjammer I had been given early for Christmas so Niall would see its bright side, its red and blue tartan checks. I walked into the ward and turned to his bed on the left and on seeing him it took all the powers I had not to run and fling myself sobbing on top of him. He had unnatural colour in his cheeks as he had just had a blood transfusion. There was worry about the supply of the blood they had at Exeter for him as he had a rare blood group and so they tried to prolong the intervals between transfusions.

The ward was darker than you would usually expect, with a line of five beds along one wall each a fair distance apart. A Christmas tree faced the sick on the opposite wall with a few baubles hanging off its branches. At a bed next to Niall was a very sick young man with his wife beside him holding his hand tightly in hers. They hadn't been married long.

I smiled and squeezed Niall's rather cold fingers very gently as his hands had needles in them for some drips. He smiled and signalled that he couldn't talk much but asked me to talk. So I told him I had heard from RADA and they had accepted me so next year we would be together again in London, he in the flat and me at Lady Hendy's, that while he regained his strength I would be there to look after him, as Anthony wasn't much good at that sort of thing; to that he gave a wry smile. Breon stood back as he had visited Niall before and realised that this was my time. Then Niall mouthed "Eileen", and I said, "Do you want her?" and he nodded. So I kissed him and said we would go directly to get her. Then I said "Goodbye Niall, I'll see you again soon". But I never would.

In the corridor it was almost impossible not to cry out and my throat hurt from keeping my anguish in. There was a lot of noise and laughter coming from behind a door on our left and as we passed the door flew open, and a man introduced himself as Niall's doctor. Behind him was an actor, Brewster Mason, with a plaster cast on a leg and a nurse on his knee, and other nurses all over him.[2] It looked to me like a modern Hogarth print of "The Prodigal Son" in the brothel. "Come in and join us. You are too young to be down there with the dying. Come and have a jolly time with us". "No, No" I said, turning to the doctor, "My brother is there looking for a nurse and his mother". "Oh, come on in", said Mason, and

---

[2] Brewster Mason (1922–1987) was an English theatre and screen actor who began his career on the London stages in 1947. From 1963 to 1987 he was a member of the Royal Shakespeare Company. When Shivaun saw him, he was fresh from his appearance in the famous British film, *The Dam Busters* (1955). His leg in plaster is an odd reminder that Mason died in 1987 as a result of a fall while he was playing the King in Shakespeare's *Richard II*.

NIALL'S LAST FIGHT 1956

the doctor didn't disagree. I'm afraid Breon said something like "You should be ashamed of yourselves" as he walked me away to the exit. There we met Sean and Eileen coming to visit. We only told them that Niall was asking for Eileen; the rest came out later in Eileen's little room in the Clarence Hotel on Cathedral Square. "You shouldn't have said anything, Breon, they may take it out on Niall", Eileen said. Then we felt even worse than before.

Sean's Notebook:

23 December

Went with Breon, Shivaun and Eileen to see Niall. Shivaun and Breon went in first two only allowed at a time; quarter of an hour later (so short a time with Niall. Hail and Farewell). Eileen and I sauntered into the hospital, and met Shivaun returning, and she brought word that Niall was talking oddly, and found difficulty forming words. A shock to us, and a dread of what it might signify. Shivaun also told us Niall was eagerly waiting for Eileen. Poor, brave Eileen; always Eileen; first me; now, Niall – Eileen, Eileen – every breeze touching the O'Casey family face, called out, or whispered Eileen. We went in and found him hardly able to form a few words. We had all been looking forward to a quiet and gay family Christmas. Breon had to remain in London for Christmas the year before, but would be with us this time, and there would be a temperate feast, a drinking of wine & draught from a cider-cup to be made by the skilled hand of Niall. All the presents were parcelled up in gay-coloured wrappings, ready to be handed out on Christmas morning, and in the evening carols would be sung standing around the piano as Shivaun played the tunes. Red berried holly was bunched on the table waiting to decorate picture or wall; and a bunch of mistletoe to be hung from the ceilings centre. All things during the season would have a special sparkle.

Breon drove Sean and me back home. We were all too upset to talk. Just sat thinking our own sad thoughts. Sean hadn't completely recovered from his two operations – even then – and I knew Eileen was a little concerned about the strain he was undergoing. But that was put aside by our continual hope for Niall. I made myself believe he would survive; he couldn't do anything else. If anything were to happen like that in our family it would be to Sean.

The next day was Christmas Day and Eileen had said we should bring Niall's presents with us and give them to him around his bed. She had bought him a lovely warm buff-coloured sweater: he was to die with it on. We wrapped any presents yet to do with heavy hearts and brought them with us.

CHRISTMAS 1956

We got as far as the corridor – and heard Christmas carols being sung – maybe around his tree. But before we got very far, Eileen hurried back to us after talking to the Sister to say Niall wasn't well enough. We took Sean back to the little hotel room, ordered up some tea for us all, and with the presents ignored on the floor, drank the tea and waited to hear when we could go and see Niall.

Sean's Notebook:

> No presents were given out when our cold Christmas came, except to Niall, who got his watch some days before, and wore it on his wrist to tick away the few stiff hours before he ceased to hear them. Christmas Day, & Lord God what a Christmas - tense, and waiting all the time. Tho' better on Christmas Eve, our boy wasn't too well on Christmas Day, and so we couldn't gather round the bed to give him his presents. Presents! They didn't mean anything to him now, stretched out, pale, under sentence of death – for he knew well what he had, and the danger he ran.
>
> Eileen kept with him, taking off his sweat-soaked pyjamas, damping and drying the hot dry body, and putting fresh pyjamas on him, waiting for the doctor – very kind and capable Dr. Haddon – to come, to give him the drug that might, and usually did – relax the tight-shut, painful throat: Eileen ready with milk & chicken essence, or beef essence; so that the boy could swallow the food within the short time his throat allowed him; he making successful efforts, encouraged by his mother's eager solicitudes, doing for her what he wouldn't do for others. Kindly, indomitable Eileen, the quiet mother battling for the life of her child; careless of her own health for his sake.

The little room at the Castle Hotel, in Exeter close around the Cathedral – listening to the bells toll the quarter, the half and the hour, we sat. None of us wanted to face the restaurant, so we ordered up some sandwiches and tea. All suppressing our worst fears and inner cries.

It was decided Breon should drive Sean and myself home, partly as Eileen didn't want to have to think about Sean and knew he would be better in his own room, what she called his home. So, we left Eileen to rest and sleep in her little bed.

We started home for Torquay in the slashing rain. It was difficult to see ahead as the rain was so heavy and the windscreen wipers weren't fast enough nor the lights strong enough for us to travel faster than 10 or 20 miles an hour. Sean sat in the backseat and I sat beside Breon to help him, to be on the lookout for fallen trees or other obstacles. Sean was nervous, and so were we.

I had hardly noticed the rain falling all that day. Sean said it was the most violent Christmas Day he remembered, the rain slashing down, the wind fierce and rowdy. As we drove on, the weather got worse and the roads were filling up with water. We splashed through pools, and when coming towards Newton Abbot we saw a car on the side of the road blinking his lights as a signal to stop. The driver asked how was it on to Exeter. Not too bad we said. "Well, it's damned bad in front of you," he said. "We've just managed to come thro' with water over the car's bonnet". We went on but soon found we were plunging into swirling water, rising as we went, with the wind rocking the car, and roaring so that we had to shout to hear one another giving opinions about the rough sea of ruffling waters facing us, as far as the eye could see. It was obviously too dangerous to risk the rising water and so finally we turned and ploughed back to Exeter, crawling down the hills, for the moving mud mixing with the waters made the road slippy.

Luckily there were rooms for us at Eileen's hotel and I think Eileen was glad to have us there with her. We all had dinner together and Sean said it was definitely good for Eileen, seeing that our presence, with the things we said about our perilous journey, kept her tense mind from continual remembrance of her poor boy sinking, sinking into sleep. She was returning to the hospital between 9 and 11 for a last look; and she came back tired, in body now as well as mind, and she too was soon sinking into sleep.

Sean's Notebook:
At two in the morning I, too, lay down, but didn't sink into sleep till after I had heard the Cathedral clock chime four of the clock. To think of all the fierce energy of the storm beating around the hospital as

Niall lay there – listening maybe to the strength of the storm and as his strength slowly left him.

The next morning on St. Stephen's day, the 26th, the roads were still impassable – we waited to hear Niall was a little better. But Eileen wanted Sean and I to go back home. She told me again she didn't want to worry about Sean as well and he would be better in his room at home. So Sean and I went together by train to Torquay, leaving the Christmas tree and the Cathedral almost without a glance. We sat opposite each other in an empty carriage and said little but looked at the large tracts of countryside flooded on either side of the train. Breon stayed behind with Eileen and he rang to say that the doctors had decided Niall should be transferred to Bart's Hospital the next day, the best in England for leukemia treatment. I was to stay behind and look after Sean and Breon would follow Eileen to London to help her. This was a shock for Sean and me as it meant we wouldn't be able to visit him, but it seemed the very best for Niall and that was what was important.

The next day while Eileen and Niall were travelling to London, Breon drove back the car and left it in the garage to do its share of waiting. Later that day he took a train to London to stay at the flat and be with Eileen.

Dr Doran and Dr Hadden had arranged for Niall's transfer to St Bartholomew's Hospital. Niall travelled up with Eileen by train. An ambulance took them to the Exeter Station and Eileen with Niall on a stretcher and a nurse were put into a compartment on their own. The nurse was a pretty one and excited about having an evening in London, Eileen said. Niall was cheerful and hopeful on the journey and Eileen said he took some orange she peeled for him.

I had often seen compartments with their blinds drawn, and seen between the gaps in the blinds nurses or a nurse with a person lying along the one side of the compartment, propped up with pillows and covered in red blankets. I had to stay behind to look after Sean though inside I was crying out to go to London to be near Niall, to be doing something to help him. It was so difficult to while away the heavy time, trying to function with some normality, to talk about other things to Sean, things that no longer interested me – or him. He listened to the news and tried to read but whenever I went into his room he was sitting in his armchair, the book open on his lap and one hand resting on it, looking forward or his head resting on his other hand.

NIALL'S LAST FIGHT 1956

Clare came in each day to cook or prepare things to cook. Sean thanked her and said we could manage but I asked her to come in each day to help a bit, to have someone else to talk to.

Breon was at his London flat and Eileen was staying at the Strand Palace Hotel, fairly near the hospital. It was where she and Sean had shared a single room when Eileen was very pregnant with me while they fought a court case against their Battersea landlord. Sean had slept on the floor and Eileen on the bed.

Sean's letter to Eileen:

30th December 1956

Mrs Eileen O'Casey

My darling,

Its hard to know what to say to you, things are so tense, but I do hope you are trying to take as much rest as you can; and eating as regularly as is possible. Breon has told me all you are doing for our poor Niall, and I can't say anything that would advise a lesser devotion. May God be with you, my dear and beloved lass.

Breon has said you would like to read a few of the reviews, or quotations from them, of 'Purple Dust', sent to me by Sally Biggs, so I enclose them with this note. I'd have written before, but I wasn't sure you'd settle down in the Strand Palace. Shivaun and I are going along fine; she doing the cooking; I getting the breakfast & washing up when Clare isn't here in the evenings. So don't worry about me. ...

The amount received from Braziller's $1430 is £512.18.2. – the American exchange came this morning, & I have entered the amount in to 'Accounts Book'. There is three more still to come. ...

Could I do anything to ease your burden, my darling? Could I go up & take your place with Niall for a day or so? It would give you a rest. Or, if not I, could Breon do this? I'd do anything, or try, anyway, for you my dearest girl.

Do you think I could write to Niall a note, or do you think I'd better not, for he has enough to do to think of himself, our dear lad. But give him my dear love, & say he is never absent from my mind. ...

God keep you, my own darling Eily.

As ever in deep love

Sean

A day of waiting. Eileen rings up to say Niall is getting all possible things done for him. That evening the consultant Dr Bodley-Scott had come to see Niall; Dr Doran had told him all about us, and Niall's bed was next to the Sister's desk, in a ward with very sick patients.[3] It was, Eileen said, light and the beds were curtained. The next morning Niall was brighter – and even able to go to the bathroom; he liked the doctor who was young and talked to him quite a lot about the possibility of getting better.

We were all hoping that he could live for a couple of years and that during that time a cure could be found. Sean said if only all the money spent on killing people could be put into research, how much further we would be towards solving many medical problems: killing instead the damned bugs and viruses that kill so many.`

NIALL'S DEATH

Eileen recalled (on pages 255–57) Niall's last hours in her book *Sean*: "The day before he died he felt much better. We were on our own. He had been through the heat-and-cold treatment and his bed was curtained off. Blankets were put over him when he was cold; when he was hot he was in a bath of sweat and had to be sponged down. All the time he had tubes attached to him that transfused pints of blood. The nurses were splendid; they got tea early for him that day because he loved it and it was wonderful to be able to swallow again. He asked me to bring him fruit in the evening. I went to the hotel where Breon was to have dinner with me, but felt too uneasy to wait for the meal; as soon as I could I dashed off. Though it seemed foolish to us as it was the first evening when we could have relaxed a little, some premonition drove me on. The fruit Niall wanted we bought at a stall in the Strand; I think Breon got the fruit for me. Then I jumped into a taxi and told the man to drive to Bart's as quickly as he could. I rushed up to the ward where Sister was surprised to see me back so soon. Niall was delighted; his throat was beginning to hurt and he seemed desperately anxious to taste the fruit. His nurse said though it was possible for him to eat it he must not swallow the pips from the grapes and must just suck the orange and swallow none of the pith. It was a breathlessly

[3] Sir Ronald Bodley Scott (1906–1982) as a young house physician showed an interest in haemotology and it became his specialty. After his service in the RAMC during the Second World War he was elected physician to St Bartholomew's in 1946 where he became an internationally known expert in leukaemia. He was successively physician to King George VI and Queen Elizabeth II. His book, *Cancer: The Facts*, was published in 1979.

quick task for me to skin the grapes and give them to Niall, also the orange and the peach. He had a savage desire to taste before his throat gave out; a savage desire to taste and live, to live – live – live. Suddenly he grew very quiet. Sensing danger, I asked Sister if I could telephone his brother as I really thought Niall was worse. 'No', she said, 'In the morning will be all right.' Then she looked at Niall and said, 'Yes. Telephone.' I did. Niall became delirious and excited. All the tubes were still attached to him. He looked strong and well; it was hard to hold him now when he wanted to get up and go places. He talked only in a gay mood. 'Let's go to America.' (he knew *Purple Dust* was on there.); or, 'Let's get the Hillman' – we had just bought this new car – 'and go anywhere.' He imagined Shivaun was with us and getting a meal; he talked about jazz, and talked and talked and talked. He tried to get out of bed, the nurse and I holding him in. Breon arrived and Niall seemed more relaxed, lurching no longer. Suddenly he regained consciousness. He knew he was going to die, and quietly and sadly said so. A nurse came and removed the tubes that were giving him blood. He received oxygen, and at intervals I was handed a mask to put over his mouth to help him breathe. I knew Breon was there, but in my mind now I see only Niall, Niall going from life. He said, 'Goodbye.' I did kiss him, and from a corner of his eye a tear was trickling, the one sign of sorrow that his fight for life was over, at the age of twenty one."

December 30. The phone rang and I went to answer it. It was Eileen who said she was so sorry but Niall had died last night: the shock froze everything in me with a terrible pain. Then Sean was by my side and I could tell as I handed him the phone he knew the very worst had happened to our Niall.

After clasping each other in despair we lay on Eileen's bed, entwined in grief, howling in the quiet of the morning. We lay distraught until we both realised we must pull ourselves together for each other. We brushed ourselves down like two lovers caught kissing and suppressed our crying gasps down low into our bellies – trying to lock our jaws. Getting a firm grip. Sean left his door open and I heard his typewriter starting its tap, tap, tappity tap. I started to tidy everything I could: wipe, sweep, order things; I even tidied Eileen's work-basket. I wanted everything to be perfect for her when she came home. Nothing for her to do. Every now and again gasps came from us. Then Clare our daily arrived, and I told her Niall had died; I couldn't hold all my tears back, but she asked if she should stay or go. "Can you stay for a while?" She did, she prepared some food for us to cook: peeled potatoes and veg. I felt I could never eat again and I am sure Dad felt the same. If we opened our mouths to eat surely we would howl. She made some strong tea and I took a cup to Sean and we sipped it together in silence. Silence was to fall over us a lot in the following days.

When I awoke the next morning, after an exhausted sleep, it hit me immediately that Niall had died. I thought that I should have died instead. He was something really special. He was not only very clever but also a young man with feeling and passion and with a wise person's solidity and reasoning. I was far behind him in intelligence and reasoning. But I also knew that Niall would want me to live as he would have lived if I had indeed died instead of him, that the twisting tormenting pain had to be endured, had to be quashed, so I could help as best as I could Eileen and Sean to survive their unimaginable loss. One of Shakespeare's songs I read when I was eight at school said "Golden girls and lads all must,/ like chimney sweepers, come to dust". But surely not at twenty-one!

Sean's Notebook:
Our dear, dear Niall died at nine o'clock on Saturday night. Eileen didn't ring up on Saturday night to tell Shivaun and me that he had gone away from us: that we had lost him; so that we might sleep quietly, unaware of our loss. He slept soundly God knows; slept more deeply than we had ever wanted him to do: a sleep from which he would never awake.

Breon and Eileen walked long into the night along the Embankment, beside the dark flowing Thames. At the hotel Eileen had a bath and resolved to go back to the hospital to see Niall, to look at him. "The Strand was fairly quiet; it was about seven in the morning, and the flower-shop at the corner was open. I went in, bought a large bunch of freesias, and took a taxi to the hospital where the Irish porter who knew me by now told me that my son was in the Chapel of Rest. I went in: Niall, laid in a coffin, looked very handsome and so young: his hair was thick and his hands looked so fine; he had just a slight mark on his forehead, like a big bruise. I laid my flowers beside his face; I was glad I had come, and drank in every moment of that last glance" (*Sean*, p. 257).

Oh, drink it in for me, too, mother, for I so long to see him to say goodbye. The cremation was to be in three days' time. The hospital authorities asked Eileen if they may have Niall's body for a day for research into the disease. Niall would have wanted this and so Eileen agreed. One day in the London flat we had been talking about death and burials and Niall had said emphatically that he wanted to be cremated –the thought of worms crawling about inside his skull repulsed him, so he and I both agreed we would be cremated.

Sean's Notebook:

December 31st

A day of struggle, typing to forget that Niall once lived. Oh, how can one forget. I try to work, writing letters, tearing up those I don't want to keep, tidying up the table. I work at looking at Television with Shivaun, (anything to distract and pass the time.), cooking prunes, getting breakfast, washing up, while Shivaun does the cooking (for we just have to eat, tho' little is food to our taste) and shopping, – but the relief is a dull bubble of distraction that soon vanishes, and Niall is the fullness of my mind again.

Sean and I watch the New Year's Eve celebrations on TV, mindless, senseless.

January 1st [1957]

Niall's body is cremated on Thursday. My poor dear Eileen. Breon good and stalwart companion is with her; close by her side. Shivaun and I remain at home in Villa Rosa, uneasy, trying to be natural, and bravely trying to hide how we feel; here we go about our life in Villa Rosa which first showed our boy out to death. Here I gave him my kiss, and in the Royal Devon and Exeter Hospital gave him the second kiss, the last till, maybe, if there be such a thing as second life I may give him the third kiss when I meet him after I, too, have gone the way of all flesh.[4]

January 3rd

Niall's body is cremated today at 2pm. It passes thro' the fiery furnace, and is utterly consumed. No miracle these days. Meshach, Shaadruch, and Abednego have ceased to live. I feel all this. Why Niall of all of us.

---

[4] Christopher Murray in *Sean O'Casey: Writer at Work* (pp. 380–381) has Sean and Shivaun travel to the Golders Green crematorium and meet with Eileen and Breon but Sean, recovering from his kidney operation, thought he would be a hindrance were he to go and Shivaun remained at home with him.

Why? My bitterest pain of remembrance is not of my loss, but of his. The loss of lovely life; just as he had entered the rich vigour and its youthful beauty. It must have been hard to suffer the thought that he would have to go; just when he had entered into its rich vigour and life's youthful beauty: Oh, it must have been agonising to have to think that he would have to go. Oh, my darling boy, so lithe, so jovial, so thoughtful, in the midst of them all, you knew you had to go away from them, away from life, and forever. My boy, my heart-loved boy. Death came to you like a god-damned thief in the day, when all was young and everything was bright, and your gay life was dancing.

He is now a handful of dust scattered over the Garden of Remembrance in Golders Green – the Tennyson & Shelley Rose Garden. Better if I had taken his place. Sean felt this most bitterly – "the young sapling gone and the old withering tree left". I felt it because Niall had so much to offer the world – I knew it and I know it – and that makes his loss even greater.

AFTERWARDS

Letters of condolence came, and we bravely looked at them – they were a distraction. Eileen got a letter from Ireland saying that he was "taken away" because she had lapsed from her faith! This so angered Eileen it anchored her dislike of the Catholic clergy forever. When she died she refused to see a priest, although we offered her one, and went bravely on her own merit to meet, maybe for a lightning second before darkness, her Niall.

Eileen and Breon came back home on January 4, 1957. At last I can hug her who had hugged Niall recently, who had held him as he died. – She could tell us all; even the pain of listening was a nearness to him. She said something shocking, that he had a massive haemorrhage – that blood even came from under his fingernails. With tears she told us how he looked – that he had asked for us – even thought we were there. This was never mentioned again and I began to think Eileen was dramatising his death. But now I think she was trying to protect me from this vision that Breon must have seen. Now we could all mourn together. Except our Breon who, in character, retired to his room as much as he could to work it all out on his own. Eileen and Breon are home again, but Niall is broken from us forever.

I looked up Acute Myeloid Leukaemia – complications. It said: if you have AML, you'll bleed and bruise more easily due to the low levels of platelets in your blood. Bleeding may also be excessive. People with advanced AML are more vulnerable to excessive bleeding inside their body, which is the second most common cause of death in people with the condition. Complications arising from infection, being immuno-compromised, are the leading cause of death. It seemed Niall had the first cause of death.

The only time I see his massive bleed mentioned, apart from Eileen's brief moment, was in a letter Sean wrote in Spring to his American friend, the literary scholar David Greene.

> 2 April 1957
>
> ... Niall died very swiftly. There are two kinds of Leucaemia, one chronic, the other acute. When he went to Barts Hosp. London, the doctors thought they could keep him with us for a few months, but, suddenly, after two days there, massive bleeding occurred (said to be rare, but it happens at times), and he died in an hour or two; but retained his fine physical form and his clear and penetrating mind up to a half hour before he died. It was just as well, for what would a few months have meant to him but constant pain, blood transfusions and a shrinking away of the handsome body. He still keeps very close to me, though I try to bury myself in work; but, without any conscious cause, memory of him sweeps over me, tears come, and I hear myself crying out his dear name. But life has to go on, and we have the fond knowledge that he had a happy and gleeful life, for all his serious thought about things, while he was with us.
>
> My love to the children, Catherine, and to you.
> As ever
> Sean [5]

Sean and I talked about Niall's trip down to see Sean to talk about Hungary and the bloody repression of its people.

Sean's Notebook:
Niall had been deeply distressed by the desolate confusion in Hungary, and couldn't understand the methods used by the Soviet Union in quelling the semi-popular, semi-fascist revolt. He had come down from

---

[5] *The Letters of Sean O'Casey, Volume III*, p. 408.

London to talk to me about (it), and we discussed the revolt, he from his angle, I from mine; but we could not agree. I was as gentle as I could be, for I have never been anxious that my opinion should be forced upon another. We went through the contest, went in, came out, went in again, till I got up from my deep armchair, and stepped over to the chair, austere and simple, where I sat when I wrote or typed, and where he sat now, facing me. I put my arms around his shoulders, pressed him warmly to my side, and told him we must cling to our own views of what has happened, which to him was a blunt and clumsy interference, and to me a sad necessity. I told him he must not be influenced by me; that his intelligence was, at least, equal to mine; and that we would not quarrel over the differences between our thoughts. Then I pressed him to me again, and bending down, kissed his bushy head of hair. How glad I am now that I didn't get testy as I sometimes do, God help me, when what is plain to me seems obscure to others. How glad I am, sadly happy, that I caressed him then, for within a few more days, my boy was dead. He had gone and left the distress of Hungary and all a long way behind him.

A letter of condolence arrived from Harold Macmillan:

10 Downing Street
Whitehall Jan 4th 1957

Dear Sean,

I have only just heard of your very sad loss & hasten to send our deepest sympathy. I remember so well Niall coming to stay with us years ago.
   Yours sincerely
   Harold Macmillan

And from the head of Botany at University College London

University College London, Gower Street WC1.
Department of Botany
Professor W.H. Pearsall D.Sc., F.R.S.
22nd January 1957

Dear Mr. O'Casey,

I feel I must seize an opportunity of writing to you to say how very sorry we, in the Botany department here, are to hear of your son's death. I think that you and your wife would at least like to know how highly I and my staff here thought of your son's work and character. He was genuinely liked and we hoped that he would continue to do well. Though in these circumstances all we can offer is our sympathy, I hope you will appreciate the fact that it is very sincere and shared by all members of the Department.

Yours sincerely
W H Pearsall[6]

And from Emmet Larkin, the young American scholar who was writing on James Larkin:

875 West End Avenue
New York, 25, N.Y.

January 9 1957

Dear Sean and Eileen,

Twice in Devon I enjoyed the hospitality of your house, and the warmth of a pleasant evening spent with you all. Dave Greene just told me the unhappy news, and it is with a heavy heart that I write my first letter to you.

I met Niall on both evenings I spent with you. We did not get a chance to talk much, Niall and I, that first visit in July of 1953. Still, I will long remember that wonderful walk in the inky darkness of the Totnes streets after midnight. We talked and laughed all the way back to my digs, and when we parted we shook strong hands in sincere silence.

Last summer I met Niall again. It was pleasant to see how he had developed in three years later. We had a wonderful dinner, and a most relaxing time afterwards in that luxurious hotel overlooking Torbay. Niall and I amused Dave by insisting on discussing socialism when the

---

[6] William Harold Pearsall FRS (1891–1964) was about to retire as Quain Professor of Botany at University College London. He was an expert in the ecology of aquatic vegetation.

whole setting called for anything but. As I remember, he, too, was concerned about the fate of British Socialism, the Labour Party, and the lack of enthusiasm among the younger people at the London School of Economics. When we parted again that evening at your house, I knew that your boy had the one quality, which over and above all others is most important – a genuine love and concern for his fellow man.

I thought of you all again this fall when I heard *Pictures in the Hallway* read here in New York. I was again reminded of Niall specifically a few days after Christmas when I visited a young cousin of mine whom I had not seen in several years. My young cousin turned out to be a jazz enthusiast, and I remembered Niall telling me about his passionate interest in jazz. Curious that chance should have placed your son in my mind when you were both, undoubtedly, going through so many trying moments. Your son was one of those people, and there have not been an abundance of them in my life, whose very being gave assurance. You meet someone, and you pass out of their life, but memory of such a man gives great pleasure. You feel that life is certainly richer because you are assured that in another little corner of the world there is now someone else whom you can depend on to fight the good fight.

Such a man was your son, and we are all the poorer for the loss of such a Goode Knighte.

With my deepest sympathy and love to you all
Emmet Larkin[7]

Sean wrote to Brooks Atkinson on February 21 and told him: "I am still full of thoughts about our Niall; he was so well-balanced, so fair-minded, so gay, and his was the shrewdest voice that used to advise on all our family problems. It has proved a deep wound, and one that will never heal, but we must still engage in the activities of life. ... We all, at least have a sorrow to share; it is the one great sacrament that unites all men together".[8] I have an undated scrap of paper on which Sean jotted down a tribute to his dead son: "We can laurel his memory only by going

---

[7] Emmet Larkin (1927–2012) later became Professor of history at the University of Chicago. His book, *James Larkin, Irish Labour Leader, 1876–1941*, appeared in 1965. The two Larkins were unrelated.

[8] *The Letters of Sean O'Casey: Volume III*, p. 396. The phrase "for fair-minded" in Krause must be an error.

forward ever as he did, by being brave as he was brave. Never halting till we fall to rest as he rests now."

Years later there came a letter from Trudi Black:

Dear Shivaun,

I found the Dartington day a powerful one. All too fleeting in many ways.

Here are some copies of the photos I mentioned. We look like neglected war evacuees! Also one of the Stomping Scholars with Niall on the trombone. I have been wanting to tell you that Niall and I started going out just before he died. We went on a trip together to Jill Lance's birthday at Dartington. He did not get in touch. I wondered why. Then I heard he was dying.

Lots of love
Trudi

Niall's death broke the family; we were adrift and unable to handle it: Sean wrote and wrote; Breon retired into himself – his studio, his room; Eileen kept going by busying herself with what had to be done but smothering her agony. I couldn't stop crying; when Eileen and Breon came home, tears started to pour out of my eyes and wouldn't stop. I tried very hard to be as stoic as Eileen. A few days after she came back I went down to Torquay with her – but when someone came over to say how sorry they were – I just cried. I noticed Eileen was upset and when her friend had gone she said, "Shivy, you must pull yourself together, it is not fair on me." I felt terrible, bereft, and the bosom I wanted to cry on was saying "It's not fair on me". This was the way she had chosen to face her searing loss – to lock in as much as she could, and I saw that it wasn't fair not to try and help her and do the same – or so I thought then. She couldn't bear hearing Sean's muffled crying from his room, maybe unaware that he was heard, so I went to him and asked him to try to stop – and by and large he did.

The first time I went into Breon and Niall's room was an experience of despair and longing for Niall just to be there. The smell of the room reminded me so much of Niall, Niall here and in the little flat in London where we had spent time together for nearly three months. Then I was bloody pleased that I had left school early, on an impulse, and gone to London.

NEXT YEAR WILL BE A GOOD ONE

Sean's Notebook:

January 22, 1949

Remembering Niall: The times I played Hurley with him outside the house of Tingrith, or cricket or football on the lawn: or clock-golf with him and Breon (later, sometimes me) on the lawns by the sea at Goodrington, near Paignton. Another time: Niall arrayed himself in a brilliant crimson football jersey, blue shorts and black stockings, barred with vivid red stripes, for a match at Dartington Hall's home ground. Solomon in all his glory wasn't arrayed like this young lad, minding me of the day when I donned a jersey of blue, barred with green hoops, white shorts and running shoes, to go forth to play my first fast hurling match, and to play well and to play fast for the honour of the club. Eileen had marched through many streets, and visited many shops, had searched high and low, before she had managed to pounce on the jersey and stockings that alone would fit our Niall for the fight in defence of his club and his school; then he was fourteen years old.

Sean wrote a threnody (with a nod to his beloved Shakespeare) -

UNDER A GREENWOOD TREE HE DIED

Never come in, never go out
Never sit at table,
Never lead us in a bright and reckless laugh.

Never go out again, walking together
Through a summer evening,
While it was yet light
Before the darkness came upon him.
A few brief moments in the garden of life,
Going where the primroses grow,
And then the night came and we lost him
In the midst of darkness.

    Walk, walk, walk my love,
    Walk with grace and softly move
    Walk thru that door and give me joy
    My own one, my soft spoken boy.[9]

NIALL'S LAST FIGHT 1956

Never come in, never go out,
Never come into my room again
To talk about a beetle or a bird.
His boy's way was the wind's way
And his young thoughts
Were long, long thoughts.

There is no voice in rain, wind, frost or snow
That says 'die' to a young heart.
Let the greenwood tree be bare and bony,
Or lush with leaf and blossom,
The young heart sings beneath it.

To go so young, and life so much within you
And around you.
Oh, where is the Lord's deliverance?
He delivered Daniel from the lion's den,
Jonah from the belly of the whale,
The Hebrew children from the fiery furnace,
But he never delivered you.

Death came to you like a damned thief
In the daytime
When all was young,
And everything was bright and brave,
And life was dancing.

> Walk, walk, walk my love,
> Walk with grace and softly move,
> Walk thru that door and give me joy,
> My own one, my soft-spoken boy.

---

9 Refrain is from a Gaelic song translated by Wolf Stephens. According to Des Geraghty (pers. comm. from Rosheen Callendèr to the author) and Jim McLean on the Mudcat Cafe website, Wolf Stephens was the pseudonym of the Irish singer and writer Dominic Behan (1928–1989, brother of Brendan). Behan first came across one of the songs he sang on his 1959 LP *Down by the Liffeyside*, "Easy and Slow", from a version Sean used in *Red Roses for Me*. See https://mudcat.org/thread.cfm?threadid=69447.

PART TWO

THE TREE SPLINTERS

Niall O'Casey.
PHOTOGRAPH: Gjon Mili

1
RADA and my prospects
1957

The Rain, it raineth every day!

TO RADA AND BACK

Life without Niall began. I was to start RADA on January 14, 1957 and went up to London a couple of days early with Eileen. Eileen stayed at a temperance hotel on Bloomsbury Square and I was back at Lady Hendy's. Eileen also had the hard job of going through Niall's things at the flat, now Anthony's alone.

Eileen had asked Charlotte Wanamaker to keep an eye on me; this led to an open invitation to go to the Wanamakers whenever I wanted, for a meal and comradeship. The Wanamaker's large flat on Regent's Park Road became my second home.

I could now drive. When Breon had tried to teach me I was so bad I drove him into a hedge. I was told I had to get a driving instructor. I did and passed my test on market day in Newton Abbot: that meant herds of nervous cows and sheep along the streets for me to navigate. To my surprise I passed first go even if I did nearly knock the inspector out on the emergency stop; the tests were easier then. Don Stewart and Ella Winter gave me their old maroon Citroen car, like the one in the movie *Rififi*. You could park almost anywhere in London, then.

Charlotte would greet me at the door of their flat in her all-encompassing white apron, with her lovely laugh and sparkling dark brown eyes. Zoe and Abby would come and take me to their room to show me what they were up to: ballet steps from Zoe, a load of school work from Abby. Glynis Johns who had owned the flat had completely mirrored the bathroom, walls and ceiling. You could see yourself vanishing into infinity left and right and see yourself from a bird's-eye view lying and looking at the ceiling: you couldn't avoid seeing yourself.

Sean was right, RADA was a lot worse than I had thought possible. I couldn't believe that you had to stand up when the teacher entered the classroom and say, for example, "Good morning Miss Carter", and she would answer, "Good morning. Please sit down". Well, one day I refused to stand up for Miss Carter and, I am afraid, I reduced her to tears. I was summoned to the office of the head, Mr John Fernald.[1] He was a charming

---

[1] John Fernald (1905–1985) was born in California but in his career was a British television playwright, London stage director, and actor. The year after Shivaun met him, he directed Ibsen's *Ghosts* at the Old Vic with Flora Robson and Michael Hordern in the principal roles.

man and admitted that this habit was archaic, especially for young adults, and he was attempting to reform it – that is, stop it. Would I please continue to do it till that time? I liked him so much I agreed and apologised to Miss Carter, who was a lovely old lady. Then the movement lessons were not too good: at one lesson we were told to "wave your arms in the air like branches of a tree. Now it's a gentle breeze, now it's getting stormy…", etc. Then we were told to get down on all fours and be cats. Having had enough of all this sweetness, I decided to be an alley cat and get into a fight. My activity was stopped and I was asked to comply and to make "cat-like movements, or leave the room". "That is what I was doing," I said. "Just do as I say".

But we had a wonderful teacher for historic dance, Medieval, Tudor, etc., called Litz Pisk. She was very knowledgeable and clever. In her classes you felt you had learned a great deal about the manners of the time as well as having a hard and complete work-out, sweating; and aching the next day.[2] Fencing was good, too, although I was quite hopeless at it.

We rehearsed a dreadful play by Enid Bagnold called *The Chalk Garden*. I had seen it with Eileen in the West End and we both thought it very poor, particularly the writing.[3] Then we approached Shakespeare – *A Midsummer Night's Dream*; in one of the scenes we presented I was cast as Helena. But enough of this, for many other things were happening with me outside the hours of drama school.

Our family rarely mentioned Niall although we all thought about him. Nearly every night I rang them up at Villa Rosa. It was usually Eileen who took the call after shouting "Sean, it's Shivy". We would talk for a while, then I could hear Sean in the background saying, "This is very expensive and you are talking a very long time. Let me have a word." Then I would be handed over to Sean and we would talk about plays I had read and what we were working on at RADA; he would ask what I thought of the books I had read and then we would discuss them and he would give his

---

[2] Litz Pisk (1909–1997) was born in Vienna and moved to Britain in 1933. Before leaving Vienna she directed the first production of Bertolt Brecht's *Rise and Fall of Mahagonny*. In Britain she taught actor movement at RADA and the Old Vic Theatre School. She worked with Vanessa Redgrave on the film *Isadora* (1968). In 1975 she published *The Actor and his Body*. See "Litz Pisk", Wikipedia; also: https://media.bloomsbury.com/rep/files/litz-pisk-background-and-selected-biography.pdf

[3] *The Chalk Garden* was however a great success when it premiered in Britain in 1956. Born in England and growing up in Jamaica, Bagnold was a novelist as well as playwright and published *National Velvet* in 1935.

opinion if I asked him for it. The plays we didn't like we would criticise and wonder what anyone saw in them. Eileen's voice was heard: "You told me to be brief and now you're talking far longer than I did. Let me say good-bye." Their phone bills were enormous, but they said it was worth it; it certainly was for me.

Most Sundays I went to Don and Ella's soirees, also dropping in on them at other times as I loved Don's dry American humour and Ella's exotic presence. Her "help" always rustled up some leftovers, often very left-over, to put on their lunch table. At that time Don's handsome son Don was with the beautiful Swedish actress Mai Zetterling, and I loved watching such a handsome couple who were so in love.[4]

In January 1957 a Northern Irish director called John Gibson, working for the BBC radio's Third Programme, was producing some plays by Sean.[5] The first was *The Plough and the Stars* with Liam Redmond and Sheila Manahan to be aired on February 24. At roughly the same time Samuel Beckett's *All That Fall* was being rehearsed for broadcast on January 13. Sam and John and his French wife were good friends. John asked me if I would like to sit in on some rehearsals and transmissions. It was then I became friendly with Jack MacGowran and Donal Donnelly.[6] I had met Jackie briefly before when he played Seamus Shields in *Shadow of a Gunman* at the Lyric Theatre, Notting Hill Gate. Jackie and Donal shared a flat and they asked me to tea there, at Hammersmith. Tea was about all you could ask for there, as it was a complete muddle, just like the room shared by Seamus Shields and Donal Davoren in *The Shadow of a Gunman*. They would have been the perfect casting at that time.

[4] Don (Duck) Stewart Jr became a writer and editor and was briefly Mai Zetterling's partner. He died in 1980. The Swedish actress Zetterling (1925–1994) had her career breakthrough when she acted in Ingmar Berman's 1944 film, *Torment*. She moved to England in the mid-1940s. She lived with Tyrone Power from 1956 to 1958 then married the English novelist David Hughes in 1958. Later in her career she became a movie director.

[5] John Gibson was born in 1925 in Kells, Co. Antrim, Northern Ireland. He was a BBC producer and director. In 1967 he directed four episodes of *Z Cars*. He died prematurely in 1974.

[6] The Irish actor Liam Redmond (1913–1989) appeared on stage at the Abbey Theatre and on Broadway. Among her other films, the Irish actress Sheila Manahan (1924–1988) was in *Only Two Can Play* (1962) with Mai Zetterling and Peter Sellers. The Irish actor Jack MacGowran (1918–1973), a sought-after film and stage actor, began his career at the Abbey Theatre and crowned it as a famous interpreter of Beckett's plays. Born in England of Irish parents, Donal Donnelly (1931–2010) graced stage and screen and became intimately associated with the plays of Brian Friel.

To make money Jackie and Donal were waiting table at a little Italian restaurant in Chelsea or Kensington and sometimes I used to meet up with them after work. One evening, when I called at the restaurant, Jackie and Donal said we would all go to the reception at Richard Harris's wedding. Where it was I can't remember but it was quite grand; the reception had been going on for hours, and Jackie, Donal and I sat down on the floor with some drinks. Richard Harris came over and hugged Jackie and Donal and joined the group on the floor, then his beautiful wife, Elizabeth Rees-Williams, in all her wedding glory, joined us.[7] I thought she was beautiful and exotic and well able for "Dicky". I had never been to a wedding before and wondered when the couple were going to go on their honeymoon; it was early morning.

In May 1957 John Gibson produced and directed *Red Roses for Me* with Donal playing Aymon, Jackie playing Rory, Richard Harris playing Mulcahy and Dermot McDowell playing the shy singer with a beautiful voice, Sammy. (*The Silver Tassie* was done in April, directed by Raymond Raikes.)[8]

A friend of Jackie and Donal's called Kate was given a job playing the piano at the Italian restaurant. It was very small and very popular, up some stairs on the first floor. Posh: tablecloths, large napkins and silverware. Good Italian food. They were all given a meal after the customers had gone and told me that I should come along and eat with them: "The owner would adore it", they said. He did. He was ebullient and also liked to relax with a glass of wine at the end of the day. Once he got going, Jackie drank till he was drunk. He was very funny when he was drunk so people loved it. He laughed as he argued in a fiery but not a malicious way. The evening usually ended with Jackie and Donal singing long into the night and Kate would jump up and accompany them. It was during this time I was taken by them to 22 Ladbroke Road, where they often went by taxi to sleep after

---

[7] Elizabeth Rees-Williams (1936–2022), described as a Welsh socialite, was married to the film actor Richard Harris (1957–1969) and later married Rex Harrison (1971–1975), Peter Aitken (1980–1985) and Jonathan Aitken (m. 2003).

[8] Dermot McDowell featured in television dramas, including the Irish series, *The Riordans* (RTE). Raymond Raikes (1910–1998) was a London-born theatre director, actor and broadcaster. After World War 2, having been an actor in repertory and West End productions, and several films, he joined the BBC drama department and directed the hugely popular *Dick Barton – Special Agent* (1946–1951) and classical drama for the Third Programme. See "Raymond Raikes", Wikipedia.

work rather than go all the way to Hammersmith. We were all welcomed by the two people who lived there, Dermot McDowell and Dee O'Connor. It was very late but no one seemed to be thinking of bed. Later when I sometimes stayed over instead of paying for a taxi, I found out beds were made for Jackie and Donal in Dermot's room. The women slept in the large windowless hall outside Dee's room, and a bed would be made for me there. Dee had a room of her own and slept by herself, waking early to go to work to keep Dermot and, it seemed, everyone else. She worked in Social Services on mental health. Dee had been married very young to someone she didn't get on with. They separated but the Pope wouldn't annul the marriage until she became "barren" which meant after menopause. She could buy an annulment but that cost a lot of money. So she was unable to marry Dermot. Dee was a practising Catholic so this also meant that they were unable to sleep together. This was more difficult for Dermot than Dee. He was a sweet gentle man but with a dramatic temper at times and he was shy of sex and didn't want to upset Dee. He was not fond of the church.

Theirs was a basement flat on a corner and rented by Dee. Dermot was an aspiring actor and opera singer, being not very good at either but with a heart as big as his huge barrel chest. Dee was little: no more than five foot four and Dermot stood six foot plus. He had a mane of hair, glasses, and a handsome face. She had a face that always smiled, with kind eyes and a small sensitive mouth. They loved each other.

It was here I met Dee's sister, Maureen Halligan. Maureen was an actress and although she was married to Ronald Ibbs she had kept her stage name.[9] She and Ronnie had been doing the Dublin Players' American tours for a few years, each one lasting for six months. Josie MacAvin was their producer; she booked the tours, sorted out the money, found accommodation and generally ran everything. There were no sets, just maybe a screen with a door in it or a window, but usually they played in "blacks"; that is, the drapes that belonged to the various theatres they played in. Josie was to become a lifelong friend and also a famous set

[9] Maureen Halligan, b.1914 died at 94 in 2008; she was a Dublin actress and casting director, responsible for *Judgment at Nuremberg* (1956). Ronald Ibbs (1915–1990) was an English film actor born in Middlesex. His most notable performance was in *Great Expectations* (1959). Halligan and Ibbs were members of the touring Dublin Players before moving to San Antonio, Texas in the early 1960s where they ran the theatre department of the University of the Incarnate Word. Halligan's obituary in the *San Antonio Express-News*, October 23, 2008, is available online.

decorator who won Ireland's first Oscar, in 1986 for the film *Out of Africa*.[10]

So, still attending RADA and living at Lady Hendy's, I was watching rehearsals for *The Plough* and John Gibson asked me to join them all at the George pub in Portland Street for a drink. Louis MacNeice the poet was sitting in a corner with a group of BBC people, and when he learnt who I was he started in on Sean.[11] I was told by Donal to ignore him, which I did, but I thought he was very rude. Sam Beckett was there and John came over and asked if I would like to join him and some others for dinner at his home. I agreed instantly partly because I was very hungry. So off I went with John and Sam, Donal and Jackie – off to Chiswick on the tube. When John beckoned us all into his home to meet his wife, Aimee, she was not pleased at all. It turned out that she was expecting four to turn up, John, Sam and Sam's publisher John Calder and his lady friend who had driven there. I think the rest of us murmured that we would leave but John wouldn't hear of it and insisted we stay. Drinks were poured, and the drinks brought from the pub were added to them. The talk was subdued and rather literary. Aimee came in and asked for someone to bath her little girl: the little girl was asked who she would like to do this and she chose me. I was delighted, pleased to get away from the uneasy talk and also to feel useful. We had a grand bath time; dried and dressed ready for bed, up she went as good as gold: Aimee settled her in.

I noticed Beckett looking at me in a quizzical way, most likely wondering what I was like under my very shy mask that had enclosed me among this company. Finally dinner was served, and down we sat around an oval mahogany table, traditionally set with silver and plate on a white lace tablecloth. My God, I was hungry. Aimee brought in an exquisitely cooked whole fish and a few vegetables. And although the fish was large it was not large enough for the eight people around the repast. Aimee had cooked for five only. No bread and butter to fill up on. I said how lovely it looked but that I wasn't very hungry. I was given the same as everyone else – a tiny bit of fish and then came the veg. I tried not to gobble it all in one mouthful.

[10] As well as winning an Oscar, Josie MacAvin (1919–2005), who began her theatrical career as a ballerina, had been nominated in 1964 and 1966 and won an Emmy Award in 1995 for *Scarlett* (1994).

[11] Louis MacNeice had reviewed *Rose and Crown* (1952) critically in the London *Observer* and Sean replied in his last volume of autobiography, *Sunset and Evening Star*; see *Autobiographies II* (London: Macmillan, 1963), p. 635.

Time to leave came. We had missed the public transport. Calder had a car and could take three people at a squeeze, apart from himself and his friend; I would have to take a cab. I didn't have enough money for that but didn't say anything. Maybe Sam noticed my hidden despair as he asked me where I lived. "I can share a cab with you, that is my direction". On our journey in the taxi we chatted away as if we had known each other for years. He asked about Sean. I told him how we were all knocked backwards after Niall's death, which was still very raw. Somehow Sam's work came up; he surely didn't ask me what I thought of it, but I remember saying how I liked his work but how I wished he could be less bleak, be more hopeful. "I wish I could. But I can't." He went on to describe a play he was thinking about that would be one person on stage, how he wanted to simplify his work more. On a later meeting he told me of his idea of just having a mouth on stage. I wondered if it maybe rather too small to see and suggested magnifying it somehow. He said I should come to Paris and he would write a play for me. This made me very embarrassed as I thought I was not nearly good enough to be in a play by him, for that is what he implied. "Oh, I'm not good enough to be in a play of yours." "I would like to show you Paris". That was twice I had been offered Paris: first by Tom Curtiss who said he would pay for me if I went to the Sorbonne, and now this offer from Sam. Both came to nothing, the first because I didn't want to "study" at a university, the second because I couldn't possibly afford to go to Paris then. Sam did mean it, though. When we got to Abercorn Place he took my hand and squeezed it saying how glad he was to meet me. I said I really loved meeting him. I offered to pay some of the fare but he brushed it aside with a goodbye, a clasp of my hand and a kiss on my hand and off he went into the night.

The next morning, March 19, I was late for RADA; I hadn't set my alarm clock. My head and dreams were full of this very gentle, clever man who had offered to write a play for me. This never happened, again. With a jolt I remembered it was the day we were to perform our scenes from *A Midsummer Night's Dream* to the staff. In a panic I rushed out and ran down the escalator to the tube. At RADA I dashed to the changing room where I pulled on my "long skirt" over my clothes and ran to the studio room. I looked through the glass porthole in the wooden door to see the class favourite walking on for me. A disaster. It was then I decided to leave. Was it to save face? I left RADA on March 29, 1957 after 11 weeks. Josie MacAvin had hinted that I could be an acting assistant stage manager on the next U.S. tour of the Dublin Players, starting in September. I didn't feel good. Gone was the exhilaration of having a play written for me.

The next day I braced myself and went to John Fernald's office; I think I was actually summoned. He was charming. I apologised for being so late and then said I would like to leave and could I mention a list of complaints – having to stand up when a teacher came in, the lame movement lessons, lack of in-depth instruction on how to approach a text, and the lack of a good library with many books and theatre magazines. He listened intently and took my list and then asked if I would reconsider leaving. I said I had to leave. And so that was another one-term at a college behind me. Whenever I met John Fernald and his charming daughter at the theatre he always said "hello" and I was always glad to see him.

WEST LONDON AND THE DUBLIN PLAYERS

After letting poor Sean and Eileen know of my rash decision, I moved out of Lady Hendy's. I went home to talk things over and convince them that I was old and wise enough to go on the tour of America. They were worried, mainly thinking I was rash and hasty due to the loss of Niall, that I couldn't settle or concentrate. Eileen went to London to meet Josie who assured Eileen she would take care of me and look after me during the tour: and she did. The only thing that worried me was that Sean and Eileen would be alone during Christmas and the sad anniversary of Niall's death. I knew I was better than Breon at being there for them.

When I came to London again I rented a small room in Notting Hill, in the same house as Kate O'Connor, with a shared loo and a shared butler's sink on the landing with cold water. No hot water and no bath. We were near to 22 Ladbroke Road and so bathed now and again there. We also ate there a lot. I accepted the job of assistant stage manager (ASM) with Sean and Eileen's approval. Eileen's letter to me:

My dearest Shivy,

I will be in London on Thursday. Please can you book me a room at the Rembrandt, or try Browns, then leave it if they have nowhere & I'll find one when I arrive.

I am on edge to see you & talk about this tour. You could only go playing parts, as it would be likely very poor production etc, they go to very out of way towns, like the companies who used to visit Totnes – so if you decide to go and not try here first, please be sure you play parts, then you get some experience, the harder the part the better in some ways, the girl in Juno is not difficult. I can't really write as I am muddled in my thoughts, and only begin to think of the snags & also we would be better talking. I hope you are eating your meals.

Love Eileen

Josie asked if I could go to Dublin with her to start collecting props, etc. Luckily JJ O'Leary – the kind gentleman who had looked after Eileen and me so well during *The Bishop's Bonfire,* offered to put me up. I went over by train to Holyhead and then by sea to Dun Laoghaire, just down the road from his house in Seaview Avenue. JJ lived just around the corner from Josie and knew her and her family well. I had a small pretty room at the back of the house. JJ didn't believe in heating, except in his very nice sitting-room on the first floor, with a three-corner window looking over the harbour and his precious sailing-boat, or should I say "yacht".

JJ was a great friend of Barry Fitzgerald, Sean's old friend from the Abbey. Now a Hollywood star, Barry stayed with JJ whenever he was in Dublin. He had left a week before, after filming a bit for the film *Rooney.*[12] I hope his room was heated. Jackie was still in town for the film, about a sportsman by night and a dustman by day. John Gregson was the lead, he of *Whisky Galore* and *Genevieve.* I thought him very dishy – but he was happily married and wasn't anyway interested in me. Josie looked after me and took me to see Jackie, often ending up in a pub on a corner right opposite the Gate Theatre in Parnell Square. It pulled down its blinds after closing time but served drinks all night – to special customers: lawyers, politicians, and police officers as well as actors and artists. Now and again it would be raided; a phone warning would come and everyone was told to hide under the tables: the Gardai would look in and leave, presumably with eyes wide shut.

Donal had come to Dublin to see Kate Binchy at the Pike Theatre, playing the young girl in Tennessee Williams's play, *The Rose Tattoo,* with Anna Manahan as the lead.[13] The Pike was in a mews garage converted to

[12] *Rooney* (1958) is a British comedy set in Dublin and adapted from a Catherine Cookson novel. Fitzgerald starred alongside John Gregson and Muriel Pavlow, while Liam Redmond and Jack MacGowran featured.
[13] Kate Binchy (b. 1937, Dublin) appeared in the films *The Lonely Passion of Judith Hearne* (1987) and *Poirot* (1989). Anna Manahan (1924–2009) received an Olivier Award nomination in 1977 for her performance in *The Plough and the Stars.* In 1998 she won a Tony Award for her performance in *The Beauty Queen of Leenane* by Martin McDonagh.

a tiny theatre, run by Alan Simpson and Carolyn Swift. *The Rose Tattoo* was their production for the Dublin Theatre Festival in 1957. We heard that the police were at the theatre, arresting Alan Simpson and closing the theatre. A whole lot of us ran there to see Alan disappearing amid a bevy of Gardai and great excitement and shouting from the crowd that had gathered. Why had this happened? The play had won in 1951 the Tony Award in America for Best Play, and the film version had won a number of Academy Awards. Well, it confirmed what I knew – how backward Ireland was at that time towards life and the arts. In this case, word had got out that John Charles McQuaid, the Catholic Archbishop of Dublin and Primate of Ireland, wanted a firmer control of the arts; that is, nothing that he deemed un-Catholic was to be even hinted at. During the play a condom is dropped on the floor – in the Dublin production an envelope was dropped on the floor that slightly confused me; it was said a condom wasn't used because one couldn't be found in Dublin but I can't believe that.

I went to the play the next night amid the excitement, and liked it a lot. The Company was raw and passionate which suited the play: in such a small space it was potent. Carolyn asked me up to their flat afterwards for tea or a drink. It was a rather grand flat and tea was upstairs in the bedroom and we sat on their enormous bed. I think Carolyn, exhausted, was in bed. I believe Alan was still in custody.[14] There was a strange unsettling atmosphere that made me want to leave, and so I did as soon as I could politely do so. They had asked if Sean would sign a letter of support and protest. I was sure he would and rang him the next day and of course he agreed. Sean contributed to The Rose Tattoo Fund in Simpson's defence and told Brooks Atkinson in a letter how "Just a week

---

[14] Alan Simpson (1921–1980), a Protestant, was born in Dublin and like Beckett was educated in Northern Ireland. With his wife Carolyn Swift he founded the Pike Theatre. He staged the first Irish production of Beckett's *Waiting for Godot* in 1955. The legal proceedings following his arrest took a terrific toll on Simpson financially and personally; he and his wife divorced and later he moved to the United States: "Alan Simpson", Wikipedia and *Dictionary of Ulster Biography* (online). The case was in the courts for 13 months before Simpson was acquitted. After the Pike Theatre closed in 1960, Carolyn Swift (born Carol Samuel in London in 1923) worked as a script editor for Radio-Telefis Eireann and ballet critic for the *Sunday Independent*; she wrote a memoir and eighteen books for children. Two days before she died in 2002, Michael D. Higgins TD (later President) urged a State apology to Swift for her treatment during the *Rose Tattoo* affair. See Roisin Ingle and Sorcha Crowley, obituary of Swift in the *Irish Times*, November 18, 2002 and Gerard Whelan, "Swift, Carolyn" in the *Dictionary of Irish Biography*.

before, I had a letter in THE IRISH TIMES replying to a Catholic teacher in a Cavan College, who had lectured about the Catholic writer and Censorship; a letter that is provoking yelping letters in the same paper. It is all very comic, but it has a dangerous effct on potential Irish writers, and we have neither a Shaw nor a Yeats in Ireland now".[15]

Sean thrived on the comedy he saw in these shocking cases of Catholic control over Ireland: he uses scenes in his plays that are created from this, but he also sees the danger and that it can produce tragic outcomes. Sean had to put up with this Catholic and conservative backlash throughout his writing career; his books were banned not only by the Censorship Board but more subversively by Customs not letting them through.

The Rose Tattoo was going to the Lyric Theatre, Belfast. I followed with Donal, who was following Kate Binchy. The *Tattoo* cast travelled on the Great Northern Railway on which Sean had worked as a navvy: Red Jack they called him then. My first time in Belfast wasn't good; it was raining and the city appeared dull and industrial. It also became very obvious that I was in Donal's way and not really appreciated there. So I didn't stay long. I also needed to get back to London and then down home, to spend time with Sean before I went off to his favourite city, New York. I did visit Mary O'Malley at her large home and was amazed to see a little theatre rigged up for her children (and maybe some young students) in her living room.[16]

Back in Dublin I said good-bye to JJ and Mrs MacAvin who had been so warm and welcoming to me. Then over the choppy waters to London for a while, to pack up my things and go home to get ready before leaving for the States.

Although Josie was sure I was going on the tour, I hadn't had a squeak out of Ronald Ibbs or indeed his wife Maureen. Then, maybe having been prompted by Josie, a letter arrived that was my form of contract.

12th July 1957
22 Ladbroke Gardens
London W11

---

[15] *The Letters of Sean O'Casey*, Volume III, pp. 435–436.
[16] Mary O'Malley (1918–2006) from Cork founded the Lyric Theatre with her husband Pearse. When Shivaun visited Belfast the theatre was in converted stables behind the O'Malleys' large house in south Belfast. N.B.: Condoms were freely available in Northern Ireland since the powerful Roman Catholic church did not hold state-wide sway as it did in the Republic.

Dear Shivaun,

I have just received confirmation from New York that the Tour is definitely booked.

Rehearsals will commence in London on Sept 1st, the Company travelling to Dublin Sept 23rd Approx for further rehearsals.

Reservations have been made on the "America" – cabin class, sailing from Cobh on Oct 2nd arriving NY Oct 8th.

The tour will end sometime in March 1958.

I can offer you ninety dollars per week for the tour, with £7 per week for rehearsal time.

There may be two non-playing weeks during the tour, for which you are offered sixty-five dollars per week, assuming there be no playing or rehearsing during that time.

In addition to ASM and/or Wardrobe duties, I hope there will be at least one part that we can find for you. As Maureen will be producing 'Shadow and Substance', she can run over Thomasina with you when you return to London.[17]

I hope you will have a very happy tour with us.
Very best wishes
Ronnie Ibbs

As far as I recall, the odd rehearsals we had were all in Dublin. I say odd as there was no sitting round a table to work out the meaning of the play, the intentions of the actors, or the build to any climaxes.

THE PROMISED LAND

I had some time to spend in the splendour of my safe and loving home. Sean wrote to his close friends who were to watch over me: Brooks and Oriana Atkinson; not George Nathan as he was too ill but I would go to bear him Sean's deep love and gratitude; Bob Ginna; to a lesser degree Bob Graff: Kathy Fannon, who had stayed with us and fallen for our Breon; Lucille Lortel, the rich friend who unbeknownst to me also helped the Dublin Players; Eugene O'Neill had died but I would see his wife Carlotta.[18]

---

[17] *Shadow and Substance* by Paul Vincent Carroll was written in 1937 and won the New York Drama Critics' Award the following year. Thomasina Concano is one of the cast of characters.

[18] Lucille Lortel, who died at 98 in 1999, was an American actress and director, founder of the White Barn Theatre in Connecticut. She produced or co-produced almost 500 plays in her career, some off-Broadway.

All the Company was to gather in Dublin for rehearsals and a few run-throughs. Eileen came over to Dublin for a week to stay with me at JJ's. I had packed what Eileen and I thought I would need for the six months in the one allotted case. Eileen had lent me one of her warm overcoats, a thick and well-cut one from Aquascutum. I didn't have a posh dress for receptions so Sean and Eileen arranged for money to be released to me from his American agent, Jane Rubin, and she would take me to buy one and some simple shoes.

October 2 came: the day of departure. Eileen and I joined Josie in a cab from Monkstown to Dublin's Heuston station. We were going by a hired coach in which all the baggage and the company fitted. There was a great fluster as all the company's luggage got stowed away. Finally it was time to go; I hugged Eileen for a long time before clambering on board, gathering all I could of her to bring along with me. The Company was all seated, waving goodbye to family and friends and off we went to the boat waiting for us at Cobh.

Here was Cobh, a very pretty town beside Cork City, holding hands so to speak. The bus pulled into The White Star Line Wharf where you waited to board one of the two tenders that took you to the huge liner out in the bay. Millions had done this before and many never came home to their native land again, but on my mind was that Sean had done this and that Eileen had also sailed to America. The SS *America* of the Cunard Line was vast even in the distance and as we approached it became a sheer towering wall of black painted metal. Gangplanks appeared from the side of the boat for us to clamber up. It was a lovely autumn day and the sea looked calm, the air was clear and crisp and familiar seagulls were circling; they reminded me of Sean at home and Breon in St. Ives.

Before I left JJ's I got a letter from Sean, the first of many he was to send me on the tour; most I still have but I lost some in my wanderings and gave one away to an Armenian friend of Bob Ginna's and Gjon Mili's who had a restaurant and loved Sean.

26 Sept 1957
Miss Shivaun O'Casey

My very dear Shivaun,

A Happy Birthday to you: and a happy and successful tour thro' the U.S.A. to you, & to all your friends. We shall miss you very much, and it will be a lonely Christmas. Never mind! It is a grand, or should be, experience for you; & a rare chance to see a great and a wonderful land: much more to me than all the Parthenons and Colosseums of Greece and of Rome: or the immemorial Castles and Cathedrals of Medieval Europe.

The one danger you may have to guard against there – human danger, that is – is the desperate & untiring generosity of Americans. From my experience, they were the most kind and good-natured of mortals.

God bless you & your friends throughout your journey.

With love of my heart Sean

Once at the top of the steps the size of the liner hit even harder. There were so many crew members hurrying us on to find our cabins. I was sharing with the youngest actress, a relative, if I remember right, of Paul Vincent Carroll, the author of *Shadow and Substance*. Not his youngest actress daughter, Helena Carroll, now living in the States. This was a large-faced, rather dull girl who didn't talk or laugh much. She had been given the part of Thomasina, the part I was "looked at" for. The great part I had landed was the Sewing Machine Man in *Juno and the Paycock*: two lines delivered almost off-stage: "You don't happen to want a sewing machine?" Boyle replies in the negative; I reply, "God help you". I wasn't too pleased about this but I was keen to tour the States. Our cabin was clean and small with a porthole that didn't open. We had two little beds, not bunk-beds, and a small sink. I had the 'flu that lasted for two days, but I left my cabin and went on a walk-around.

We had six days on board and once the 'flu had gone I loved it. Nothing but blue sea forever. Dolphins following, and flying fish – amazing, using their fins as wings to keep them up, and the dolphins looking so happy and jumping so high – looping gracefully along.

It was a great rest with nothing to do but walk the deck, sit wrapped up on the deck, and eat breakfast, lunch and dinner. I didn't drink so the bars were somewhere I never went. Here on the boat I got to know better the members of the group. I knew Josie well and Maureen a little. Ronnie Ibbs and Maureen were married and the head of the whole shebang but Josie was really in control of everything, apart from directing the plays. Ronnie was involved in himself and Maureen pretended to be airy-fairy and theatrical but I think she was crafty enough really. The plays they were touring were *Arms and the Man* by GBS, *Shadow and Substance* and *Juno and the Paycock.* At the start, I have to say, they were a mix of talents, although all technically professional – that is, members of Equity. Ronnie was an old hand who had played Hamlet at the Gate Theatre Dublin with Maureen as Ophelia. A smooth actor who could have been a lot better if he had demanded more of himself. Maureen another out-front actor, slick and again falling into clichés. Lollie May who was playing Juno was the best of the group, who had a talent and worked on the character honestly and with a serious vigour: she had given up theatre for a steady income and a 9 to 5 job and had been given a six-month leave of absence to do what she loved most in the world – act. Her Captain Boyle was a terrible actor called John Kelly, an old Irish ham: all surface and getting all the cheap laughs he could muster. The Joxer, Eddie Byrne, tried. Other actors on the tour were mediocre, to be kind, except for a young energetic actor, Maurice Good who kept apart and on the tour made friends with the bus driver, Ernie. Aileen Harte and Grania O'Shannon were good, not great, but what could they do among so many who didn't cut the mustard? The productions were for easy popular success for mainly Irish-American audiences. And Dermot McDowell was there, my old friend from 22 Ladbroke Grove. He was a godsend, not a good actor but full of joie de vivre who with the help of Maurice, cut through any bitchiness that rose up and down like the ripples on the sea I was looking at. But my God he did have a temper when roused: and I couldn't blame him. So, I had the company of Josie and Dermot and soon became friendly with Lollie May (although she liked to keep herself to herself and dine with Eddie Byrne). Grania and Aileen were a part of the Josie group.[19]

---

[19] Lollie May at the outset of her career had an uncredited part in the movie, *The History of Mr Polly* (1949), starring John Mills; she later played Lady Johnson-Marshall in the BBC TV eco-drama series, *The Country Boy* (1989). John Kelly (1904–1977) appeared in the British film, *Someone at the Door* (1950) and in two episodes of the 1963 BBC TV series, *No Cloak - No Dagger*. Eddie Byrne had worked with Barry Fitzgerald in *Rooney*; he was a character actor in great demand and appeared in four other films released in 1958. Maurice Good, born in Dublin in 1932, appeared in *Quatermass and the Pit* (1967) and other films; his TV appearances included *Z Cars*, *Coronation Street* and *The Avengers*; he emigrated to Newfoundland, Canada where he taught and acted, and died in 2013. Aileen Harte was a stage actress, drama teacher, then television actress; she played in the RTE serial *Tolka Row*, 1964-68. Grania O'Shannon, who died in Dublin in 2010, became an assistant director in major films between 1960 and 1970.

THE GREAT STORM AND NEW YORK EMERGES

One morning I awoke by being tossed from side to side. Water covered our porthole, and the girl whose name I have forgotten was green and moaning. Stewards were running up and down the corridors knocking on doors and telling us NOT to go on deck and to move about carefully, holding on. I felt fine, dressed and started out to breakfast, holding on to the bars along the corridors and up the stairs. The restaurant was empty; I put it down to being too early or too late. All the tables had metal fences around their edges and the chairs were battened down. Eventually a waiter arrived to say there was nothing cooked as most of the staff and crew were sea-sick, but he could make me some tea and toast.

It was getting really rough now – like trying to eat on a see-saw. I put very little tea in the cup and watched all the plates and cups move from side to side on the few tables that were laid. I was the only person there at that moment, and two waiters. Very excited, I asked if I could see the storm. The steward came back to say that if I followed him he would take me to a room under the captain's bridge where a few people would be looking at the waves. We went along a corridor with windows looking on to the deck; when swirling water broke over the deck, it was as if the ship were sinking, and when the boat heaved itself up, the angry water would gush out through the gunnels. I hung on for dear life to all the rails along the walls and around the side of the viewing platform, a space under the bridge with extremely thick glass reaching as one enormous piece across the front of the observation room. As I saw a mountain of water in front of me, I held my breath in amazement; this would surely sink us. I saw and felt us climbing up the side of the mountain and hovering for a moment at the summit. I looked down into a chasm before we crashed through and down. Had we sunk? Then I felt the ship heaving up beneath me, ready to face another mountain of solid water. It was far too extraordinary for me to be frightened, the strength of the water and the wind was so vast and strong: this big liner was as if a speck in all this angry sea surging forward to find the coast miles away to crash against its rocks. Luckily she was strong and well-built. In a day the storm had passed; I was told we had ridden out the storm instead of going the long way around it. So I could tell Sean that I went through a storm on the way to the States just as he had done in 1936. Later that next day the sun came out.

The waves had been 60 footers I was told by the captain and it had slowed us down so we may have added a day to our journey. Actually, the SS *America* made up some time after the storm and we lost only about half a day. She did this by not using her stabilisers so a few people continued to feel queasy, though luckily not me.

I awoke early to a lot of hustle and bustle. I grabbed my coat and climbed up to the fore-deck. The sun was rising on a clear New York day. People had started to gather. We could see land and soon were between Staten Island and the top of Long Island on my right. Suddenly the land each side gave way to an expanse of water with the Statue of Liberty lit by the morning sun. There below her was Ellis Island, where people had been processed not so very long ago. And then I saw the miniature New York skyline: the old skyline with the tallest building still the Empire State Building; and from that cathedral-like top, falling away from it, were other spires and strangely shaped tops of buildings, sticking up like geological statues. And there was the Chrysler building shining its metal roofed light into the morning. I thought of our Niall and how excited he would be here; again I wished I had died instead of him. I did know that was stupid and that he would want me alive just as much as he would want his own life back.

I felt very excited. We had gone through a fierce storm and were safe. As this large creature of a ship gracefully steamed along into the Hudson River, the buildings grew bigger and bigger. The SS *America* had its own pier waiting for her – the United States Line pier. Crowds of people, looking very small, were waiting and waving. I ran down to get my suitcase. It was October 8, 1957.

The crowds flowed and shoved towards the gang-planks, and the sailors made them stand back in an orderly manner. I felt as if I was in a Hollywood movie – the hilarity, the tears, the hugs. I waited with Grania and Aileen and slowly the group gathered among the swirling bodies. Cabs had to be got for us all. I stuck with Josie and when everyone else was cabbed and on their way, I literally fell into one of the large Yellow Cabs with her and a lot of luggage. The cab drivers were all local. "Where you from ladies?" "Dublin", Josie said. "What are you doing over here?" "We will be touring America with some Irish plays." "You don't say!"

The hotel wasn't very far away. It was full of cowboys and cowgirls in all their very best finery. The only thing they didn't have with them in the hotel were their horses. Wowee! Here was the America of my youth in front of my eyes, when we had all watched so many cowboy films. "Oh", said Josie, "This is nothing; last time the Circus was in town and there was an elephant in the lobby". That didn't diminish my delight of sharing the hotel with the frontier of America, mainly cowboys and cowgirls in their gallon hats, tasselled shirts and jackets, Texan boots, spurs, chaps, and lassos.

Waiting for me were messages from Bob Ginna and Kathy Fannon wanting to see me. I also had letters from Eileen. Josie wrote to Eileen soon after to reassure her. Later that morning I was in a Yellow Cab with Kathy and Bob on the way to NBC's offices in Rockefeller Center. Josie was very busy from the moment she hit land, organising things for the tour; she gave me the week off. All the others vanished about their own business.

Kathy Fannon had come to visit us in Devon, after Bob Ginna and Gjon Mili's visit but after we had moved to St. Marychurch. She stayed with us for a long time and had a "grah" for Breon (the Irish for crush). Breon didn't feel the same but we all liked Kathy a lot. We went up in the lift many floors to her office overlooking the Plaza way below, with the skaters looking minuscule against the white ice. She rang up Sean and Eileen on her office phone. This was untold extravagance as international calls cost the earth then. We spoke; that is, I spoke, Kathy spoke and Bob spoke a little but mainly me, for over an hour. We could have spoken for longer but Eileen and Sean thought that even this length of time would be difficult for Kathy to explain, if she ever had to. I was full of thoughts of Niall, who had longed to come to the USA, to Chicago and New Orleans, to immerse himself in their traditional jazz. I imagined him here with me, taking me to all the jazz clubs he could find; I was far too timid to go to the jazz clubs on my own. I suggested once to Bob that I would like to go but it must have slipped by him. So slowly Niall also slipped away, left this life he never had a chance to live and I went on to live my life. Luckily, I was kept busy by all Sean and Eileen's old friends – and also later my duties as an ASM and a very bit actor for the Dublin Players.

That evening I met up with Bob. He came to the hotel lobby with his pipe, in his red, checked with green peak cap, his broad grin, and his chuckle. His fiancée Margaret was with him, very pretty and bright and funny. He took us up-town to a restaurant renowned for its fish. After checking with us Bob ordered the restaurant special, lobsters. I heard a knocking on the floor and looked down to see many lobsters walking towards us: "You have to choose your lobster, Shivy." "Oh my god, I can't do that – it's like, you know, the one that is going to be killed." I was a coward and said, "Please choose any one". I was glad when they took them away and tried to forget the sight of the poor things. Drinks were ordered and a splendid meal was taken in a warm, shining restaurant – mirrors glistening and wooden tables polished like glass. We all bundled into a cab and they dropped me off at the hotel. I slept as soon as I lay down.

The next day I was to meet Sean's agent Jane Rubin who had been instructed to take me shopping for shoes and a dress that I could wear to receptions, etc. I was told to get a cab to Saks Fifth Avenue, where she would meet me. She was a rather dumpy dull lady in a pale brown mink coat and matching hat. She took me to the women's fashion floor where I found a pencil-skirted dress with a box-pleated back that slightly billowed out. It was a heavy black silk with a soft silk lining. Thinking of it now, it was rather grown up for me at 17. There wasn't any fashion for young people then – that came later in the Sixties – except the prom skirts and white socks that I thought were horrible. We bought a pair of black leather court shoes with a two-inch heels. So with Eileen's lovely wool coat I was all set. I soon bought a pair of galoshes; it had started to snow.

At a distance from home I was beginning to understand what I needed immediately after Niall died: I had needed to talk it through. Breon and Niall were very different in character: Breon was the opposite of the outgoing Niall; he wanted to be solitary much of the time, appearing for meals and only when needed by Eileen or Sean. He was a quiet helper. After Niall died I was alone with Sean at first but we both foolishly tried to be brave to protect each other. When Eileen came home I had her, until she told me that I must pull myself together as it wasn't fair on her to cry so much. This meant I felt I couldn't speak to them about how desperately unhappy I was as it would undoubtedly upset their own sorrow in some way. Breon had made it clear that we wouldn't talk about Niall, that Niall was not to be sentimentalised; he hated Sean's outpouring of grief in his laments written about Niall; he wanted this to be private.

LUCILLE LORTEL AND PAUL SHYRE

I met Lucille Lortel who had put money into Paul's productions of Sean's work. At that point she hadn't met either Eileen or Sean but had written to them both. After Sean's death she became a close friend of Eileen's. She had married a millionaire called Louis Schweitzer who had made a large amount of his fortune from making the filter paper for cigarettes. Lucille had given up a career in the theatre and had agreed not to have children in order to marry him. He had bought Lucille an off-Broadway theatre, The Theatre De Lys, later renamed The Lucille Lortel Theatre. We met at The Pierre Hotel where she had an apartment overlooking Central Park. We went to Pierre's restaurant. At the table her sweeping sable coat was ceremoniously taken from her small, nicely plump figure. She was well known here and given a lot of attention, especially by the head-waiter. I was almost tongue-tied but able to talk about Sean and Eileen when prompted. At the end of this rather formal meal she asked for her usual "doggy bag". "I didn't know you had a dog. What kind is it?" "Oh no dear, we don't have a dog – this is for Louis". My God, I thought, Louis got the leftovers! After eating, our coats were returned; she handed the doggy bag to a young porter in the lobby to take up to Louis as she was going to the theatre, and waved goodbye to me as she drove off. Around the corner I hailed a cab and told him to take me to my hotel as I fell back into the seat, glad to be alone.

Paul Shyre had arranged for me to see the readings that he had adapted from Sean's first volume of his autobiography, *I Knock at the Door*, playing until November 10 and that Lucille had produced. The year before he had put on the staged readings of Sean's second volume of autobiography, *Pictures in the Hallway*, produced by Playhouse Theatre: it had won a Drama Desk Award. I had met Paul before when he visited home; he was a quiet young man, then only about thirty, fairly short, but then I am 5'11" and so not many people are taller than me. He had close cut dark hair and gentle smile. I have no idea of his background, just that he was clever and ambitious and liked Sean's work enough to risk putting it on. This year his readings won the Obie Award – a special citation for bringing O'Casey to off-Broadway with both *Pictures in the Hallway* and *I Knock at the Door*. So his work with Sean had been successful for him as well as for us.

I was to see *I Knock at the Door* at the Balasco, a Broadway theatre on West 44th Street, with the American actors Rae Allen, George Brenlin, Staats Cotsworth, Aline McMahon and Shyre himself. I met Paul for lunch, after which we went to the Museum of Modern Art and saw *Guernica*, a powerful and terrible cartoon-like vision. We ended up for tea at the Palm Court of the Plaza Hotel, on the corner of Fifth Avenue and Central Park South. The Palm Court was in a central marble-floored square, full of potted palm trees that protected the tables from human traffic. The people eating were generally conservatively suited and the women over made up and coiffed. The only people moving around were the waiters – in black with long white aprons. That night the readings were very well done and simply presented, with a circle of black high stools and lecterns to hold the scripts. The actors all knew their parts but it gave the feeling of a reading. Sometimes if they had a scene together one of the cast would walk over with their script and stand by their partner. Simple lighting and music on a flute gave all the atmosphere needed. The words were the important thing and you visualised the scenes. The audience loved it.

The main thing Sean and Eileen wanted me to do was to see Sean's *Purple Dust* at the Cherry Lane Theatre, off Broadway. This production had opened on December 27 as Niall lay dying in St Bartholomew's Hospital. It was to run for just over a year, until January 1958, the longest run of any of Sean's plays. I had already met the director Philip Burton and he was to be there tonight to meet me again. He was the schoolmaster who had spotted Richard Burton's talent when he was his pupil in Wales. He had taken him under his wing and took him up into the Welsh hills to proclaim Shakespeare. The young actor, born Richard Jenkins, had taken his mentor's surname. Philip was a tall energetic and enthusiastic Welshman who I liked a lot. It was a good production but not brilliant. There had, of course, been a cast change and Paul wished I had seen the original cast. The sets and costumes were rather shoddy, maybe as it was done on a shoestring. But that really isn't an excuse in my books. It was done simply and the play came across well with all its humour and Irish mystic pagan past. The audience loved it and the theatre rang with their laughter. After the show I told Philip how much I had liked it and was rushed back to see all the cast and technicians before we went out for a drink in a huge bar with sawdust on the floor. Paul introduced me to a lovely, very funny stagehand who had volunteered to work backstage. Paul jokingly said, "She says she is going to be a big star". To which Barbra Streisand replied, "Yes, I am".

Jason Robards was drinking at this same sawdust-strewn bar with lots of other thespians and he was very drunk indeed. There was a lot of drinking in the theatre, and in all the arts, then. I had seen it in London with Jack MacGowran, Richard Harris and Peter O'Toole, but this was the first time I had seen it in New York. I didn't like to drink too much or do drugs and never had any desire to join in. It was starting to snow heavily now as Paul took me in a car up the Hudson River (near to where I was later to live with my son) to a line of horses and their traps along the side of Central Park. "We have to do this, to ride through Central Park in the snow". So up we climbed, a rug was put over our legs and with "Tally-ho" we trotted off, and round and about the park: past lakes and grottos and a skating rink. It was a strange park full of very large granite rocks that poked out through the snow. It was thrilling; we could have been in Scandinavia or even Russia. The snow was still falling and it was getting late. I patted the horse on its nose and we hailed a cab, I dropped Paul at his apartment and the cab drove silently through shrouded Manhattan to my hotel.

OLD FRIENDS AND NEW

I was getting ready to meet our old friends Brooks and Oriana at the famous theatrical restaurant Sardi's. I had found out where it was and I decided to get a cab; the address written down on a piece of paper said Sardi's was on West 44th, between 8th and 9th Avenues. I also decided that this was an evening to dress up; it was the press-night of *Romanoff and Juliet* at the Plymouth Theatre; Peter Ustinov had written it and was starring in it and George Kaufman was directing it. The cab dropped me off on the corner of 44th Street. When I stepped out my feet fell into snow that covered my black court shoes. I walked as quickly as I could down the sidewalk, my feet soon wet through as my lovely new shoes weren't meant for this kind of weather. It was beautiful seeing the snow cascade down between the buildings and Sardi's sign was well lit up and easy to spot. I pushed through the doors and asked for Brooks Atkinson. I looked at my feet and to my horror saw that the dye from the sodden shoes had crept up my skin-coloured nylons about four inches. Well what the heck – there was nothing I could do – a new look for New York.

Brooks stood up and we hugged, and there was Oriana, laughing and brimming over with anticipated fun. I told them about my legs and they laughed, so I laughed too. Oriana pointed out famous people to me; they had sat me on the banquette facing the room and they sat each side of me. She pointed to the walls that were covered in well-framed caricatures of actors, actresses, writers and even Brooks; there wasn't one of Sean but there was one of Eugene O'Neill and that was good. They were drawn by a succession of cartoonists and were very different to signed photos. Sitting near us was Siobhan McKenna, also in black but with a broad-brimmed white hat still on her head. She looked animated and at ease as "the talk of the town". The year before, she had been nominated for the Distinguished Actress award for her part in *The Chalk Garden*; it was won by Julie Harris, who I had loved so much when she visited us in Devon, for her Joan in *The Lark*.[20] Siobhan didn't recognise me at first; we had met when I was a young girl during the rehearsals for *Purple Dust*. But Brooks introduced us. She asked how Sean and Eileen were after Niall's death. A difficult moment for me as Niall's loss suddenly flooded over me, but I managed, I think, to say they were coping as best as they could.

The play was funny with light and easy sets and costumes, but without Peter Ustinov's performance I don't think it would have been much to watch: it was a parable of lovers from different lands at odds with each other, in this case the son of a Russian ambassador and the daughter of an American diplomat falling in love. A play with humour similar to Noel Coward's inoffensive jokes, but no bite like Shaw. By the end everyone was happy and chatting as they went out.

I had to go back to Sardi's to meet Louis Schweitzer (Lucille's Louis who ate food from doggy bags), to be interviewed for his radio programme about Sean and *I Knock at the Door*. Louis interviewed me and I said how well I had liked the readings and that the adaptation by Paul Shyre was good and the staging and acting excellent. Then he offered to drop me back at my hotel in his taxi. He owned a taxi; that is, he paid a special driver a full-time salary with also the possibility of picking up other fares when Louis didn't need him. He had decorated the inside of the cab with carpet, cushions and tassels and magazines. Later he did this with a gondola in Venice and Christmas cards would come depicting Louis and Lucille floating down the Grand Canal. I never got to have a ride in that.

In the morning before I met up with Brooks and Oriana I went to visit Sean's very dear friend, George Jean Nathan. Although they had corresponded before Sean's journey to New York in 1936, it was at their meeting in the city that the friendship became so close. Sean had started his visit to New York to oversee the production of *Within the Gates* by being put up at the Majestic Hotel near the National Theatre where rehearsals were taking place. But soon after his first meeting with Sean,

---

[20] *The Lark* (1952) by Jean Anouilh was performed on Broadway in 1955 with Julie Harris as Joan and Boris Karloff as Pierre Cauchon; Lillian Hellman made the English adaptation and Leonard Bernstein provided the incidental music.

George Jean Nathan insisted Sean should move to the hotel where he lived so that they would be closer and able to meet and talk more. So Sean moved to a room at the Royalton Hotel on the East side of 44th Street. Every night he was made welcome in Nathan's apartment; there he met Eugene O'Neill, a young Thomas Quinn Curtiss, the critic Richard Watts, the playwrights Maxwell Anderson and Elmer Rice and, of course, the leading lady in his play, Lillian Gish.

It was to this same apartment I was walking, not knowing what to expect. I knew Nathan was very ill and that he had recently married an actress called Julie Haydon, who was younger than him and a devout Catholic. She was devoted to him and looked after him.[21] I was nervous and didn't feel up to the task of bringing Sean's great love and respect personally to his friend. Nathan had never come down to Devon to see Sean and Sean had never travelled again to New York or up to London to meet him on the few occasions he was there. So Nathan had never met Eileen, Breon, Niall or me. I knew he was revered as a critic and all theatre people were in dread as to what he would say about a production. Sean told me about going to the theatre with him: he folded his cloak and put his hat in the little hat-shelf under the seat. As soon as the curtain started to fall on the first act he said to Sean, "Come on, we're leaving". He took up his hat and cloak and strode out, leaving Sean to hurry behind him. Sean had never done this before but evidently this event was looked out for by theatre managers as it was often "the death knell" for a production.

I was told by the doorman of the Royalton Hotel what floor to go to, and when the lift opened I stepped straight into Nathan's large apartment, with black and white marble floor tiles. Julie met me and took me through to an area where Nathan was sitting in a wheelchair waiting for me. As often happens with me, I suddenly felt very shy and was at a loss as to what to say. He had slight difficulty in speaking but was perfectly clear. I gave him all Sean's love, and he asked me how he was after Niall's sudden death. I described as best as I could the change it had brought on him and Eileen, and us all, but that in spite of his grief he was working on a new play. When after a while Julie said that Jean was getting tired now, I immediately thought I must have bored him. He motioned to a book on the table saying that it was hot off the press. I praised the fact and said we all waited to read it. Sean said later that I should have asked for it and he

[21] Chicago-born stage and television actress Julie Haydon (1910–1994) married Nathan (73) at the age of 45.

would have signed it as that was obviously why it was sitting there. But I didn't think to do that. He then said he would like to write an autobiography called *The Spittoon on the Dining Room Table*, and laughed: and so did I, and then thanked them both and said good-bye.

The next night I went to see the newly published play by Eugene O'Neill, a personal play that he hadn't wanted printed until 25 years after his death, but his widow had decided it was all right to do so now, four years after his death. It was called *Long Day's Journey into Night*. What a lovely title. There was Jason Robards Jr being riveting as O'Neill's older alcoholic brother, Jamie. What a terribly sad and tormenting play. Another towering performance by Frederic March and a sad Ophelia-like mother played by Florence Eldridge. It was a wonderful and devastating evening and stayed with me over many of the miles we travelled.

Although Eugene O'Neill was dead, his widow Carlotta was very keen to meet me. I was sent a note stating the place and the time. It was some residential block of apartments on Central Park's Southside, with a doorman and a large atrium. I went with Bob Ginna and when we got there we were told to wait and after about thirty minutes this thin fragile lady dressed all in black appeared from the elevator. She even wore black lace gloves and a black hat. She was intense and we sat down on a sofa in the atrium. I wasn't invited to her room or apartment: maybe it was a hotel. She asked about Sean but mainly wanted to talk non-stop about her dear Eugene – how awful everything was (even at times he himself, I seem to remember). Before we parted she gave me copies of photos of him as a boy and the pair of them together, he looking very handsome and her beautiful, and one of him with his spotty dog. She also gave me a lovely little book he had made from his memories about the dog after it had died, a dog he obviously adored. Then this fragile lady dressed all in black was gone.

THE TOUR BEGINS

A great hustle and bustle in the hotel lobby as the "Irish troopers" arrived down from their rooms with their luggage to wait for the hired Greyhound bus that was to be our home for six months. Ernie the driver was thirty or forty and very helpful and upbeat. It was obvious there was a pecking order and I stood back to let everyone on before I clambered up. Great movement as people grabbed the seats they wanted, or the best they could get. The oldest man in the company, John Kelly, had opted for the seat in the front behind the driver on the Left. Big and tall John had various ailments, mainly to do with suppurating varicose veins on his legs and he also had a penchant for pink gin. Charlie Blair, the Stage and Company Manager, had the seat on the right with a clear view of the road; in charge from the beginning, top dog, Charlie was camp and cocky. His job was to run the shows and he took charge of all the calls and made sure everyone was on time to climb on to the bus. He was a cruel man with a biting tongue when he wanted. I settled near the back, behind Aileen Hart, a good-looking strong actress, and on my right Grania O'Shannon, the daughter of Cathal O'Shannon, a Union man who Sean had known. Lollie May sat in front of Grania. Maureen Halligan, the grand leading lady of the company, sat on the very back seat that ran the width of the bus where she could recline or sit upright at the top of the aisle and watch over us all – mainly her wayward husband. He sat a little further down behind Grania and loved to flirt with her and Aileen. Grania was a tease and having no real intention of messing with Ronnie, she loved to gain his interest and ruffle Maureen's feathers. I felt sorry for Maureen; she was astute though, and her sharp tongue could fire barbs into the air at Grania and her Ronnie: she had Ronnie in the palm of her hand. There were a lot of "leading" people, as they all took differing parts of importance in the various plays. Dermot, not far away, was keeping his eye on me for Josie, for Josie went ahead in a car as the Production Manager to find suitable accommodation and get the venues ready for our arrival. He was, of course, an old friend and was very kind and had a great sense of humour and was often chuckling at the absurdities as they cropped up. Not only did he sing many songs, both operatic and folk but he was full of quotes from plays, in particular Shaw and Sean. We all had two seats to ourselves, so you could curl up and sleep if you wanted.

Great noise and excitement and after a lot of shouting and fussing by Charlie Blair, Ernie revved up the old engine and we were off. It was October 14, 1957. I was wide awake on that first journey; sorry to be leaving New York so soon but keen to see the sights of the USA.

Josie's letter to Eileen:

16 October 1957

My dear Eileen,

Many thanks for the beautiful roses, it was good of you to remember us.

RADA AND MY PROSPECTS, 1957

The enclosed is a good detailed map which will help you follow the tour.

Shivaun is very happy and is doing fine work. She seems to be getting more of a thrill from the road than anyone who has ever travelled with us. She doesn't waste a minute – even sketching as we drive & yesterday she was wishing she had her paints – can you see us rushing to a date and Shivaun in a dream wishing to paint!!

However when the work has to be done there is no one in the company more faster.

Love to yourself & best wishes to Sean O'Casey

Josie

Our first date was not too far away when compared to some later journeys, although quite a drive up in Berkshire County to a small town called Williamstown, sitting among gentler hills with mountains in the distance, a white clapboard church with tower and clock and Grecian columns in front. Clapboard houses with verandas and no fences around them to show the dividing line between people's property: just open ground and paths through manicured lawns leading to the road. In the countryside around the fields were white picket fences and wooden Dutch barns, often painted a dull red. It was all very picturesque.

We had the evening to get over this first drive as we didn't perform until the following evening and we were to stay and sleep there after the show and leave in the morning. Breaking us in slowly, maybe. I remember the first date still: setting up the props for *Juno*, and feeling nervous while prompting and anxious about my tiny part. Josie was there to greet us at the College Theatre and the actors looked around as we unpacked the things needed before heading for the hotel for two nights. Many of the colleges we were to visit they had played before on their previous tours and so knew many of the people involved. Josie was in charge of collecting the money and of giving it to Charlie Blair in its envelopes to give out at the end of each week. After some weeks on the tour Josie suggested that I could drive ahead with her if there was enough leeway between dates and my duties could be completed and not interfered with. The tour was a chance to get to know this remarkable woman and meeting various Americans and places and undreamt-of adventures.

Our pit stops were usually at a chain of diners called Howard Johnson with orange roofs and a kind of portico or small tower with a green pointed roof. They had 58 varieties of ice cream! The portions for dinner or breakfast were far too big. If you ordered pancakes you got what they called a stack, which was about four or five sitting on top of each other, with butter and maple syrup on the side, or else strawberries and phoney-looking whipped cream.

I was getting a very good wage, $90 a week, and for the two weeks we had off over Christmas we got $65 a week: a fortune for me. We paid for our lodgings and food out of that but the group bookings Josie managed to get worked out as really cheap. At the eating places and hotels they had bowls of free matches advertising themselves, as most people smoked then, and I started collecting them for Sean; by the end of the tour I had a two-foot Mexican woven basket full of them and it sailed to Sean over the Atlantic in the hold of the *Queen Elizabeth*.

After Williamstown we dipped down to Boston before heading up again to Buffalo and Niagara Falls, then Cleveland, Ohio. We were to stay three days in Boston and after the show I was taken by the mayor to the Waterfront – where he gave me an orchid and told me that he wouldn't have banned Sean's play *Within the Gates* in 1935 if he had been in office then. Boston had also banned Eugene O'Neill's *Strange Interlude* in the 1920s: this had forced the producers to take it out of Boston to the small town of Quincy, Massachusetts. As the play was 4 to 5 hours long they had a long interval in which the audience could have dinner – and the place opposite the theatre was the first Howard Johnson diner and this helped the restaurant to fame and expansion. Boston was the first stop on a scheduled tour of *Within the Gates* in thirteen cities, and so when the Catholic mayor and a gaggle of priests banned it as "lewd and blasphemous", it scuppered the whole tour, as other cities followed suit and banned the play. In the play a bishop comes in touch with his illegitimate daughter from a relationship when he was young. So here in Boston, back in 1935, and before that in 1928 when Yeats refused to do *The Silver Tassie* at the Abbey, was a pattern that followed Sean about.

Two ladies who were mad about Sean rang me and asked to meet - they had heard we had a day off before leaving town. Mrs Jane Manty worked at Helena Rubinstein's Beauty Salon and had arranged for me to have the works, and her friend, Mrs Florence Castleman, was a fighter for desegregation.[22] Florence wanted me to stay the night with her and

[22] In 1947, Florence Castleman was identified as on the administrative staff of the Samuel Adams School in Boston, one of the many schools that Walter Steele (eminent in the American Coalition of Patriotic, Civic, and Fraternal Societies, *Contd.*

promised Josie they would deliver me back in time to catch the bus the next day, and I was swept away. While being pummelled and washed I was introduced to Mrs Edward G. Robinson, who told me her film star husband loved my father and so did she: loved his work but also what he stood for during these taxing times in the States. The Reds-under-the-bed scare and segregation were at the top of an ugly list. Odd to me then was how many people in this vast land were scared and so often sorely bigoted. They often gained the majority vote, and this scaremongering enabled Joseph McCarthy, another of those "good Catholics" I was becoming aware of, to run his trials and set up the Black List that damned anyone who had been a Communist or had any sympathies for the left – damned them to shame and the loss of their jobs and often to suicide. We knew many people who had suffered – my friends the Wanamakers, and Ella and Don, and Joe Losey; but also the American philosopher Barrows Dunham.[23] With these brave souls stood Charlie Chaplin and Paul Robeson. How was it possible that these two great people could be persecuted?

After the beauty treatment Florence took me to a department store and bought me a dark blue tweed suit, a short-sleeved red top that didn't tuck in, and more bizarrely a real leopard skin hat (that I later gave to Charlotte Wanamaker) and a fake leopardskin cravat thing you put around your neck with the one end slotting into the other. Florence drove me off to her home to the suburbs where I was staying for the night. It was a one-storey modern bungalow with grounds around it. Inside it was simply and comfortably furnished; but it didn't seem to me that she was wealthy and I thought she shouldn't have bought me all that stuff. She talked a lot and she cooked. I think there was a husband there somewhere. She found presents for me to take home: a whole collection of Jelly Roll Morton LPs, as Niall had loved jazz, and some Columbian terracotta figurines and heads stitched onto a belt to hang on the wall. Then bed and a sound sleep. Woken early; breakfast; a hair-raising drive to the bus as we were late; then fond goodbyes.

[22] *Contd.*, and managing editor of the *National Republic* magazine) accused of being Communist-inspired: *Testimony of Walter S. Steele Regarding Communist Activities in the United States before the Committee on Un-American Activities House of Representatives*, July 21, 1947 (Washington DC, 1947), p. 52.

[23] Barrows Dunham (1905–1995) was an American professor of philosophy. He wrote the highly popular *Man against Myth* (1947) and *Heroes and Heretics* (1963); he was fired from Temple University in 1953 after refusing to name names before McCarthy's House Un-American Activities Committee.

I staggered into the bus in all my finery and everyone laughed, my bobbed hair and yes, I was made-up still – I don't think I had taken it off. The suit, the bloody hat. Well, I was able to take hat and the neck cravat off as soon as Florence was out of sight. The suit wasn't bad if a bit conventional, and it was warm. What two very extraordinary lovely ladies they were.

THE MID-WEST

We had been driving all over the top right hand side of the U.S. Through New England, Connecticut, Buffalo New York, Niagara Falls, Chicago, Boston, Harrisburg, Madison and Cleveland, among some of our one-night stops. In what order we wove in and out I have no longer any idea. Chicago was bitterly cold, the wind whistled around my legs and up into my skirt. Here the Company bumped into their old friend Carroll O'Connor, famous later as Archie Bunker in *All in the Family*, the famous TV sitcom. Born in Manhattan, he had been on one of the early tours and owed a lot to Ronnie and Maureen. Years later he wanted to make a film of *Juno and the Paycock* but several years after Sean's death, Eileen had been led to make a disastrous contract with Peter O'Toole by which the TV rights were tied up, and in a roundabout way the film rights too. Peter forbade two TV productions being made while Eileen was still alive but allowed one to be done to honour the 100th anniversary of Sean's birth in 1980, but he got the money for it as per the contract. Peter had written a film script under an assumed name; he wanted initially to play Captain Boyle but later as he got too old for that he still wanted a major input to any production. But because of his track record at the time, no producers would touch it with him involved, as they could not insure against his unreliability. Finally after Eileen's death and many attempts with many lawyers, Peter asked if we would buy back the rights, and this we did a year before Breon's death; so at least Breon knew it was back with us.

A letter from Eileen came telling me she had found a flat in London! Mainly for her use but also the family's. One of some small pied-à-terre flats used by politicians and businessmen. The daughter of Mona Hilliam, Nancy Joan Hilliam, had a large flat in the main building looking out over Cromwell Road. Mona and Eileen were great friends from their Cochran Young Ladies days. Mona had married B.C. Hilliam of Flotsam and Jetsam fame.[24] When Joan heard of this vacant flat she immediately recommended

---

[24] B.C. Hilliam (1890–1968), the English singer and musician, was Mr Flotsam in the Mr Flotsam and Mr Jetsam comedy duo; Mona Barrett-Leonard was his second wife.

it for Eileen. It was a reasonable rent. For a while Captain Townsend lived underneath us, he that Princess Margaret was so cruelly forbidden to marry.

Sean's letter to me

November 27 1957

Darling Shivaun,

Well, you have gone a long way over a big part of the world by now – a kind of terrestrial Sputnik; watched Niagara, and lately in the Windy City - Chicago.[25] ... Drums of Father Ned is with Brendan Smith; and all the Irish papers have announced it is to be performed next Tostal.[26] No actors have yet been mentioned & I don't yet know who will direct it. I daresay they aren't hurrying for the event won't be till next May. ... Eileen has been busy with the new flat, & Breon is to do decorating of it next week. ...We all miss you greatly, and when Eileen goes to London, & Breon is out, the flat is very lonely. Never mind – after St Patrick's Day (or before) you should be home with us again.

My deep love, darling, go with you.

Dad (Sean)

Things had been happening at home that these loving letters hide and that were hidden from me until I got home. To quell some of his sorrow, Sean would still cry or keen in his own room. This upset Eileen and she became so enraged that she started to drink. Eileen had always harboured a suspicion, quite unfounded, that she would become a secret drinker like her mother: so she set about it. Where Breon fitted into this sad routine I don't know but I imagine they kept it from him or he would stay at his studio room in town.

The letters from Grannie's Irish friends saying that if Eileen had stuck to her faith Niall would not have died must have hurt her terribly – such

---

[25] The Soviet Union launched Sputnik the first artificial Earth satellite on October 4, 1957. Chicago is indeed windy, but its nickname, the Windy City, derives from the reputed windiness of the local politicians.

[26] The Dublin Theatre Festival was founded in 1957 by Brendan Smith, an impresario who also ran the Olympia Theatre, Dublin. (*An Tóstal*: the gathering, or festival.) Smith approached Sean about the possibility of staging the world premiere of his newest play in the Festival.

an injustice to a wonderful and caring mother. Things became unbearable for her and she swallowed a lot of pills to be with her Niall and had to be rushed to hospital to have her stomach pumped. Sean was beside himself and was told by Dr Doran that he should consider Eileen more. I think they both needed help but it wasn't available then; Dr Doran went on to say that this attempted suicide or cry for help should remain a secret between them. So, you see, no counselling then, just advice from a dearly loved doctor. Suicide maybe had a shameful air about it for Dr Doran – although I know Sean never thought it shameful; but rather courageous in many cases, as something difficult and terrifying to do. The result was more bottling up of emotions – more pretence of feeling normal. Sean had to stop his keening but no mention was ever made of Eileen's friend, the bottle; she couldn't stop trying to deaden her feeling with a secret drink, mainly at night and disguised in a glass of milk. And so, ignorant of Eileen's pain and Sean's turmoil, I continued my working journey, distracted by all I had to do for the Company and at all the new and astonishing things I kept encountering. But I was relieved to receive this letter from Eileen with its comic account of the doomed attempt to decorate the London flat.

November 30 1957

Shivay dearest one, I am sorry I have left you so long without a letter, but I have been somehow meaning to write every day. I went to London for two days last week to paint the flat. Charlotte was going to get two ladders & a plank & take them along & we were to start; well, we bought 2 big tins of paint and went back to 31 [Abbey Lodge, where Charlotte lived]. The next morning I got there [Abbey Lodge] at about 10.30am for Charlotte & we started off.

 Charlotte took paint & a basket with rags etc. in & I followed with Charlotte's best coat (we were to call at Harrods on the way & she wanted to wear it in Harrods) on my arm and various bits and pieces. I heard a cry from Charlotte & she rushed back saying, 'Don't go out there please; I have done something awful'. I of course went out and one pot of paint had literally spilt all over the carpet & for miles around the Abbey Lodge passage; I had coat on my arm still & I rubbed it against the wall where paint had splashed all over; it was amazing how far that b——— paint had gone. Well we were there until 1.30pm with

turps & rags. I tackled coat also & we got it all cleared up – we were wrecks & reeked of turps! And so did the hall. ...
Now dearest Charlotte Jessie and all send their love to you.
My love dear and take care of yourself.
A big hug & x Eileen X

SOUTHWARDS

As we drove south, the weather became hotter and sometimes humid. The brown moss hung from the trees and reminded me of the harrowing song, "Strange Fruit Hanging from the Poplar Trees". As soon as I saw the large painted clapboard mansions on the right-side of the tracks – and the contrast with the small dusty-brown little shanty houses on the wrong-side of the tracks, with mostly black people in the fields as far as I could see, some actually picking cotton – slavery and injustice screamed at me. Now and again, I saw a poor white family, some also in the fields. On the white side, for that is what it was, apartheid, you saw the black people working for the mansions, in and outside of them. I did nothing about it except look and be ashamed for such a rich country to put up with and condone such a thing. Stopping the bus at a small town before the big city of Houston, I was sitting having a coffee with Maurice and Dermot when three very large Texans, with, I kid you not, red sunburnt napes of fat necks, came in and sat down. The word "nigger" floated gently into my ears. On asking, I learned that blacks weren't welcome in this cafe. So I paid my bill and left immediately. I went and sat on a bench. Noticing that I got some strange looks, a black man sotto voce told me that I was sitting on a bench reserved for Blacks Only; my bench was over there and it would please him if I used mine. I soon learnt that even if I stayed on the bench, making a small gesture like that embarrassed the black people and angered the white people. Then I saw a water fountain that had a notice painted above it, Whites Only, but I couldn't see another fountain for the rest to drink from. I didn't like the place at all. I thought that segregation to be a narrowing bitter thing that helped no-one. All the time I noticed, Whites Only, No Blacks, and the smouldering fear it engendered between the members of the human race.

One night, late after our show had finished, as we drove along, we noticed lots of people parking their cars, getting out, and walking towards a large burning cross. Around the cross were many people in white sheets and horrible pointed pillowcases over their heads with round holes cut out so they could see. The dreaded Ku Klux Klan. Here were some of its bombastic self-righteous members – bullies with nothing better to do than to downgrade other people. How frightening it must be for the black people minding their own business and how dangerous for the black people taking a stand.[27]

In the cities of Houston and later Austin, you noticed segregation in a much subtler way. Most people in the centre of the city where we hung out were white, except doormen, cleaners, maids and some waiters - and of course the shoeshine boys. I had seen these in New York and they reminded me of the movies. Here I was near to the jazz Niall had loved and no time or help to ferret it out. I needed Alan Lomax to appear to grab me and show me around. I had met him the year before at the Wanamakers. Charlotte had warned me, very seriously, that he was a womaniser – and not to go home with him. That scared me and I refused his kind offer.

At one of the do's after the performance, amongst the green sherbet and the green cookies all made to celebrate the Irish Company, we met the heir to the hot sauce, Tabasco, a Mr McIlhenny. He was about to go off with his entourage of three to Mexico to look at a Mayan dig. I would have loved to go and was offered a ride but my work had to be honoured. Another night a doctor took us all to his house: at each side of the door to this modern building stood on guard two giant cacti, at least twice as tall as me: that is about 12 feet. Inside was a cavernous room: high ceilinged with a central fireplace, that is, set in the centre of the room, with a large log fire burning as it gets cold at night in the desert. I was famished and there was no food anywhere. I asked if he had anything we could eat, and maybe upset by his inhospitality he ordered in steaks, chips and salad from an oasis in the desert. It arrived about an hour later and we all devoured it as if starved. He fancied me, I think, and wrote a letter saying that he had a wife, etc: this was a shock to me as all I had wanted was some food.

Colleges were our main dates, especially Catholic Colleges. At one Texas college that we played in San Antonio, it was a delightful surprise to see such free and joyful nuns – in full habit; in those days that meant a long heavy dress and white starched wimples and headdresses. Here, if needed, they would hoist their skirts up and tuck them into their belts, just like

---

[27] Racial segregation in Texas persisted in various and gradually declining ways until the civil rights movement of the 1960s.

washerwomen, and would help with the scenery or shin up a ladder to adjust the lights. I wasn't very familiar with nuns; the only nuns I knew were Eileen's relations, but I never saw that kind of joyful abandonment before in nuns.

Maureen and Ronnie were well known at this particular San Antonio university (they later retired there to teach and remained until their deaths) so the bus with all its props, etc. was safely housed there, at the University of the Incarnate Word. The Alamo didn't impress me much; more fighting, more killing. Then came the Christmas break! Time off; two weeks in all with two-thirds pay. Josie asked if I wanted to go with her and Grania and Aileen on a trip to Mexico.

Very early in the morning, before the sun came up and under Josie's orders, we girls drove off in the big old American Chrysler that had seen much better days. We nosed into Mexico at the Laredo border crossing and suddenly we were in another world. From the more conventional dress colours I was used to seeing in the States we had gone through to an outpouring of bright vibrant colour in the clothes, the shops, the cars – everything. In this border town the streets were full of shops and stalls for the tourists: brightly coloured straw baskets and hats, animals from straw and painted tin, bright skirts and shawls, and white embroidered blouses, shirts, and tops, and blankets and rugs: also the stalls selling steaming food and brightly coloured sweets. I wanted to stop and wander the shops but Josie said we needed to get on to Mexico City, where we were to stay for a time.

It was still morning when Josie pulled in off the road for her to rest for a while and for all of us to stretch our legs. We were all tired and in need of a shower, as it was very hot. Before we had time to take in the arid parched land around us vanishing into the distance to some distant purple hills and with cacti of many species growing here, a small, very dilapidated black car pulled up about fifteen feet behind us. Out of it came a very tall Mexican in a large black sombrero, black shirt buttoned neatly up to his neck, black trousers with flares from the knees Mexican-style, a heavy belt with holsters and guns and slung across his chest a belt full of bullets crossing his largish tummy. He had greasy dark hair, possibly dyed, and a hanging moustache, and when he smiled a few blackish teeth. We said "Adios", and he answered with a nod.[28] Then, as if it was a circus trick, about six other men emerged from the little car – with guns, bullets and

[28] The Mexican would have expected "Hello!"("Hola!") rather than "Goodbye!" ("Adios!").

hats. None of them quite so grandly dressed as the tall black figure but oddly assorted clothes, sizes and ages. None of us spoke Spanish – Josie was the best. I heard her, as she shook his hand, explain we were all Catholics – and had a few days to spend in Mexico. Josie, being a devout "pagan" Catholic, had rosary beads and a St. Christopher tied to the front mirror and lots of holy medals. He saw them. They loitered around for a while, and we all felt awkward, especially Grania and Aileen who had their hair in curlers. Then as quickly as they clambered out they shoved themselves into the small car and sped off, leaving a trail of flying dust behind them that slowly settled on us. I suppose they were lower grade bandits who felt that our pickings weren't worth the effort, especially from such good Catholic women.

Amazed, we continued through small villages, and suddenly by lunchtime we were all very hungry. There was no town near but Josie spotted a small muddy house with a petrol pump and with a sign that signalled they sold food. Outside were parked colourfully decorated lorries. Coming in from the glaring sunlight it is dark. Gradually I see men drinking and a woman behind a counter in charge. Josie asks in broken Spanish if she has food. Only one dish and it is very hot. Josie is game and so a bowl with enough for us all is placed on the table with four plates and spoons. Everyone is looking at us, the truck drivers seemed unable to stop giggling. As I take my first mouthful of this kind of curry I feel my mouth and throat burning as never before – I try not to choke but my eyes are running and the whole place erupts into laughter. Aileen and Grania ate gingerly but Josie seemed defiantly fine. I remained hungry but Josie finished to the admiration of the audience. We asked for bread and water and I apologised for leaving my food. When we got back in the car my throat and ears were still on fire.

As we were driving down into Mexico City we noticed some sort of celebration at the side of the road. A gathering of dusty people, with ribbons and flowers in their hair, a band and singing. Josie pulled us up. There before us were the poorest people I had ever seen, much poorer looking even than the sharecroppers. Their clothes were patched rags and the little children had thin legs and distended tummies – everyone had red sore eyes and dust in their hair, clothes and skin; but they were rejoicing. We asked an official-looking person about it. He told us that the charity he worked for had supplied a water hole and tap, so now they could get water. Till then they had drunk the water from the cacti.

RADA AND MY PROSPECTS, 1957

Leaving behind the singing and dancing, we drove on into Mexico City. Wealth sat right next to poverty here. Here, where water was so scarce, there were gardens with green grass being continually doused by sprinklers. On the pavements sat whole families and their few possessions, covered by precarious tent-like constructions. This was everywhere – and most people ignored it, they were so used to it, I supposed. Children – what beautiful brown-eyed children – ran after the car or followed us as we walked, asking for anything. We gave what we could, though not much I'm afraid.

The hotel Josie found was The Hotel Frimont, Jesus Teran 35, MEXICO 1 O.F. I know because I found a letter from Ismail, the tallest and handsomest of the waiters had sent me in Spanish (that I got translated when I got back to England.) It is a lovely letter, funny and an affectionate send-up. We had a lovely evening together at a fiesta where I got drunk for the first time on a very strong drink. I was so happy with the music and the dancing that I suppose I didn't realise what I was drinking: so I was dancing about wildly on a raised dais, rather like a boxing ring with no ropes, the band playing, skirts swirling, feet stamping, being whirled around mainly by Ismail. Luckily Josie and the girls stepped in and persuaded me to come back to the hotel with them. I had little resistance and was thankful. I don't remember if I ever answered the letter – there was no reason to but I had obviously written to him first. I must add that nothing happened and he exaggerated our friendship to a ridiculous degree.

Miss Shivaun,

Your welcomed letter of the 10.1.58 here at hand from which I have derived the greatest possible joy.

Like a flash I seemed to live again in my imagination 'the (ecstasy??) of our fleeting romance', as the poet would term it. My thoughts are ever with you all, especially you, Shivaun, indeed shall always hold the memory of you most dear.

Unfortunately time and distance must inevitably separate us. Meanwhile I shall keep the grateful recollection of my happy sojourn with you. Your gay laughter. High spirits as a lingering consolation.

May it please the gods that one day you will find yourself here in Mexico, where the good will to love, cherish & appreciate is ever paramount. Please do send me a recent photograph of yourself. I can assure you it will be treasured on the ranch as tho' it were a Leonardo da Vinci Masterpiece. The future I hope will guide you someplace in the world where we can meet again.

Greetings to all your friends and to you, my fleeting love. The tender affection of your Romeo.

Ismail.

P.S. Greetings from Godolfo to his most beloved Helena [Aileen], imploring her to respond to his entreaty since he already feels the pangs of nostalgia acutely. A few understanding words would give him the hope he so sorely needs to alleviate his present suffering.

They must have been doubled up writing this letter. Maybe they were both back at his ranch in Cuaothemoc. What rhetoric!

We were packing our things in the car to leave the hotel to great consternation among the male staff of waiters, "You must come and see Ismail, he is so sick with sorrow he is ill in bed!" We went up amid a lot of laughter and said goodbye to a bad actor. We waved goodbye to our admirers and off we sped with Josie at the wheel. The fiesta with the local people had been the night before we left, a fitting goodbye. I had seen the impressive and ornate Cathedral, entering the main door over the black and white square paving stones, marvelling at the wedding cake beauty of the inside while Josie prayed. In a museum I saw the work of Diego Rivera and Jose Clemente Orozco, among beautiful Colombian and old Aztec art. But it was the streets with all the smells of the cooking that I remember most and shopping in the local shops Josie took me to for Mexican shirts and ponchos and a tin painted cockerel for Sean, a Mexican black lace dress for Eileen, and a white one for me.

We now had left Mexico City behind us and were driving through arid countryside. Then in a flash, or so it seemed, we were in almost tropical surroundings – lush yuccas, and huge red, white and pink poinsettia bushes. Many of the women wore these flowers in their hair and looked grand and beautiful. Josie pulled up at a hotel sign, and announced "This looks like a good place to stay." Out she got and soon came back to say that although the hotel was still under construction we could stay in a couple of the little adobe houses that were finished and the wife of the caretaker would provide food for us. We were the only people there. They filled the swimming pool for us, and as soon as the water was deep enough Josie was in it and I followed. What cool delight.

One evening the young caretaker came to say that there was an important man asking to see me; he had a message from Israel Antillon Pipeto. Josie was worried and I wasn't keen to meet this mysterious man, but not one to shy away from something from fear or apprehension, I agreed to go with the caretaker. When we got near to reception he pointed out a bigger house than we were staying in. I knocked at the door and a voice said, "Come in" – the speaker spoke good English. Lounging on a double bed was a rather unprepossessing man, with his shirt open revealing a large scar. He told me his name (which I forget) and asked if it meant anything to me. But it did not. He proceeded to tell me about himself: he was a fighter for freedom and that is how he had got his scar. He had heard of my interest in Orozco and that I had been shocked by the poverty I had seen. He said Israel had sent him to replace him! I didn't like him and didn't believe he was a person to trust. He told me a scary story about a spider with hoof-like feet that if it dropped on you with all four feet at once you died in an instant. Luckily I think he was as put off by me as I by him and so when I said I had to go or my friends would come to fetch me he let me go with no trouble at all. I was relieved because I did think he thought I was an easy lay. All the girls were glad to see me back, unscathed and still a virgin.

We had stayed for a week at this Cuernavaca hotel doing nothing except talk, read, swim and lounge in the sun. We stayed another couple of nights in Mexico City at the same hotel but our friends had left for home as I suppose the rush of tourists was over. I went out on my own to investigate the city. It was a perfect day, not too hot, and I had been at the art gallery. As it was getting late I decided to hail a taxi. I told the driver the name of the hotel, he nodded, and I jumped in. Soon we stopped to pick up someone else with lots of shopping – she sits in the front and they talk. We are driving down a hill towards a cross-road and I see another car coming from the right along the road crossing ours. Our car speeds up and to my horror so does the other car – faster and faster. I cry out to stop. We whistle over the crossing a moment before the other car. The lady and driver laugh. I feel sick. Before we reach the hotel we have picked up and dropped off at various places at least six people – one had a live chicken with its legs tied together, sitting next to me, flapping until he put it under his arm. Everyone was jolly and chatty – but I had no idea what they said, maybe "What an odd tall foreigner with nothing to say, just smiles and laughs."

Josie was keen to see a bullfight and I went with her. It was crowded, as full as a football match would be in England. I wasn't looking forward to it as I liked bulls and had made a friend of a bull when I was little. The ceremony began. Horses with elaborate saddles and the men riding them holding kinds of spears. Then in marched the matador with his cloak and sword. Huge resounding cheers. A small black bull was released into the ring – it was furious. It seemed as if it had been taunted before it ran in otherwise I think it would have been more placid. The matador danced around flashing his red cloak and the bull charged. It passed under the cloak. This went on and on until the bull was dizzy and exhausted. The final charge, the bull stopped. The matador skewered the bull in the head with his very sharp sword and the fine animal fell at his feet. The crowd went mad. I felt very sad for the bull. Such a cruel thing to do to a graceful dignified animal fighting for his life. We left the bull ring and walked to our hotel. We passed the back of the ring and a large wooden gate was wide open and a horrible sight: the blood flooding from the carcass, running out of the gate and to our feet; the bull was hung up and being skinned. Red carcass, red blood, with the men talking and laughing as they did their butchering

Somehow Josie got the mail sent to us in Mexico and before Christmas this letter arrived, with the merest hint of the theatrical furore to come in Dublin.

December 16 1957

Darling Shivaun,

'The Drums of Father Ned' is to be in the Gaiety Theatre, &, Mr Brendan Smith, Director of the Festival, tells me Jim Fitzgerald is to direct the play. Hilton Edwards directs the play to be done built on Joyce's 'Ulysses'.[29] I'm sure Brendan Smith will do all he can to make

---

[29] Jim Fitzgerald (1929–2003) was a stage director and TV producer; the *Irish Times* published his obituary on September 20, 2003. Born in London, Hilton Edwards (1903–1982) had his early career as a stage and film actor in England. In the late 1920s he settled in Ireland and with his partner Micheál Mac Liammóir (also born in London, as Alfred Willmore) founded the Gate Theatre in Dublin.

the production a success. ... An American in Dublin has written to say that talk about it has started in Dublin – in the pubs, and also in various places. I haven't a script to send you. I have only three, & two are gone; so I've only one to be kept in case I may have to refer to it, & make possible changes during rehearsals. ... I'm looking forward to seeing the Spring again, and of meeting you in the midst of the daffodils.

Do take care of yourself darling.

All my love to you   Dad (Sean)

Then came the day for our long drive back to the States. We drove down from Mexico City and through dry hills to flat parched land, this time to the border town of El Paso. What a crowded, dusty, colourful town this was – a play-place for Americans after cheap drinks and drugs and also bursting with shops for tourists: with sombreros, raffia animals, blankets, jewellery, etc. We made our way to Austin, Texas, slept a night at a motel and the next morning met the bus at the university.

2
Fare thee well, America
1958

FARE THEE WELL, AMERICA, 1958

OFF AGAIN

I wasn't looking forward to climbing aboard the bus again, thankfully now touring to the middle of March, which was only three months away. The bus often had an uncomfortable atmosphere as people grew weary of the trek across the States. Maureen, sitting at the back, started making comical but barbed remarks; Ronnie, now slightly bored with no one to dally with, answering back. I think this banter kept them going as they certainly respected each other's idiosyncrasies. Add to this duet the cruel biting tongue of our SM Charlie Blair, the groans of John Kelly with his sore legs, dressing and undressing his bandages to tend to the oozing varicose veins and taking courage from his bottle of pink gin taken from his bag full of ointments, bandages, biscuits and God knows what else.

Backwards and forwards: Louisiana, Atlanta Georgia, the University of Mississippi and then over again to Oklahoma. I had received a few letters from young college graduates. One from a Grinnell College, Iowa student read: "Having watched you as an actor and been able to catch a rather fleeting glimpse of you as a real person, I must show gratitude for the spark of inspiration you have given me. And please do not relegate this to infatuation or neurosis on my part. ..." The fleeting glimpse of me could hardly inspire anyone in their right mind: on and off in a blink of an eye with my two lines. The sewing machine was meant to be played by a man so they put me in a trench coat and a black beret, which was slightly odd.

I suppose I was miffed at not having a real part in any of the plays, and was learning little about theatre on this tour. However, I learnt how important it was to really care about what you were doing and the importance of pragmatic imagination in directing and acting. This company had been directed to overdo the comedy; it copied past Irish productions, but because they all had Irish accents the audiences applauded. Just remember, I told myself, what you are seeing – speeding along the roads, high up in our bus was an America I would most likely never see again.

We crossed over the South from Texas to New Mexico on our way to Santa Fe. Another date was added: we were to play *Arms and the Man* for the US soldiers in the White Sands Missile base. We were told it was a very secure base and we couldn't wander about; we would drive in, set up, play the play, pack up and leave. Fine by me – I didn't even want to breathe while we were there as it was where the first nuclear blast had been set off – The Manhattan Project – the location where the final assembly of the prototype Fat Man plutonium bomb took place – tested July 16, 1945, the first nuclear weapon tested in the world: and sadly not the last. Two of its scientists died from radiation poisoning after a mishap. Bombs designed and tested here were given the go-ahead by President Truman to be dropped on Japanese citizens in Hiroshima and Nagasaki: burnt to cinders, or maimed, and their descendants inheriting deformities for decades, that are still occurring.

The sands were really white and the sun reflecting off them made it very dry and hot. The dunes in the distance were blown into high undulating shapes. It was a long drive through desert roads to the high fenced entrance; then lots of paperwork before we were chaperoned in by army jeeps to an ugly building where it turned out we were to perform in a bleak hall. We were shown to the rooms for the cast to make up with toilets and showers. A meal was arranged for us before the performance – very formal with higher ranking people. I remember a very silent place with very few plants growing; no birds, no cicadas. But maybe apprehension closed my ears.

Niall had died from leukemia brought on, we were told, by two main possibilities: first, radiation from nuclear testing in the Pacific that produced a cloud of radiation dust carried by winds over to England. We weren't allowed to eat lamb or beef from various areas for months. Niall sunbathed and got badly burnt (too badly as I look back on it). The second possibility was also nuclear. When he was on army operations just before his release from the British Army of the Rhine, some US attachment had a small nuclear device that had a mishap: it exploded or leaked. Niall said one of the lads had been killed. For me any kind of nuclear warhead was horrendous. Nothing was said about this; I even think I may be imagining it: do I remember Niall telling me this, almost as a satirical joke, to demonstrate how the army was so inefficient? After the show was over, and we were all safely in the bus, how glad I was to hear the heavy wired gates clang shut behind us as we left this bone-dry place.

At our motel I showered for a long time and then joined the group. We were off early the following morning for Santa Fe and Josie, driving along with us in the car, was determined that we stop to see the Grand Canyon. We drew up at the parking area among the cacti and the tumbleweed

FARE THEE WELL, AMERICA, 1958

(amazing stuff never rooting but always rolling along) and walked to the edge of the canyon. It was a surreal sight – a vast area with cliffs going down into a sea of mist. The canyon was filled by a vast misty blanket, tinged with pink and yellow from the rising sun rays. We weren't able to wait to see the mist lift to reveal the depths of this huge presence; we had to set off to Santa Fe to make our next date.

Meanwhile, letters arrived from Eileen telling me of a storm gathering in Ireland over *The Drums of Father Ned*.

January 16 1958

My dearest Shivy,

Your lovely long letter, darling how can I ever write such a letter. Mexico sounds all I ever thought it was, I hope I make it one day. I doubt if I would like a bullfight, although it is supposed to be superb theatre in colour & parade. ... Well by the time you get this you will maybe have heard Sean willy nilly is in the middle of a fight. The Bishop of Dublin has refused to give his blessing to the Tostal if Joyce or O'Casey are produced; this being Ulysses & 'The Night is Whispering' (Sean has gone back to the original title) but the Tostal Committee have decided to do them & have them apart from the blessing: but it's not over yet![1] Jim Fitzgerald is to produce & had just been down to see us; and he is discussing casting etc. as if all were to carry on; but there is sure to be a fight. I only say to keep it to yourself until the story breaks out. Sean is tired & would sooner there was no fight; it's a mild and good humoured play, needless to say the Bishop didn't read it. ...

My love dearest one

Eileen X

[1] Indeed, it was not. John Charles McQuaid was the Archbishop, not Bishop, of Dublin, and held immense secular as well as spiritual sway in the Republic of Ireland which for decades had been a theocracy for all intents and purposes. James Joyce (whose novel *Ulysses* was to have been staged in a dramatisation by Alan McClelland) represented obscenity, free thinking and faithlessness while Sean represented atheistic Communism which the Catholic Church denounced at every available opportunity; both writers were accused of profound disrespect for the Church. Readers can listen on YouTube to Sean giving his account in 1962 of the Tostal affair: "Famous Irish Writers" in the Great Audio Moments: Voices of Yesteryear series: https://www.youtube.com/watch?v=ENwntXstZNw. The recorded interview ends with Sean exclaiming: "There's nobody writing plays worth a damn in Ireland now".

January 23 1958

Darling Shivaun,

... I know very little about what happened over 'The Night is Whispering' – I've practically decided to go back to the old name I gave it – beyond what appeared in the papers – that Dublin's Archbishop informed the Tostal Council he would not say a Votive Mass if they were to do a play by Joyce and O'Casey. There were a few references in the papers, and a lot of Press-men pestered me to tell them all about it; refusing to believe they knew as much as I did. All I definitely know is that the Tostal Council have decided to go on with this program.[2] They can hardly do anything else, unless they abandon the Drama Festival altogether; or produce all foreign plays – Ibsen, Strindberg, Chekhov, or the like, which would hardly give it an Irish flavour. <u>Now</u> the Protestant Church is holding meetings to decide whether <u>they</u> will hold the Tostal inaugural services or no – a bonny brave crew! I enclose the only cutting I have about this business - one from the Sunday Review, published in the 'Irish Times'. Brendan Smith has practically said that the Press have exaggerated a 'lot'. I can't say whether they did or no, for Brendan has told me nothing more; and Jim Fitzgerald, who was with us last week knew nothing more either. 'A Hush Hush business'. ...

It is very cold here now, below freezing point, & I keep close to the frontier of the fire. ... However, cold as I am, I send my warm love to you, & look forward eagerly to seeing you, darling, again.

Ever your Dad xxxx

On January 24, Sean was asked by the Globe Theatre Co. Dublin to authorise Jim Fitzgerald to make changes to the play of his own specifications. Sean had no knowledge of the Globe Theatre's interest in staging the play during the Festival. On the same day, Sean wrote to both the Globe Theatre and Brendan Smith crushing the idea that anyone should have authority to structurally alter his play.[3]

[2] It is both ironic and pertinent that *The Drums of Father Ned* (aka *The Night is Whispering*) is itself about a Tostal or Festival of Irish culture; without reading the play, the Archbishop clearly had been apprised of the element of pagan joy in the script.

[3] Christopher Murray gives us a comprehensive account of the Tostal affair in *Seán O'Casey: Writer at Work*, pp. 386–404.

FARE THEE WELL, AMERICA, 1958

I imagine Brendan Smith, if no one else, must have realised they would be left without the main attraction to the Festival. The press had announced that a new play by O'Casey was to have its world premiere at the Festival. So he wrote to ask Sean to reconsider, but Sean remained steadfast. Indeed, in July Sean proceeded to ban any professional productions of his plays in Ireland (amateur productions would be allowed). Beckett also banned his plays. The Abbey was frantic as they made money from Sean's early plays, but nothing would move Sean, who also suffered from loss of revenue. He didn't lift the ban until 1964. Let all lie sleeping in Drumcondra, for the Archbishop had won, for now.

Before Santa Fe we played Tucson, Arizona. I remember nothing of this, except the pictures of adobe houses, the soft red and yellow of the sandstone, and the cacti, some as tall as the two storey houses.[4] I wasn't drawn to this parched landscape as Georgia Keefe was, although I saw a beauty in it and in the native Americans who still lived there, marginalised and still controlled by the white settlers.

In Santa Fe I bought as much turquoise as I could afford for Breon and his jewellery making, from the female American Indians who squatted on the pavements selling threaded beads of it. Josie took me to a trading post where I spent money I had saved on two traditional necklaces of silver and turquoise, one inlaid for Eileen, the other for me. Also a small saddle blanket that seemed to be woven by the Navajos although we were in the Pueblo tribes area. I may not remember all the Catholic Colleges we visited, or all the varieties of theatres and halls we played, but I do remember visiting a Pueblo reservation with Josie, just outside Santa Fe. Josie and I were taken by her friend who had also accompanied us to the trading post. He worked for the Indian population for a human rights group. He drove us there in a big old American Chevrolet, rusty and red like the landscape. The reservation was smaller than I had anticipated, surrounded by an adobe wall, not too high. Some of the teenagers from the tribe were on top of it watching the tribal dancing that was being performed for about forty tourists. I was shocked to see the dancers' costumes as they were mainly made of cheap taffeta and brightly coloured braids manufactured by their colonisers. The leather headdresses were

---

[4] The *Tucson Citizen* of January 20, 1958 reported that Shaw's *Arms and the Man* played to an audience of 2500. Grania O'Shannon as a Bulgarian debutante "had tremendous appeal and a very winning way"; Lollie May, Aileen Harte and Maurice Good were all lauded for their performances.

grand and old, as were some of the basic clothes, often hidden by the cheaper brighter taffeta skirts. I wondered if, maybe, they were not wearing their traditional ceremonial clothes because this dance was for tourists and not a ritual gathering. After the dances were over we were introduced to the Chief, a tall, wise-looking, imposing man with bright sensitive eyes in his handsome chiselled face. He was most gracious and invited us to share a meal with him. Josie and I entered his adobe house and swinging in a small hammock was a beautiful child of about two years old, asleep and clad in an all-in-one romper suit of pale blue and cream. Then I saw a large television set, with an old man sitting glued to its screen, with his back to us, wrapped in a lovely Indian blanket with a single feather stuck in the back of his thick braided hair. He briefly turned to greet us and then went back to looking.

The Chief was the only person eating with us and we were served by his wife, dressed simply in traditional dress with a tie around her waist. Josie's friend, let's call him Tom, talked intently with the Chief about what to do for the young people of the tribe living in the reserve. The young were frustrated and felt angry about their lack of opportunities and freedoms. They were often categorized as delinquents and many of them were stealing in order to buy drink. It was a big problem for the Chief; it was a mess and he felt his responsibility keenly. They were squeezed into a reservation that wasn't good land, making it difficult to grow much food. They were unable to move freely as was their old tradition – when they had different grounds for different seasons. They had few horses and, with the meagre means to grow their own food, were reliant on the unsympathetic state and government for their survival. They are still fighting for their rights as I write – for what is rightfully theirs and for their dignity. It was sad to leave them doing nothing at all to help.

After Santa Fe we had a long ride across to Atlanta, Georgia and on to Chapel Hill, North Carolina. We were then back on the east coast and nearing our final stopping point, New York City. I couldn't wait to get off the bus for good and to spend a couple of weeks in New York before sailing home; the tour was wearing thin for we were retracing our ground a bit, I suppose due to available dates.

We went through the salt lakes of Utah, through Nebraska and through long flat fields of potatoes while crossing Idaho. We were in Raleigh, North Carolina on the 21st and 22nd February. Anthony Harvey came over from Chapel Hill, the young student who wrote to Sean a lot! He was very nice, small and delicate, with vibrant energy.[5] He introduced me to friends of his who had written a screenplay about two teenagers with mental difficulties who fell in love at the home where they were being looked after. They thought I would be perfect for the girl. I read the script – I didn't say no but wondered how on earth I could ever play the part of this American girl: a few months of letters from Anthony and it all petered out. I wasn't that sorry.

Travelling became more of a blur as the tour drew to an end, like the streaming view from a train window as the landscape flashes by. The long road journeys, stops in motels and small hotels - all much the same: the roadside diners and here again, Howard Johnson. I was longing for home now and to set my eyes on Eileen and Sean to see how they were coping with their lives with Niall torn away from them. We pass billboards, wooden houses, the land slowly getting greener and less dry. Down now to counting weeks before we are deposited in New York City.

While we were working our way towards the tour's end we were hit by a very cold snap and masses of snow. We were on the way to a college up a mountain; it was snowing hard when the heating system in the bus broke, and then the bus itself broke down in the middle of nowhere. Soon the cold began to creep into the bus and into us. We wrapped newspaper around our legs and John Kelly took swigs from his gin. Luckily a truck drove by and Ernie asked them to stop at the first gas station and ask for help for us. In an hour or more, help finally came in the shape of a large tractor-like vehicle and we were towed to our college where we were greeted and taken in to de-freeze with hot drinks. We had to stop there two days waiting for the bus to be mended and off we went again.

February 17 1958

Darling Shivaun,

Delighted to read that you are going along fine. Tho' I hope you were warmly clad when you were in the cold bus. Thanks, a lot, for the

[5] Anthony E. Harvey was a student at Yale University Divinity School when he corresponded with Sean, who wrote him copious replies to questions and observations. In one May 1955 letter to Harvey concerning a black actor who played Bentham in *Juno and the Paycock* in New York in 1955, Sean wrote that despite the apparent dramatic difficulty involved, he would be honoured were his play acted by "Chinese, Negroes, Indonesians, or any other race interested in the work", in seeming anticipation either of the colour-blind school of acting three quarters of a century later, or of multiculturalism. See *The Letters of Sean O'Casey, Volume III*, pp. 28, 135 and index.

colored Cock [a painted tin Mexican cock]. He stands on the desk near me; &, at night, when the lights go on, he sparkles with many gleams of color. He looks grand & proud, and suits his master well.

... The Tostal program has fallen flat. The Council Tostal program wanted me to alter the play to what they said was their requirements, which I couldn't do; & so had to withdraw it. ... Now the council have decided to drop the Joyce play 'Bloomsday', built out of 'Ulysses', & all is disappointment. I enclose clippings that will explain it to you from the 'Irish Times'. There's a rumor now that Samuel Beckett is to withdraw his too on account of the ban of the others. It's a pity, because my play was, I imagine, the gentlest one I've written, 'just an idle laughing play', as I call it in a verse-prologue.[6] ... Take care of yourself in N.Y., and by the way, try to think out what you will say at the Broadcast or Television show there. Get an idea of what may be asked; and collect a few thoughts about possible answers

My deep love, darling, as ever

Sean xxxxx

I was shocked at the news about Ireland's backward action, possibly more so than Sean as he was more used to what Ireland could and did do to restrain free speech in the arts – and in its people. I had experienced the hypocrisy and hatred of the Irish critics with their response to *The Bishop's Bonfire*. Later, the Pike Theatre incident involving *The Rose Tattoo* showed me that the fear and narrow-mindedness was not just a vendetta against Sean. Like the Pike Theatre closure, the Tostal banning was instigated by the Catholic Church with a nod of approval from the (Anglican) Church of Ireland. It was, of course, a loss financially for Sean and Eileen, who were now looking very earnestly indeed towards America for their immediate keep.

[6] This letter carries the same date as the letter Sean wrote to the *Irish Times* after he withdrew his play from the Festival and in which he gives his version of events: see *The Letters of Sean O'Casey, Volume III*, pp. 539–542. (See David Krause's own account on pp. 512–515.) It is generally accepted that Sean correctly interpreted the request from the Festival organisers for changes to the play as an oblique way of inducing Sean to withdraw his play; in short, to succumb to a banning. Samuel Beckett did indeed withdraw his mime work, *Act Without Words I*, and a reading of *All That Fall* in sympathy, and after the Joyce dramatisation was also dropped from the programme. The entire festival was then cancelled. Deirdre Falvey has recounted the affair from Beckett's perspective in the *Irish Times*, April 19, 2025.

FARE THEE WELL, AMERICA, 1958

BEFORE US, MANHATTAN

The advice from Sean and Eileen about being interviewed was because I had been asked back in October, and I had agreed, to do an interview for NBC TV when I got back to New York. In anticipation of my return, NBC got in touch.

December 6 1957

Miss Shivaun O'Casey
Ronald A. Wilford Associates
119 West 57th Street
New York 19, New York

Dear Miss O'Casey,

Thank you for replying to my letter and for your willingness to be interviewed. We are still very much interested, despite the unavoidable delay. When you return to New York, would you please call me at N.B.C.

By chance I discovered that you have a friend at N.B.C. – Kathy Fannon. I took the liberty of discussing you with her this afternoon.

I hope we can get together on an interview.

Very truly yours
Piers Anderson

The show was called *Outlook* and I was interested in having a go at being on television. I had given a couple of local radio interviews on the tour and I enjoyed them.

It was nearly over, the monotony of the bus, the confined home on wheels. I wasn't the only one thinking of being back in New York and then home. Not much more than a week till March 5!

Here we were coming into New York City as if coming from the airport. Over the high road looking down at the penitentiary – Roosevelt Island[7] – the low bridge over the East River: and there was before us the outline of Manhattan from the east side: skyscrapers shooting up into the clear

---

7   Known as Welfare Island at the time of Shivaun's visit, the two-mile long island between Manhattan and Queens was named after the President in 1973. There was a prison on the two-mile island from the 19th century until 1935 and convicts housed there included Emma Goldman, Dutch Schultz, Billie Holiday and Mae West.

blue sky. We had finished our six-month stint as travelling players and we were to spend one night at the old Hotel Sutton, 330 East 56th Street, where we had first spent the night on US soil with the cowgirls and cowboys. Most of the group were going back to Dublin the next day. John Kelly was staying on for a bit and so was Josie: she had many friends and her brother, Michael, lived nearby. Maureen went to Hollywood to play in a Disney Production and she also got a part in Playhouse Ninety – Ann Todd and James Mason had the leads.[8]

I decided I wanted to be independent and I found a room in a hotel so small that I had to climb over my trunk and cases to get into my bed. Here I lay my head for nearly three weeks, and during this time I barely saw it as I was out all day and evening. I rang Bob Ginna and Kathy Fannon and soon was busy.

Josie changed my return ticket for me and the next available sailing was on for March 19 on the polished and ship-shape *Queen Elizabeth*. The first evening Kathy had arranged for me to go with her to have dinner with a fellow NBC worker called Beatrice Cunningham. She was very thin and tall with an interesting face dominated by large eyes, a high forehead and long dark thin hair scraped back into a tight bun. She had been a model for *Vogue*, discovered on a bus; the pictures of her as a model are amazing with legs that went on forever.[9] Beatrice was later to marry Wolfgang Suschitzky, our old friend who was the cameraman on the NBC documentary and the Barry Fitzgerald interview with Sean. Sean liked him a lot as he did his other photographer friend, Gjon Mili, because he tolerated the two to click away at him. Beatrice's apartment was a lovely compact New York one-bedroom in the centre of Manhattan. She served up oyster stew and it was very good. Here in New York oysters were not considered a delicacy or precious; oyster bars were still dotted about as

[8] Maureen Halligan played an uncredited role in *Darby O'Gill and the Little People* (1959) that starred Sean Connery and a host of Irish actors. *Not the Glory*, set in 1939, was an American television play by David Shaw (adapted from the novel by Pierre Boulle) broadcast on May 8, 1958 in the CBS Playhouse 90 series.

[9] Beatrice Cunningham (1923–1989) was a location manager and producer at NBC. In the 1950s she was associate producer of a series called *Conversations with Elder Wise Men* and in 1965 Marcel Duchamp was the interlocutor. At some point during the making of the programme in the Philadelphia Museum of Art, Duchamp gave her a drawing (now referred to as the Cunningham Drawing) associated with his major 3-D work, *Large Glass*. See https://www.tate.org.uk/research/tate-papers/10/an-unpublished-drawing-by-duchamp-hell-in-philadelphia

they were when Sean visited in 1937, and he remembered having oysters at these bars with George Jean Nathan.

These last days in the US are now a muddle of activity: little sleep, great food when it appeared, otherwise no thought of it, walking for miles. I visited Brooks at his office and he introduced me to a young journalist called Arthur Gelb (who later became the head of the *New York Times*).[10] I was rung by Jane Rubin, Sean's American agent, who wanted me to meet Marc Blitzstein, the composer for the musical of *Juno*, and Joseph Stein, the lyricist. They wanted to play me some of the pieces so I could talk to Sean about them. I met them in a rehearsal studio somewhere midtown. It was dark and sparse with an upright piano. Joe Stein rushed at me with bursting energy, glittering eyes divided by a large nose, full of explanation about their concepts, etc. Marc Blitzstein was very nervous, a sensitive, small, well-built man with a dark moustache, but when he played all his nerves vanished and off he went with great bravado. It was modern music inasmuch as he used discordance a lot. I knew very little about music but I liked its passion: it was unlike most "musical" music, more operatic.[11] But when the lyrics started, sung by Joe Stein, they were dreadful – not funny but just bad, I thought.[12] Of course I didn't say anything then but I later told Sean what I thought. In the 1980s I went to a revival in a theatre downstairs at Union Square. I had been correct. Here I saw the whole thing with the dialogue and the songs: it was odd that they had kept mainly to Sean's dialogue when they spoke but when they sang the more catchy lyrics, they didn't fit at all, and definitely not the music: two very different things going on along with the musical score. So it was no wonder it wasn't a success even with its wonderful cast of Shirley Booth as Juno, Melvyn Douglas as Boyle and my old buddy Jackie as Joxer.[13] I think Joe Stein's lyrics are wrong and if they were to be re-written while the score and

[10] Arthur Gelb (1924–2014) was probably in the drama department of the *New York Times* when he met Shivaun. He and his wife Barbara Gelb published a biography of Eugene O'Neill in 1974. He was later managing editor of the *Times*, 1986–1989.
[11] Marc Blitzstein (1905–1964) was an American composer and also librettist, most famous for his 1954 off-Broadway adaptation of Brecht's *Threepenny Opera*. He was also a film composer.
[12] Joseph Stein (b. 1912) began as a radio scriptwriter for famous performers including Phil Silvers and Jackie Gleason. He then wrote the script for musicals, so successfully that he several times won the Tony Award for Best Musical, which included *Fiddler on the Roof* and *Zorba*. He died in 2010, aged 98.
[13] *Juno* the musical opened on Broadway in 1959 and ran for only 16 performances.

choreography were retained, bringing it nearer to the form of *Porgy and Bess*, it would be far better.

The last letters to the US from Eileen and Breon arrived.

March 8 1958

Shivaun dearest,

I haven't written as I knew Sean & Breon had written most of the news. ... Now darling Charlotte begged me to ask you to bring a jar of her favourite face cream. It's an enormous looking jar.
 From Saks 5th Avenue
 Cosmetic Department 1lb size.
 'Scandia Cream. Rose'
 18 dollars. All purpose cream.
I have written to Jane asking her to let you have 100 dollars to use & Charlotte will pay you back when you return – if not too much trouble to get a little dress suit and baby 2nd size for Madeleine, she loves some yellow in it, but that doesn't matter, she has baby in May. I don't need anything. I think I am same size again now 16. If you do T.V. show darling try to be prepared a bit, it's much better for you. ... I would like to meet you at Southampton. Am sending this to Jane Rubin c/o . –
 My love dearest
 Eileen x
 P.S. Am kept at it over this withdrawal of Sean's play, usual phone and press, & really don't want Sean to answer

So I have to buy a dress for Madeleine's baby, a jacket for Sean, something for Eileen, sheets, and for Breon? This last was answered by his letter the following day – books of paintings by Edward Hopper and Marsden Hartley and on American painters generally – all helpfully sold at the Museum of Modern Art.

Jasus! Thank goodness I'm going home by boat. I was filled up by the art at the MET and MOMA and there bought the books for Breon. I went to Saks and bought Charlotte's expensive, heavy pot of face-cream, towels and linen, and Sean a lovely tweed jacket – only partially lined – that looked great on him.

Among all this was my television interview: a whole day of talking and

FARE THEE WELL, AMERICA, 1958

being filmed at some NBC Studio. I remember the interviewer, who I suppose must have been Piers Anderson. He was nice but nervous. I wore a sombre grey, black, white check woollen sack dress. I was asked about Shaw and explained I never met him but described Eileen's time with the great man as he lay dying. Then out of the blue, as we went from question to question sitting in our comfortable chairs, he asked "Was Sean a Communist?" "Well, anyone that has read his books and articles would know he was", I answered. There was a strong silence. "Have I said anything I shouldn't?' I asked. Oh, no, no, and on the interview went for a while more.

Kathy Fannon's letter to me:

May 1 1958, Thursday

Dear Shivaun,

... Mr Anderson did not call me when he first ran the film of the interview. I've not seen it but he did call me yesterday to say it would be going on May 11th, then the enclosed press release came out today. Piers said he was unhappy with himself in the interview but that you came across very nicely, & especially telling of Shaw's death. He also said, you were 'beautiful'. They will probably use about 12 minutes of the total they took of you, which is quite nice really. ...

My love to all the family

Kathy

I never saw the programme. And I never heard anything about it, so it must not have been too good. Ah well, only a day wasted.

Time was passing very quickly for me now and suddenly it was St. Patrick's Day and I was to go with Kathy and Beatrice to Bob Ginna's flat to celebrate and also to watch the documentary the two Bobs made of Sean for NBC. Bob's father was there. He had an amiable broad face like Bob's but greying ginger hair. Bob and he had green ties on with golden harps on the bright green. "My God Bob, what a tie!", I said as he met me at his door. He shushed me and said it was to please his father. Siobhan McKenna was there; she was appearing in *The Rope Dancers*. Drinks had been passed around, when his Dad asked, "Why are both Siobhans wearing black?" Siobhan's immediate reply was "We are in mourning for Ireland". He looked puzzled but joined in the laughter. The time came to sit, with glasses in our hands, to watch the Sean documentary. To our surprise and horror a documentary on De Valera started. Bob Graff was mortified and rang NBC. It turned out that Beatrice had delivered the wrong reels to be televised. Dev was very monotonous so it was turned off. The next day a notice in the *New York Times* read: "Several hundred puzzled O'Casey fans telephoned NBC to find out what happened to the Sean O'Casey documentary. 'It was a clerical error'." That was the explanation: poor old Sean. Even when it was all clear to go and not banned like the interview on the *Ed Sullivan Show* that was put a stop to, but simply cancelled by mistake by a friend.

One final memory was a visit to a Harold Clurman class. In New York famous directors and teachers gave classes to actors who weren't working. This was a scene study class where actors work on their own or with partners to present a scene and then are critiqued by the said famous person.[14] An excellent practice. I was taken by Bob Ginna to the small theatre studio, and was told it was a great privilege. A small energetic man came up and shook hands and told me how he admired my father. I was very impressed. He had arranged for two scenes to be shown. The first was between two men. In the second was a very pretty girl who was rather all over the place. He critiqued them both but didn't give the young girl much advice. He invited Bob and me to his apartment and this very pretty girl came with us, draped in a very expensive-looking fur coat. The thing that remains most prominent in my mind was that his very long pile orange carpet was impossible to walk on in the high heels that I was wearing. You had to lift your feet up as if walking in snow or nonchalantly kick off your heels and walk in bare feet. We had a drink but didn't stay long as it seemed the young girl and he had one objective on their minds.

GOODBYE MANHATTAN AND HELLO LADY ASTOR

No time now except for quick goodbyes and packing all my stuff: a tin trunk, two suitcases and a red Mexican raffia basket full of all the folder matches I had collected for Sean from dinners and hotels during the tour. On March 19 early in the morning Bob Ginna and Kathy arrived outside my hotel with one of the large yellow cabs. The luggage just about all got

[14] Harold Clurman (1901–1980) was an American theatre director and drama critic. In 1931 he co-founded the New York Group Theatre of which Lee Strasberg was a member and which favoured an intense style of acting and left-wing politics. He directed more than forty plays. See "Harold Clurman", Wikipedia.

FARE THEE WELL, AMERICA, 1958

in with suitcases below our feet and I drove with my two friends down the West Side and alongside the Hudson River to the huge docked liner, RMS *Queen Elizabeth*. Cabin D33. It was all bustle and action. We looked over the ship until the hooters went for visitors to leave ship – what hugs and kisses. I watched my two friends walk down the gangplank to the dockside. Crowds of people waving and crying. The engines were turning and the boat pulled slowly away from the big, heaving, never-sleeping city I had begun to know a little. Bob and Kathy were gone – Staten Island was gone – the Statue of Liberty was gone – the New York skyline was gone – we were leaving the coast and entering the Atlantic Ocean. Goodbye until another time.

The crossing back was easy with no violent storms. The lady I shared with was a retired nurse who had looked after Marlon Brando when he had what she called "a breakdown". She told me how clever he was but retained a professional silence as to anything else. He was my favourite actor then and I was one of the few who loved his performance of Mark Antony in the film of Shakespeare's *Julius Caesar*. I had given Sean a Marlon Brando haircut with the little hair he had and he looked good with it. Being on my own, and avoiding the only other member of the Dublin Players on board, John Kelly, I had time to explore. I went past a gate on deck and talked with a young man smoking a cigarette outside an open door that led, I soon discovered, to the first-class passengers' swimming pool. He said if I came in the mornings before 10am he would let me in to swim. I did this every day; I usually swam completely alone in a big clean pool – thinking of the fathoms of deep ocean beneath me, miles of deep water with all sorts of fishes and ocean life I had never heard of going about their watery lives. On deck again I saw porpoises following the ship and more flying fish beating their little fin-wings madly. Eyeing in awe the vast blue of the sea, the magnitude of the flat heaving surface transfixed me.

On one day of the five it took us to cross this deep sea, a note was delivered to me by a purser. "Lady Astor requests your presence for pre-dinner drinks in the first class lounge." The date given was for the next day and I was instructed to bring this card with me. The purser waited for my reply. I agreed as I was curious to meet this lady, a friend of Sean and GBS, with a big house on Plymouth Hoe, that was her Parliamentary constituency. When the time came I put on my grey tailored skirt and white ironed blouse and my red Gamba shoes. I set out to climb the decks to the first-class area, up and nearer to God. I was shown to her cabin door. I took a breath and knocked. After rather a long time and just before I was to knock again the door was opened by her maid in a black costume with an apron and white cap. There was a tense atmosphere coming from the large room beyond and some noises. I asked if this was the right place for Lady Astor? Yes it was and it was also the right day and hour "but her ladyship is a little behind and would like you to go to the lounge where she will join you shortly and she will be wearing this dress so you can recognise her". What a horrible dress it was, too, she showed me: made for a small thin figure, it was a pale-blue fitted cocktail dress covered in blue lace and with chiffon flounces looking as if they were churlishly copying the waves of the sea.

I was shown the lounge and to a seat; it was the lounge adjacent to the dining room, and I waited. And waited. Finally she appeared and asked after Sean and Eileen. I assured her they sounded well and I was looking forward to seeing them soon. We were joined by some other first-class acquaintances of hers, also in their cocktail dresses and coiffed hair, the men in black dinner suits and bow ties. I was in the midst of a Conservative Party jolly and very much the plain Jane of the company.[15] I was feeling very hungry and the smells from the kitchen behind us were making me more so. There was a cold buffet laid out at the entrance to the dining area, with salmon and chicken done up with decorated patterns made with cucumber, etc. Also lobsters and shrimps making patterns on another platter. The table on which these extravagant luxuries were displayed was swathed in a starched white cloth with flowers around the edge. The Campari and soda I had ordered arrived, and I had barely taken a sip when the bell for dinner was rung and they all got up – and so did I. "Well, goodbye", said Lady Astor, "It was good to meet you and please give my regards to your father and of course to your beautiful mother". I could barely speak I thought she was so rude. In my haste to get away from her stiff formality I went through a swing door and found myself in the busy steaming kitchen where all hell was happening. No gentility here, orders flying about, cursing and a frantic ordered chaos. Every now and again waiters were coming through the swing door I had taken in my embarrassed haste, with emptied glasses: others going through another swing door with the ordered food. "Is there another way out?" I pleaded.

[15] Nancy, Lady Astor (née Langhorne, 1879–1964) was elected as a Conservative Party MP in 1919, the first woman to sit as an MP, which she did until 1945. She veered to the far right in her politics.

FARE THEE WELL, AMERICA, 1958

"No, I'm afraid not, you have to go through the OUT swing door". And so I did to titters from some waiters, and my eyes to the floor, and dashed for the glass doors I now recognised as the door I had come in by. I passed by all the first-class citizens going in the other direction to their dinner. I managed to get a sandwich from the cabin-class kitchen and was glad to be back in normality even if rather hungry.

The next day we were to see land: Land's End, in fact. There it was – home. We sailed past Devon along the English Channel, around the Isle of Wight, over the Solent and up Southampton Waters. Land was on both sides and this great hefty lady of a ship was steering through it gracefully. More and more boats appeared of all kinds and somewhere along this slow journey a tug boat arrived to show us the way. No big container ships back then clogging up the Channel, the cargoes were still in the holds of ships, to be craned out bit by bit by the dockers. Our ladyship with her three red funnels puffing out grey smoke crept towards her dock.

I was ready to leave with my suitcase as soon as I could make my way among the crowd to the cabin class gangplank. And there was Eileen, looking lovely in her new grey fine-wool swing coat. Now I am in her arms at last. How good to feel her warmth again and to see she looked well. I spotted Lady Astor with her maid waiting as her chauffeur-driven car pulled up to bundle her in and drive her, maybe, to Plymouth. Her blue dress must be neatly folded in tissue paper in her monogrammed trunk. Eileen said she should say hello, so off she went while I guarded my luggage and waited for the rest of it to come from the hold. When Eileen came back and saw what other luggage had appeared, she said "We'll never be able to take all this on the train, we'd better take a car to get us home". And so we did. Eileen and I sat in the back seat with luggage piled on the front seat, in the boot and even under our legs. We held hands and talked all the way. "You must find a job as soon as possible", Eileen suddenly said. "Work! Work's for horses", the driver said, "Give the girl a chance to rest a bit before she searches for work!" I heard Eileen's lovely peel of laughter again. How good to be back.

Sean heard the car pull up the drive and was on the top of the flight of concrete steps that led to our front door to welcome us. He looked older, even a little thinner, but well. The familiar hug, familiar smell of Erinmore tobacco, and then the searching look close up to my face so his one functioning eye could take a good look. Here we all were back together again ... but with a huge part forever missing.

3
Now what?
1958

NOW WHAT? 1958

HOW TO GET A JOB?

As Breon now lived in a room in Torquay town with a view of the harbour, I took the boys' room, much bigger than Eileen's with its two beds. Here I rested and waited to hear back from places I had written to for work. It was in this room that I made a set for Act 1 of Chekhov's *The Seagull*: I was proud when Sean showed it to a visitor saying how much he liked it. I wanted to act and knew Sean would rather I became a designer. At school I had been considered a good actress and I had got into RADA at 16 but I had gone into my shell. I wrote to all the regional companies asking for any job, preferably as an acting ASM.

No replies came, so I busied myself helping Breon with his Torre Abbey Exhibition of Modern Art: dyeing material to cover screens Breon had borrowed, designing and printing posters and flyers and distributing them, hanging fabric from the beams to cover the walls. Finally the opening day came. Mai Zetterling arrived to open it and it all went swimmingly with good local press cover. Breon organised one other similar exhibition the following year before he moved to St. Ives and sucked me into helping him: painting sheets of plywood to go around the hall to distract from the nasty colours on the walls and helping to hang the pictures on to this plywood. The Scottish actress Adrienne Corri was coming to open the exhibition and all the local press were there with their flashbulb cameras to get her picture. She was very pretty and I think she thought Breon was rather handsome.[1]

In between times, I had a lot of time to discover more about the sad fate of *The Drums of Father Ned* while sitting with Sean in his room. I became aware of the upset the issue of the play caused in our family. It was a sorry story of an Ireland in the fifties, when the church and state held hands: in particular the Taoiseach De Valera and the Archbishop of Dublin, the Most Reverend Dr. John Charles McQuaid. Today we know more about McQuaid than was known publicly then. A few knew of him helping priests who had fondled or had sex with children. Back then there was a

---

[1] Adrienne Corri (1931–2016), born in Glasgow of an English mother and Italian father, was a much recognised face on television and cinema screens. Her screen credits include *Doctor Zhivago* (1965), *A Clockwork Orange* (1971) and *The Human Factor* (1979).

thick velvet curtain to shield all horrors that went on in that most holy fraternity.

Eileen kept insisting that I should look for an acting job, but how? By now it was May and Sam Wanamaker offered me a job looking after his office in London and since we had the flat it was possible to take it on. Up again in London I felt nearer to the action but certainly not part of it. The flat was lovely and very central, almost next door to the Victoria and Albert Museum where in my free time I often went to look at their amazing art book collection. You could ask for any book and with gloves on you could look through the Matisse in *Verve*, Picasso's Beasts, and go through prints, etc.[2] It was a beautiful place to go.

Sam's office was at 24 Coleman Street, EC2. He was running WW Productions Ltd. (Wiman and Wanamaker). Anna Deere Wiman was a very wealthy American with, maybe, a crush on Sam. Every time I met her, she was brought in by a male helper and driver and could hardly walk. She had to be helped to the table and although she managed to talk and laugh she never ate more than a morsel but always had a drink to hand. She was always well turned out and held together by an air of deep sadness and loneliness.[3] For "work", all I had to do was to sit alone in Sam's office, open his mail and answer the phone and take messages: every day I would update him. One day he rang and asked me to type a letter. Type a letter! I couldn't type or spell. It took me a full day and lots of headed paper to finalise it and send it off. Then I typed one to Sean.

May 21 1958

Dear dad,

I am practising typing while sitting waiting for the telephone to ring, that is about all I have to do. This is an extraordinary typewriter, if

[2] Between 1930 and 1937 Picasso created 100 etchings depicting brutal passions embodied and expressed through the figure of the Minotaur. *Verve* was a French art magazine that ran to 38 issues between 1937 and 1960. It offered high-quality lithographic colour reproductions of artworks and Henri Matisse was its most featured artist.

[3] Anna Deere Wiman (1920–1963), born in Illinois and a great-great granddaughter of John Deere, of agricultural machinery fame, began as a dancer in Hollywood and then moved to England where she became a theatre manager and producer. Between 1957 and 1959 she ran the New Shakespeare Culture Centre in Liverpool. She died young at the age of forty-three. See her obituary in *The Dispatch*, Moline Illinois, March 25, 1963 and her entry in Encyclopedia.com

NOW WHAT? 1958

you press it to(o) hard it jumps places, it's called touch control. It also has a red half to the ribbon, if you pull a lever the ribbon rises and the hammers strike out red. ...

Everyone seems to be praising the Moscow Arts Theatre. I am going to try and see it sometime this week so I can see for myself what it is really like, I never trust public opinion, and I can tell mummy all about it before she comes up, and I can also tell you. Charlotte saw 'The Cherry Orchard' and thought that the leading lady was poor and so was the leading man, but that the rest of the cast were wonderful, especially the teamwork of the smaller parts (I suppose that is where the long rehearsal periods help). ... Did you know that this is their first time over here for sixty years? That must be before the revolution.[4]

I have decided to learn Russian. I think it will be the most useful in the years to come because Russia is the main Communist power today and from now on it will be a struggle between them and the Conservatives and India (and Africa). And since Indian is too difficult and not so important I have decided on Russian.* ... The sun is shining up here and everything is carrying on as usual. A few people, in comparison to what it should be, are lobbying their M.P.'s against the H bomb. I don't think much, or anything, can get a rise out of the English, or even less out of anyone settling here.

Would you ask mummy to bring up a copy of 'Three Sisters' when she comes up, please.

With lots of love from Shivy

*If only ...

The Moscow Arts Company was at Sadler's Wells, brought over I believe by Peter Daubeny before he started his International Theatre Seasons at the Aldwych.[5] This was a company I had heard so much about with their Stanislavski training connected to Chekhov. I went to everything they did and saw the best character acting and teamwork I was ever likely to see. I

---

[4] The London revival of *The Cherry Orchard* at the Sadler's Wells Theatre by the Moscow Art Theatre ran for 12 performances from May 15 and was performed in Russian. The MAT also staged *Three Sisters* and *Uncle Vanya*.

[5] (Sir) Peter Daubeny (1921–1975), an aspiring actor, though born in Germany, lost his left arm in 1943 while serving in the Coldstream Guards at Salerno, the scene of the Allied invasion of Italy. In the light of his injury, he turned his considerable talents to stage productions. He brought a wide range of distinguished performers to London, including the MAT.

fell madly in love with the young leading actor but he was in love with the young starlet and I looked on adoringly as they sped off on his motorbike. The sets and costumes may have been old-fashioned, but the acting, lighting and sound effects were out of this world. I thought their performances bigger than life and yet absolutely real. The way the young male actor said Peter's line, "All Russia is our orchard Anya", showed that of course she was in love with him. He also played the doctor in *Uncle Vanya* and the scene between him and Yelena was so painfully beautiful. And the storm! First the curtains started to blow then a distant thud before rain fell and then loud claps of thunder, billowing curtains and lashing rain; the whole of the theatre vibrated. I went backstage to see how it was done and met my old fellow students from Central School of Arts and Crafts coming out. Among them was Veronica who became an expert dyer and fabric printer and John Gunter, who later designed Peter Gill's 1966 production of Shaw's *O'Flaherty V.C.* that I was in at the Mermaid.[6] Well, the storm was made with four enormous kettle drums and thunder sheets and rainmakers (peas in a wooden box): it was the size and skill of the people using them that made such a terrible storm. No money was spared on the arts in Russia at that time.

Ella Winter invited the whole company to her place and we were all invited to the Russian embassy to a function held in their honour. (Odd looking among the crowd was a deeply tanned Douglas Fairbanks Jnr.) This company inspired me. Later I would be enveloped in the magic of the Berliner Ensemble, some of the many companies I watched thanks to the Peter Daubeny's World Theatre Seasons at the Aldwych Theatre in the 1960s. I had seen other very good and memorable productions but with these two companies the benefits of having a permanent company shone out and produced timing and characterisation that were extraordinary. But nothing would hide the fact and the sinking feeling within me that kept repeating I was out of work again and again Eileen was worried. Sean was encouraging my Russian interest.

[6] John Gunter (1938–2016), born in Essex, became a much acclaimed stage designer whose work was for the Royal Court, National and Mermaid theatres and for the Royal Shakespeare Company; he designed operas as well as plays. Peter Gill (b. 1939) is a Welsh stage director and playwright; he is called the unsung hero of British theatre by Michael Billington in a tribute published in the *Guardian*, September 4, 2019.

10 June 1958
Shivaun O'Casey

Darling Shivaun,

I hope you had a good time at the Soviet Reception. By the way, if you are in earnest about learning Russian, I'd advise making enquiries about the SCR: Soviet Cultural Relations Society, who, I believe hold Russian classes. They are at:
 14 Kensington Square, London W.8. I've been attached to it for years.
...
 I hope you are looking after yourself. I am wearing the Brittany Beret now. ...
 As ever Dad, or Sean XXXXXX

ALAN SCHNEIDER

I was home again and I had been offered a job by the American director Alan Schneider to be his assistant on a new play he was directing. Rehearsals were to start in July in London with a pre-West End tour in August. I admired him so much from seeing his productions at Dartington. I went home before my work started and wrote more application letters to repertory theatres.

When I returned from the United States I was oblivious to Eileen's mood changing during the evenings. I was just happy to be with her again and to go about with her as we had always done. Sean said nothing about it to me. One evening after clearing and washing-up the supper things with Sean, him washing and me drying, we went to his room to talk. He sat in his armchair by the electric fire and started to light his pipe for a relaxing smoke. I sat down in his chair opposite. Suddenly Eileen broke in, angry and accusing. "Look at you 'intellectuals' both 'discussing' important things and thinking you are so clever!" A long shocked pause. "I suppose I'm not good enough to take part in the discussions! Well, I tell you, I am not stupid!" This was a blast from nowhere, a punch in the stomach. This was not the warm understanding mother I knew; who *was* this harridan? Sean put his head in his hands in a way that made me think something like this had happened to him before; he begged her to come and sit with us and said that he wanted that very much. After more pleading she roughly pulled a chair to sit behind his armchair and facing me over the table, with a look of defiance and what I felt was hatred in her glance. Sean started to talk again trying to shift things into a positive mode again. She sat for a while and then flounced out. I didn't know what to say. Finally Sean said quietly that she had been like this on and off for a while. "She is upset, and finding the evenings difficult." He never mentioned drink. Niall's death had hit her unbearably hard and the bad thing about our family was that we were all being very brave and keeping our deep sorrow inside so not to upset anyone. This was the worst thing to do and her sorrow had burst out.

At that moment I wanted to ignore it and pretend it didn't happen. Sean said to leave her for a while. But I decided to face up to it, plucked up my courage with difficulty, and went to find her. She was making noises that seemed as if she wanted to be heard. I hated embarrassing or awkward situations, or shocking discoveries, but I knew that if you talked it out it was usually a relief. I asked her why she was being so unreasonable. It was then I noticed that she was drinking. I took up the glass she was drinking from and took a sip; it was alcohol disguised in milk. She started to defend herself. "I am just like my mother, a silent drinker, and it is getting worse as I get on". My God, what to do? I thought of Sean who so hated people who were drunk, with his memories of his brother Mike and the destruction he had seen around him caused by alcohol, and the brutality, very often against women; he hated how Eileen's mother drank and made Eileen's life miserable. She went to take a drink from her glass. "Try and stop drinking that, Eileen, just try to stop it." "I told you, I'm like Grannie." "You are definitely not like her. You can stop it if you want to. You are not in the least like your mother." Some such words were said and ended in us embracing and crying our eyes out. This went on over and over again for some weeks. In the day time she was the warm kind Eileen but I, and I think Sean, dreaded the evenings. We watched the television that had been given to them by Sidney Bernstein. On the box we stared at Perry Mason, one of the favourites to halt the night bringing on its loneliness, and we all tried to solve the mystery acted out before us before the end, usually getting it wrong. Needless to say, Sean was the best at getting it right. He sat right next to the set and to one side so we could see as well as possible, straining to make something out from the black and white figures and listening intently to the words for clues. Things were a little better before I had to go to London to start work with Alan Schneider.

NOW WHAT? 1958

When I came home after the tour of Schneider's production of *The Deserters*, I felt things had changed a great deal and Sean and Eileen were back again sharing their lives and, importantly, laughing again. To both their credits, mainly Eileen's, they pulled through it themselves without help and the long struggle to embrace the unrequited longing for Niall bound them closer together into a friendship of deep understanding, respect and love that lasted till Sean died.

We rehearsed Schneider's play in the West End. No pay, only expenses. I liked Alan a lot and we got on well. *The Deserters* was a pretty bad play altogether. The action takes place in a convent in, I think, France. The Mother Superior, played by Elizabeth Sellars, was holed up with two other nuns during the WW2 in France. Into their midst comes a handsome American deserter and later two Germans who want to catch him and kill him. A lot of talk about what is right and what is wrong and a tantalising hint that the young nun and American deserter might love each other.[7]

During rehearsals I sat next to Alan to take notes for him, so he could watch all the time, and not take his eyes off the action. Not just a *few* notes but *masses* of notes for the actors, not the technical team. Each actor had their own page for their notes. "You are to make my notes polite", he told me. "When I say 'tell that smuck to move when I told him', you'll write 'Please move as mentioned on such and such a line'." This I did. At all rehearsals, previews. and even performances on the tour, I took notes and handed them to the appropriate actors for them to look at before Alan came round to their dressing rooms to go through them with them. Albert Lieven, who played the Nazi officer, always took them from me with a quizzical smile.[8] During rehearsals Elizabeth Sellars' manager, or guru, attended by agreement with management, and sat in the circle and

---

[7] *The Deserters* was written by the American playwright (and director), Norman Thaddeus Vane (1928–2015). The play opened in London and then toured English cities, doing, in Vane's own words, "so-so business": "Enviable Debauchery: Interview with Norman Thaddeus Vane", *Hidden Films*, January 20, 2012. (https://hidden-films.com/2012/01/20/enviable-debauchery-interview-with-norman-thaddeus-vane/) The Glaswegian actress, Elizabeth Sellars (b.1921), became well-known in film and on TV from the 1950s through the 1980s. She died in 2019 at the age of 98.

[8] Albert Lieven (1906–1971), born in East Prussia, began his acting career in Germany before fleeing to the United Kingdom with his wife in 1937 (both were Jewish). His English career began on stage before he became a prolific actor in films; among his credits are *The Life and Death of Colonel Blimp* (1943); he often played Nazi officers. He returned to Germany in 1951 but continued to appear in British as well as German movies.

watched. Alan didn't like him as he gave Alan notes to do with Miss Sellars being centre stage and, later on, being well lit.

I became friendly with the young actress playing the pretty nun. She was called Joanna Dunham and had been at Slade studying art before becoming an actress. The other nun was played by an American actress called Jane Gordon, and we all palled up on the tour.[9]

We were on tour for about a month, and I was given another job; I had to go and buy red roses for the ladies in the cast on each first night. My experiences weren't as bizarre as Eileen's when she toured with the D'Oyly Carte – no dead body under the bed as she had at her first digs.[10] Joanna and I were late booking digs for the first date and ended up with a little rigid lady whose house was full of nearly life-size holy statues: on the landings, in the dining-sitting room, and in our bedroom, where we had a large Mary standing guard over us.

Sean's letter to me:

August 1958

P.S. drawn and written in bed.
Darling Shivaun,

In bed! And wretched programs on the Radio, or, rather more wretched than usual. Much better today, and was up for an hour or so.

So much for me. You have entered a new field, for this one is really your first experience of a tour with a genuine theatre company – the Ibbs one was really a tour of the USA. I hope you may not have too tiring a time, and that the experience will be, at least, a fairly happy one. Anyway Alan is a different director from Ibbs, Thank God. It is indeed something to work for with him. Give him my warm regards & good wishes like those of the old trumpeter in My Heart's in the Highlands.

---

[9] Joanna Dunham (1936–2014) from Bedfordshire, came to prominence soon after her role in *The Deserters* when she performed in *Romeo and Juliet* at the Old Vic in 1962. On the strength of seeing her as Juliet, Marilyn Monroe recommended her for the part of Mary Magdalene in *The Greatest Story Ever Told* (1965), a Hollywood box office hit. She ended her acting career and became a painter.

[10] Eileen recounts the story in her autobiography, *Eileen*, pp. 59–60.

Take care of yourself darling, and rest well & wisely. My deep love as ever goes with you.

Dad, Sean

Sean had had a very bad attack of bronchitis, and it took hold badly this time. As he still smoked, inhaling his pipe now instead of cigarettes, his lungs were not the best. But when he got over these relapses he walked quickly and didn't wheeze or get out of breath.

Our digs in Manchester were run by a very warm and friendly landlady, very theatrical herself, but our lavatory was built in the corner of the dining room where all the guests ate. Just thin plywood walls and the door straight into the lav – you washed your hands in the kitchen. When people went, you heard everything as if they were sitting with you at the table. It was a jolly place, though, and gave an excellent breakfast which we shared with people from another show in town, and we laughed as we all shared our experiences of touring.

When we were up north, Jo (Joanna) and I visited the Brontes' house near Leeds. I was amazed by the beauty of the moors and the house and village. It was not now the dangerous desolate place it was back when the Brontes lived there: the water was evidently contaminated then and the graveyard ill-drained opposite their Rectory. The northern landscapes were so beautiful, not at all what I had imagined. Not a Black Country at all. I hadn't seen this when I was young and stayed with my friend Jane in Doncaster, unaware maybe of what was outside as inside I was so miserably missing Eileen.

Our last stop, Brighton, was lovely. Jane Gordon found us a self-catering apartment that looked over the pebbled beach and the sea. It was a romantic windy place, with many lovely windows, like the windows on a galley ship. It was the beginning of September and the sea would be rough one day and calm another – but there was a bite in the air and autumn was coming in. I left after the first night there and it was a great place to say goodbye and wish them all good luck in London.

Sean's letter to me:

2 September 1958

My dearest lass,

Yes, I'm on my feet again, at last, & having an occasional look at the wonders of St. Marychurch. However, I have to take care still. I do hope you may have good weather in Brighton.

I received Dave Krause and his geologist friend in bed, in State, like a king on his throne, covered with a gay Mexican bed-spread. He is to spend near a year in Ireland. Brendan Behan rang up today looking for you. He is in London, but goes back to Ireland tomorrow. He is to have a book – a biography, 'Borstal Boy', published soon; and I wish it good success, for the lad has something in him; and might have more, if he set himself to be a little more sensible. 'The Playboy' musical [*The Heart's a Wonder*] is coming to the Westminster Theatre in two weeks time. The Irish critics have hailed it as a musical masterpiece, and expect it to have the success of 'My Fair Lady'. The Tostal of 1959 is to be spread over April, May, June, July, August & September – leaving Christmas a day free. I wonder what dramas they will work into next year. At the moment, I'm writing – or typing – a chapter about the ban on 'The D of F Ned'; built on an article by Quid Nunc in 'The Irish Times', saying that O'Casey withdrew the play himself, and the clergy had nothing to do with it. ...

Your sketch of note-taking in the dark is very fine: the look on each face is really good; the one stretching forward, tense, the other, calm, waiting for the remarks. Very good indeed. ...

Sean

My deep love.

P.S. You have a talent with the pencil, my love.

As the tour ended in Brighton and I left before their last night, it seemed to me that all hope of London's West End had faded. Nothing and nobody, not even Alan, could make anything out of such a play. I was sorry to leave Jo, as we had become good friends but I would see her again in London over many years. While I was working in Bristol (my next job) she took over from Judi Dench as Juliet in Zeffirelli's 1960 stage production of *Romeo and Juliet*: I saw it and loved it – she was earnest and vulnerable. Soon she was cast as Mary Magdalene in the big Hollywood movie *The Greatest Story Ever Told*. I was very pleased and very impressed. I met her in her lovely Regency house on Highbury Fields, with graceful windows that reached down to the floor. She had babies before I had, a girl and a boy. After I had my baby, Ruben, we met up in her house, designed by her architect husband, Harry Osborne. In 1989 when she toured with me to

NOW WHAT? 1958

East Berlin with a rather too-long show about my Dad, she helped me run the show and sat drawing the actors and the streets. We picked up bits of the tumbled wall on the East side while they were selling them on the West side. The last time I saw Jo was before I moved away from London and she was just beginning to show signs of memory loss, like her mother before her. She painted until she died and exhibited her paintings, working for the Alzheimer's Society.

EILEEN GOES TO NEW YORK

After the tour I went home for a while and the feeling of being cut off from working in the theatre came back. Sean was old and in poor health so I wanted to be with him and learn from him, but I needed work and the theatre thing was there and I couldn't ignore it. Jane Gordon had told me about movement classes that she went to at Cambridge Circus given by Yat Malmgren. He had been a lead dancer of the Jooss Ballet and taught a theory of movement by Laban who originally used it to annotate dance movements; Yat helped to bring it into context for actors.[11] Sean and Eileen agreed that I should go up to London for a couple of months after I had written some more letters to theatre companies. I thought I might do some voice classes too, but never got round to that: I could only find individual lessons and they were too expensive. Yat's lessons were interesting and unusual – roughly using different movements to express different feelings. I had done some ballet at school but not much but most of the actors like me were pretty awful. I managed the floor exercises and the upright walking ones, but I didn't understand the theory at all.

Eileen's letter to me:

October 1958

Dearest Shivaun,

... Now don't think me mad, (I am slightly) while you are waiting

[11] Yat Malmgren (1916–2002) was a dancer and acting teacher in his native Sweden and in Berlin and Paris. As a dancer, he toured throughout the UK with Ballets Jooss. He collaborated with Rudolf Laban (1879–1958) in developing a theory of movement. When through injury his dancing career ended, he taught at the International School of Ballet in London and conducted movement classes in Covent Garden attended by distinguished British actors, including Sean Connery and Anthony Hopkins. He cofounded the Drama Centre in London in 1963 with Christopher Fettes and John Blatchley. See his obituary in the *Guardian*:
https://www.theguardian.com/news/2002/jun/13/guardianobituaries.obituaries

around and not doing anything why don't you take some lessons in Fencing – voice production & dancing. You need all these things for Performance/perfection (?) & all three are good for you.

Fencing is taught at Polytechnic in Regent Street. Voice production and singing is more expensive you can get cheap classes at Poly but in this case maybe a better person. I was going to Miss Warren at Aeolian Hall, (still may one day) Sam told me she was good.

Dancing again. You could go to private class in day – or ask Charlotte, but I am sure The Stage must be littered with adverts for lessons. You don't need too cheap a type of person, work it out; but you could be at it all the time and don't tell me to move isn't important & <u>don't</u> tell me they can teach you nothing.

There is also a dancing times which would have adverts. You would also be using your body & slimming in a way.

I know you think of pottery, also, why not? This would be near you.

London is really so easy this way & a lot of good: Polytechnics have good classes & almost enough to at least move, fencing I am sure is good for quickness. ...   Love & love Eileen

This letter really made me feel bad. I felt incapable of doing all she suggested. I hated the idea of fencing and as for movement being slimming, I was size 10 and didn't need to lose weight. Also I had very little money left from the US tour and none saved from the expenses of Alan's tour. The flat was free and that was a blessing and it was warm and bright. I ended up continuing with Yat and taking an etching class at the Chelsea Art School for nothing. But I only went three times. I arrived to be taught by Middlemarsh, or somebody, who did a famous etching of a drowning chicken. When I went to my first class he was there, very distraught and theatrical: I was the only person to turn up. He quickly gave me a copper plate and roughly explained what I should do: the etching tools, the blocking wax, the acid bath, and left like his chicken in the whirlpool – never to be seen by me again. He didn't tell me how long to leave the plate in the acid and a passing student showed me how to ink up and use the press. I made two prints, one of a bowl of fruit and the other of Paddington Station. When I showed them to Breon he actually thought they were rather good.

Eileen was going to New York! I was at home before Eileen left for New York to see the opening of *Cock-a-Doodle Dandy* at the Carnegie

Playhouse directed by Philip Burton (who had directed the successful *Purple Dust*) and a production of *Shadow of a Gunman* sponsored by the Actors Studio with Lee Strasberg's daughter, Susan Strasberg, playing Minnie. This was directed by Jack Garfein.[12]

Eileen was to fly to New York and she was very excited. This is the first time she would be in New York since she was a Cochran Young Lady. This is also where she had read *Juno and the Paycock*. She had been cast by George M. Cohan to play a maid in a touring production, and the leading lady was to read for Mary and asked Eileen to help her with an Irish accent; Eileen, who had heard the Irish nuns and whose mother had a slight Mayo accent, tried to help her. Eileen fell in love with the play and was determined to get to meet Sean O'Casey via her lover Lee Ephraim as soon as she got back to London. Lee kept Eileen to some degree but would never divorce his sick wife, so young Eileen, who wanted children, was in limbo.[13] When she did get back, the first things she asked Lee to do was to get her to read for Mary and to meet Sean O'Casey. She did and Sean fell in love with her: this vulnerable, kind, beautiful girl. The long and short of it was they married when Eileen was a little pregnant; she had always wanted children; Sean became a lover, protector and friend.

Just as well Eileen was flying, since she got very bad sea-sickness. Eileen was to be put up by Lucille at the Pierre Hotel – luxury. John Cavanagh, the dress designer, whose mother was born in the same Mayo town as Eileen's mother, Kathleen Carey, and who designed for the Royals, gave her a lovely dusty pink satin evening coat with a small pale mink collar; it had a lovely ochrey yellow lining.[14] She bought a Dior dress that had a built-in corset and underslip; so you didn't need any underwear. She must have looked grand for the first night as she was a beautiful woman

---

[12] The fame of the American actress Susan Strasberg (1938–1999) in her lifetime rivalled that of her drama coach and theatre director father, Lee Strasberg. Jack Garfein (1930–2019), having survived (as Jakob Garfein, born in Czecholovakia) Auschwitz and other concentration camps, became an associate of Lee Strasberg's, a member of the Actors Studio, and a distinguished film and theatre director.

[13] Lee Ephraim (b. Kentucky 1876 or 77; d. London 1953) was active as a theatrical producer in the 1930s and 1940s. Consult the index of *Eileen* for an account of the love affair.

[14] John Cavanagh (1914–2003) lived in London where he was possibly born despite his claim to County Mayo beginnings. He designed dresses for members of the Royal family, including a "Coronation collection" for the enthronement of Queen Elizabeth in 1953. Eileen mentions him in her memoir, *Eileen*, p. 183.

anyway. One of the sacrifices of living with Sean was not enough money to buy the clothes she loved. She used to buy *Vogue* and we would pore over it. After Sean's death, when his work was making money in Germany, she started to shop at Kenzo and buy some things she had longed for.[15] She always looked amazing. She often bought things for me, saying it was important to have lovely things when you were young.

So off she flew on November 5, 1958 to represent Sean and act as his ambassador. When Eileen was away, Breon looked after Sean and I helped a little when I was home. Looking after Sean really meant shopping and cooking, reading his letters to him if he asked, and of course talking with him a lot. One thing I did was cook him something he longed for – a sweet omelette; that is, an omelette with jam inside and sprinkled with sugar with marks burnt on the top. Sean had a very sweet tooth and usually had four to six teaspoons of sugar in his tea, sometimes surreptitiously adding another, to our shouts of, "No, too much!" He didn't drink coffee.

There was a lot of press coverage about Lee Strasberg's daughter playing Minnie, and Eileen gave interviews. Eileen was reserved about both productions. We were all particularly sad that *Cock-a-Doodle Dandy* had such a bad first showing: first productions of works are so important. For Sean it was a big blow as it was his favourite play and he had hoped it would be a success and get recognised as a good work, and maybe open the door to his later work being done and put a stop to the continual cry that he wrote nothing of worth since he left the Emerald Isle. Ah well! *Cock-a-Doodle Dandy* opened on November 12. "What a shame Cock didn't get all that good notices," I wrote to Eileen on November 15. "Still it is such a difficult play to act one can hardly expect it to be perfect the first time. Maybe biz will catch up later (Let's hope that 'Shadow' is a financial success anyway.)"

Brooks reviewed *Cock-a-Doodle Dandy* in the *New York Times* on November 13 under the heading "O'Casey's Defense of Joy". Here is part of what he wrote: "Since it was written on the amiable assumption that all actors are as pungent as Barry Fitzgerald and F.J. McCormack, it also sets the theatre serious problems. ... The Celtic tone is uneven throughout the cast. Probably there is nothing that Philip Burton, the director, can do about that. And some of the actors are first rate, Irish or not; Paul Shyre as an addle-headed soothsayer & moralist; George Abeling as a harsh,

---

[15] Kenzo is a luxury French fashion house begun by Kenzo Takada (1939–2020), a Japanese designer who moved to Paris.

bellowing priest; Anne Marie as a giggling Irish-spirited servant; Rae Allen as a fiery-eyed young wife to an old codger; Gaby Rodgers as a shameless hussy; Jack Betts as a mysterious messenger who is not intimidated by superstition or authority ... ". From this review it seems as if the two main comic-tragic parts of the husband and the turf-dealer were not too good. They are central to the play, as is the young girl, Loreleen.

The play, of course, ran another risk. *Cock-a-Doodle Dandy* had played in Toronto before coming to New York. An account of "an incident" there was reprinted in the *New York Times* that reminded me of when a member of the audience watching a production of mine, *A Pound on Demand*, in New York in 1990, yelled out: "There isn't a prostitute from one end of Ireland to the other!")[16]

SHOUTERS AT PLAY CHIDED BY O'CASEY

Toronto Evening Telegram, October 6 1958
Dramatist Scores Manners of Couples Who Interrupted His Drama in Toronto.

Sean O'Casey said yesterday the two couples who caused a commotion at a performance here of his play, "Cock-a-Doodle Dandy", had bad manners. The playwright added:

"The couples had a right to oppose my views; they had a right to express themselves, but not to interrupt the players."

Mr. O'Casey was interviewed by telephone by The Telegram here at his home in Torquay, England.

Two men leaped to their feet in the third act of the performance here Saturday night and cried "you're a liar", when a dying girl returns from the shrine of Lourdes, France, without being cured and rejects the belief in miracle healing.

They had urged the audience to leave at the second intermission. The men continued their shouts until escorted out.

[16] This shout from the audience in 1990 echoes the furious objection the avid theatregoer Joseph Holloway made to Lyle Donaghy, the Irish poet, after watching the premiere of *The Plough and the Stars* at the Abbey Theatre in 1926. Donaghy told Lady Gregory that Holloway called the play "abominable" because "There are no streetwalkers in Dublin", to which Donaghy replied: "I was accosted by one only last night". Unfazed, Holloway said: "There were none in Dublin till the Tommies [British soldiers] brought them over". Benedict Kiely quotes the whole exchange in his review of Robert Hogan and Michael J. O'Neill (eds), *Joseph Holloway's Abbey Theatre* (1967) in *The Northwest Review* 9:2 (1968): 114.

Mr O'Casey said yesterday "the play is based on fact." He said commotion at his plays is not new to him. He said he wrote the play to amuse people and was not trying to put across any message. ...

The first objections came from the couples when a priest knocks down and accidentally kills a man who has been living with a common-law wife.

An understudy in the play, Elsa Dawson, said the couples complained during the intermission at the front of the theatre and said the play should be banned.

"Does the church know about it?" they asked.

... the men apparently considered the play anti-Roman Catholic. A few members of the audience had walked out at every performance. ...

Eileen returned exhilarated by all she had done and seen: a wonderful ambassador for Sean, wooing almost everyone she met with her beauty and warmth and wit. She was a very flirtatious and sexy lady. She craved and needed attention for herself, especially from men; it didn't really matter what they looked like.

SEAN AND BARRY FITZGERALD

Christmas came and went and soon after New Year a film crew arrived to film a conversation between Barry Fitzgerald and Sean. Sean had refused to go to Dublin for this, so Barry came to him with his friend, and our friend, J.J. O'Leary, to look after him and with whom Barry always stayed when in Dublin. The two young men who were the producers of the documentary were charming and enthusiastic and were called Tom Hayes and Jim O'Connor.[17] They called the documentary, which was about the Abbey Theatre, *The Cradle of Genius*, and used the burnt out ruin of the old theatre as its background – except for this interview. The Abbey Theatre had burned down in 1951 and when Sean was rung up about it by reporters, he first asked, "Did anyone get hurt?"; after being assured that no one was hurt he said: "Then it is a good thing, it was an old place and needs new life."

The hubbub of the preparations for filming again invaded Sean's quiet life. For Eileen and myself it brought the excitement of meeting all the people involved and for me an interest in the whole process. The interview was to take place in Sean's room and so for a couple of nights he slept in Eileen's bedroom and she slept in the front room on the Hille sofa bed.

[17] The documentary film-maker Tom Hayes (1926–2008) was born in Co. Limerick. Details of Jim O'Connor's career are proving hard to come by.

NOW WHAT? 1958

Sean was relieved that the cinematographer was Wolfgang Suschitzky whom he had liked so much when he filmed the NBC Wisdom series in the same spot when Niall was alive. This put Sean at ease to a certain extent as the producer, Paul Rotha, was a withdrawn and rather humourless person.[18] I found the final documentary uninteresting and dull except for the Barry and Sean bit: Eileen described it as like "an advertisement for Irish tweed", as so many people were dressed in that cloth.[19]

To see Sean and Barry fall into each other's arms when they met affected everyone, as we all looked on in silence; Sean clapped him on the back as if he couldn't get enough of him. Then Sean came out and gave Eileen a very sad look; he took a moment to gather himself and then went back in. He was shocked by how ill Barry was with Parkinson's disease and felt very sorry that he had in effect forced Barry to make the journey to him. But then Sean could not have made the trip to Dublin, so they never would have met; although it was a great joy, it was also a great sadness to Sean. What was it for Barry? J.J. had made the journey as comfortable as possible and was watching over him all the time, but Sean worried about how much this visit might take out of him. But, he was here and the interview was to take place. Sean then found out that it was difficult for Barry to retain things, difficult for him to talk easily; so Sean had to lead the story of the first night of *The Plough* and managed to end up with *Juno* and Barry joining in and singing with him the song Captain Boyle sings while frying his sausage:

> When the robins nest agen,
> And the flowers are in bloom . . .
> He's promised he'll come back to me,
> When the robins nest agen!

The days that followed Barry's departure Sean would repeat over and over again to Eileen that they should have let him know how ill Barry was and they should not have let poor Barry make such a journey. Eileen would

[18] Paul Rotha (born Paul Thompson in London; d.1984) was a British documentary filmmaker; he often collaborated with the cinematographer Wolfgang Suschitzky.
[19] Yet Christopher Murray in his biography, *Sean O'Casey: Writer at Work* (Montreal, Kingston: McGill-Queen's University Press, 2004), p. xiii calls *The Cradle of Genius* "that wonderful piece of film". It featured several distinguished Abbey actors and was nominated for the 1962 Academy Award for Best Documentary Short.

say that he had come all the way from Los Angeles to Dublin and maybe it brought him a short time of joy and comradeship. I must say, that is what I felt when I saw their embrace and also when I watch the film – a glimpse of what they had lived through together in Dublin in the 1920s.

4
At home in Bristol
1959–1960

Listening to my buttie Mozart.

THE BRISTOL OLD VIC

A letter had come on December from the Bristol Old Vic that gave hope for work.[1]

17 December 1958

The Bristol Old Vic

Dear Miss O'Casey,

I have not written before as we had nothing to offer you but it looks now as though there may be an opportunity if you would care to assist generally in making scenic props, e.g. flowers, etc, and possibly make hats, jewellery and trimmings for the wardrobe, together with some scenic painting. We usually have a budding designer with the company doing this, and this has just fallen vacant.

I am just off to Tel-Aviv to do a production, but our Production Manager, Mr. Nat Brenner, will see you about the middle of January if you are free and interested. Perhaps you could let him know.

Yours sincerely

John Moody, Director[2]

I was starting to feel nervous. With tummy wobbles I went for my interview. I was asked by Brenner if I could make props and assist in painting the scenery when needed, and what experience I had of all this. Of course, full of bravado, I said yes, and showed him a letter of recommendation Sam Wanamaker had kindly written. Nat said he would accept me if I wanted the job: I said I did, and we shook hands.[3] While I

---

[1] The Bristol Old Vic company was established in 1946 as an offshoot of the London Old Vic Theatre. However, the theatre itself is the oldest continuously operating theatre in the English-speaking world, having opened on King Street in 1766 as the Theatre Royal, with a prologue from the stage written by David Garrick.

[2] John Moody was Director of the Bristol Old Vic, 1954–1959. After that, he was appointed Director of Productions at the Welsh National Opera, 1959–1969, resigning to become a full-time painter. See the Theatre Collection of the University of Bristol and "John Moody (opera director)", Wikipedia.

[3] In 1952, Brenner had directed the BBC Television movie of *Tess of the D'Urbervilles*, starring Barbara Jefford as Tess. Brenner once took a cut in pay at the Bristol Old Vic in order to afford hiring Peter O'Toole: see Mark Hennessey's account of the proposed Peter O'Toole Memorial service in the *Irish Times*, May 17, 2014. Brenner, something of a legendary figure, became Principal of the Bristol Old Vic in 1963.

was there I was given tickets to see *As You Like It*. There were interesting sets by Daphne Dare – very minimal, with the forest trees and bushes made from wooden structures with chicken wire on them to make the shape of the leaves.[4] I was shown around by the person I would be replacing, Fluff Browne.[5] We ended up in the pub and there was Peter O'Toole with the beautiful, tall and elegant Siân Phillips. I think he remembered me, and I think I said "Hello". He had a handsome angular face with a bush of hair and an interesting crooked nose. Then I caught the train back home.

The offer sounded grander than it turned out to be: there was no chance of any design, except in so far as I could add to any props and hats I made, which was my main job. I didn't make this clear to Sean or Eileen who still thought I might design a production. However, it turned out to be a great experience, making props, hats, jewellery etc., painting scenery, printing fabrics and being a small part of a good solid, three-week repertory company. I accepted and was to make £7.10.00 a week (about £170 in today's money), not near what I had been paid on the American tour. But it was a steady job with regular payments.

Breon and I were at home with Eileen and Sean to see Christmas come and go. I was feeling even more nervous about what would face me in the making and painting line. The Old Vic recommended some digs for me to start from, and Eileen and I chose some in Redlands, Bristol, so at least I had somewhere to sleep. I would be 19 the next September.

In January I arrived the day before my work was due to start. The digs we had chosen were in a respectable middle-class area, a street of sturdy Edwardian red-brick semi-detached houses. The house was owned by an elderly couple who had decided to let a few rooms in their rather large house. They were a sweet couple; the husband who had managed a bank was retired, and they thought that letting rooms to theatre people would be "interesting" and make their lives more "vibrant". My room was at the top of the three-story building, with its cable window looking out over the treetops, bare now, to the road in front. It was a large room with a wash basin and a small gas fire (for which you needed change). It had a pleasant bed, a chair and a table with a wardrobe for my clothes. They gave me supper on this first night – otherwise it was just breakfast – and

---

[4] The costume and production designs by the Somerset-born Daphne Dare (1929–2000) later included the movies *Doctor Who* (1963), *Kes* (1969) and *Hidden Agenda* (1990).

[5] Catherine (Fluff) Browne designed productions at BOV between 1957 and 1967. See her listing in the online site *Theatricalia*: Plays, People, Places.

told me how to get to the Vic in the morning. I actually slept that night, to be called to arms by the loud ringing of my alarm clock.

You entered backstage via a small alley called Rackhay, cobbled, with bits of old vegetables scattered about. This was a part of the Bristol Dock area where the ships offloaded vegetables and fruit. I liked the smell of rotting fruit filling the cobblestone street. At the end of this narrow alley was a very large oak door and in this large heavy door was set the small stage door. A little window slid to the side if you needed to talk to the little, very old, respectably-dressed man. His shirt was slightly fraying at the cuffs and his suit was a bit too big for him. This was Billy – always amiable even if he was confused or overwhelmed by his responsibilities. He shook my hand and told me to go up the broad wooden stairs, through some other large doors that led to the stage, and into the scene dock where Daphne Dare would help me.

She was talking to a handsome man and looking at a model of the set for *The Taming of the Shrew*: this was to be the first play I worked on here. The first reading was the day after next. The man was the theatre's designer, Pat Robertson, and Daphne was the other designer but also the scene painter. Daphne designed about three shows in a season, Pat about nine and visiting designers one or two.[6]

I immediately liked Daphne and Pat; they were friendly and funny, relaxed as well as being intensely serious about the look and feel of their productions, both perfectionists. Daphne took me up to the dressing rooms that were on two levels. Up we climbed to the level of the Fly-floor, where I met the king of this domain, Frank Fresko the Flyman.[7] Just before we had entered the flydoor there was a little door to the right to a small room with a little paned window looking out along a roof gully, with slate tiles slanting up each side, and along which and above the slanting roofs you could see the sky. A work bench ran along under this window, and on the

---

[6] Pat Robertson (1922–2009) came to the Bristol Old Vic in 1950 or 1951 and was there until 1960 when he left and freelanced before in 1964 joining the Nottingham Playhouse, by then co-directed by John Neville and Frank Dunlop. See his obituary in the *Guardian*, April 22, 2009: https://www.theguardian.com/stage/2009/apr/22/obituary-patrick-robertson. His designs are listed in *Theatricalia*: https://theatricalia.com/person/50p/patrick-robertson

[7] The flyman is now called the flyperson and he or she operates the weighted system of raising or lowering scenery on the stage. Fresko is listed in *Theatricalia* as having been involved in three productions 1957–1961 at BOV and Theatre Royal (London) suggesting he might have been an actor as well as flyman.

wall to the right shelves full of bits of material, trimmings, bottles and brushes, boxes full of odds and bits, two canvas wig-stands, glues, wire etc. This was my prop room and I felt immediately at home. I followed Daphne through to the fly floor and through a door to a large, light, L-shaped room, with a very large cutting table, sewing machines, a large sink, ironing board, always at the ready, and a drying cabinet, where you could hang shirts. Along the other leg of the L was a narrower space, with the two high-powered sewing machines, and at the end another table where the costume designer, Rosemary Vercoe, worked when she was doing the costumes for a show. But the Queen of all before her was the costumière, Doris Nicholas, petite and neat, with her auburn hair screwed back in a bun. She was profoundly deaf and mainly relied on lip-reading. She was a brilliant cutter and maker of costumes.[8] She and her assistant were washing and ironing clothes for the Christmas show that was running at the time, called *Christmas in King Street*, directed by the departed Director, Denis Carey. A new Director was to arrive called John Hale, but his first production wasn't until April with *Hay Fever*. *The Taming of the Shrew* was to be directed by an old friend of my art teacher at Dartington, Frank Dunlop, who saw me play Janet in *The Lady's Not for Burning*.[9]

Eileen's letter to me:

January 27 1959 2.30–5pm

My dearest Shivy,

I'm on duty!! [at Breon's Arts Council exhibition] So far there are quite a nice few people. Well dearest I hope you are O.K. you won't really

---

[8] Rosemary Vercoe (b. London 1917) later became a frequent and distinguished collaborator, with Pat Robertson, of Jonathan Miller, particularly in productions of Shakespeare and Chekhov. She started at the Bristol Old Vic in 1951, the same year as did Pat Robertson whom she married in 1958. She died in 2013 at the age of 96. See her obituary in the *Guardian*: https://www.theguardian.com/stage/2013/aug/14/rosemary-vercoe. Doris Nicholas had been costumière with the Royal Shakespeare Company in the 1950s before working at the BOV; she became Wardrobe Mistress with the Nottingham Playhouse in the 1960s.

[9] Denis Carey (1909–1986), appointed in 1949, departed BOV as director in 1954; as an actor his TV credits include *I, Claudius*, *The Barchester Chronicles* and *Doctor Who*, and his movie credits *The Day of the Jackal* (1973) and *Lamb* (1985). John Hale (b.1926, London), stage hand, stage manager, director, novelist, playwright, movie scriptwriter (*Anne of the Thousand Days*, 1969) was Artistic Director of BOV 1959–1961 but directed plays there between 1958 and 1968. For Frank Dunlop, see Part One, chapters 5 and 7 above.

know where you are for a bit I am sure; still Bristol itself once you leave that centre bit is nice. I was relieved you liked your digs, so at least it's somewhere until you are lucky & as you say better not rush and be sorry.

... We have the young playwright Millard Lampell who is Charlotte's friend and knows Jack Garfein, who produced Gunman & is Carrol Baker's husband, coming this Saturday to see Sean and I.[10] We had a usual letter from Garfein to-day telling us how badly he had been treated & how dreadful it was to take a play off playing to full houses. Let's hope 'Juno' [the musical] makes it, I really want this for everyone concerned in this case. I didn't care about any individuals in Shadow. Of course I wanted play to succeed in C-A-D-D's [*Cock-a-Doodle Dandy's*] case.

... Are shops nice in Bristol, well you can't say yet & are best away! (I will write again dearest.) Take care of yourself. It seems rather blank when you go; Breon was home last even. That is nice. When he goes as well it seems quiet.

Love and X Eileen X

I was busy preparing for the first production and I was very glad Eileen was busy helping Breon and was doing so much work for Sean. She needed that recognition as she loved to be in a theatrical society.

The first show was to open on February 24. As the men's hats for *Taming of the Shrew* were black felt and appeared from the costume store and the women's headgear was fairly straightforward; not much in the head department for me to do, so I was commandeered to help Daphne with the scene painting. In those days the sets were mainly built with canvas stretched on wooden frames and painted to represent an exterior or interior of a building; doors were painted with panels and made to look like wood with paint finishes. These sets had the advantage of being light and quick to set up and also quick to strike or dismantle; they were held upright by adjustable wooden staves stuck into stage weights with sandbags on top to secure them and tied together with rope tied around

[10] Millard Lampell (1919–1997) began his stage career in the leftwing, pro-labour unions Almanac Singers with Pete Seeger, Lee Hays and Woody Guthrie; he was blacklisted during the McCarthy era. He wrote television plays and the stage play, *The Wall* (adapted from the John Hersey novel), which opened on Broadway in October 1960 with George C. Scott and Yvonne Mitchell in the leading roles. For Jack Garfein, who was married to the actress Carroll Baker 1955–1969, see Part Two, ch. 3 above.

hooks attached to the sides of the flats. I learnt from Daphne how to stir a powder paint into water and "size" (a fish glue that had to be melted and boiled before using) till the right consistency was learnt. Then there was the matching of the colours. The paint was mixed in galvanised buckets that could be heated on the gas-burner when the paint had set to soften it up again: often I went to stir an old batch and a horrible stench would hit me and fill the paint dock. Len the lighting man would shout out his objections.

At my digs I was joined by Peter Wyngarde and his young friend Alan Bates.[11] So I had hit the jackpot with the digs - the "star" was staying here. During their stay we had many talks. Peter knew Sean's work and asked about him as a father. One night, however, the conversation turned a little sinister, about ghosts and strange happenings, and as soon as I could leave for my room without offence I steered away from a darkness I felt looming. In my room I felt sorry for his friend – a very handsome well-dressed man with a little dog. Before I left these digs the husband told me he was a Mason, and, although it was meant to be very secret, he showed me his regalia – apron, etc. and showed me the secret handshake. I found this a little creepy as well. Nice as the couple were, I wanted a place of my own where I could paint as I wanted to and where Eileen and Breon could stay when they visited.

One of the scenes in Pat's designs for *The Taming of the Shrew* had a statue of a cherub standing in the middle of a square and Frank Dunlop decided he wanted Petruccio to take a cornucopia out of the cherub's hand and hit people with it. I was told to make this cornucopia. Pat drew a picture of a trumpet-like thing with fruit and flowers pouring out of it. While I was trying to work out how the heck to make it so that it was strong enough to be beaten about, Frank the flyman said that Ernie the electrician had soldering equipment in his workroom under the stage and often made armatures for things that needed strength. He was sure Ernie would help if I asked him nicely. Sure enough he did and all I had to do then was cover it with felt, make the fruit and flowers to stick in it, and paint it so it all became more rigid and looked like a part of the statue. It survived the three weeks of battering and I was chuffed when Pat said that

[11] The famous stage and movie actor Sir Alan Bates (1934–2003) needs no introduction; the stage and television actor Peter Wyngarde (1927–2018), born Cyril Goldbert, was a stylish figure in British life and an immensely familiar face on British television when in the 1970s he played the sleuth Jason King in two series.

my prop was a much better standard than the previous prop-makers, as they usually fell apart. *The Taming of the Shrew* had another surprise. Doris came in with a pair of felt slippers and told me that I had to make lifts inside as Peter Wyngarde was smaller than he liked and wore lifts in his shoes and boots: Frank wanted him to put on slippers and he couldn't suddenly lose height. I did my best and with thick soles and about three inches inside, sloping down to only ½ inch at the toes, they passed muster with Mr. Wyngarde. Every show threw up new things to be thought through. An older actor came to my room in a panic during a performance with his false teeth plate broken: I glued it together as best I could with my strongest glue and it lasted the night.[12]

Sean's letters to me:

5 March 1959

Darling Shivaun,

Terrible – the weather here! Rain slashing down and the wind shaking the windows. I am a prisoner. The other day, I ventured out, and had to fly home at half-top-speed in the best I can make now; and that means panting. No news here. George Devine is busy with CockaDoodle; but I don't yet know anything about the proposed caste. ... I'm writing for the advent of the "Musical" [*Juno*], which is to go on, I'm told a week from now; greatly improved (I'm told) by the new Director. ...

It was fine and gratifying to learn that you had done so well with your designing. I was worrying about you; how you would get on, & it was a cheering thing to hear from you that you had done so well. I always thought that pencil, brush, & colours were your best gift, & always hoped you go for it fully. I always thought you clever at designing, & I still do; more firmly than ever my darling. Take care of yourself: take what rest you can; and eat well.

My deep love as ever
Dad Sean

12 March 1959

Darling Shivaun,

---

[12] The full cast and crew of *The Taming of the Shrew* can be found in *Theatricalia*: https://theatricalia.com/play/1f/the-taming-of-the-shrew/production/994

Sean and Shivaun, 1955
PHOTOGRAPH: Robert Emmett Ginna

TOP: Eileen and Sean outside "Villa Rosa", 1955.
PHOTOGRPH: Wolfgang Suschitzky

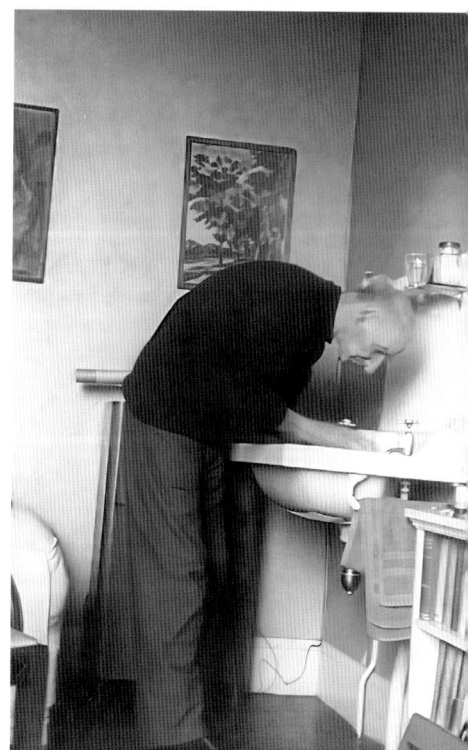

Sean washing his eyes to open them properly

TOP: I am interviewed for NBC TV, New York, 1958

Samuel Beckett

Eileen with Joseph Stein (LEFT) and Marc Blitzstein, discussing their *Juno*, the musical, 1958

Barry Fitzgerald and Sean meet after thirty years in "Villa Rosa", 1959.
PHOTOGRAPH: Wolfgang Suschitzky

TOP: Sean with his trusted GP and friend, Dr Doran

Sean and Sam Wanamaker consult about the London production of *Purple Dust*, 1953.
PHOTOGRAPH: Haywood Magee/Getty Images

TOP: At a Shelbourne Hotel reception during the filming of *Young Cassidy*, with Shelagh Richards behind me, Gabriel Fallon and Arthur Shields, 1964

I am on the set of *Young Cassidy* with Thomas Quinn Curtiss; Rod Taylor on the car bonnet

Eileen and Sean in Sean's armchair, "Villa Rosa", September 1964, the month he died.

AT HOME IN BRISTOL, 1959–1960

Here's the clipping from the London TIMES. [Re the musical, *Juno*.] Nothing to evoke a cheer; but it may turn out better that the Revieus would suggest; as so often before, we must wait. Soon as the fuller ones come from New York, I'll send them along to you.

It was very pleasant to see your name on the Bristol Old Vic program. I'm so glad you have done so well; for it was really a big & hard test to go through from home; and it will be a very healthy & useful experience in life as we all have to live it; each fighting a way forward.
...

My love to you darling
Dad Sean

It was not to turn out better than the reviews would suggest. The musical of *Juno and the Paycock* had been directed by José Ferrer, the dances and musical numbers staged by Agnes de Mille. In its cast were Melvyn Douglas as the Captain, Shirley Booth as Juno, Jean Stapleton as Maisie Madigan and our old friend Jack MacGowran as Joxer. It opened at The Winter Garden Theatre on March 9. It closed on March 21 after 16 performances.[13] Another hope gone.

It was during March and the start of Spring that with Daphne's help I found a top floor flat in Saville Place, a rented unfurnished flat, and it was much cheaper than the digs. The landlord's name was Mr. Virgin and his assistant was Miss Hayword. The rooms were attic rooms but without too low a ceiling. The main room had a dormer window that looked out over the deep valley falling down to the River Avon that ran through Bristol; the view stretched over the countryside and beyond into the hills in the far distance, below which the steam trains of the Great Western Railway puffed along, one way to Torquay and Cornwall, the other way to London. There was no heat and no hot water – so I had to buy an electric hot water heater. Breon came up to help me paint it and we had a ball mixing up bright colours. First he had painted all the walls white, then added colour on single walls: shocking pink in the loo, orange in the hall, ultramarine on one wall in the bedroom. The electric fire did its best to warm the flat up. Eileen bought me some vinyl flooring that you just lay down in sheets for the main room, and when the wind blew it rose and fell like the sea.

[13] Eileen in her book *Sean* (p. 268) described the production as "a very rocky experience" and thought that the curt title *Juno* was a mistake, as was a production that treated the resulting adaptation as a musical comedy instead of a musical play.

Breon liked staying there and Eileen now stayed with me when she came up, so we saw much more of each other. Peter Wyngarde was directing the next play, Eugene O'Neill's *Long Day's Journey into Night*. It was to open March 17. There were no props or hats for me to make for this, so I assisted Daphne painting the sets in the scene dock. This was just off stage left, and made it possible to sometimes hear rehearsals or sometimes watch from the wings. A Canadian actor, William Hutt, had come over to play the lead James Tyrone, and Dorothy Reynolds was to play his wife. A young John Charlesworth played Edmund (the part based on O'Neill himself) and Ronald Hines his elder brother, James Jnr.[14]

Pat Robertson made a beautiful set with the colours of a moonlit night, Prussian blues and black in varying degrees, the backlit cloth behind giving the sense of distance over the sea, and the fog. Dorothy Reynolds was so good as Mary, unexpectedly for me as she was usually cast in funny parts or writing with Julian Slade, but she was a damned good actress. It was near impossible to be as electrifying as Jason Robards in the part of the tortured brother, James Jnr., but Ronald Hines played the older brother well and all the cast worked so well together that they drew you into the sad destructive story. Breon came to see it.

17 March 1959

Dear Shiv,

Tony and I are coming to Bristol Fri night – Sat–Sun of Easter. Would you book two (three if you want to come) seats for L.D.J.I.N. for Sat night? I would sooner pay and get good ones for this play.

I am going to London Tues 24th & have an interview with the lady of the Beaux Arts (don't tell anyone as nothing will come of it, I expect)

---

[14] William Hutt (1920–2007) played James Tyrone decades later (1994) in a filmed Stratford Festival (Ontario) production; a bridge in Stratford is named after him to commemorate his long years on the Stratford stage, often playing in Shakespeare. Dorothy Reynolds (1913–1977) was an English author as well as actress, and wrote musicals with the composer Julian Slade, the best-known being the hugely successful *Salad Days* (1954). John Charlesworth (b. Hull, 1935) had by this time achieved fame as a child actor in the movies *Scrooge* and *Tom Brown's Schooldays*, both 1951, and in the Billy Bunter TV series, 1952–1955. In 1960 at the age of 24, he took his own life and left a self-accusing suicide note. Trained at RADA, Ronald Hines (1929–2017) acted with the major London theatre companies before becoming a busy TV actor, most famously in the BBC series *Not in Front of the Children*, 1967–1970.

on the Wed. Then I thought I might join the march to Aldermaston (!)[15] I suppose there's no chance of your coming too? I will have to work out some way of taking the van, & then I would give you a lift back to Bristol. Aldermaston is halfway between London and Bristol, just off the A4.

Breon

Then two shows appeared that needed hats! John Hale's first production needed them for the ladies in Coward's *Hay Fever* and after that they were needed for *The Importance of Being Earnest*. I had to make all the hats for *Hay Fever* without a hat block – just a canvas wig block. The nightmare was the large floppy hat for Dorothy Reynolds as Judith Bliss. My design worked well so I was gaining a little confidence. Daphne designed *The Importance of Being Earnest*. The hats were straw and I copied some of Fluff's creations.

Dorothy Reynolds was at Bristol for the Season; Wilde's play, directed by John Neville, was a very happy production with all notes for the cast being given at the pub across the road.[16] John Hale was settling in. When he started on *Hay Fever* we all heard for the first time the calls of "All on deck!" and "On the green everybody!" – nautical and cricket terms flew about during his stay at the Old Vic.

HOME AND AWAY

Now came John Hale's big showpiece, *Cyrano de Bergerac*, and he was running and flapping about during all the weeks of rehearsal. Peter Wyngarde came back to play Cyrano and was excellent. After the opening, I took a short break and went home. On my trip down to home I took the very late train. I was tired. The train's carriages still had corridors off which the compartments sat, each with two seats facing each other and racks with string netting hanging from cast iron supports, like bunks. I

[15] Aldermaston in Berkshire was home to the Atomic Weapons Research Establishment. Anti-nuclear weapons demonstrations took the form of protest marches from London to Aldermaston, a distance of 52 miles. The inaugural march was in early April 1958 and by the early 1960 tens of thousands made the journey.

[16] John Neville (1925–2011), born in London and a RADA graduate, early distinguished himself at the Old Vic, London, and Old Vic, Bristol, particularly in Shakespeare roles. He later became a well-known television actor (*The First Churchills*, 1969) and movie actor (*The Adventures of Baron Munchausen*, 1988). In 1972 he emigrated to Canada, took out citizenship, and devoted himself primarily to Canadian theatre.

opened my eyes to find a man leaning over me holding onto the luggage rack with one hand and taking out his cock from his flies with the other. Saying, "Excuse me", I slid from under him and went determinedly to the sliding door and walked along the corridor, leaving my case where it was. All the compartments were empty, then I saw a compartment with its blinds drawn and a notice etched on the window that read "Ladies Only". I slid back the door to find a smoke-filled compartment full of sailors. "Seen a ghost?", one asked me, for I was shaking and must have been white. "A man ... ", I started to say. "Don't worry love, come and join us. Safety in numbers." And I did. One sailor kindly went and retrieved my small suitcase and coat and we settled down to a lovely journey as far as Newton Abbot where Eileen was standing on the platform to meet me. She was surprised to see the sailors leaning out of the windows cheering and waving me goodbye.

It was always a comfort to come home, to smell the familiar polish and tobacco smoke faintly added to by any flowers that Eileen had in vases throughout the flat. Cups of tea; hugs; assurances. Then the catching up with the local news and the world of the theatre concerning Sean, in America and in Ireland. Then I returned to my life in Bristol.

A great shock greeted us when we started the clear-up after *Cyrano*. It was May 20 and Spring was here and we heard Pat was leaving! Daphne and I were struck hard and I couldn't believe it. Daphne wasn't appointed, which I thought was very bad show, and it started putting me off the people running the Vic. She was a dear kind woman and although upset decided to stay on for a while longer. Frank Dunlop arrived with Carl Toms the designer to produce *No Bed for Bacon* to open on June 9.[17] Once the show had opened I was off home for the summer break. Sleeping in Niall's bed had a nearness to him and a sadness – remembering him sitting up in bed after the strange doctor had told him he had only a few weeks to live: just like that. Blankness. Shock.

At home Sean was finishing his one-act play *The Moon Shines on Kylenamoe*, and his previous two last plays: *Figuro in the Night* and *Behind the Green Curtains*. The excitement in the flat was to do with the forthcoming production of *Cock-a-Doodle Dandy* directed by George

---

[17] Carl Toms (1927–1999) was an English set and costume designer. After service in World War Two, he attended the Royal College of Art and then trained with Michel Saint-Denis at the Old Vic School. Thereafter he became a distinguished figure in the theatre, winning a Tony Award and collaborating with Tom Stoppard. See "Carl Toms", Wikipedia. *No Bed for Bacon* is by Caryl Brahms.

AT HOME IN BRISTOL, 1959–1960

Devine for the Royal Court. It was to open for the Edinburgh Festival and then play at George's theatre, the Royal Court. This was Sean's favourite play and the first professional production in England. George asked him to write some words for the programme so he was busy. His eyes were getting worse and as I had very good eyesight I helped him relieve his pain by pulling out his ingrown eyelashes. He sat in a chair pulled up against the window and I put on the magnifying glasses given to Sean by his eye man. I looked at his soft poor eyes. He pointed to where the offending lash was, a tiny speck in his red sore lid, and I would carefully pull it out. Sometimes they were difficult to get hold of and some had little ulcers around them and I hated it if I nipped a bit of the thin surrounding skin by mistake. When I did pull one out he would cry out with relief as his eye watered with the effort.

The great thing with Sean was his daily walk; there was nothing wrong with his legs. One of our usual routes took us along the seafront in St. Marychurch, a high paved walkway on top of the steep cliffs overlooking Torbay. I held his arm, walking on his good side – he was deaf in his right ear. He held his walking stick painted white in his right hand more as a signal of his poor eyesight than as an aid to walking. It was useful as well for pointing out things much as Mrs Gamp's umbrella was good for poking things: "Look, I believe that's our friend the robin out to take the sun, remind me to put out some fat for him when we get back home … What's that flying overhead?" We admired a row of cottages set a little back from the front. Polished windows, flowers in the small gardens, the odd cat sunning herself on a stoop. "Isn't that a good sight, not like the wretched homes for workers where I lived in Dublin." I squeezed his arm. We looked over the sea to the horizon as people sauntered by. Coming back, rounding the wall to our driveway, which took us to our flat and tea, we stopped to look at the stones that built the wall. We looked long and hard at all the fossils revealed by the mason's chisel that split the rocks to size: fish, shells, plants and seeds, millions of years old. The odd bit of lichen and moss clinging on and the tiny red spider mites darting over them. "Niall showed me these, he was always observing and discovering. I miss him so – we all do." A seagull squealed overhead.

"Second to a painter I would have liked to study nature, and I have a little. I have learnt a lot from you children. From Brooks and Geoffrey Dobbie I have learnt about birds and from Leonard Elmhirst I have learnt about trees and shrubs: and, of course, Lady Gregory, there was a woman who knew so many wonders and had a great patience in explaining them all to me."

"How about we go in for a cup of tea? Your mother will wonder where we are."

So, off we strode with the tall cypresses bowing overhead on our right and the tall hedge protecting Mr. Norman's lawn and garden on our left. We climbed the concrete steps to our top-floor flat, not forgetting to comment on our petunias flowering in their boxes with the bees buzzing over them.

"We're back, Eileen, it was a grand walk." He hung his muffler on the coat on a hook on the back of his door and his cap on the hook: he always wore a cap to protect his eyes from the bright sun, or any light that could prick them like needles. He rubbed his hands together and gave Eileen a hug and a pat on her bottom, and we all sat down to tea. "Don't forget the fat for the robin, Shivy."

Breon wanted me to visit him in his new studio in St. Ives. What excitement. – The train journey from Newton Abbot was lovely – Devon, green, lush red soil and gentle hills; the vast Plymouth Sound; the Tamar Bridge, another of Brunel's masterpieces and bigger than the Bristol Suspension Bridge; then, slowly, fewer trees, lots of rhododendron, grey rocks and a windswept cleaner look. As on our Dartmoor, the trees were leaning the way of the most common wind-sou'-westerly. Here, I was to find, the sand was yellow. At St Erth Breon met me in his orange van and we drove the short distance to St. Ives, crowded with visitors as it was the summer season but nothing like the tourists that flock there now. The biggest problem that faced the town council then were the beatniks sleeping on the beaches. I immediately liked little St. Ives, snugly settled on the steep hills that sloped down to the harbour and the beaches.

Breon's studio was on Porthmeor beach. The buildings where Breon lived and which artists had recently commandeered, were tall and made out of wooden slats. Some were still being used by the fisherman for their nets to hang and dry and to let the fishermen easily see the holes that needed mending. Breon had a camp bed and had borrowed another for me; he had a sleeping bag and I had blankets. To stop some of the wind whistling through, he had attached newspaper and tarpaulin on some of the walls, especially alongside his bed. He was excited and a little anxious but here he was among fellow artists able to find his way.[18]

In the evening we bought fish and chips and ate them on the harbour wall. A couple of boats had come in with their catch and a lovely donkey pulling a little cart came down to the sandy floor of the near harbour; the tide was half way out, and the crates of fish were hoiked into the cart. Off the donkey trotted, he really needed no steering, up the hill behind us to the fish market. Breon took me into a low slung Inn called The Sloop for a beer, then to bed.

A week of swimming and surfing on body-boards, and I did nothing much else but read – and I felt very healthy indeed. A visit to Denis Mitchell's studio was a highlight: Bre did the odd bit of work for him. Denis was a sculptor who made wonderful abstract shapes in solid polished brass, wood, and I have a small marble statue of his. He was a kind, cheery, loveable man with a Rembrandt-like face, a great laugh and a twinkle in his eyes.

In the autumn, Breon had some news: he was working for Barbara Hepworth three days a week and two days a week for Denis.[19]

When I got home a letter was waiting for me from John Floyd, company stage manager of the Bristol Old Vic.

Dear Shivaun,

I regret to say that the new designer has taken over your work-room. I know this is going to be rather a blow for you but John H[ale] and Nat [Brenner] feel the new designer must work and be on tap in the theatre. I did try and get Mark King (the new designer) to take Roy's old office [Roy Phillips was the resident stage manager], but he felt he would be too cramped and of course there is no daylight. Obviously we want to make him comfortable, but at the same time I don't want you to suffer. In the past years the prop lady has worked in the

---

[18] On his website, Breon O'Casey (April 30, 1928–May 22, 2011) vividly remembers his St Ives studio in the course of offering his own biography and recalling his career as a painter, sculptor, jewellery maker and weaver: http://www.breon-ocasey.co.uk/biography.html

[19] Denis Mitchell (1912–1993), a distinguished member of the St Ives group of pre-war and post-war artists, was an English sculptor whose work was much exhibited. He was principal assistant for ten years (1949–1959) to the major modernist English sculptor Barbara Hepworth (1903–1975) who moved to St Ives during World War Two with her husband, the abstract painter Ben Nicholson. There is an amusing anecdote concerning Breon and Hepworth on the Pangolin London site devoted to Breon: https://www.pangolinlondon.com/usr/library/documents/main/breon-o-casey-catalogue-email.pdf

wardrobe where Rosemary [Vercoe] had her table. How about that? If this is no use, perhaps you would like to move into Roy's office? Well now, have you had a good holiday? I met a lady friend of yours in London last week, Kathleen O'Connor. Who was M.D. for 'The Hostage', she sends her love & she says you owe her a letter.
Love John

We were to have a resident designer very different to lovely Pat both in temperament and talent. It was a blow and it made me realise that I was rather a small cog in the theatre's machine. I was tempted by the life Breon was living in St. Ives and considered giving up the theatre and turning my energy to my own art. But I worried about money: Breon wasn't making much and was virtually being kept by Sean and Eileen, and although they helped me out a lot I wasn't quite as dependent as him on their generosity. They were supporting Breon because they believed he had talent and would earn a living in the end, which he did. I agreed full-heartedly with what they were doing as I thought Breon very talented. I focused on the Bristol Old Vic and the possibility of getting a grant to go to Drama School from the Bristol County Council after I had been resident in Bristol for a while longer.

At the Shakespeare Memorial Theatre during Stratford's centenary season, Tony Richardson directed *Othello* with scenery by Loudon Sainthill.[20] Othello was acted by the remarkable Paul Robeson with Sam Wanamaker as Iago, Angela Baddeley as Emilia and Mary Ure as Desdemona.

Sam and Charlotte asked Eileen and me to come and stay in their house in the Cotswolds where they were living while Sam played Iago. What a beautiful house it was, with a dovecote built into the roof. It was always exciting being with Sam as he was bursting with energy and ideas and talked about the production he was doing. I had listened to Paul Robeson singing many times on our wind-up gramophone: "Swing low, sweet chariot, comin' for to carry me home". Sean loved his voice and also his upstanding dignity and his principles as a man. He had been banned from coming to England for 23 years, blacklisted as a Communist by the Joseph

[20] Loudon Sainthill (1918–1969) was an Australian artist and set and costume designer for the Old Vic, Haymarket, Savoy and other theatres. In 1958 he was set decorator for the film *Expresso Bongo* (1958) starring Cliff Richard and Laurence Harvey and interior set designer for the 1959 film *Look Back in Anger*, starring Richard Burton, Claire Bloom and Mary Ure and directed by Tony Richardson.

McCarthy witch hunts. It was a triumph for us to have him here among us; I saw him as a truly great man. So to listen to Sam talk about him and his wife was like honey that we passed on to Sean back at home to taste. It was said his wife wasn't very well, so while he was in Stratford he was resting with her as much as he could. Sam pointed out a large poster he had hung on a wall of a matador nearing the kill with a huge black bull, and telling us that that's how he saw Iago, as a matador running circles around Othello until he finally gave the coup-de-grace.

It was a breathtaking production with the lean, mean Iago and the large passionate Othello. Eileen and I went back to see Sam in his dressing room and to go home with him: and Paul Robeson came in – I was tongue-tied, what a majestic warm man he was. He said he loved Sean and all he stood for and after talking about the evening and Sean's great works, he told Eileen that he was going to Russia for treatment for his wife, Essie. It turned out his wife had operable cancer and he had a physical breakdown brought about by all the McCarthy years of hassle and harassment. It was a shameful time for America: the trials, the deaths caused by them, the hypocrisy of the government at the time to let such an evil man take such devastating control. In a message read out in Carnegie Hall to celebrate his 75th birthday Paul said "Though I have not been able to be active for several years, I want you to know that I am the same Paul, dedicated as ever to the worldwide cause of humanity for freedom, peace and brotherhood."

Before I knew it I was back in Bristol and with my new friends in my temporary prop home. With birthday money from Eileen I was able to buy a car. Breon came to Bristol to help and found a Ford van like the one Niall had driven back from London with me sitting next to him when he was so sick with leukemia. We didn't get this new van inspected - we just bought it from a local garage for £30. While Breon was driving back to my place the steering went funny and the clutch didn't work, so he turned back and drove slowly to the garage. We left it with them to replace the steering rod and clutch: the garage man was mortified, as when he tapped the steering rods they all fell apart. He was apologetic and didn't charge for the repairs. We never told Sean or Eileen and I used that garage all the time I was in Bristol

The next show was *The Clandestine Marriage* by George Colman and David Garrick.[21] I was glad I wasn't Mark King as the whole technical

[21] This comedy of manners inspired by Hogarth pictures opened at Drury Lane in 1766.

team had decided they disliked him. He was a bit of a tosspot. He seemed wrapped up in his own brilliance.[22] After Pat Robertson's carefully designed sets, his were fussy. I have a designer friend who when she taught would look at a student's model and if she found something unnecessary would say, "Let's try it without this", and take something out; then she would say "What a relief!" She called this her Relief Test: and Mark King's set designs and costume designs needed a lot of that. There were masses of hats and headdresses to make and I decided to exaggerate some of them a little, to heighten the comedy and this resulted in some getting applauded on their entrance.

Some new actors came for the season: Leonard Rossiter, Annette Crosbie, Peter Bowles, Michael Griffith (who was to marry Annette), Ewan Hooper and lovely Susan Engel.[23] Susan often came to Daphne's flat during the weekend when Daphne cooked wonderful Sunday lunches in her lovely little proper flat at the top of one of the large houses in Royal York Crescent. It was with her cooking that I started to understand new elements and delights, such as garlic and rosemary with leg of lamb. Robin Phillips, Annette Crosbie were also invited, and once or twice Susan brought Henry Woolf with her.[24] Daphne's feasts were delicious jolly affairs.

Meanwhile, Sean's *Cock-a-Doodle Dandy*, directed by George Devine, was to play at the Edinburgh Festival before opening in the Royal Court

[22] Mark King (1931–2014) was born in India where he grew up during the last days of the Raj. At seventeen he sailed to England to study art in Bournemouth. He became resident scenic designer at the Oxford Playhouse, Bristol Old Vic and the Scottish National Opera. He then moved to Paris to become a fulltime painter. His paintings are sold through Doubletake Gallery, Minneapolis; on its website can be found his biography.

[23] Ewan Hooper (1935–2023) was a Scottish actor; his Wikipedia entry directs us to *Dracula Has Risen from the Grave*, a 1968 Hammer Film production, for his best-known performance. Susan Engel, aged 90 at the time of writing, is an Austrian-born British actress with innumerable credits in theatre for the Royal Shakespeare Company, the Old Vic and National Theatre; in films; on television (including *Doctor Who*); and on radio. Annette Crosbie, aged 91, is a multi-award-winning Scottish film and television actor, familiar to those who watched the BBC sitcom, *One Foot in the Grave*, 1990–2000. In her mid-eighties she appeared in *After Life*, a black comedy series written by Ricky Gervais.

[24] Robin Phillips (1940–2015) was born in Surrey and trained at the BOV, but established his reputation as artistic director of the Stratford Festival in Ontario, Canada, 1975–1981; he was also a film and television actor. Henry Woolf (1930–2021), though London-born, spent his mature years in Canada like Phillips. He was a stage and film actor and drama teacher, a close friend and collaborator of Harold Pinter's for many years.

AT HOME IN BRISTOL, 1959–1960

Theatre London on September 17, and we all held our breath in hopes that it would be a good production and do well.

Sean's letter to me

18 September 1959

Dearest Shivaun,

... I believe 'Cockadoodle Dandy' had a fine send off last night; all notices good – so Eileen reports from a talk she had with George's secretary. He says all 'are feeling on top of the world'. Well lets hope they'll be able to stay there for a while.

Enclosed, as promised, check for £20. Mum is writing to you too. We expect to go to London next Tuesday. I'm not looking forward to it. Rather be here among the birds – not so jaunty now as they have been: the grim winteer is cumen in. ...

Monsieur Kruschev seems to be doing well, &, maybe Americans and Soviet people will merge, if not as comrades, well, as friends. I am hopeful and delighted.

Thank God the *Cock* was strutting about with good reviews and packed audiences. I was pleased for Sean as he had so many sad productions and outcomes in his life. Sean was to go to London and stay in the flat with Eileen to see his eye man and also his play.

After *Romeo and Juliet* (Romeo played by the Canadian actor, Paul Massie), the next play, *The Man-Eaters* by Anne Piper, had no props or hats and only one set. So I took a few days off and went up to London to be with Sean and Eileen in the little flat.

After a bit of a skirmish about how we would all fit in I was welcomed. Sean slept in the bedroom and Eileen and I shared the front room: she on the daybed and I on a camp bed. Harry Craig from Macmillan and his wife, Jackie McGowran and Gloria Nugent had come to tea or drinks with us early one evening. The talk was flowing fast when there was a knock on the door and Sean Kenny, who had designed the sets for *Cock-a-Doodle Dandy*, appeared with Peter Hall in tow. They sat for a while and then Sean Kenny looked at his watch and said they had to rush to another appointment. Eileen had asked Peter Hall if he would like to read a recently published volume of Sean's new plays that Sean had been talking about with Jackie. He said "Yes, of course". Eileen later sent him a copy.

Sean never heard a word from Peter Hall from that day to his death - Sean was passé I suppose. It would have been wonderful for Sean so late in his life to have had some acknowledgment, especially in the form of a production.[25] We no longer expected that, but I did expect courtesy and a thank you, even if just to say that the new plays weren't for him.

Sean's Notebook:
Kenny pronounced the name of Peter Hall with such awe that I heard a faint distant fanfare of silver flutes and golden stringed guitars, sounding up from below and down from above. Was this the pale-faced an emanation, an apparition, from some milk wood or Fairy Land forlorn? ... flowers in the O'Casey garden were not for Peter Hall to pick. I often wondered why he came at all: possibly to see a Ta ra ra rara avis in a Tiny Zoo. ... I wonder why so many authors and artists of all kinds, after critics and community have given them a name delight in putting on a aura of awesomeness as if it were a cloak, to canopy them from the common touch, or an old school tie? – We are lost in breathless adoration for these mortal gods. These authors seem to have their heads meshed in moonlight and to walk on dew".

Sean then ruminated ruefully on the role of what he called the Commercial Grandees of the Theatre, and the role of money and the unequal distribution of subsidies in the whole business, the neglect of repertory companies and jobbing actors and the inflated role of directors and producers. I had some bitter thoughts about the dramatis personae of the scene in the London flat. I had known Jackie MacGowran since I first came to London in 1956, and here he was with his wife to be, Aileen Gloria Nugent. A disappointment to me as I had thought he would marry my friend Josie MacAvin. Gloria's father was Sir Walter Nugent, 4th Baronet of Multyfarnham, Co. Westmeath, and an Irish M.P. at Westminster, 1907–1918. Gloria mixed with the Irish horsey lot and was a friend of the Hon. Garech Browne son of Lord Oranmore. These titled names sounded hilarious to me; later Eileen knew him as Garech a Brún; when he took Sean's tapes away to "Do things with them – like record them on his 'label'", he did nothing with them, and only with pressure

---

[25] The theatre director Hall, later Sir Peter Hall, was twenty-nine at the time; his obituary in *The Times* in 2017 called him "the most important figure in British theatre for half a century".

from me did Eileen finally get them back.[26]

Before that evening with Peter Hall, I had met Sean Kenny several times with Jackie. At some point after this brief encounter Eileen and I were invited to come to his basement flat, somewhere in Chelsea. It seemed we surprised him as he had to rush off somewhere – always rushing off – but he asked Eileen to stay to be with his wife Jan Walker. His wife was very young and very beautiful in a delicate way. Before he had fled the scene, Sean mentioned they had met when she was sixteen and he was enraptured by her fragile beauty. But here he was, leaving her with two adorable boys, one a toddler, the other in arms, with two people she had never met before. The toddler looked like a miniature Sean – with just as much energy and charm. The mother looked exhausted and miserable, unable to cope with her babies and the emotional toll of living with an ego-driven drinker. I knew he drank because I had seen him with Jackie and the drinking clients at the George. It was a time when drinking was considered exhilarating and creative among many "artists"; and drunk artists were "entertaining", and if they performed well while drunk, people would nudge them in that direction. The London club called The Establishment opened in 1961 – with Sean Kenny among the elite behind the venture – and was a heaving place full of bright young things and old young things.[27] When I went in I couldn't get back out quick enough. But here we were in the Kenny basement. I made some tea, and Eileen, who was a magician with babies and children, changed the baby's nappy and set him on her lap where he stopped crying and fell fast asleep. The little sturdy toddler sat between us, and Eileen fed him some sugary tea from her saucer. When we left we felt very bad indeed.

But the play's the thing and I went to see *Cock-a-Doodle Dandy* with Sean and Eileen and was thrilled to be with them both: only the second time I had been at a theatre with Sean although I had been to theatres hundreds of times with Eileen. The other time I had sat next to Sean in a theatre was at the dress rehearsal of Sam's production of *Purple Dust*. It was a very good production of *Dandy* and the audience loved it; it was a success although not quite big enough a success for it to make it to the

[26] The year Shivaun met his friend Gloria (1959), Browne had co-founded Claddagh Records, a label that became significant in promoting Irish traditional music; he helped to form the famous group, The Chieftains.

[27] The Establishment club, offering jazz music and satirical comedy, was opened in 1961 in Soho by Peter Cook and Nicholas Luard, both associated with the satirical magazine *Private Eye* which was founded the same year.

West End. The play had good reviews but some criticised the cast. One of the problems was the wonderful actor Wilfrid Lawson, who had a fearful drink problem.[28] Some nights he was incoherent and messed up the comic timing but like the girl with the curl in the middle of her forehead, "When he was good he was very very good". On our night he was good, thank the Lord. Eileen had seen the play at the Lyceum in Edinburgh, and had helped to sober up Wilfred Lawson before the curtain went up on the first performance with masses of coffee and encouragement. Sean Kenny's sets worked all right, although my father and the rest of us thought they lacked imagination, being "realistic": a white Irish cottage as Paul Henry would have painted it. The main objection held by all of us, though, was the Cock and his costume: it was made to look like a caricature of a real cock - a very large black rooster with big awkward feet with claws and a paunch protruding in his front: this wasn't the blast of a life force described in the play; unlike Sean's dancing, prancing, flying Cock, this Cock was earthbound. Sean and Eileen had seen Diaghilev's production of *The Firebird* and that is what Sean had in mind.[29] But *Dandy* was very well directed by George Devine and we could all hold our heads up. We all went backstage and the cast gathered round Sean as he spoke to them and answered many questions. There is a lovely picture taken of him with Pauline Flanagan: what a great actress she was! (She played in a company I formed in the 1990s, when she was Bessie Burgess in my production of The *Plough and the Stars*.)[30]

The Times gave the Edinburgh production a long thumbs-up review on September 8. It won the Lord Harwood Award for Best New Play at the Edinburgh Festival. Great for Sean. The Chief producer at the Festival, Robert Ponsonby, sent a telegram to Sean thanking him for allowing them

[28] By the late 1950s, Wilfrid Lawson (1900–1966) had become a familiar face in BBC television drama even as his parts on television and in films diminished due to his alcoholism. His was an intense, even unnerving presence, giving the impression of someone struggling to keep control: but a hugely memorable actor.

[29] Nonetheless, Sean Kenny (1929–1973) from Tipperary became an immense influence on stage plays, including musicals. In 1966 he married the actress Judy Huxtable who left him and married Peter Cook. In 1973, Kenny designed the Mermaid Theatre's production of *Juno and the Paycock*.

[30] Pauline Flanagan (1925–2003) was born and raised in Sligo but later as an actress made her reputation in the United States where in 1957 she made the first of many Broadway appearances, in Dylan Thomas' *Under Milk Wood*. Years later in 1995, she was in an off-Broadway production of *Juno and the Paycock*. She reached her biggest audience in *Ryan's Hope*, an American TV soap opera in 1979 and 1981.

to have such a grand drama finale. I think we should have moved to Edinburgh!

While Sean and Eileen were in London they visited Bernard Miles and Josephine Wilson at the Mermaid Theatre to talk about another O'Casey Festival.[31]

Back to Bristol and the jewel of a theatre in shoddy little King Street. Pat Robertson was back for the next production, Ben Jonson's *The Silent Woman*, in which Robin Phillips was to play the silent woman. Robin had always been a regular visitor to the wardrobe and prop room; we were now very good friends. He was camp but funny and easy to get along with. I am not sure when he moved into the spare room in my flat as a friend, but at some point that happened and maybe it wasn't a good idea although it did help to pay the rent. I remember being confused as to why he showed no interest in me sexually. It made me feel rather undesirable but luckily I didn't dwell too much on it and put it to the back of my mind along with wondering about his sexuality. But he hasn't a boyfriend either, I thought. I was rather innocent. When Sean and Eileen were in Bristol over Christmas and New Year Eileen rather pointedly told me how good the homosexual men (as they were called then) were to her when she was touring as a young girl. She got sciatica and they had ironed her with a warm iron.

One weekend we drove to visit Robin's parents. He loved his mother but I gathered he feared his father. They lived in a little cottage on the edge of a small estate that was owned by the Hollywood actor Stewart Granger and his wife. His parents worked full time for them, the mother as housekeeper and the father as gardener and handyman. The Grangers were away but Robin insisted I come with him to see the large redbrick house. It was just like a Hollywood set of an English house – I saw nothing in it I admired or wanted, but it was friendly enough and comfortable. Robin had an elder sister, tall like me, who he missed and adored. Although I liked his mother I was glad to leave as the atmosphere of his home was tense and oppressive when the father arrived. It was as if everyone was acting out a lie.

For this production Pat and Frank Fresko restored the 17th century "drums" on the fly floor to make them able once again to fly one flat out as another flew in, simultaneously. The riggings for each flat went around

---

[31] The stage and film actors Bernard Miles and his wife Josephine Wilson established the modern Mermaid Theatre in St John's Wood in spring 1959.

the wooden slatted drum in opposite ways. It was brilliant and Pat used it in his designs for this play. Pat also designed the costumes that were as colourful and simple as his sets, traditional shapes with patterns made from stuck-on felt. Daphne designed the next production, Willis Hall's new World War Two play, *The Long the Short and the Tall*, later a movie. Where had Mark gone to? He had vanished. In his place, Daphne again was overlooked, and a woman appeared called Jane Graham, much more amenable but who also produced fussy, complicated designs without clear shapes or meaning.

CHRISTMAS WITH SEAN AND EILEEN

Sean and Eileen had decided to spend Christmas in Bristol to be near me. They arrived on Christmas Eve and I went to their hotel for an early evening meal. This was our third Christmas and New Year without Niall. Eileen suffered the most during this time: All the memories rushed back for her because he died during a time when people every year celebrate and do not grieve.

In the afternoon we all went for a walk and looked at the lit-up Christmas tree standing on College Green in front of the hotel, reminding Sean, I am sure, of the tree he saw in Niall's ward in Exeter Hospital – and the title of his Lament for Niall, "Under a Greenwood Tree". They were both tired. They stayed for nine days, over the worst time of the year for them. On New Year's Day we all did our best to distract ourselves. I had my van and we drove to my flat. Up the three flights of rickety stairs to see the home I had made myself, to look out of the window over the rooftops to the hills over the valley, and, as if on cue, a little train puffing along the hill blowing out its stream of white smoke. I showed Sean the few sketches I had in my books and excused the lack of any more to the fact that I worked long hours at the theatre. Over the week, as I had time off, I drove them to see the Bristol Zoo and my favourite gorilla, to the Suspension Bridge, and to Wookey Hole. We walked up and down Park Street many times and up to the University, looked into the Cathedral and the museums. Every afternoon Sean had a rest and Eileen and I looked at the shops, or she came to my prop room with me to see if anything needed doing or mending.

The big event was Sean going with Eileen to see *Hooray for Daisy* by Dorothy Reynolds and Julian Slade, that had opened on December 23. I was sorry that Christmas and their visit coincided with this show and not a better play or production. But there were a lot of props made by me, mainly the pantomime cow Daisy. Ernie the electrician had helped me with the head, soldering together a firm frame: there were several levers and pulleys inside that made her ears move, her eyelids move, her tongue come out, and, of course, her mouth opened and shut – and she cried. It was the first time Sean had been to the theatre since *Dandy* and years since he had seen anything apart from his own work, so it was indeed an event. I got them lovely seats near the front, but I forgot they were for the matinee, and when we turned up in the evening and they settled down in their seats they discovered they weren't theirs. The house was sold out so there were no other seats at all. I was called from backstage and was very upset but the theatre was lovely and settled them down again, this time on two chairs at the back of the stalls, in front of the gangway, so they had a wonderful view. That is, Eileen did, for I imagine Sean could see little wherever he sat. But the show was full of song, dance and music and with a delighted audience full of children – so they loved it. It turned out to be the very best thing they could have seen to lift them: seeing children enjoying themselves.

After the new year had started, they went back home and I followed in the old van to stay for a few days. Once again I saw Sean make himself his boiled egg for lunch and scrub the potatoes for our dinner. Every night I helped him with the washing up: he washed and I dried as we talked and looked out over the lights of St. Marychurch that reminded him of New York. Last thing, he put out the milk bottles for his friend the milkman. Breon said he thought Sean never really laughed again after Niall died - not the same abandoned laughter of the past, anyway. Breon said he thinks it was because the laughter might have changed to tears. I think Breon felt like that for a long time too. He would never talk about Niall's death, or ever had photos of Niall in his room. It was only in 2011, the year Breon died and I slept in his room to help him, that I saw the Gjon Mili photo of Niall sitting on Breon's bookcase so he could see it from his bed. I feel it gave Breon a sense of calm in facing his own death – as Niall had been so very brave when only 21.

Sean's letter to Ron Ayling:

January 1960

Dear Ron,

> ... the London Office of *LIFE*, the American magazine, rang me up to say I was among the last three selected for possible award of the Nobel Prize. They wanted to come down and take pictures in case I was the final recipient. I refused this request, and, in any case wouldn't have submitted to such an ordeal. ...
> As ever,
> Sean[32]

Ella had been very excited about this, but Sean asked her to get a message to the Committee to say that if it was offered he should have to reject it as James Joyce was never offered it. The Group Theatre in Belfast were also pushing for the prize to be given to Sean. It meant nothing to him.

A BIT OF A SHOCK

Hooray for Daisy was still playing when I got back to Bristol. A shocking and unexpected thing then happened. One evening when Robin came home to the flat he sat me down and put a very pretty coral and pearl Victorian ring on my finger. "Let's be engaged", he said. I was unprepared and slightly embarrassed; as fun as he was I didn't imagine him as my husband. "All right", I replied, and he hugged me. No kissing, just a hug. "This doesn't mean I sleep with you," he said. "I could never sleep with you until we are married". How very old-fashioned, I thought, but actually was a little bit glad as I had no feelings of that nature towards him. I didn't give this much thought, although Eileen was not too tranquil about a step none of us had considered, and me being stubborn, once I had agreed I was against getting out of it. Then parcels started to arrive for me from his parents and neighbours with ugly things in them, like lace tablecloths and I can only describe them as trinkets. "What on earth are these?", "Oh, they are bottom drawer presents." "What?" "Bottom drawer presents for our wedding." "What on earth do you mean?" "Well, people send presents if you are engaged". "I've never heard of such a thing. How embarrassing." I put them in "the bottomless drawer" and tried to forget them. Robin wrote and thanked them for me because I was damned if I

---

[32] *The Letters of Sean O'Casey: Volume IV*, ed. David Krause (London: Macmillan, 1975), p. 96. Ronald Ayling (1932–2022) became close enough to Sean to be a witness of Sean's will and after Sean's death to become literary advisor to the O'Casey Estate. He became Professor of English at the University of Alberta, Canada, and published widely on Sean and other members of what was known as the Irish Literary Revival.

would. Some people at the theatre looked bemused, but most didn't turn a hair. He made me a ridiculous dress that I felt obliged to wear and told me I should always wear my hair up high to distract from my rather large chin – charming!

Rehearsals for *A Taste of Honey* started in January, a new play by a very young author. It had been put on by Joan Littlewood at her Stratford East Theatre. Joan had (as it turned out she usually did) reworked it and "put it into shape". It was an excellent play for a first effort, with two good women's parts. The author, Shelagh Delaney, came down during the last week of rehearsals with a friend called Una Collins. Now and again, Shelagh or both of them would come into my little room for a chat. I liked Shelagh a lot: she was tall and without much of a bust like myself but with thick dark curly hair and dark soft eyes. Una was short and rather bossy, although nice enough; she was also dark but had a way of not looking directly at you. She was introduced as a costume designer; she had done the costumes for *A Taste of Honey* at Stratford East and was designing Shelagh's next play, *A Lion in Love*, at the Bristol Hippodrome. She had also worked on *Oh, My Papa* here at the BOV before my time. I thought Shelagh was a fine writer and addressing the subject of homosexuality so well, with humour and sadness, that at that time was brave. Robin's part was that of the young gay boy who was very like him so it was perfect casting. *A Lion in Love* was not well reviewed by the male critics of the time, a bad thing for the theatre as she could have written many good plays. Later she wrote the screenplays for Lindsay Anderson's 1967 movie *The White Bus* and Albert Finney's movie of the same year, *Charlie Bubbles*. The casting director for *The White Bus*, Miriam Brickman, wanted me to play the young girl but Lindsay chose Rita Tushingham. When Eileen was in an old people's home and Lindsey was visiting when I was there, he told me, "I should have cast you in *The White Bus* like Miriam said". That's two good jobs missed: that and *The Father*, never made by Joe Losey.

By this time Daphne, Robin and I were very often together, Daphne often feeding us. Daphne herself forged two important work partnerships, one with Ken Loach and then with Robin who took her to Stratford Ontario, Canada with him when he became the artistic director there. But I was beginning to get cold feet about this "engagement" to Robin and the dreaded Bottom Drawer presents. But I was also romantically building up a dreamy picture of living with a young successful actor. But when a school friend, Speth (Elspeth Edwards), wrote to ask "How's Bristol and the theatre and your fiancee, or are you married?" I went cold all over. This was followed by a card from Jackie MacGowran which ran "Hallo from Stratford Shivaun. Congratulations on your engagement. Be happy love, Jackie" Then I remembered Donal Donnelly and my unrequited love, and how much I had loved him, much more than Robin, and I knew I was digging a very bad hole for myself – and for Robin.

For the production of Schiller's *Mary Stuart* (1800) I had to make a lifemask of Gwen Watford, to make a severed head to be held up after the execution. I had never done one before but got careful instructions from Daphne: made all the preparations and assumed a confident air. Miss Watford was very nervous: I gently placed two straws up her nose and protected her hair, covered her face in Vaseline and put the collar of card that Daphne had shown me how to fit around the hairline of her head. I slowly spooned and poured the plaster of Paris onto her face and persuaded her to stay still until it had set, which didn't take long. It worked but she was annoyed that some small amounts of the plaster of Paris had got into her hair – she wasn't the easiest person to deal with. John Standing and his elegant wife added glamour to this season. A lovely young woman called Prunella Scales came to direct *The Woodcarvers* by Oliver Goldsmith (not the Irish poet and playwright), a very dull play. She had acted in *The Man Eaters* (a production in which I had to make a dead runover cat!). She had spent a lot of time in the wardrobe making a new canvas cover roof for her little sports car and it was a joy to chat and laugh with her. Daphne was designing this production and I was doing a lot of the painting so we met amid the work.[33]

The productions kept on coming and going as if on a conveyor belt –our friend Brendan Behan's *The Hostage*, Ronald Gow's *The Edwardians* (a tedious nothing),[34] Goldsmith's *She Stoops to Conquer*. John Hale hadn't

---

[33] The London-born Gwen Watford (1927–1994) was a versatile stage actress (discovered by John Gielgud when still a schoolgirl) who also became a well-known face in British television drama in the 1960s through the 1980s. John Standing (b. 1934, born John Leon, later 4th baronet) was an active stage, television and movie actor in a career stretching from Peter Brook's *Titus Andronicus* at the Shakespeare Memorial Theatre (1955) to *Game of Thrones* (HBO, 2011). Prunella Scales (b. 1932) began her theatrical career as an assistant stage manager at BOV, breaking into television in the early 1960s, and achieving greatest fame as Basil's wife Sybil in *Fawlty Towers* (1975–1979).

[34] Sean in February 1935 had in the *New Statesman* savagely attacked an earlier long-running hit play by Gow, *Love on the Dole*, which caused a bitter row among commentators: see *The Letters of Sean O'Casey, Volume I*, p. 528.

AT HOME IN BRISTOL, 1959–1960

in him any fire or ideas about theatre that interested me. I was beginning to feel I couldn't learn much more at a theatre that didn't even consider the needs and careers of the technical people working there. I knew Sean had hoped that my job might lead to designing a production, or even costumes. But I had realised in my first month on the job that was never to be: if, after Pat Robertson left they didn't install Daphne Dare as the resident designer, and after Mark King's silent exit another RD, Jane Graham, appeared, and they still overlooked Daphne as the hard working and reliable second designer, it was obvious I had no hope of moving up the Bristol Old Vic's rickety ladder. Anyway I wanted to act – and started to find a way towards that and to leave Bristol behind. I looked into the Further Education Awards from the Bristol Council

BLASTINGS AND BIRTHDAYS

In March 1960, Ed Sullivan, the American TV personality, rejected the filmed conversation between Sean and Barry Fitzgerald in the documentary film salute to the Abbey Theatre, *Cradle of Genius*, which he had originally intended to use on the St. Patrick's Night edition of his famous *Ed Sullivan Show*, in the month of Sean's eightieth birthday. It seemed that Ed Sullivan, himself of Irish descent, had knuckled under to pressure from the Irish-American organisations which, according to Sullivan, characterised O'Casey as "rather a shabby expression of Ireland". This was not surprising, as Mr. Sullivan was a weak man politically and after a guest was seen to be subversive he worked with the anti-Communist newsletter *Counter Attack* and would check potential guests on his show with its right-wing editor, Theodore Kirkpatrick. Soon after and while Sean was still alive, Bob Dylan withdrew from the programme as they wouldn't let him sing his song, "John Birch Paranoid Blues". Good for him, I wish Sean had known of this – or maybe he did.[35]

[35] Theodore Kirkpatrick was the managing editor of *Counterattack: The Newsletter of Facts on Communism* which began in 1947. For Sullivan's preventative use of the newsletter, see https://www.britannica.com/art/television-in-the-United-States/The-red-scare. See also "*Counterattack* (newsletter)", Wikipedia. Prominent Irish-American politicians (mostly observing Catholics) were simultaneously fiercely ant-Communist and anti-English and Sullivan said that they had told him that O'Casey "had been used by English communists": O'Connor, *Sean O'Casey*, p. 366. *The Torbay Express and South Devon Echo* of March 14, 1960 quoted Sean's muscular reaction to the news: "Who the hell is this fellow Sullivan – I've never heard of him, so how the hell could I have appeared in his show?" According to this report, Sullivan had received objections "from representatives of Irish and Protestant groups". "What right have they to butt in?" Sean demanded.

Sean wanted a quiet eightieth birthday on March 30 and refused interviews in prestigious quarters. A local newspaper, the *Torbay Express and South Devon Echo*, explained on the eve of the birthday:

SEAN O'CASEY IS 80 TO-MORROW.

Today on the eve of his 80th birthday, playwright Sean O'Casey was keeping away from the telephone.

The bell in his Torquay flat rang often as newspaper representatives in Britain and overseas, sought to speak to the man who, eight decades after his birth into poverty in Dublin, is still active on his pinnacle of achievement as one of the greatest dramatists.

When a Herald Express reporter telephoned to-day, he received the same polite reply as was given to others by Mrs. O'Casey. She went off to consult her husband, but returned to say. "He wishes you well, but he is not speaking to any of the newspapers."

To-morrow, she explained, would be just like any other day for him, and added: "He's quite young. You would think he was 900 or something like that'"

This week many inches of space in newspapers throughout Britain have been given to reviews of the newly-published biography "Sean O'Casey: The Man and His Work." by David Krause, an American scholar, who was able to live in Dublin for more than a year, gathering material and writing the book. In it he describes Mr. O'Casey as "a proud rebel with a mighty rage for life who in the midst of tragic surroundings made himself a great comic artist."

There were still flowers all over the flat when I arrived home to spend the weekend after the event. Eileen told me someone had sent him 80 roses – she had put them in the bath as she searched for enough vases to hold them all.[36] She gave some to Clare, the sweet gentle lady who cleaned for Eileen. A group of artists from Ireland had sent him a silver "tassie"; and Sam Beckett wrote a note to the *Irish Times*: "From Paris, To my great

---

[36] In *Sean* (p. 281), Eileen identified the sender as Joan Littlewood of the Theatre Workshop.

compatriot, Sean O'Casey, from France where he is honoured, I send my enduring gratitude and homage". Sean was taken aback and moved by this.[37]

---

[37] David Krause in his introduction to the year 1960 in *The Letters of Sean O'Casey: Volume IV* (p. 90) wrote: "As if to redeem his reputation in his homeland, a group of eighteen courageous [sic] writers and actors presented him with a silver tankard or 'tassie'", suggesting the risk it took in the Ireland of time to flout the Irish establishment and praise O'Casey. The Littlewood roses suggested, too, that although a new drama had come into being, O'Casey's rebelliousness and his stand against Irish religious and state censorship were still remembered and honoured.

5
Last days in Bristol
1960–1961

LAST DAYS IN BRISTOL, 1960–1961

DECISION TIME

The talk at the theatre was the upcoming production of *Romeo and Julie* tour to the Baalbeck Festival in Beirut, Lebanon. In this revival Daphne was to design the costumes and Robin was to play Romeo. I was annoyed that I wasn't going, although it was quite obvious I wasn't really needed. Instead of my work at the BOV giving me a desire to design, it put me off.

Meanwhile, a letter came from Sean and from the weak and wobbly handwriting you could tell he didn't feel well.

19 June 1960

Darling Shivaun,

Enclosed is the new "Drums of Father Ned" in Paper-back format. I like it very much. It was I declared for P-back knowing that a cloth-covered edition would cost (minimum) 15/6; so 8/6 is a decidedly better and more reasonable price. Macmillan's think it will have a big sale. They have now undertaken to publish the 3 plays still in MS. The design on cover is, at least, modern, touching thie new idea of symbolic expression – a big step forward in designing for Macmillan's.[1]

Bob Hogan, who produced it in Indiana – comes here on Monday for a visit, then on to Dublin. Strange what an attraction Dublin has for so many.[2]

All quiet here on the Western Front: sun shining, but weather warning of thunder-storms and cold front tomorrow. Wore my red cap-peaked today in sun.

Enclosure 10/- – bit short

Love as ever Dad Sean

Sean and Eileen's world was more interesting to me than mine. If the Bristol Old Vic had been something more than just a good professional three-weekly rep, I maybe would have pushed to do something more there; that is, step up once in a while from prop making and painting. It was

[1] *The Drums of Father Ned* was published in 1960 by St Martin's Press, a division of Macmillan. The plays to be published in 1961 were *Behind the Green Curtains*, *Figuro in the Night* and *The Moon Shines on Kylenamoe*.
[2] Robert Hogan (1930–1999) was a publisher, editor, critic and playwright. He travelled to Ireland where he met Sean and became a champion of his work; he eventually retired to Bray, Wicklow. He edited *The Dictionary of Irish Literature* (1979; 2nd 2-volume edition, 1996). The obituary of this versatile man appeared in the *Irish Times*, March 8, 1999.

great Daphne was designing for *Romeo* and was going to the Festival. I had learnt a trade from her as a set painter. I was now determined to follow my first wish to learn how to act.

The whole theatre was in a whirl. The costumes, hats and headdresses checked and checked again, then carefully laid in large wicker hampers lined with oilskin. The props were packed, the furniture and set dressings all packed: now it was all ready to go. The actors' suitcases stood together: the big truck arrived to take it all on the first leg of the journey to Baalbeck. Later, the actors and technical staff started to gather, a coach arrived, they clambered in bursting with great excitement, and those left behind waved the tour group away – and then for me at last a sense of relief, not annoyance but relief.

Back home: at last within the comfort of home and no one to worry about, I definitely felt I wanted out from Bristol. I talked it over with Sean and Eileen. I would try for a grant from Bristol County Council. Eileen wrote to Peggy Ashcroft for advice as to what school to go to. A letter came back to say she strongly recommended studying with John Blatchley, who taught at The Central School of Speech and Drama at Swiss Cottage. He was an ex-pupil of Michael St. Denis who Sean and Eileen knew from the 1930s in London. I wrote off and was sent all the information about how to apply. I should ask for an audition in January; a good time for me as the Panto would be on.

I would keep it all under my hat at the theatre until I heard if I had got in or not, then hopefully I would hand in my notice. I felt positive and excited again. Sean Kenny had said I could work for him (of course for nothing) in my spare time, at his studio in Soho. I had in mind I could do this as well as learning how to act. The design bit pleased Sean.

Robin reported from Beirut on July 16: "My dear Shiv, It is quite wonderful, and oh so very hot. Incense hovering in the evening air, and Jasmine flowers blooming everywhere. Wonderful journey out stopped and shopped in Athens. Had those press conferences. Love to you and all, Robin"

Rhinoceros by Ionesco was being staged in September. For *Rhinoceros* I had to make two life-size rhino heads that peeked out from either side of the stage at certain points. I must say they were very impressive. Plot of *Rhinoceros*: over three acts, people of a small village turn into rhinos, except for one man, an everyman sort of chap, who drinks, etc. Said to be a critique of Communism, Fascism and Nazism before WW2. Mind you, without the Commies' help in the war, it may have had a different end. I agreed with Sean that the play was ridiculous. Actually I found most of the work connected to the Theatre of the Absurd – well, absurd, and dull as regards colour and content. John Hale obviously thought differently as we were soon to do another of Ionesco's plays, *The Killer*. During rehearsals Mr and Mrs Ionesco visited John. There was a great fuss and I saw three people climb the back stairs to the stage, Ionesco, his wife and his daughter, and heard clapping. They reminded me of the wooden Russian dolls that nestled into each other. All small and plumpish, he being the tallest by a smidgeon.

Away from the theatre, my most urgent thing for me to do was to get a meeting with the arts grants department at the Bristol County Council, set conveniently near the theatre in a large ominous building curving round one side of College Green. It turned out that I was eligible for a full grant which meant fees and keep money, with a letter from The Bristol Old Vic stating that I had been working there and on the payroll for two years; it would be over two years by the time I left. But they couldn't process the grant until I had been accepted by a College or Drama School. This was very good news, indeed. Now I started to think what parts to do for my audition.

In November 1960 came a play called *The Tinker* by Laurence Dobie and Robert Sloman. It was during this production that Robin came clean with me telling me he was "homosexual", the word used then. I should have admitted to myself what I really knew all along but didn't want to face it: then there was one of my biggest traps in my life: my belief that people can change. So sadness and tears at what definitely couldn't be. I felt as if I had been led up a garden path. Why on earth had he bought a ring and suggest we get engaged? I not only felt foolish, I definitely *was* foolish. Amongst my feeling of betrayal was also a feeling of relief, as the bloody "bottom drawer presents" were an embarrassment and the thought of marriage at 21 was a nightmare fantasy I was glad to wake from. It meant we had a row and our friendship abruptly ended for a while. Robin told me he had to tell me because a young Canadian actor who was to be in *Romeo and Juliet* had told him he must. It was this young man in his decency who made Robin "come out" to me. I thank him for that and also for supporting Robin.

Our friendship soon went back to what it naturally had been until he started to become rather famous and then we lost touch. Years later I learned how extremely asleep I was. In April 1960 Bill Gaskill had come to Bristol University to direct *The Happy Haven* by John Arden, who was their writer in residence. He used many of the Bristol Old Vic actors and Robin played a dog.[3] On three theatrical occasions much later, Bill Gaskill came up to me and said something like "When you and Robin Phillips were together and I was directing *The Happy Haven*, we fucked every day!" "Well, good for you", I replied every time. And although I felt sorry for Robin at such an ugly violation of privacy, as Bill seemed so aggressive, I wasn't upset in any other way. Robin moved out and I was alone again and had to pay the full rent. For a while I felt very hard done by as I had so obviously been blind to the reality.

With *The Tinker* production came along the actor, Ed Judd.[4] It was another ridiculous play: Harry and Paul in an exploit to publicise Rag Week climb the clock tower (smacks of *The Master Builder*), Paul falls to his death and Harry is sent down for his part in it. That was it.[5]

At the first night party two things happened that I remember. The head of The Bristol Old Vic Drama School, Duncan Ross, did a tap dance on the wooden bar-top.[6] And Ed Judd sat me down and talked me through why it was such a good thing Robin had left me: "Let's face it, he's not worth bothering about!" He told me how much I had ahead of me, that I should try for Central School to take their acting course – and then he made me laugh. How grateful I was that he took time and cleared my air; I felt much better in myself. A new page turned over.

Before the panto we had to work on *One Way Pendulum*, of the absurdist genre. People riding camels to hounds, collecting weight machines to make them sing the Hallelujah Chorus; and some replica of

[3] William (Bill) Gaskill (1930–2016) after the Bristol University staging went on to direct for the Royal Shakespeare Company and Royal Court Theatre.

[4] Born in China, Edward Judd (1932–2009) was a successful English film actor between 1948 and 1988 and a TV actor in the 1970s and 1980s before he faded from public view thereafter.

[5] The play failed in the West End but was adapted as a British movie, *The Wild and the Willing* (1961), starring two newcomers, Ian McShane and John Hurt, who later made good on their early promise. The play fitted the contemporary British theatrical demand for realism and the social class theme.

[6] Duncan Ross (1918–1987) was Principal of the Bristol Old Vic Theatre School, 1956–1961. He acted with the Birmingham Repertory Company (1942–1946) and the Royal Shakespeare Company (1946–1947) before moving to Bristol. In 1962 he left for the United States where he taught at the University of Washington, Seattle, and the University of Southern California. He appeared in the American TV series *Cheers* (1982), *Remington Steele* (1982) and *The Winds of War* (1983).

the Old Bailey, where the son of the house is tried for murder because "He kills people so he can wear black mourning". A little play, signifying nothing.

Then the panto! Great excitement for me with Jessie Matthews, she of the Cochran Young Ladies, she with the long legs and high kicks, coming to play the Fairy Godmother. Everyone else knew her as Mrs Dale in *Mrs Dale's Diary*, but she took me back to Eileen's stories of Cocky and his "young ladies". When Eileen came up they had a long chat together in her dressing room.

DAVID PHETHEAN AND *THE DRUMS OF FATHER NED*

In May, David Phethean, who ran The Queen's Theatre in Hornchurch, east London had visited Bristol looking for talent. I met him and after a long talk I gave him a copy of Sean's *The Drums of Father Ned* to read.[7]

July 16 1960

Dear Siobhan (sic),

Very many thanks for 'The Drums of Father Ned'! I must apologise for not writing at once to say so. You can imagine with what pleasurable anticipation I sat down in the train to read it. ... I managed to read two acts before getting back here, and I will read the last act this weekend. It is marvellous stuff. Your Dad must have been in a more mellow mood when he wrote it, tho' the wit is as sharp as ever. I can't agree with you that it doesn't necessarily require the true brogue. The 'ths' are liberally spread around! – and I couldn't bear to hear it mangled and muffled by Kensingtorians – More later.
Best wishes to you both
David P

August 8 1960

Dear Shivaun,

I would like to do 'Drums of Father Ned' here in October or November, providing (a) your Dad agrees (b) I can get the Irish actors. I think I can get the latter providing I give them enough notice. Apart from the

[7] David Phethean (1918–2001) was an English actor and director. In the 1960s he appeared in such popular TV series as *Dixon of Dock Green*, *Poison Island* and *Softly Softly*. He directed many plays at the BOV between 1958 and 1986.

performance mentioned in the script has there been any other this side of the Atlantic? On T.V? – or anywhere? If you would be so kind as to let me have your Dad's address I will write to ask him his opinion – and my sincere thanks for allowing me to keep your very special copy for so long.

Best wishes to self & Robin ... and thank you for your help.

David P

Two years after its rejection by the Dublin Tostal, the successful two-week run of *Father Ned* at the Queen's Theatre, Hornchurch, Essex, from November 8, 1960, directed by David, was the first performance in Europe. Richard Findlater, drama critic for *The Observer*, usually took a dim view of O'Casey's later plays.[8] But in "Hurrah for Hornchurch", his review in *Time & Tide* for November 26, 1960, Findlater described the play as "A summery comedy unaccountably banned in Ireland two years ago by a bigoted archbishop and thereafter (more predictably) ignored by British managers . ... *The Drums of Father Ned*, to be sure, is not a masterpiece, but this high-spirited little extravaganza flares out in bright, broad comedy with a stirring affirmation of life by the grand old man that has more real charity than is usual in his work . ..." I got away from Bristol to go to London for a few nights to see it. What a lovely company I walked into – a warm bubbling atmosphere. The play was designed by David Jones. It was well directed with so much colour, energy and enjoyment. The "Pre-rumble" as Sean called it in the printed copy of the play was excellent and its dark comedy set the scene for the lighter rest of the play. No banning from any old Archbishop stopped Father Ned's drum; no banning, even, from the Lord Chamberlain (although he did ban a performance of *Figuro in the Night* at a Festival of Irish Comedy in London in 1963), no protests but good reviews and good houses. Not good enough for a move to the West End, but the play had a successful production while Sean was still alive, which was a wonder.

While Robin was making the weight machines sing the Hallelujah Chorus, Daphne and I, and the wardrobe, were busy working on the upcoming panto. I must say I made the most beautiful seahorse with a cane frame and stretched organdie over it, so you could see the person within the lovely shape of the seahorse. Breon came to see the production

---

[8] Richard Findlater (1921–1985) was also the author of numerous biographies of actors and books of theatre history.

LAST DAYS IN BRISTOL, 1960–1961

and thought the seahorse was great. Praise from Breon meant a lot to me. Sean's letter to me:

December 3 1960

Darling Shivaun,

Up outa bed again and doing a little. I hope you are minding yourself, & taking as much real rest as you can from a busy life. I daresay, you are now in the midst of the Pantomime properties & dress: Breon is to be here at Christmas, & Eileen & I look forward to seeing you shortly afterwards – or at Christmas, if you can come. Jane Rubin tells us 'Drums Under the Windows' is doing 'nicely' in New York, so, even tho' the theatre is a small one is very satisfying. I've refused to do a television interview for Canada as I'm tired of these exhibitions. Brendan Behan was on the B.B.C. Television last Sunday. He was quite sober, and did well, interviewed by E. Andrews. This boy wanted me to do a similar show; but I refused, & said a few things in the letter of refusal.[9] Dublin didn't seem to take to 'The Hostage'; but what is Dublin these days! No one cares about what Dublin says. I enclose a 10/- note for a gallon of petrol or a hair-do.

Do mind yourself, darling, & don't forget the visit after Christmas (or on Christmas).

My warm regards to Robin.
As ever, with love
Dad, Sean

I was able to join Sean and Eileen for Christmas and with Breon there

[9] Sean's dating of the Behan TV interview by Eamonn Andrews to Sunday November 27, 1960 should solve the dating problem for both the Irish Film Institute and Trinity College Dublin who have suggested that the interview, apparently released as a 35-minute BBC TV Special in 1962, was conducted sometime between 1959 and 1962, though they also note that Telefis Eireann broadcast the interview on November 29, 1960. See: https://www.tcd.ie/irishfilm/print.php?search=keyword&q=brendan&exactMatch=& Also: https://ifi.ie/film/quare-fellow-and-meet-the-quare-fellow-the/ According to the author of a profile in the *Sunday Times* of October 13, 2002, Andrews, the well-known Irish presenter of BBC programmes, scared away potential interviewees who feared they would be outshone. Liam Fay adds: "Playwright Sean O'Casey refused to participate in the proposed show unless he could interview Andrews". It is less likely that Sean was intimidated (he may have known that Andrews was a Dubliner) than that he refused for his own reasons.

too, it was a pleasant time, although, of course, we all silently missed our Niall. This would be the fourth New Year without him.

THE 1961 SEASON

Arnold Wesker's *Roots* started the season and a young actress came down to play Beatie Bryant, Eileen Atkins.[10] She was lovely and so good in the part. It was directed by Duncan Ross of the long wooden bar-top. Duncan had the stage manager fry onions before the audience came in and waft the smell out into the auditorium. Exciting as the production was, and good and solid as the play was, for me it dulled over constant hearing, whereas with Shakespeare I am always finding new possibilities and sudden understandings. *Richard II* was next, Richard Gale playing the king. But more interesting was the arrival of Freddie Jones, an energetic, funny, larger-than-life character who had a "gra" on Daphne. This was lucky, as it meant I saw a lot of him and had some jolly Indian meals, with Freddie eating the hottest curries available, while I looked on in disbelief as he actually enjoyed steaming and sweating. He was a well-needed shot of life at the BOV. A laid-back intellectual, Michael Mellinger, appeared, and other new faces and talents.[11]

Still, my mind wandered more and more towards London, especially as we had the flat there. The flat was situated on Cromwell Road, smack in the middle of Kensington. I now had experience with professional productions and some of the visiting directors did really good work, but the artistic director was not a visionary by any means, unlike Michel St. Denis, whose work had an encompassing purpose, combining the play, the direction and design with the method of acting to mount the full theatrical experience. Here at Bristol each show was an ad hoc experience, the actors bringing their separate skills and different styles together; they were all

[10] *Roots* (1958) reflected the working-class and regional dialect preoccupations of British theatre at the time. Eileen Atkins, born in London and aged 90 at the time of writing, had joined the Royal Shakespeare Company in 1957. She went on to appear in many distinguished television and film dramas, co-create the famous ITV series, *Upstairs, Downstairs* (1971–1975), and write screenplays (*Mrs Dalloway*, 1997).

[11] The English actor Richard Gale (1921–1983) and German-born actor Michael Mellinger (1929-2004) were at BOV through the 1960–1961 season; Mellinger soon after played Kisch in the James Bond film, *Goldfinger* (1964). The TV, stage and film actor Freddie Jones died in 2019 at the age of 91. On stage he most famously played Sir in *The Dresser* (1980), on the cinema screen Bytes in *The Elephant Man* (1980), and on the small screen Sandy Thomas in ITV's *Emmerdale* (2005–2018).

LAST DAYS IN BRISTOL, 1960–1961

experienced and dedicated people of the theatre without a leader. Yes, John Hale brought a clutch of absurdist dramas to the Vic stage but neither Ionesco nor N.F. Simpson thrilled me. I wanted panache, colour and a drama that said something positive and, yes, political. Shakespeare, of course, but also some of the less known works of O'Neill, Shaw, and the young John Arden: Sean's later works would be a big ask. In his way, David Phethean had made a warm inclusive company in Hornchurch, and although I only saw a few productions there, the atmosphere was exciting.

Jackie MacGowran was to arrive soon in Bristol to play the lead in yet another Ionesco play, *The Killer*. He was to play Berenger, another downtrodden everyman. A murder play of great dullness. Berenger discovers "Utopia", but in it is a killer who lures people by offering to show them a picture of "The Colonel" – and then drowns them. He drowns Berenger's supposed girlfriend, so Berenger leaves Utopia and spends hours tracking down the Killer. He confronts him, a little man, & argues against murder & it is unclear what the outcome is. Was it another play against Communism and Nazism? Peter Birrel played The Killer.[12]

I was meant to keep an eye on Jackie for his wife Gloria. Jack was a recovering alcoholic and on some very strong suppressant pills that reacted badly if you did drink any alcohol. That was a treatment then. At that time it was difficult to refuse a drink in a pub – "Drink up and be a man". One day during rehearsal I was urgently called from the scene dock to poor Jackie, convulsing on the stage to the horror and anxiety of those all around. An ambulance came and the next day he was back on track. Gloria came down to be with him. It was the sort of play that would drive a teetotaller to drink.

Sean's letter to me:

Darling Shivaun.

Damnable weather here; painful to look at the sour mug of the sky. Hope you may be able to come to us some week-end soon. Well, Kennedy has had a setback in Cuba. Instead of weakening Fidel Castro, he seems to be weakening himself – willy nilly, he has to go back from the incoming tide(s), washing away old things & ideas, & carrying in

---

[12] Peter Birrel (né Cohen, 1935) was a busy English television actor for forty years before his death in 2004; his widow is Stephanie Cole who played Dr Ellingham's aunt Joan (2004–2009) in TV's *Doc Martin*.

new ones.[13]

I've just written a short article on Spring Thoughts, 'The Time the Lilac Blooms', for May Day article in 'The Literary Gazette', & a short one of remarks to the younger generation, for 'Izvestia's' 'Book of the Day': article I call, 'Pioneer & Konsomnd'.[14]

Enclosed a few cuttings. Behan is to appear in Court in about 10 days in Toronto. He'll be lucky if he escapes a jail sentence.[15] Also enclosed a £1 for a few sweets; also enclosed my deep blessing.

Dad Sean

Breon and his wife Doreen rented a lovely tiny house in Teetotal Street in St Ives. It really was tiny: a bedroom, kitchen and sitting room above a boat shed that had once been a tackle and net space. There was now a loo and bath set in this space and a bed for visitors. In a letter, he confided that Barbara Hepworth was doing a television film: "hellish boring. Anyway, I'm sick and tired of her damned statues". Later in May, Hepworth had an exhibition: "I have to do extra days for her. What a life we sculpture assistants have".

I can't remember when my auditions were for the Central School but I remember entering the room and seeing John Blatchley coming towards me to greet me.[16] Other people were sitting at a large table. John asked me what I was doing for them – I said the Nurse from *Romeo and Juliet* and something else I can't remember; he told me to take my time; I liked

[13] After an attack on Cuban airfields by American bombers, over 1400 paramilitaries, Cuban exiles funded by the CIA and partially trained by U.S. military personnel, landed in Cuba in the Bay of Pigs on April 17, 1961; they were defeated by Castro within three days. "The invasion defeat solidified Castro's role as a national hero". See "Bay of Pigs Invasion", Wikipedia.

[14] *The Literary Gazette* was a 19th-century Russian language literary journal resuscitated in 1929 and which became the organ of the government-controlled Union of Soviet Writers, becoming political as well as literary after 1947: see "*Literaturnaya Gazeta*", Wikipedia. *Izvestia* is a daily Russian broadsheet founded in 1917 and until 1991 the chief organ of the Soviet Union government, as *Pravda* was that of the Communist Party.

[15] A copious, entertaining and sobering account of Behan's tumultuous stay in Toronto March–April 1961 has been written by Kevin Plummer for "Historicist", *Torontoist* July 27, 2013. Behan was arrested for assault during a drink-fuelled rampage, and the diabetic playwright was hospitalised and almost died in a city hospital; he was fined and released in April. See: https://torontoist.com/2013/07/historicist-one-drink-too-many-and-a-thousand-not-enough/

[16] The actor, director and writer John Blatchley (1922–1994) was born in Australia; he wrote the BBC TV series, *The Black Arrow* (1951, 1958).

LAST DAYS IN BRISTOL, 1960–1961

him immediately. After I had done my bit he sat me down to take questions from him and Yat Malmgren. I was shocked and delighted that he said I would be accepted for the coming year! I was brave and asked if it would be possible to work some evenings at Sean Kenny's workshop while I was there. He stressed that only if it didn't in any way interfere with my coursework. Of course I never got it together to work with Sean Kenny. But now I could go with the acceptance letter in hand to get the Bristol Council going on authorising my grant.

Bernard Miles's Mermaid Theatre in London was to have an O'Casey Festival starting in July with *The Bishop's Bonfire*. This was a relief for Sean and Eileen - mainly Eileen with the tax worries. She never thought about putting money aside from Sean's earnings for the tax, so the money just went. Mostly all spent before the tax bill landed on the mat. In those days if you had a good year you were taxed for all the earnings within that year; if the next year was very bad, you got none of that tax back. Sean argued that for artists it should be deducted over three or four years, something that is better organised now.

My letter to Sean:

Dear Daddy,

I got your new book of plays today. Thank you very much. I have just read 'Behind the Green Curtains' again and liked it very much, it is very funny.

It has been a lovely sunny day today and I have made a Gooseberry Pie. Robin is staying with me so it isn't so lonely & it is very nice.

How are you? I hope you aren't working too hard & ignoring the sun. How is Mum getting on with Miles & the exhibition? I hope they get Cyril [Cusack] to play the Codger.

Val May is taking on here next season from Nottingham[17] and Frank Dunlop is taking on Nottingham.

I have given in my notice, & will leave in three weeks or so.

I enclose the silly clipping about the book.

My love to Mum & thank her very much for the £3 and everything.

Looking forward to seeing you both.

Love Shivaun xxx

---

[17] The English theatre and artistic director Valentine (Val) May (1927–2012) headed up BOV between 1961 and 1975, and then the Yvonne Arnaud Theatre, 1975–1992.

A SUMMER DRIVE THROUGH FRANCE

I was nervous of going back to acting. I hadn't acted since RADA in 1956, as I couldn't count the very few lines in *Juno* I had with the Dublin Players. I was impatient to start. I was going to learn from John Blatchley, recommended by Peggy Ashcroft as the only worthwhile teacher around.

Fluff Brown, who had worked in my place at the BOV before me, asked me if I would come with her in her car to the south of France. I had time on my hands while waiting for Bristol County Council and the offer of an exciting holiday! After talking to Sean and Eileen I said Yes to Fluff. Charlotte said her two lovely friends, Ben and Norma Barzman, had offered Fluff and me a roof in their newly bought, but yet unlived in by them, villa near Cannes. It was sitting there empty; the water worked, the electricity worked, but nothing had been done to it since they bought it. It had two mattresses they had used while settling things there and some bedding, a few cups and saucers, etc.

Eileen came to help me pack. Fluff picked me up in her little grey Citroen, and off we went to the early morning ferry in Southampton or maybe Portsmouth. Fluff drove and I was her pilot and not allowed to drive her car. Our journey after leaving the ferry and after a peaceful crossing, was tense. Fluff was apprehensive when driving a right-hand drive on the French roads, with lorries and cars whizzing by and honking their horns at every opportunity. We circled Paris and just kept going. Fluff was of the kind who once started didn't like to stop for anything, so we only pulled in when absolutely necessary, to pee or fill the car with petrol. After many hours, and one or two near misses, we reached the outskirts of Marseilles and found the road to Nice. How beautiful it all was, so many reminders around me of artists' paintings: the declining sun, long shadows, red parched earth, and the smell of dry earth and crushed herbs, and of the sea.

At Cannes we did as Norma had instructed and took the road toward Grasse and finally came to a "Provencal gate" within an old stone arch and before a long driveway winding up to the main house, with large cypresses all along one side. We spoke to the guardian, who got in the car to come with us and explain what was working and what to do. It was so romantic. This overgrown villa in its neglected shabby glory. There was a bath and there was hot water. We were given a key. The room allotted to us had a stone balcony and the branches of a fruit tree dipped over the balustrade, full of a fruit I had never seen before: I took a bite and it was delicious. I learnt later from a shop that they were kumquats.

The Barzmans were living in Paris. I had met them at Sam and Charlotte's when the whole family burst forth into the sitting room – a blast of bubbling energy. Norma had a baby in her arms and rushing, tumbling toddlers; curly-headed vibrancy. Norma had the same warmth as Charlotte. The difference was that Norma seemed confident and free, in a sexy and contented marriage, whereas there was an underlying sadness behind Charlotte's bright eyes and deep chuckle.

The Barzmans, all of them, were arriving on June 26 from Paris to take up residence for the summer. The Barzmans had fled the U.S. just in time to avoid the House Un-American Activities Committee. They had been warned by Marilyn Monroe and Groucho Marx of their imminent danger. One of the Hollywood Ten, who had served 6 months in jail, squealed, testifying about the Barzmans in 1951. The HUAC put the USA's artistic future on wobbly grounds: how much more could have been achieved without its ignorant suppression.[18]

Fluff and I weren't the perfect holiday pair; she wanted to pick up handsome men and I didn't – too risky in my eyes. I wanted to see museums and visit Gordon Craig, the great set designer who had worked with Yeats. To visit Gordon I had to be driven to Vence and she would have to wait in the car; she wasn't too pleased. I remember putting a spanner in the works when she suggested we go along with two rather diminutive sailors. "You can go if you want but I am definitely NOT up for it", I said. She became quite heated about it but I was adamant. So that was brushed into the sand and a very grumpy pair drove back to the Villa. I was just happy being in its garden or on the balcony plucking fruit

[18] Ben Barzman (1910–1989) was a Canadian screenwriter, journalist and novelist who took U.S. citizenship when working in California, writing screenplays for such Hollywood films as *Back to Bataan* (1945), *The Boy with Green Hair* (1948), *El Cid* (1961) and *The Blue Max* (1966). He was a member of the U.S. Communist Party when he met his future wife, Norma, in 1942. He was blacklisted by the HUAC in 1951 and had his American citizenship revoked from 1954 for nine years. He and Norma moved to Paris (where they befriended Picasso, Yves Montand and Simone Signoret) and then the south of France. Norma herself (born in New York in 1920), actress and writer, was a member of the Communist Party from 1943–1949 and her passport was revoked from 1951 for seven years. She and her husband had their names removed from the credits of certain films. Norma long outlived her husband (dying in 2023 at 103) and remained unrepentant about her Communist affiliations. See Tom Teicholz, "The Hollywood Blacklist in Exile", *Jewish Journal*, August 15, 2014; "Ben Barzman", "Norma Barzman" in Wikipedia.

from the kumquat tree and reading. Fluff wanted excitement so I was a total drag.

She did drive me to Vence, where I bought some berries and soft fruit at the market for Gordon Craig. We drove slowly up to his little house. Tom Curtiss had written to him to say I would call on that particular day. I didn't have his phone number to make a time, so it was like a cold call. I nervously pushed open the little creaking gate and walked along a narrow path to what looked like a bungalow compared to our large villa. I knocked at the door, and his face popped out through a window to my right, his mass of white hair, sharp beaky nose balancing a pair of glasses, his hair topped with his black felt hat. "Have you come to interview me?" My heart sank. "No, I am Shivaun O'Casey, Sean's daughter. Tom Curtiss arranged for me to come and pay my respects". By then the door had opened and his daughter (I think) explained that he was waiting for an interviewer to come any minute now. "Oh. Well, let me give you this fruit". I looked at it and in the heat it had become slightly soggy. "And I'll say goodbye." "Wait and I will ask Mr. Craig." Then ensued a kerfuffle – "I need my shirt button", etc. Then the great man appeared at the door, flustered but wanting to talk for a short while. We sat on a bench beneath the window that he had shot out of like a cuckoo from a Swiss clock. We talked of Sean and, of course, Tom. I stuttered out how very much I admired his work and then the interviewer arrived and his attention whooshed away from me to the interviewer; I had vanished in his eyes and I made an awkward exit to a waiting Fluff. On our way back to Cannes we stopped at The Colombe d'Or restaurant to try to see the art. I mentioned Tom and the proprietor came to say he had no tables free, everyone booked way ahead. I explained that we couldn't afford to eat there, much as we would like to, but wanted to see some of his art collection. He was charming and took us into each room where we looked above the heads of the diners, at lovely works by Matisse, Picasso, Braque, etc., small and domestic-sized gems. He then took us out to see the swimming pool, it had a wonderful mural by Miro along one side-wall. I thanked him and we shook hands: I thought one day I would try to eat there surrounded by this art, but I never did.

That Wednesday afternoon the Barzmans arrived with all their tumbling children. They took us out for an early meal at the restaurant they had recommended to us. It was very exciting to talk and laugh with such an extraordinary couple and to spend one night all together at the villa. Early next morning we left the romantic villa behind and headed for Paris. I can't remember where we stayed for the two nights: I know Fluff had a friend to see and Tom took me to his local: he lived in the Tour d'Argent, I met him outside the door to the restaurant, not the back-door to his apartment. He was just the same smiling Tom with his one-inch American crew-cut and his bustling walk. After a hug we went inside to a reception desk. The restaurant was up at the top of the building. It all rushed back to me, the meals we had with Eileen and Tom on my first visit abroad. I had forgotten how grand it was. I was expected to have the same pressed duck with the familiar card with the poor duck's number written. Then the stunning view towards Notre Dame. Dusk was falling, the lights beginning to come on, and I relaxed, glad to be with such an old friend of our family. A perfect end to my holiday. The next day Friday, we had to get up early to catch the 11.30 ferry home.

TURNING TIDES

Hallelujah! I had been given a grant. Back in Bristol to pack-up my home of nearly three years, I was asked by Nat Brenner if I could work on the next production in August. It was, I believe, a situation where the theatre and its staff had been hired to house a production. It was a production of a play by Lawrence Durrell called *Sappho* (1950). It was the personal project of Margaret Rawlings: and the pay was so-so. I readily agreed as I badly needed the money. Daphne was helping with the painting of the sets, mainly rostra, and Robin was involved in some way. As there is little record of the production I assume it was financed by Miss Rawlings, who was married to a wealthy man who owned Metal Boxes. Her pretty daughter, Jane Barlow, was in the play.[19] *The New York Times* said about the play (not this production): "The dramatic fantasy of Lawrence Durrell ... has not followed the sensational Lesbian line, but has contrived a moral fable that is chiefly political in its implications, with mystical and religious overtones soundly based on normal sexuality." That's as may be, but this verse play didn't grab me.

I visited Margaret Rawlings with Robin in her apartment at the Dorchester hotel. It was very large with windows looking over Hyde Park;

[19] Japanese-born Margaret Rawlings, Lady Barlow (1906–1996), was an English stage actress married to Sir Robert Barlow; she was the co-founder of Equity, the arts and entertainment trade union. Her daughter Jane (b. 1943) became a businesswoman, married a distinguished Italian architect, became Jane Sacchi, and supervises the letting of their restored 12th-century medieval tower near Florence.

luxurious but not to my taste. What I liked then as I do now are books and pictures and simple furniture: comfort but simplicity. No books and bad pictures do bother me. My favourite rooms are workrooms and kitchens. Margaret was welcoming but what I remember most was her talking about a large polar bear rug on the floor. By now in my mind it has grown a head with bared teeth. It was a gift for her daughter as "it is the best thing to seduce someone on". I laughed a little, not knowing if it was a joke or a truth.

John Hale wanted to take my flat on – I told him it was the third storey up rather rickety stairs (thinking of his wife and his children); and the roof had often leaked. I liked his wife. She came to look over the flat and thanked me. I left them the double mattress and the huge table, floor coverings and curtains, and, most importantly, the water heater. On my last night I looked out of my window and thought, I will be sorry to leave this view. ...

Back in the St Marychurch flat life went on as usual: productions happening or being hoped for, and visitors appearing now and again to talk with "the great man". It was never dull. When on their own Sean's and Eileen's talk was easy, funny or serious; it never dried up as they were both great talkers.

The Mermaid production of *The Bishop's Bonfire* opened on July 26, and it got mixed notices but played to full houses. Sean told Ron Ayling that it "was denounced over the radio by Richard Findlater as worthless, slapstick rubbish, and a lot more" but that "this kind of review stimulates me into a laughable desire to reply to Richard, who left himself open on many counts to an intelligent and satirical antagonist: but I had to let him go in peace." Otherwise, "The play went very well, surprising Bernard Miles into ecstasies of delight; bringing crowded houses, rocking with laughter, and more money into the Mermaid Theatre till than ever fell into it before".[20]

Sean had agreed to the Festival as he liked Bernard and Nellie (Josephine). In his introduction to the play in his collection of Sean's plays, *Seven Plays by Sean O'Casey*, Ron Ayling wrote: "London theatre goers saw the *Bishop's Bonfire* in a weak production at The Mermaid in 1961". Ron forgot that mixed reviews don't necessarily mean a bad play or a bad production. Eileen went and told Sean it was excellent, and I went and thought the production was top-notch. It was a shame that Ron was so

[20] *The Letters of Sean O'Casey, Volume IV*, pp. 242–243.

wrong shipped in the assessment that he printed in his Introduction, as it hurts the play and its director and isn't fair to the production.

There was talk of the two Bobs making a film from Sean's Autobiographies. But when I was home I noticed Sean seemed upset and I heard him talking to Eileen asking her what she thought about the situation. I hadn't seen him get so personally aggrieved about anything. When I asked her, Eileen told me that he had been hurt by something Paul Shyre had done. That was a particular blow as Paul's productions in New York had helped Sean and Eileen during arid times: "He has fiddled Sean", she said. It was difficult talking to Sean about it; the glasses would be taken off and his right hand would wipe across his eyes and then ruffle the little hair he had on his head: and he tried to explain.[21]

Now I was old enough to see the distress things like this caused Sean: I note this one in particular as Paul had become a friend of the family; in my eyes it was a betrayal. The affair of *The Drums of Father Ned* paled into significance compared to this, as Paul was our friend. The film option was signed and then it vanished for a couple of years and our lives went on.

Twenty-odd years later when I was living in New York, I bumped into Paul and his partner as we came out of the same theatre. I had avoided him once before but didn't want to be too churlish, so said hello. He contacted me and asked me to his flat. There it was, exactly the same, only the cushions had faded and everything looked rundown and worn. I felt sorry for him. He was obviously ill and looked strange with his hair dyed like a redhead (it had been dark) and his face looked very pale beneath it. He asked me to audition for a part in a reading he was doing about The Shakespeare & Company bookshop in Paris. Could I read for the part of Gertrude Stein's partner, Alice B. Toklas? I auditioned in front of a camera. He said he thought I was a good actress and offered me the part. We performed it for one night, and I am proud to say I got the laugh I expected. It didn't go anywhere. In 1989 Paul died of septicemia due to his poor health with AIDS. It was a horrible and scary time with people dying too fast and often from that cruel disease. I am glad I did contact him as maybe he was sad about what he had done, with Miss Rubin's help, to Sean.

---

[21] Sean's long letter to Brooks Atkinson explains his grievance. See *The Letters of Sean O'Casey, Volume IV*, pp. 232–233.

6
Another bash at acting school
1961–1962

A visitor

ANOTHER BASH AT ACTING SCHOOL, 1961–1962

OFF TO SWISS COTTAGE

There was a hiccup in the grant from Bristol Council – they had rung to say that surely my father was well enough off to finance me. I went for another interview to explain how infrequent Sean's money was and how unpredictable. Also, that I was now 21 and independent and had worked for over two years at the Bristol Old Vic. They agreed that my parents' income, even if it was small, should not impede my grant.

I drove up in my van to the little flat in London a few days before school started. For some reason Robin was staying with me. This must have been fine for a short time but the space was very limited and eventually he obviously had to go. He went to stay in Ned Sherrin's flat in Mayfair and slowly I saw less and less of him as I became more involved in my own work and my new friends.[1] Daphne Dare moved to London soon after and lived in a lovely semi-basement flat near Kensington High Street. She later worked with Ken Loach on his kitchen-sink film, *Kes* (1969). I made a few things for her when she was designing for *Dr. Who* and the extra cash was great.

There stood the Central School of Speech and Drama,[2] set back off the street from the main Finchley Road in Swiss Cottage and attached to the Swiss Cottage Theatre where Sean and Eileen had seen Gordon Craig's productions and met the musician Martin Shaw who then composed the music for Sean's *The Silver Tassie* in 1929.[3] I climbed the steps into the lobby of the school and found the students gathered there: everyone seemed as nervous as I was, most were younger by two or three years and I felt rather old. I found a few who were nearer my age and who had worked at various jobs before applying. We were ushered into a large room to hear the person I had come to study with: John Blatchley whose introductory talk was excellent. The gathering of our year of aspiring young actors was nerve wracking for all of us I think – very few looked

---

[1] Ned Sherrin (1931–2007) was an English theatre director, author and broadcaster. He had joined the BBC in 1957 and in 1962 produced the satirical *That Was the Week That Was*. He directed stage plays in the West End in the 1970s and 1980s.

[2] The CSS&D became the Royal Central School of Speech and Drama in 2012.

[3] The Londoner Martin Shaw (1875–1958) was a composer and conductor who collaborated with Ellen Terry and Isadora Duncan as well as Sean.

assured and comfortable. We were a motley bunch: tall, short, fat and thin; some beautiful but most ordinary enough; but all of us had craned forward to listen and learn.

I had learnt nothing about men from my relationship with Robin. Possibly the emphasis Eileen placed on being admired by the opposite sex may have pushed me to try to prove that I could get a man, even with my fairly plain looks and boyish figure. So I took in the students and wondered if any would be suitable to point my cap at. I didn't want anyone younger than me so it boiled down to a physically and mentally clumsy American, the interesting and talented Ian Hogg (but he had a firm fiancée) and another man who was married.[4] It was rather disappointing but it also meant that there was no mad rush as no one seemed to want to be romantically involved. The following year stronger men appeared in the new group and added to the dynamics of the school.

In our group was a quirky young man called Marc Karlin who lived in a very nice flat in Hampstead near my friends Don and Ella Stewart. He took a lot of flak from the assistant movement teacher, Christopher Fettes, but he shrugged, grinned and ruffled his hair.[5] This was not my idea of teaching. When Yat Malmgren, the principal movement teacher, gave a criticism it was more in sorrow than in anger and therefore gentler, and so you wanted to please him and do as he wished.[6]

In the first year we had a lot of work to do on our bodies and our voices, the tools of our trade. Acting and its theories developed gradually with Blatchley; he taught acting techniques based on Copeau[7] via St Denis and Stanislavski. Blatchley had an endearing habit of pushing his glasses up

[4] The English-born Ian Hogg (b. 1937) joined the Royal Shakespeare Company after graduating from CSS&D and before becoming a familiar face in many popular television series, including *Taggart*, *David Copperfield* and *Doctor Who*.

[5] Marc Karlin (1943–1999), born in Switzerland and growing up in France, became a highly respected independent and counter-culture film-maker. See https://spiritofmarckarlin.com/bio/ and https://www2.bfi.org.uk/news-opinion/sight-sound-magazine/features/marc-karlin-act-remembering

[6] Soon after Shivaun's experience, Christopher Fettes (born in Edinburgh, 1937) co-founded the Drama Centre in London in 1963 with Yat Malmgren whose students were to include Pierce Brosnan, Simon Callow, Helen McCrory and Colin Firth. Before his stint with CSS&D, he was with Joan Littlewood's Theatre Workshop and the Royal Court Theatre. For Malmgren and Fettes, see http://www.soulamericanactor.com/essay07.shtml

[7] The immense influence of the French actor and stage director Jacques Copeau (1879–1949), who founded the Théâtre du Vieux-Colombier in Paris, stretched as far as the UK and USA.

ANOTHER BASH AT ACTING SCHOOL, 1961–1962

on his nose and giving his head a little twitch. He seemed astonished and amazed at what he had got himself into. He was a clever and informative director who I later tried to emulate when I directed. Harold Lang and his assistants, Nicholas Amer and Greville Hallam, got us doing acting exercises that made us aware of what everyone else around us was doing and saying.[8] For classes we could wear tights with our leotards and sometimes our excellent circular long heavy skirts made from charcoal grey heavy wool, but for improvisation with Catherine Cluzout, the pretty very young wife of John Blatchley, we were allowed to wear only our rather baggy and unattractive cotton leotards that meant bare arms and legs. The men all wore jock-straps to stop their bits peeking out. I was painfully aware of pubic hairs which seemed to push out from everywhere. We had all swum in the nude at Dartington and I think I would have felt easier if we had all been naked. These lessons in mime were fascinating but it wasn't till the second year that Miss Cluzout came to me and said "Now, you see, you have realized your improvisation". I still remember what I had done: I was walking along a street and I let my hand drag along the railings, and I could visualize and feel it all as if the railings and the street were really there.

Breon was now teaching at a secondary school and had a growing family in St Ives. He was grateful when Sean sent him some money. Sean's old butty Barry Fitzgerald had died on January 14, 1961 aged only 72, and later that year Sean learnt that Barry had left him £5000 in his will. Sean was deeply touched by this. Sean and Eileen decided they should buy a house for Breon and his family with it and asked me if I minded. Of course I didn't. It was obviously a good thing to do. Breon finally bought a lovely two-storey terrace house with views over rooftops to the harbour. There

---

[8] Film buffs will readily recognise the face of Harold Lang (1923–1970) from many British 1950s B-films, mostly made before he went to teach at CSS&D. His importance in the latter role is discussed in Yat Malmgren's obituary: https://www.theguardian.com/news/2002/jun/13/guardianobituaries.obituaries Nicholas Amer was born in 1923 as Thomas Amer; he became a distinguished Shakespearian actor with the Old Vic and other companies and carved out a career in cinema and television as well; he died at the age of 96. Greville Hallam (1934–1982) acted with BOV in the 1955–1956 and 1958–1959 seasons. He became a London theatrical agent. In 1982 his life was cut short when he was brutally murdered by James Monahan. During his prison stretch, Monahan wrote *Guardian* columns from 1998 under a pseudonym. His real name, which was revealed in 2009, was known to the editors but withheld from the paper's readers, as it controversially transpired.

was a small garden in front and a yard behind leading to a walkway where the children played if they were too young to walk by themselves down the steep steps to the yellow sanded Porthmeor beach.

He had settled down with Doreen Corscadden, a Northern Irish woman from Portrush. She was a very handsome woman with large dark eyes and straight black shiny hair and a slim figure that she admired and we all admired. She had come to Cornwall with her young daughter, Alison, from her broken first marriage. I understood that her husband gave her enough to live on and to look after his little girl. When living with Breon they rented a house in Teetotal Street, St Ives, but now they all seem happy in their new home: and I was delighted that brother Breon now had a house and it was filled with a wife and two daughters and another on the way. So much for my belief that two children should be the limit, due to overpopulation and lack of natural resources for multiplying humanity! (A belief I still hold!) A few years later they were to have a son, Brendan. Eileen and Sean didn't wholeheartedly take to Doreen nor I believe her to them. Luckily while Sean was alive all was well even if they weren't over enthusiastic. Eileen adored Alison, Oona and all her grandchildren – she just loved children.

Breon's letter to me:

Dear Shivy,

I've been trying to ring you up for ages. I want you to do me a favour, IF, and only IF, you have the time.

Could you submit my picture you got from Boulets to the London Group Exhibition?[9] Sending in day this coming Monday. It would mean ringing Boulets & finding out if they could do it for you; or where to get sending-in forms (Boulets may have them) You might give it a bit of a dust too.

It's not all that important, so don't put yourself out (too much), and then when Boulets send you the bill, you could forward it to me. Forge my signature on the forms.

Do you have Anthony's address?

I've applied for the job of part-time telephonist here for the summer,

---

[9] The London Group Exhibition was held at the RBA Gallery in Suffolk Street, March 9–29, 1961. Among the artists exhibited were Vanessa Bell, Duncan Grant and David Hockney (though the latter was not a member of the London Group). The Royal Society of British Artists (RBA) was set up in 1823 as an alternative to the Royal Academy.

but as I couldn't tell them what 9x9 was, I don't suppose I'll get it. This fucking jewellery. Am in the middle of making a SUPERB grandfather clock, also remaking the case of an American striker, also got an ex time-bomb clock and 2 ex gaslamp clocks to make. I gave all my classes at school a lecture last week: How the Clock's Work. Poor little buggers. They were bored stiff.

Breon

After my meeting with John Blatchley I learnt it would be too difficult to work for Sean Kenny as well as study. As I was not to be paid I decided to drop the idea and didn't get back to design until I designed and directed Sam Beckett's *Happy Days* in New York in 1990. Of course, Sean was disappointed.

It was fascinating how many theatrical people Sean and Eileen knew were connected in some way to the school. John Blatchley and Frank Dunlop had both been students at the Old Vic School (1947–1951), run by Michael St Denis with the director being Glen Byam Shaw (who Eileen had held hands with in the stalls during the rehearsals for *The Miracle*, directed by Reinhardt). Frank Dunlop went on to be Laurence Olivier's assistant when the National Theatre was founded. George Devine was also connected to the Old Vic School and later formed the Royal Court's writing theatre. John went on to work for Glen, etc. Frank directed *The Bishop's Bonfire* at the Mermaid Theatre (1961). George Devine directed *Cock-a-Doodle Dandy* in 1959; he fell in love with Jocelyn Herbert and they lived together.[10] Jocelyn's father, the playwright A.P. Herbert, knew Eileen well when she was in his play *Mother of Pearl* early on in her marriage with Sean, directed by Charles B. Cochran. (Jocelyn became a very close friend of Eileen's after George Devine died; she read at Eileen's funeral with a bunch of lilies of the valley in her hand, afterwards placing them on her coffin): One of the students at Central was Stephen Fagan, the grandchild of James Fagan who had produced Sean's first plays in London, the Dublin trilogy. The grandfather had a wife called Mary Grey

---

[10] After serving in the Second World War, the English actor, teacher and director George Devine (1910–1966), co-founded the English Stage Company which mounted *Look Back in Anger* (1956) at the Royal Court Theatre and nurtured the new generation of British dramatists. After his tenure at the Old Vic Theatre School, Glen Byam Shaw (1904–1986) became director of the Shakespeare Memorial Theatre (1952–1959) before becoming the director of productions at Sadler's Wells Opera.

whom neither Sean nor Eileen liked as she took against Eileen when she played Minnie and Nora in Sean's plays.[11] Then there was Amaryllis Garnett, the niece of Virginia Woolf and daughter of David Garnett who went to interview Sean in his room on 422 North Circular Road in 1926.[12] And of course, Yat with his Jooss Ballet and Dartington Hall connections.

With Blatchley a lot of time was spent around the table or seated in a circle. Marking the text akin to a musical score, we divided it up into sections or "beats": names were given to each section to clarify what the character was doing within the section of the play, something active not inward or static, as the action had to move the play along. I learnt from Blatchley something basic which I had instinctively done in my limited experience in school plays: to listen to the other characters and "contact" them. Eileen told me when she played Minnie, her Davoren, Harry Hutchinson, had cross eyes and never looked directly at her but over her shoulder or above her head.[13] I had noticed on the American tour and with a few actors at Bristol, actors who did exactly that. He also taught us that you can address someone with your back to them as long as you are "in contact" with them mentally. But the substance is in the doing and this is what we were given at school: practice to make a fool of ourselves in front of our fellow students, to risk something and fail, possibly to succeed.

Blatchley took classes in scenarios/improvisation. We wrote short monologues as scenarios; some of the students had a flair for writing dialogue: Christopher Bond, who became a writer and adapted *Sweeney Todd* for the stage, wrote very pertinent scenarios. Julie Whitby also, who became a published poet.[14] In the third year we were sent to the zoo to study two animals in order to "physicalise" them and transform them into a human character. I chose a lion and a raven. The raven was alone in a

---

[11] A.P. Herbert (1890–1971) was a famous humorist and reformist politician as well as playwright. It was in James Fagan's presence that Eileen first met Sean: see her account of that first meeting and of the actress Mary Grey's animosity in *Eileen*, pp. 81–84. Stephen Fagan became a television dramatist.

[12] The actress Amaryllis Garnett (1943–1973) was the daughter of Angelica and David Garnett and granddaughter of Vanessa Bell and Duncan Grant. See "Amaryllis Garnett": IMDb and Wikipedia.

[13] Eileen, perhaps kindly, omits Hutchinson's cross eyes in her memory of the performance of *The Shadow of a Gunman*: see *Eileen*, p. 89.

[14] Christopher Bond (b. 1945) went on to become a playwright and stage director. Stephen Sondheim used Bond's 1970 dramatic retelling of the Victorian story of Sweeney Todd as the basis of his 1979 musical, *Sweeney Todd: The Demon Barber of Fleet Street*. *The Violet Room* (1994) and *Poems for Lovers* (1999) are among Julie's Whitby's volumes of poetry.

ANOTHER BASH AT ACTING SCHOOL, 1961–1962

square cage; this was upsetting as ravens are very clever, sociable beings, and I think it was going mad. It did elaborate dances and calls, and I wanted to set it free. The lion wasn't much better. He paced up and down the small cage as people would do in a prison or an asylum. But he had a weapon; when a crowd had gathered to watch him go up and down he would suddenly stop, and miraculously release a cascade of pee or scent over us all. It only happened to me once, then I took to standing back to watch the cries and consternation among the crowd as it happened again and again. Good on him, I thought. I turned the lion into an impatient mistress waiting for her tardy lover. Masks were studied in the third year.

I am shocked at how little I remember of this time; I can't even remember when we did certain scenes and plays. In *Roots*, evidently I played the sister, Jenny, in Act III. I only know this because I found the old copy of the play with the stage directions marked. No beats noted, so I think it must have been very early on in the first year. I do remember playing Queen Anne in the scene where Richard III interrupts the hearse and the Queen's journey to bury her husband the late King. I remember spitting in the actor's face, and him objecting, so Blatchley told me to fake it. I also remember a Blatchley critique: "You have very long arms, and the black jumper you are wearing stops six inches above the wrists, and made them look even longer. Watch out for that in the future". For weeks my arms felt as long as an orang-utan's. Christopher Fettes told me that I had "very bound feet". and to work on freeing them. He was right, but what with exceptionally long arms and bound feet I saw a possibility of maybe being a comedian. I was brought back from daydreaming while looking at my legs one day when, exercising on my back in a gruelling Fettes movement class, his unmistakable voice cut in, "We all know you have lovely legs". "Fuck you", I thought.

52A CROMWELL ROAD

Being back in London meant I saw more of the Wanamakers and Ella and Don Stewart. It meant I visited museums again, especially the V&A library; the gem and stone collection at the Natural History Museum was also a favourite. And I also saw more of Joan Hilliam, who had a larger flat in the main house at 52a Cromwell Road where Eileen had her pied-à-terre. We all liked the caretaker's wife, Mrs Meakins. She did most of the work and was a sturdy woman with a broad honest face. The caretaker, Mr. Meakins, was lazy; he always had the stub end of a cigarette hanging from the side of his mouth; around his thin lips was a yellow nicotine stain. She was always neat; he wore an old navy suit, the front covered in cigarette ash over greasy stains down the front from food. They had a son called Cyril who reminded me in build and conceit of Mr. Fledgeby in *Our Mutual Friend*. He maintained a spruce appearance. Cyril spent a lot of his time clad in a rayon amber and black dressing gown and neat leather slippers, with a cigarette in a long black holder held in a thin hand. Most afternoons or evenings when I came home and climbed the fire-escape to my door, his light would be on and there he lay on his bed propped up on one arm looking at me. He never pulled his curtains but left them open so we could all admire the sight. Mrs Meakins also had had a daughter whom she had loved deeply; working on the buses as a conductress during the war she was killed by a bomb. Mrs Meakins gave me her ring which I still keep for her.

It worried me when Sean now wrote very short letters with no pictures. He was getting frailer and had more bronchial attacks that took him to his bed. Also, I knew his back ached a lot as well as his eyes when he was writing and he had to break off and lie down to stop the aches. We tried to think of better chairs to support his back, but because of his very bad eyes he had to bend over so his nose nearly touched the paper or his typewriter in order to see anything at all – so there really wasn't a chair that could help him. Eileen was still active and engaged.

My letter to Eileen:

6 November 1961

Dear Eileen,

I have decided I am getting rather old to write Mummy. It is rather cold here, all the trees are bare and braving the weather, but I am fully dressed and huddled up against it. I have got the tickets for 'Mourning Becomes Electra' on Friday 24th Nov. Joan said she could come so I got 4. [For Robin, Shivaun, Joan and Eileen.] Tickets for 'Oresteia' seem to be impossible to get – but Charlotte is trying for me. They are even sold out for the Sat Mat.[15] I am longing for you to come up: the shops are getting lovely with lights and Christmas decorations – it's rather exciting. Why don't they do it so nicely all the year around?

---

[15] The trilogy by Aeschylus, *Oresteia*, opened at the Old Vic, London on November 7, 1961.

ANOTHER BASH AT ACTING SCHOOL, 1961–1962

Went down to Hornchurch last night to see the 1st night of a terrible play called 'Kind Sir'.[16] It was a nice evening though; on the way back we ate fish and chips & had a chicken when I got back. There were some 'old folks' watching the play & they kept shouting out and saying – 'Oh, she knows', & 'Oh, dear', when shocking things happened, which livened it up a bit.
How is daddy, he seemed quite well when I rang. ...
All my love
Shivaun xxxx

I sat with Eileen during the performance of *Mourning Becomes Electra*. It was a good production of a brilliant play directed by Val May. Eileen didn't like the performance of Barbara Jefford but I did.[17] This was the second O'Neill play I had seen (although I had read *The Great God Brown*, *Anna Christie*, *Desire Under the Elms*, *The Moon for the Misbegotten*, etc.). The only other play I had seen was *Long Day's Journey into Night*. This was very different, a play that rose up with his imagination. Eileen told me that Sean had taken from this play the idea of the gates on the curtain opening and closing for his play *Within the Gates*, which he acknowledged in the published version.

At some point before Christmas 1961 Robin gave me a puppy he had bought at the Hornchurch Market – "I can't possibly look after a dog, I am out all day. Oh well, I can take it back and they may drown it." So I had to take it. He had called it Cratchit. In my memory it happened while he was playing Cratchit in *A Christmas Carol* at Queen's Theatre, Hornchurch. I can't find any reference to this but what matters is that I was stuck with a very real sweet little puppy – and had to try to look after it.[18] I loved animals and had always wanted a dog – but not at this moment in my life. I had little idea of how to look after it, let alone how to train it. I saw less and less of Robin as he got more work; one of the last times I

[16] *Kind Sir*, first staged in 1953, was written in 1950 by Norman Krasna. Charles Boyer and Mary Martin were in the original cast on Broadway, where it got tepid reviews.
[17] *Mourning Becomes Electra* opened at the Old Vic on November 21, 1961. Barbara Jefford (1930–2020) appeared at the Royal Shakespeare Company and the National Theatre as well as the Old Vic, and gained wider fame as Molly Bloom in Joseph Strick's film of Joyce's *Ulysses* (1967).
[18] *A Christmas Carol* was staged by the Hornchurch Repertory Company from November 28 to December 8, 1961; Robin Phillips played Bob Cratchit and Douglas Livingstone played Ebenezer Scrooge.

saw him was at Ned Sherrin's flat near Mount Street, where he was staying. I am actually surprised to see so much mention of him in letters as I have forgotten how present he was in my first year at Central. I didn't share his ideas any more for directing: the imposing of gratuitous ideas on to a play I saw as a ruse to bring attention to the production. But maybe I was wrong as I read in an obituary for him in 2015 that "he was recognised for the simplicity of his productions – with barely any sets" – designed mainly by my old friend Daphne Dare who went over to Canada to work with him.

Poor Cratchit – he was at the window when I came home and jumped all over me. I took him out for walks and for a pee before bed. But as I was out all day he couldn't keep his pee in and the newspaper I put down was often very wet. He was very good in that he did pee on it and not all over the flat. Dear Mrs. Meakins pitied him and offered to take him for a walk around the block in the middle of the day. But he did rather cramp my style; hanging out after school was no longer possible for me. Not a bad thing, maybe.

SEAN'S DECLINE AND WISDOM

Cratchit came with me to Devon for the Christmas break and he had a much better time. Long walks along the beach and in the parks. Neither Eileen nor I could get him to come to us when we called. He was most likely so ecstatic about being free and in the air. Cratchit walked with Sean and myself on our daily walks and he liked Sean's room best; I often found them lying on the bed together. He came back to London with me until July when I begged Eileen and Sean to have him in Devon. He went down there when Mrs Earle had been persuaded by Eileen to come and help look after her and Sean. [Mrs Earle was Eileen's former dresser and something of a second mother to her.] I drove him down. Mrs Earle was doing the cooking and was there when Eileen went out. One night Cratchit rushed into Sean's room and sped around the flat in a terror and Eileen noticed that he had Mrs. Earle's false teeth stuck in his mouth. Mrs Earle was screaming, "Get them quick before he breaks them!" But Sean and Eileen were so incapacitated with laughter they could hardly move. Finally Sean managed to catch Cratchit, and unstick the teeth from his frightened mouth. Eileen took him and calmed him down as he licked her face all over in gratitude.

It was clear to me that Sean would never write another play. He wrote every day answering letters, and writing in his notebook, writing the odd article, but to start a play would be just too much. When his eyes throbbed too badly he would lie down on his bed with a handkerchief tied around his eyes, or sit and listen to the radio with his eyes shut. He always turned on the six o'clock news and would pass the evening listening to talks or music.

Sean had started to record his memories around the songs that were included in his Autobiography and a few others. In London in 1959 Bernard Miles had recorded Sean singing a song and talking and it was then he suggested Sean should try to use a tape recorder for his work. Sean said he couldn't envisage writing like that. But singing, now that was different. How he loved to sing and to talk about song: what it meant, the memories it brought back, and then the idea struck him and took root: to record the songs of his past. So Sean and Eileen started to set up the Grundig tape recorder. Donald Aldous, our local recording expert who now lived in Torquay, explained to Eileen how to work it.[19]

The first evening they came to do a recording, Eileen says Sean put on his best coloured cap and new pale-blue jersey and stood up to talk: "No! Not like that Sean", she said, "Just relax, this isn't a performance". And so they set off on their journey, over time making several tapes full of song and thoughts. Eileen, who had a lovely contralto voice, sang "Nora" and "Far Away", a song often sung by his mother. The originals sit quietly now in the National Library of Ireland. I have copies and the transcripts. We used some of them in the documentary about Sean called *Under a Colored Cap*.

Sitting with Sean after supper, by the electric fire full on, the old question would come: "Would you like a piece of fudge?" Of course – out it came from the top right-hand drawer of his old Dublin desk used to pile books on, and we sat contentedly munching and talking. Being with him was being with someone who simply loved you for what you were; he often told me I reminded him of his sister, Bella, I was like her in looks and also had her stubborn streak – a bit reckless too, jumping into things, such as relations with insignificant people and trying to forge them into significant relationships. I believe this comes from a sense of not being quite strong enough in your belief in yourself and feeling you need to live through someone else, later noticing that not only weren't they up to your

---

[19] Donald Aldous (d.1990) was a British audio journalist and author of *Sound Systems* (1984).

expectations but they definitely weren't going to change. Eileen said she didn't think that after Sean died she could ever find anyone with a mind or humour like his, or anyone who loved her so much. I started to panic when I thought of a life without him: whose advice could I trust on literature, on politics? No one's, for no one I knew was as clever and well-informed as he was. The thought of having to trust my own judgement was frightful – although I made myself look hard at the prospect and accept it, and all I could do was soldier on and do my best.

Sean was shrinking – I was now taller than him, as I pointed out. His clothes were all a little big for him and he had become comfortable in roomy shirts and trousers and didn't want things fitting any more. He always looked good in his Winceyette checked shirts and woollen jumpers, his trousers pulled high up at the waist with his braces, his jackets and caps. In the cold he would sit covered in his red indoor coat, the one I had made him.

His brain was sharp and precise: I can't recall him ever forgetting words, or using the wrong words for things as I do now and Eileen did then. We called Eileen Mrs Malaprop. She would often laugh at her own mistakes. I am following in her footsteps. Janet, who looked after Eileen when she was in her eighties, made up a list of Eileen's malapropisms. "Shivaun always says I get words mixed up like Mrs. Mallows or whatever her name is", Eileen remarked. Here are some of Eileen's choicer malapropisms: "Many of the people who go to my hairdresser like that 'baffoon' style (for bouffant)"; "He's a big business typhoon" (tycoon); "I've been pushing the buzzer insensibly (incessantly) all afternoon."; "I was nonpulsed (nonplussed) for a moment"; "Gordon Blair did all those lovely cookery books." (Cordon Bleu); "I couldn't bear to be inconstant" (incontinent); "I hope I never get All timers Disease" (Alzheimers). By contrast, Sean's command of words stayed with him to the end. Songs, Shakespeare, the Bible and St Paul, quotes, poems were all a part of the daily talk with him. Not deadly serious, just talk and spiky humour.

Eileen had the 'flu before Christmas 1961 and on New Year's Day Sean fell ill with the dreaded bronchitis: lots of coughing and green phlegm. This always took a long time to heal but this time it took longer. It was a regular feature of the winter and each winter it got a little worse.

Sean's letter to me:

28 January 1962

My dearest Shivaun,

Thank you for your letter, The 'Daffodils in Picher' is very well done, it is graceful & true, and shows your hand hasn't lost its cunning. I liked it very much indeed. I've often told you that you had a decided talent for colour, line, & form: & I'm sure of this still, darling. You should do more of this work, letting neither Robin nor Cratchit get in the way. If they do, shove them aside ruthlessly – as I did long ago when I began to try to write plays. You needn't lose your sympathy with anything; but do refuse to lose your time, for within this practice (which is DOING) lies your talent. Well, that lesson will do, dear, for one letter.

I am, I think, getting better and feeling more myself in the body and mind which is called 'Sean'; but Dr. Doran warns against doing too much, bar resting. Some fluid round a lung will take some time to go.

Under another cover, I'm sending you 'Drama' magazine of University of Kansas, which has a number of articles about me.

Take care of yourself, my darling, and get plenty of rest.

I enclose £1 for a hairdo or something.

My love, as ever,

To you Dad Sean

P.S. A gift for designing, whether one be Director, actress, or Costume-maker, is always a serviceable thing in the theatre. There is a Candle of Vision for a Director, for an actor, for a Designer, and for a Costume-maker, this candle is always there, but a flame appears only after hard practice and hard study. The Candles are the Headlights of the Theatre.

A fragment of Theatre-philosophy, though I should be adding the Candle of Vision essential for those teaching the young their first ways.

Dad Sean

Eileen's also gave advice; she made me be very careful about premarital sex. I was confused by the knowledge of Eileen's "affairs" or "dalliances", which Sean appeared to put up with in the past, and her recent liaison with Leonard Elmhirst and more recently, Geoffrey Dobbie the market-gardener, who ran a plot of land where she got vegetables and flowers and a kiss in the dark. Although I never talked to Sean about Eileen, I can imagine that Sean, being twenty years older than her, knew he couldn't satisfy her need for sexual fun, especially now his health was bad and his prostate had been removed. He liked Geoffrey who came and chatted to him about trees and birds, and he was the one person apart from the family that Sean didn't mind looking after him when he was ill. But for poor Geoffrey it was different, he fell in love with Eileen – who didn't with him – and after Sean's death he wanted to be with her but not she with him.

By this time I was becoming involved in another disastrous relationship. During my teens I was aware that I was not that attractive to boys. I was painfully unlike my very beautiful and sexy mother who if she dropped a hanky, a man would dive to pick it up; if I dropped one I would most likely end up picking it up myself. The words of the visitor were still remembered – "It's a shame Shivaun has taken after Sean and not you". What Eileen told me about Edith Evans, the great actress, stuck in my mind. Evans played many leading parts where she was meant to be beautiful. "She was rather plain", Eileen said, "with big feet, but as soon as she came on to the stage you thought she was the most beautiful lady ever!". Eileen had been told that before she went on stage she would stand in front of a mirror and say to herself "You are beautiful" until she believed it. I tried this once when at the Caprice, the very swanky restaurant. When I walked in, quite a few people turned to look at me. I thought it must have worked, but think now I must have looked like a young girl trying to walk in a straight line while tipsy. "Are you all right?" Eileen asked as we sat down.

Among our motley Central group was a tall insecure American called Gordon who looked older than me and was balding. He had a large face and large awkward big feet. I honestly didn't have a clue then that he was gay. He was good company and had a certain charisma. We often went out with Amaryllis Garnett and a younger man, Lionel. One of our haunts was the very cheap Greek cafe in Soho called Jimmy's. Amaryllis delighted us every visit by lighting the paper of the Amaretti biscuits and seeing it rise into the air; she was very cool and smoked Gauloises cigarettes. Gordon started to impose himself on my life and, against all Sean's wisdom, I let him. Gordon's parents were fairly well off; his father had a factory that made mouldings for the building trade. He first lived in a very nice room at the rear of an early Victorian Crescent near Paddington Station; its windows went down to the floor level and could open out onto a communal garden. I was still a virgin. I felt I should have sex even if I wasn't madly in love with him as it seemed to be the done thing and I was

ANOTHER BASH AT ACTING SCHOOL, 1961–1962

getting on in years. Finally we went to bed together and it was not the best – for as he got on top of me he said, rather brusquely, "Don't look at me and don't move". This was not how it was meant to be. I could have been a sex-doll for all the affection he showed to me. Better to remain a virgin I thought. Well, such was my stubborn nature and his need to control me, that I stuck with him in a kind of couple for a good year or more.

By the summer of 1962 it was decided, and I had to agree, that Cratchit had to go. He was half corgi plus another dog with longer legs. Eileen found a young girl who was mad to have a dog and train him. Her father was a butcher so Cratchit had lots of meat. They were members of the Salvation Army and played on the St. Marychurch promenade on the cliff tops overlooking Torbay. Sean and Eileen would walk past surreptitiously to see him there and Cratchit had been trained so well that he sat beside the collection box and wagged his tail every time someone put money into it. We all felt relieved that he now had a much better life. So when I came down in mid July to stay for a while before going off to do some holiday work I saw my happy tail-wagging dog in his new element.

PANCAKES AT BEAULIEU

Gordon, Amaryllis and I went down to Beaulieu, Lord Montague's pile where he had given us permission to set up a stall in the grounds, at no cost, to sell pancakes. It was the brainchild of Amaryllis, who had seen crêpes being made in Paris in the autumn, and thought why couldn't they be sold all the year round, and why not by us? In London and other towns you had to get a license for this sort of thing and this was difficult and expensive, especially for a short period of time during the summer holidays. It may have been Amaryllis or Gordon who thought of Lord Montague, whom we visited and took tea with his wife and him and a pretty toddler running about. He was friendly and relaxed – in fact quite unstuffy. He accepted us and showed us an empty Gatehouse, set in some fenced-off grass to the left of the public entrance where he said we could stay for nothing. We set to work to design our stand. Not being able to find the flat grills that Amaryllis said were used in France together with the flat stick they turned with their hands to get the required thickness of the crêpe, we had to compromise with gas jets and heavy iron pancake pans. Gordon got the thing made and I made the canopy out of blue and white striped canvas and Amaryllis and I painted the signs. We were all set to go and to make some money during the holidays like grownups. My grant was to be assessed early and I had written asking for it to be granted for the following year, so this extra money would help a bit if I was refused. I believe Amaryllis and Gordon paid their fees privately.

Eileen wrote to me from St Ives in early August: "A letter came from Bristol & I did open it, as I thought where you were I better see if it was important to answer – they will give grant another year, if the report at school is good. Do you think you would want me to send it on or shall I leave it in the flat next week?" She came to visit me at Beaulieu to check us out and met Lord Montague and over drinks charmed him. But things weren't all smooth in the little Gatehouse. We cooked spaghetti on our one gas-jet. Gordon had a temper that burst out at times – Amaryllis was calm but often tearful, maybe because of him. There was a young man who worked for Lord Montague who asked us all over for a meal one night to meet some of his friends. He offered the use of his bathroom, a luxury as we didn't have either a bath or a shower at the gatehouse. I was last up. What heaven to be in a hot bath again. I very foolishly decided to shave my legs with, I suppose, his razor, and kept cutting myself; my legs wouldn't stop bleeding. They were all waiting downstairs and shouting for me to hurry up as dinner was ready. Gordon was very angry. Finally I went down, hoping no one would notice my bleeding legs, I had put my stockings back on and that helped a bit. By now I felt very uncomfortable indeed. But our host was charming and I think he quite liked me, and maybe saw I was miserable.

Another evening we were asked by a couple to go to their beach house right on the sea. What an amazing place it was. You walked from the road down a long wooden walkway to this modern house overlooking The Sound. Its large windows brought the pebbled beach, the rough grasses and sea-pinks almost into the room, and there was the sea making noises as it came and went and tousled the pebbles, calm on that evening but how amazing it must have been to see a storm. Unhappily Gordon mixed his drinks. First he became loud and aggressive, then very sick. It was a sad thing to happen on such a sublime evening and in such a place. We weren't invited back. Now I was well warned of this nasty side to his nature and of his controlling streak. He didn't like women much but wanted them to admire him.

Sean was ill again in August. When I got home, Sean was still weak but up out of bed. We were so pleased to see each other, after a big hug he took my face in his hands and slowly looked at it, so close up, to try to see me, what I looked like, what I felt like. He explained that only a pinprick of sight was still there in the one eye left with any vision at all. Our eyes did meet. His brain was so active that I felt he could see everything – his glance was so keen, but the pale blue was not his iris but the bluey fog of intense blindness.

When coming back to Beaulieu I realised that Amaryllis and Gordon had been sleeping together. When I asked Amaryllis, nonchalantly, what her hair pins were doing in our bed of sleeping bags, she just shrugged her flexible, free flowing shoulders with an enigmatic smile. Very Bloomsbury, I thought. It turned out to be nearer the Bloomsbury sexual playground than I imagined, as during the next term I called in unannounced at Gordon's new pad, two rooms above a pub in Westbourne Park, near to Portobello Road and close to my old hangout at 22 Ladbroke Road. After climbing the stairs I opened the door to find Gordon with Lionel, a boy in our group, quickly doing up their flies. Gordon was furious with me. "How dare you come here without letting me know!" Difficult, since he didn't have a phone, and not forgetting how he made my flat his home whenever he wanted and without a by-your-leave.

At Beaulieu the tourist numbers were lessening and we all wanted a break before school started again, so we packed up the pancake paraphernalia to leave. Before we left, Amaryllis' father, David Garnett, came down for a day and took us all out for a meal. He was commanding and charming in a slightly egotistical way. He was much older than Amaryllis' mother, so we both had older fathers. But he was a picture of health compared to Sean. He ordered steak for us all and when it arrived he took out his own knife, a rather beautiful knife that folded up like a penknife, saying he always had it on him to make cutting steaks easier, leaving the rest of us to struggle with the restaurant knives as best as we could.

He did mention meeting Sean in Dublin at his room in North Circular Road after *Juno* had first been produced. He had also gathered together 938 T. E. Lawrence letters and included the lovely letter Lawrence wrote to Nancy Astor praising Sean's *Within the Gates*.[20] Angelica Bell had

---

[20] Lawrence of Arabia wrote to Lady Astor: "If you see O'Casey again ... will you bless him from me? For I have seen his Park play twice. ... This play is London (and inhuman nature): all of us, in fact: and about as helpless. ... Bless him again. he is a great man, still in movement. ... I have learned a great deal from him", *The Letters of T.E. Lawrence*, ed. David Garnett (London: Jonathan Cape), p. 790.

married David when she was very young. I met her a couple of times with Amaryllis and liked her gentleness and her caring for Amaryllis. She decorated a room they had rented for Amaryllis in Hampstead and made it look lovely, even doing a mosaic around the fireplace. Amaryllis made a lampshade from a very large balloon over which she put paper maché with tissue paper; when it was fully covered and dry she had popped the balloon and there was a lovely spherical lampshade. Gordon was enamoured of the Bloomsbury Group, and, I believe, Amaryllis; he really had no interest at all in Sean's work or his life. They were much better suited than Gordon and myself.

After we closed shop, so to speak, Gordon and Amaryllis persuaded us to drive to Charleston. This we did. A very beautiful house, now well known to the public.[21] But with all its decorative splendour on walls and furniture, we were greeted by a very surly housekeeper, who lived in situ and looked after the place both when the family was there and when it wasn't. Amaryllis told us she was always like that but I imagine to suddenly have three people land on you and having to produce something for the three to eat, could have provoked her disdain. In the centre of the highly-decorated table for breakfast was a bowl of oranges. Amaryllis took one and cut it in half and sucked it dry. "We do this every morning," she said.

During the day she took us to meet Leonard Woolf, Virginia's husband. We met down at their woodland house, the house he and Virginia had made for themselves out of wattle and daub with its earthen floor, it was right in the middle of a handsome deciduous wood. Then he took us to the small river where Virginia had drowned herself. A shiver went through me; what a sad desperate thing to do, so young and with so much before her. Free and wealthy and able to do much as she wanted: all this can't stop the weight of depression or the sense of hopelessness it must bring, can it? The wicked irony was that Amaryllis, the beautiful, talented Amaryllis was to drown in the Thames by her boathouse moored off Chelsea. She was only thirty. It was a shock to everyone who knew her.

---

[21] Charleston, near Lewes, Sussex, became the home in 1916 of the painter Vanessa Bell, her lover Duncan Grant, and his partner David Garnett. The house subsequently became a mustering place for the Bloomsbury group of artists and is now a draw for tourists as well as a gallery for exhibitions and venue for assorted artistic events.

ANOTHER BASH AT ACTING SCHOOL, 1961–1962

Her mother Angelica wondered if she had slipped off the gangplank, or whether she had meant to do it. I understand she left no note.[22]

Eileen's letter to me

My dearest Shivaun,

I was sorry you didn't manage to ring yesterday, as I am going out for a meal with Ron [Ayling] tonight and may miss you. Sean is alright except for his sistitus [cystitis], which is really very painful & he worries it will get bad. I go to London on Weds and may stay over a week, and see Plough as well [as Red Roses].[23] I would like to if he is O.K. and not actually in bed. – If you really were coming dear and would stay the day, Ron would go; Gordon could stay at Claire's and be quite happy & come here for lunch and all day, but dearest not here while Sean is as he is. ...

I am looking forward to seeing R. Roses. ... I think readings should be good. [Sunday readings at the Mermaid of *I Knock at the Door*]

Now dearest please be calm, cool and collected and don't go off the deep-end. Sean really loves to have you – you know; he won't ask anyone to stay unless they really do want to and he wants them. His eyes are really much worse and he really can't read. – only a little ...

My love dearest
Eileen xx
P.S. I just saw your picture in Express with Amaryllis – it's grand
Love again E xxx

Sean's letter to me (roughly the same day):

Darling Shivaun,

Enclosed is the usual, with a £1 that jumped outside of the cheque.

[22] After a turbulent short life which ran high in France, Italy and Morocco and on no discernible income, this gifted young woman during a spell of depression drowned in the river Thames at the age of 29, either accidentally or, like her great-aunt, Virginia Woolf, by her own hand. A friend, Liz Hodgkinson, remembered her in a *Daily Mail* article of May 22, 2012, a fortnight after Angelica's death. See:
https://www.dailymail.co.uk/femail/article-2148482/Poisoned-legacy-Bloomsbury-Set-How-woman-haunted-tragic-lives-friends—dazzling-sisters-descended-bohemian-artists-notorious-sex-lives.html

[23] Bernard Miles's 1962 festival of O'Casey plays at the Mermaid included *Purple Dust* (August 15), *Red Roses for Me* (September 4) and *The Plough and the Stars* (September 25): see Christopher Murray, *Sean O'Casey: Writer at Work*, pp. 420–421.

By the way, when Eileen goes up next week try to look after her: she is now my guide in walking, my eyes in reading, in many other things besides; and is very precious to me. I have filled 4 tapes on the recorder, Eileen arranging the machine and singing two songs.

It's funny to listen to the croaking songs of the Green Crow.

I think I told you the Sextant Film of 'Johnny Cassidy' has been abandoned – a pity but 'Best made plans o' mice & men', etc. & we have to put up with the disappointment.

Dr. Krause comes here tomorrow for a last interview about the letters. I shall be very glad to see him, & so renew for a short time a link-line to Ireland.

My love as ever to you my darling
Dad Sean

News of the Sextant film being abandoned was not good. But luckily the Mermaid festival was on.

Breon's letter to me:

28 September 1962 [My birthday]
9 Teetotal Street

Dear Shivaun,

Many Happy Returns of the Day. Hope the Central isn't too bad. I'm afraid your present from me will be a little late as I want to send it to a jewelry exhibition. Hope you don't mind. I enclose a drawing of it.

Yours Breon
Everyone here sends their best wishes.

7
The last lap
1962–1963

SEAN AND BOYS

I went with Eileen to see *Red Roses for Me* at the Mermaid O'Casey Festival. It was a production that grabbed you and took you from the beginning to the end without flagging. It had what Frank Dunlop called "pace" and with it excitement, humour and passion.[1] My old heart throb Donal Donnelly played the lead, Aymon, based on Sean as a young man. Donal was not good looking in the conventional sense; he was rather small and with a comic energy, but he was wonderful, and the cast included another great actor, Leonard Rossiter as Brennan on the Moor.[2] All the productions did well and on one Sunday Bernard put on the reading of Paul Shyre's adaptation of *I Knock at the Door*. The cast included Sian Phillips, Peter O'Toole, Donal and Jackie MacGowran and it played brilliantly.

Then the Brecht Company came to London and I saw two breathtaking productions. As with the Moscow Arts Company, their actors were so well tuned and clever – no one was an embarrassment, they were all good. They embodied their characters and enlarged them enough to reach us right up in the gods. The physical work of the actors was impressive – like a well-tuned orchestra. Their rehearsal periods were massive, and they kept going back to the productions again and again; but it didn't make them tired and lifeless; on the contrary they were alive and awake. Ekkehard Schall as the title character in *The Resistible Rise of Arturo Ui* (1940) – and the character of the old actor teaching Ui how to perform his speeches – was priceless. But it was also threatening, as the wooden gestures turned into the Hitler salute. Then Helen Weigel as Volumnia in *Coriolanus*: her reaction when she heard he was dead – such a small movement with such resonance.[3]

[1] The director was Julius Gellner (1899–1983), born in Austria-Hungary, and directing plays in London by 1943. He directed *Henry V* at the Mermaid in 1960.

[2] After a long career in stage drama, Leonard Rossiter (1926–1984) gained widespread popularity as Rupert Rigsby in the ITV series, *Rising Damp* (1974–1978) and as the title character in the BBC series, *The Fall and Rise of Reginald Perrin* (1976–1979). In 1977, Rossiter was the title character in *The Immortal Haydon*, a one-man show devised for the stage by Gellner. He died of a hypertrophic cardiomyopathy while waiting to go onstage in Joe Orton's *Loot* at the Lyric theatre, London.

[3] Helene Weigel (1900–1971) was Brecht's second wife and founded with him the Berliner Ensemble. *Arturo Ui* was premiered in West Germany in 1958 after Brecht's death in 1956; Schall (1930–2005) was a stage and screen director as well as actor.

THE LAST LAP, 1962–1963

As for my own life, Sean hadn't taken to Gordon at all and tried to tell me several times to forget "boys" altogether and concentrate on my work. My choice of men was pretty deplorable, I have to say. A letter of warning came from Sean in a letter that I still try to listen to.

21 Jan 1963

Darling Shivaun,

Since speaking to you, I have – like St. Paul – examined myself to find out if I am 'stupid' and 'silly'; and I find I'm neither. Rather am I a wise old, experienced old Green Crow.

My darling, you are an educated lass; more, you are well read, clever, and skilled with your hands, & you have a fine and analytical mind when you like to use it; – But you have a weakness – you sometimes imagine a goose to be a swan. You should always guard against this; and let no other lass, no lad, or anything else cast a spell over you: keep your mind free, observe, analyse, and see others as they are.

Now I'll leave you to guess as to (the) implication of what I've written; written solely in deep love for you, my dearest one.

We are frozen up here, but doing our best to keep calm. I hope things aren't too bad with you; that you keep yourself warm and go calmly about in your car.

I enclose a little – £2 notes to give you a chance to see we think of you.

My love as ever, dear Shivaun

Dad Sean

Dear Sean,

Like Patience herself I have been thinking and I don't see what you have against Geese!* I don't try and change geese into swans I just like geese.

Maybe I like the way they scratch and run at things with their necks stretched out, better than a perfectly white swan, with all its strength.

It can't be helped towards what our affections go, it is something unruly that I find it difficult to put an answer to.

Also I am not good at being on my own. I seem to need someone, (that is really my biggest weakness) I am trying to become better. I will have to, because one is really always on one's own, however many people you may have around you, isn't one?

Thank you for your lovely letter and I will think about what you said.

Two men from the Daily Mail came to the school today & wanted to interview me – they forced me into it before I knew what I was doing; they took a photo & cross-examined me as the photos were being taken all very quickly.

I saw it today. & it makes me out to be a perfect fool, how they twist things around. I should never have let them do it, but it is so difficult in the Foyer, with everyone buzzing around, to causing a scene! I wish to christ I had though! It's really nasty. I ENCLOSE IT . ...

Love Shivaun

*He must have put the letter down on his lap and looked to heaven in despair.

It was always lovely being with Breon and I went with him to visit the shops he already sold at, and also the V&A. He did quite well. The shop at the top of the King's Road bought earrings and silver chains. Whenever I am alone with Breon it brings back the feeling of Niall being near and the youth we all spent together. I wonder if he felt like that: just walking and talking and laughing off any rejections by the shops.

In March Sean was invited to London by Lovat Dickson of Macmillans to discuss the paperback publication of the autobiographies that summer, but Sean pleaded his blindness and old age: "83 years of wear and tear stand in the way and, I fear that when next I go to London it will be either on a stretcher or in a coffin. You see, I now knock at the door of blindness, so I amn't able to read any longer, and write a little, but type a lot by guesswork." Eileen could go on his behalf or perhaps Mr Dickson could find his way to Torquay. Eileen went.[4]

In an effort to write, Sean now followed the pen with a finger, writing, as he said, by touch. Copying out his letters to me, it seems I sent him a lot of drawings of daffodils. Not as many, though, as the pound notes he sent to me for imaginary "hair-do's". I never went to a hairdresser then, just grew my hair long, especially when I was at Drama School as it was meant to be useful for different styles; we couldn't have wigs.

In a March 1963 letter to me, Sean sent an enclosure of an article, "I

---

[4] Lovat Dickson (1902–1987) – born in Australia, reared in Rhodesia, educated in England and employed in his early adulthood in Canada – was general manager of Macmillan as well as a well-known author.

THE LAST LAP, 1962–1963

will not attack the Abbey Theatre" by Michael MacLiammoir. In it he says that the O'Casey story was fantastic. "If everybody did what O'Casey did", he said, "go off to a foreign country just because a play was turned down, nobody would live anywhere. Imagine going to live in Devonshire because somebody didn't like *The Silver Tassie"*. In fact, Sean left Dublin in 1926 for London soon after the rows *The Plough and the Stars* created with some of the Irish nationalists of the time. How glad I am that he left Dublin at that time and moved to London. In London he met Eileen and wrote *The Silver Tassie*. I say it yet again: Sean left Ireland before he started work on his great anti-war play set during the Great War. He had things in his mind appertaining to the Great War while in Dublin, after spending time in hospital where many of his fellow patients were severely injured Irish soldiers. Sean had been given a Union bed by Jim Larkin to have his tubercular glands removed from his neck. While in London, when his friend Billy McElroy sang that ballad by Robbie Burns ("Gae bring tae me a pint o' wine,/And fill it in a silver tassie"), Sean had a song to wrap his play around, and he rushed home to his little flat in Chelsea and set to. The problem with people like MacLiammoir is they put these false stories into people's brains and they become "fact". Many times I have had to correct people who told me that Sean left Dublin because the *Tassie* was rejected. Also to correct their mistaken belief that he hated Ireland, and was a bitter angry man.

David Krause sent a letter to the *Irish Times* where MacLiammoir's remarks had appeared on March 30. Sean sent me a copy after it was published on April 3 under the title "The O'Casey that was". In it David wrote: "Surely a man of Mr. MacLiammoir's theatrical knowledge should know that Sean O'Casey left Ireland in 1926, two years before The Silver Tassie was rejected by the Abbey in 1928. Furthermore, O'Casey did not go to Devonshire until 1938, when he moved to Totnes in order to live near the school, Dartington Hall, that he had chosen for his children. At the time when the Abbey rejected his play, he was living in a London flat, struggling to support a wife and a small child solely by his writing, a perhaps daring and fantastic endeavour. These facts are on record, and they should be respected."[5]

Sean also sent me a copy of MacLiammoir's reply in which he said that

[5] *The Letters of Sean O'Casey, Volume IV*, p. 386. In fact, when Sean received notice of the Abbey's rejection he was living in his London house, 19 Woronzow Road, St John's Wood.

387

he was saddened that his remarks drove David to protest. "Nobody would be more rapturously received in his native city than O'Casey; I, incidentally, would be one of the first among the cheering crowds. ..." Sean wrote to David three days after the *Irish Times* letter: "I wonder why he made such lying, venomous remarks? I have never said anything to him, never mentioned him in a book, article or speech, never even spoke to him in my life, so he had no reason for lies. One would think, speaking in a university, before students, that a Dr. of Lit. would at least respect the integrity that his literary honour awarded him". He went on to be very sarcastic about gay men (MacLiammoir was very publicly gay).[6] As far as I could see, Sean just didn't fully understand sexual orientations that veered from the norm. He was old-fashioned in that respect. Yet I remember he and Eileen being deeply upset at the treatment of John Gielgud when he was charged for being with a man in a gentleman's toilet and supporting his brother Val Gielgud in defending him. In the past he had agreed with George Bernard Shaw that Wilde should not be sent to jail; he believed homosexuality should not be criminalised.

I hated Ireland for what it suppressed and what it honoured. I resolved in my young dogmatism, at least, never to marry an Irishman - especially a Catholic one. Not forgetting that the man I admired more than anybody was Irish.

TROUBLE AT MILL

The last term of the year was coming to an end at Central School when a bombshell hit us. Called into the rehearsal hall, we were told that Yat Malmgren had been dismissed. Gwyneth Thurburn, the President of the School, had been concerned about his movement classes, convinced that some of the exercises stiffened our necks and hence our throats and could cause the dreaded nodules on our vocal cords. She said they had resulted in boys from C Stage having to rest their voices! Strange that she didn't

---

[6] Micheal MacLiammoir (1899–1978) was born Alfred Willmore in east London but early went to Ireland, became infatuated, changed his name to a rough Gaelic approximation of his birth name, and put it about that he had been born in Cork. (The extent of his appropriation of the Irish perspective can be measured in his reference to England as "a foreign country".) At first a child actor, then a painter and children's author, MacLiammoir became an adult actor and stage director, in Dublin and the West End. His partner was Hilton Edwards, with whom he founded the Gate Theatre in Dublin. He and Edwards were publicly accepted and honoured in Ireland despite their gay relationship and the general animus and laws in Ireland against homosexuality at that time.

even consider that the antiquated voice method she taught that used "bone-props" to keep your mouth wide open while you tried to articulate, had any part in causing tension. So Yat and Christopher Fettes were to go and Blatchley and Miss Cluzout to leave in sympathy: and Malcolm Williamson our music teacher to go: and Harold Lang and his assistants to go: none to come back – ever.[7]

We were left in shock. I had come to study with John Blatchley and now his team was to leave. I said we had to form a group to talk about what to do, that we had to ask John Blatchley and Yat to form a new school so that we could all continue our training with them. Most of the students in our year and the year below agreed. I am not sure when we got it together enough to resign from the School but I imagine that due to grants we waited until we had talks with Blatchley and Yat. That day Carol Jenkins, a clever and gifted American from Tennessee, Gordon and I asked John for an urgent meeting.[8] The announcement was on July 3 and we were invited to visit John for a cup of tea on July 5. We begged him to continue to teach us, to form a new school. I think he was genuinely surprised. He told us that he and Yat had in mind to form a new school in three or four years' time but that they had no finances in place and no venue. We asked if we started to raise some money and found a venue, would he consider it. He said he had to talk to Yat. So we waited and went back the following morning. On July 6, Blatchley, Miss Cluzout, Yat and Fettes met B Stage: that is, us. After an intake of breath Blatchley said if we could find suitable premises they would set in motion the opening of their new school. Delighted, we set to.

Carol Jenkins, Gordon, a student named Jane Glassey, and I started our

[7] Gwyneth Thurburn (b. 1899) was Principal of the CSS&D from 1942 to 1967; among her students were Laurence Olivier and Robert Helpmann; she died in 1993 at the age of 91. The distinguished composer Malcolm Williamson (1931–2003) briefly taught at the Central School in the early 1960s. He was born in Australia but moved to London in 1950. He was the first non-Briton to be appointed Master of the Queen's Music, in 1975, a controversial tenure from the start. His obituary appears in the *Guardian*, March 4, 2003. See also: https://musicianguide.com/biographies/1608003913/Malcolm-Williamson.html

[8] After three years at CSS&D, Carol Jenkins (b. 1938) returned to the U.S. and soon made the first of several appearances on Broadway. She later appeared in popular American TV series, including *Fame* (1982–1987), *Matlock* (1986–1995) and *Max Headroom* (1987–1988). She now teaches at the University of Tennessee. See her entry in Wikipedia and her biography in the Department of Theatre, on the UT website: https://theatre.utk.edu/people/carol-mayo-jenkins/ where she is credited with co-founding the Drama Centre, London.

search.[9] We scoured estate agents and also just drove around looking. Gordon and I found a lovely schoolhouse in Wapping: Victorian, with Boys and Girls carved in stone over two separate archways. It was opposite a small green and near the Thames. Blatchley and Christopher immediately turned it down as being too far away from NW London, where they both lived. Time was ticking by. One day while driving along Prince of Wales Road I noticed a fine columned facade that reminded me of Coopers Hall in Bristol. Jane and I went to speak to the caretaker. We were told it was possibly going to be sold to the Greek Orthodox Church. We spoke to John who liked the idea. Then Jane did wonders: she talked to the Methodist caretaker like a UN negotiator; it turned out she too was a Methodist. She then helped to instruct Blatchley, Yat and Christopher, and with their combined charms, respectability and gravitas, they obtained the use of the building on a lease. We had found a home for a new school and a procedure could be set in place for the selection of students and all that the legality of moving from one school to another would involve. Drama Centre, London had a home!

We were still working at Central as the term hadn't ended. Our voice teacher, a nice enough woman, Marjorie, tried to talk us into staying, scaring us with the possibility of grants being stopped. She seemed to be reassured that we would stay and went to Miss Thurburn with this news and the pressure from Central on us to stay subsided a bit.

The time came for those who wanted to leave and start at the new school to resign. Nineteen in all were seriously inclined. I remember a meeting with Yat and an accountant. Yat was very keen now for the new school to happen and the accountant said that it was not impossible *but* that the school would have to get recognition from the Ministry of Education, and that in the meantime the transfer of county grants would be up to each Council. So far so good, but the forming of this new school had a way to go

With the help of the accountant, William Rosser-James, a questionnaire was drawn up for students, who now had to decide whether they would be resigning: 1. Do you believe in Blatchley? 2. Are you prepared to resign unconditionally? 3. Will you return to Central should Blatchley refuse to accept you? 4. Do you want to follow Blatchley? 5. Can you afford the

---

[9] Jane Glassey trained as a actor but after graduation became a stage director. With her husband, the actor David Whitworth, she ran the Richmond Drama School from 1987 to 2007.

fees? 6. Can you still afford to if you have to pay back your grant? 7. Are you completely unable financially? 8. Can you afford to pay part of the fees? What I put down I don't know. Most likely Yes to everything. I knew I would somehow make it work. Throughout my career, I didn't let lack of money stop me, often to my own severe cost.

Blatchley, Yat and Christopher Fettes accepted all our B Stage who had resigned: 19 in all. But C Stage was a larger group of students and in order to keep this group to a manageable size for the new school, some would not be able to attend. This was in order to keep the teaching staff low and affordable: in addition to Yat, Fettes, Miss Clouzot, Blatchley, there would be a music teacher, a voice teacher and some visiting directors. Blatchley had agreed to do the first year for no pay. All these possibilities were to remain secret until Blatchley notified Gwyneth Thurban officially. This was a problem and I am sure rumours abounded.

My flat now became the headquarters for money raising, which we did with great vigour. Too quickly and without enough thought, the requests went out, until we were reined in by a horrified Yat. In *After the Revolution: A Critical History of Drama Centre* (London, 2003), pp.33-34, Vladimir Mirodan explained the nature of the challenge: "For Yat, Fettes and Rosser-James, their principal advisor, the key to the progress of the venture is the establishment of a legal structure which will give the revolutionary chaos a shape and the teachers a measure of control. On 16 July Christopher Fettes sends a letter to the students outlining their plan: in order to underpin the future school a company limited by guarantee will need to be formed, controlled by a Council of Management (Board of Directors) which at this stage includes Blatchley, Yat and Fettes. As a legally constituted body the company will be entitled to receive tuition fees as well as borrow money at commercial rates of interest. The company will be registered as a charity, enabling it to maximise the impact of donations. Once established, the company will engage the services of the three main teachers on five year contracts; salaries also listed, although at this stage these must be considered theoretical."[10] By the end of July all operations leave my flat and are transferred to Yat and Fettes. Eileen and

---

[10] The stage director and author Vladimir Mirodan was Principal of the Drama Centre (where he had taken the Directors' Course) from 2001 to 2011. His doctoral thesis at Royal Holloway, University of London was *The Laban-Malmgren System of Character Analysis*. See: https://arts-london.academia.edu/VladimirMirodan and https://loop.frontiersin.org/people/203057/bio

Sean could breathe a sigh of relief. On July 30, Fettes writes a letter to all the parents of the new students. Everyone was on high alert; some students were accosted and threatened by the Central School staff, who were horrified by our unforeseen reaction. We slept little and gathered in students' rooms near Central. The Company was duly recognised as a charity.

We did have the serious responsibility of persuading our councils to transfer our grants to this newly standing school. Rosser-James, aware of Sean's worsening finances, promised to write to press my case. I wrote to Dorothy Elmhirst for some help but she regretted that their money was spoken for on behalf of the London Academy of Music and Dramatic Art. Luckily for me, another student from C Stage, Celia Bannerman, also had a grant from Bristol. Her family house was in Bristol and Celia was working there during the break and she was much more pragmatic than me.[11] She was in contact with Bristol Corporation and also asked Rosser-James to write on her behalf. But Bristol Corporation along with other bureaucratic institutions now took their summer break. Most teachers were on holiday. All seemed shut down until everything and everyone returned from their summer breaks in late September.

GORDON, GREECE AND TURKEY

Gordon wanted to drive to Venice and then go by boat to Greece and Turkey. Of course, he would need my car and I was easily persuaded. I didn't think of the cost and was easily manipulated (another thing Sean warned me against). I assume Gordon hadn't much of a problem with money and possibly he told me he would pay the petrol costs, or something, as he had decided not to go back to his home in California for a break; so maybe the airfares were at his disposal.

We set out at the end of August 1963 for a two-week break. By the time my Singer Sports car reached the outskirts of Venice it badly needed repairs, something I hadn't planned for. We found a garage and left it there to be mended and to be picked up by us on September 12. Venice and all its ethereal beauty was like a dream – a very expensive dream. We found

---

[11] From Oxfordshire, Celia Bannerman (b. 1944) went on to train at the Drama Centre. She began her professional career in explosive style, appearing in short order in major productions at the Theatre Royal, Haymarket; she later added appearances in television series and in movies, including *The Tamarind Seed* (1974). She has directed at the Bristol Old Vic, Stratford East and the National Theatre.

a lovely pensione where the woman who owned it took pity on us, thinking we were madly in love and let us have a charming attic room for very little for the night, before we caught the ferry to Athens on the following day. I thought how lovely it would be to be here with someone you really loved and who really loved you.

The next morning after the nice lady gave us breakfast, we had a coffee in St. Mark's Square that cost us all the money we had put by for food for the day. We looked at the amazing gallery with Caravaggios, etc. I didn't know what to admire most, the pictures or the beautiful decorated rooms that held them and the views through the windows, with their diamond shaped leaded glass, framing the watery canals. Again I felt sorry that this was a strange and sometimes scary relationship, most likely for both of us. But why didn't I reject him? My memory is of a time-bomb always about to go off from my bigger than life fellow traveller.

When evening came we boarded the ferry from St. Mark's Square. The sun was setting as we left Venice. As all the lights of the city came on, I watched this delicate jewel slowly sink into the sea and slowly vanish We didn't want to spend our limited money on a cabin and so opted for the deck. We hadn't realised that this meant that no food was available to us. The kitchen kindly gave us some watermelon and as we sat and ate it people started to offer us some of the food they had brought with them: we made friends with a man from Lesbos, where we were heading, who spoke perfect French: Gordon spoke French so they communicated: his name was Jean.

September 7, 1963

Dear Sean & Eileen,

We are in Chios waiting to get a little boat to Cesme, in Turkey; and then get a train to Izmir, from where we will visit Pergamon & Ephesus: two archaeological sites with old Greek temple remains, also theatres, libraries, etc. At Pergamon the Romans built an amphitheatre over a small ravine so that they could watch Crocodile and Hippopotamus fights – gruesome.

We started off here about 5 days ago. We took a bus to the other side of the island to a place called Marmara – it was a real dead hole with a stony inlet and a few boats. So we got a taxi and were taken a little along the coast to a very pretty little village with a house built right on the pebbles of the shore. We walked down and got a little room. It was one of the two rooms that formed the house, for the women cooked and ate outside & only seemed to use the houses for sleeping in. So we swam, and it really was lovely, & ate. And in the evening we got a bill for the food and the prices were as high as in Athens! They must have seen us coming because however pretty the place the people were as morose as hell, & as we ate gigantic wasps swarmed around us and a gentle breeze blew real Greek dust all over the food. As we were lying on the beach deciding to leave, and go to Lesbos, a marvellous old lady came up with a plate full of peaches & a tomato which she washed in the spring on the way over, she gave them to us to eat with our bread, which she must have seen us buying off the little boy with a donkey who was visiting houses on the beach. Later, when we went to give her a bottle of beer, she and her husband refused it, saying it upset their stomachs & loaded us with almonds and a sweet smelling herbs. This nearly made us stay.

But luckily we didn't as Lesbos, Mytilene (as it is now called) was marvellous. Very green, covered in Olive Trees, friendly people, lovely painted boats in vivid orange, yellow, green & black, & ten times cheaper. We got in touch with the Greek who was on the boat from Athens who spoke French. He showed us around and took us to a party in a little house on the edge of a hill overlooking the town. And they fed us marvellous Greek food. All broke into song periodically (one would start & slowly all the others would join in, wrapt, a few shut-eyed ones.) Then they danced in the little hall and insisted we dance too, which we did. The Mother of the House was very nice, a huge fat toothless lady always sitting on the steps (stairs) of her house a little back from everyone, laughing at everything her even fatter husband said before he even said it. He broke into song too, like some strange bellowing old bull, singing about love. None of them spoke English our only link being through our friend Jean. We nodded periodically like two stone Buddhas to show our appreciation, which was very often looked for, especially by mum. She never ate or drank a thing the whole evening just went and got things with the help of her daughter. It must be an old-fashioned Greek custom.

At the end it was too late for a bus & so after being laden with flowers & smelly herbs we shook hands and nodded to our hosts & started to amble back with the party of guests into town. We walked in the balmy cool of the evening home.

Finally we got back, but there on the quay were more friends eating and drinking, so we had to sit down & eat more. Finally exhausted & dead tired we made our excuses & dragged ourselves home to bed, having got up at 5 in the morning to get there.

How are you both? Eileen write to me in Athens and tell me how you all are. Co. American Express
Constitution Square
Athens.
I am very well – my love
Shivaun xxxx

We arrived in Izmir, Turkey by boat on September 7. It was a hot sunny day and Gordon's military friend Mort was there in the square to meet us. He told me immediately to put on a dress or a skirt – to cover my legs and arms, as it was seen here as immoral for a woman to bare her flesh. He had booked us into a small clean hotel on the square and I changed. He left to go back to his military work and Gordon and I went for something to eat at a local cafe. There were no females there, just men smoking hookahs. We ordered our meal and finally one large plate arrived and was placed in front of Gordon. He asked where my food was; there was silence as they didn't appear to know what he was saying; then one of the men who spoke English explained that I was expected to eat what my male partner left on the plate. No way. Politely we persuaded the waiter to bring a plate for me and we put some of Gordon's food on to my plate and we started to eat while the men shot us looks of amusement or distaste as they smoked.

Mort told me not to wander into the Arab section of the town, advising me to stick to the square and the larger streets. He went off with Gordon. I glanced up a side street, narrow, with little shops and exotic merchandise spilling onto the street: fruit, spices and materials. I decided to explore. I bought lots of beads, mainly for Breon, 2 donkey bags and the "krisses", woven belts and tassels. Everyone was very helpful and friendly and I could only wonder why Mort was so fearful. Fear breeds mistrust on both sides.

The next day Mort had arranged for a small white bus to pick up Gordon and me and an older man dressed in old khaki shorts, white canvas hat, white jacket with lots of pockets, serious walking boots and a rucksack. He was an archaeologist going to see Ephesus and the Roman-built Amphitheatre at Pergamon like us, only with far more knowledge. As we drove along the coast I saw some women lying in the water with all their clothes on – mainly black – like dark porpoises. The little girls (I assumed they were girls) were also in clothes but two little boys wore nothing. They all looked so happy.

Ephesus: what a wonder. Sitting on the edge of a blue sea, these pillars of white marble, some arches still surviving; the sculpted stone shone in the sunlight. Our archaeologist friend was busy taking pictures as we walked all over it, awestruck. Even the latrines were beautiful, now out in the open, a carved marble bench carved and sanded to fit the bums of the Greeks with comfort. A marble gully would have taken the rich shit away to be piled up and used as compost on the surrounding fields. The site had a serenity and we were the only three there, with a driver and a guide. After some hours we were driven back another way to the Amphitheatre: it was so well preserved and so very handsome. It was carved in a curve; we were told that this enhanced the sound. The guide went down a long way on to the stage, we were almost at the top seats – he dropped a coin and we heard it clearly. He then spoke some lines and we heard it all; clear not muffled: and this was outside; conditions notorious for being difficult for sound – without mics!

We had run out of money here in Turkey. Mort told us to go to the British consulate, and we did. We entered another era: back to colonial times. A grey-haired, waxed-moustached man in tropical kit greeted us in his office. The light creeping through the wooden shutters showed the dust floating in the air, stirred up by two wooden ceiling fans trying to cool the shaded room. "Having a bit of trouble on the money front, I've been told", he said. Gordon explained who we were and that we needed to get back to Athens for him to access money at the American Express Office. "Well, here's what we do in cases like yours. We have a little pot of discretionary money. I can give you £10." "We'll pay it back!" "No! No! We do it this way to keep it simple. No going back and forth. It is non-refundable. Now let's have a drink. Whisky? I don't often get to talk to visitors here." So we sat under the whirring fans, getting slightly blurry, until, luckily, he was called to another meeting and we had to leave. "Jolly good! Keep sober. Bye."

The ferry took us directly to Athens during the day. We had one night there and then a night ferry to Venice, arriving at dawn with the sun rising behind Venice. We went to the American Express Office to get Eileen's letter and some money she had wired through. It wasn't there, so Gordon had to withdraw some on his card. Then after a quick breakfast we took a vaporetto through the canals to the dry land and picked up my car from the garage. We took turns to drive to Paris where we spent two nights. I went out with Tom Curtis to the Tour d'Argent and had another of their pressed duck. I loved Tom from when I was little, his non-stop talk of theatre, film and Paris life. The next day I took Gordon with me to have a meal with Sam Beckett. As Gordon went ahead Sam said, "I had hoped you'd be alone." "I'm sorry Sam, I should have warned you, I am sorry." "Remember I always like to meet with you." It was slightly stilted after that but I was glad to have seen Sam again – and looking so well.

RETURN TO LONDON, THEN MURDER MOST FOUL

It was time to go down to Devon for a while before the final term started in our new premises. I listened to Sean and Eileen recording songs on the tapes. While I was away travelling in the sun, Sean got a letter from Teresa Sacco, his editor at Macmillan asking if he would be interested in a request from Penguin about a new series of plays by 20th-century dramatists. They wanted to include one of his plays with one by Yeats and one by Synge. They would avoid the plays already published in the St. Martin's Library, and asked for *Cock-a-Doodle Dandy* to go beside *The Countess Cathleen* and *The Playboy of the Western World*. He was delighted and replied: "Dear Teresa, Since you agree in principle with the Penguin proposal, it is alright with me, so go ahead with the deal. O'Casey among the Penguins! Well, they are very remarkable birds, and O'Casey is a remarkable bird, too, and the Green Crow should show up well against the snows."

I felt duty bound to go to London and see what I could do to get the school ready for use. The grant from Bristol was not only very important for me but also for the start of the new school. Although they had some students paying their own fees, many more were reliant on grants for fees and also for their living allowance. It was on September 21 that Bristol County Council agreed grants for Celia Bannerman and myself, thanks in the main to Celia and her visits during the summer before they closed for their break, with her persuasive ways and her intelligent beauty.

On September 28 the bush telegraph buzzed that a meeting was to take place at Jane Glassey's place near the large buildings of our old school. We were all so relieved and joyous that we had managed to get John, Yat and Christopher to form a school for us. They had taken our trust and very bravely succeeded in setting the foundations for a bona-fide stable seat of learning for the theatre arts that existed until it closed in 2022. We all gathered, groups C and B, and were allotted tasks to perform. Many of us helped to clean the premises, sweeping, wiping and rubbing the loos and sinks. Celia Bannerman ran up waving a letter, jumping, ecstatic. Her cheque had come through for her living allowance. What a relief. When I got home there was mine waiting on the mat. Immediately I rang Eileen and Sean. This first grant release meant others followed and by the year's end the school was recognised by the Ministry of Education.

Our Group B was now called Group 1, and Group C became Group 2. The number was to remain with the group forever: I am still a member of Group 1. Group 1 was to present twelve different plays and Group 2 nine.

What excitement and relief on the first morning. We had done it, thank the Lord. It was all organised, the Timetable was up and work had to be done. We found the vestry dressing room and changed into our leotards, tights and ballet pumps. There were 21 of us in Group 1, and we all walked into the large church hall where the Methodist banner read "The Lord God Omnipotent Reigneth"'. John Blatchley, Yat Malmgren and Christopher Fettes – thank you for your faith in us all and for working so hard to make it happen properly and with such wisdom. In comes Yat from the back of the hall from behind a curtain: he has a smile upon his face as he says: "To work!" We took our places, he shuttled us around a bit, making sure we all had the right amount of room and bingo, off we went. We had all registered and were given a talk by Rosser-James about the grants and the financial situation.

Eileen's letter to me:

October 1963

Shivy dearest,

I do hope all was O.K. at school. Thank you for your letter. Sean isn't all that well & really has taken a bit against Mrs. E [Earle] & her cooking, he feels sick a good deal, but it is likely the drugs. I hope to get to London for a day next week & to Breon a day, Mrs E goes on Tues week until Feb: winter is hard to travel. I hope Gordon comes with you at Xmas, you can rest and sleep. I hope Sean is O.K. anyhow there will be only me here. I wondered if we couldn't try and arrange for you to go away for your last week. You could give me 3 or 4 days in London & then go off yourself. Anyhow don't let's worry too much over my days. It will be lovely to have you & I hope Gordon as well. I may see you next week.

Eileen x

Breon talked to Mrs. Earle's son, Charlie, over the phone, who told him that the work with Eileen was really too much for Mrs Earle who was well into her eighties – and he thought she should come home. Poor Mrs Earle, she wanted to do all she could.

My letter to Sean:

21 November 1963

Dearest Sean,

Why don't you live nearer? I miss you both so much – if only I could see more of you. You're down there, & my work up here – my heart is torn in twain.

We are very busy indeed, so much to do. I was told by Yat (who used to be a leading dancer & choreographer for the pre-war Jooss Ballet) that I could be a modern dancer, I have improved so much. And I can now hold a song together. I love singing. I haven't got a beautiful voice, but it isn't too bad. Solange is very worrying – so difficult.

I am going to give a lecture on Aristophanes – my favourite Greek Dramatist – & I think I will show a scene from his play 'Peace'.

Stravinsky's opera is called, 'History of Soldier' or in French 'Histoire du le Soldier', (or something). It isn't very long, is an early work, a small orchestra. 4 or 5 instruments: 1 oboe, etc. A sort of Ballad Opera, done on T.V. several times. It has a narrator. Richard Burton narrated it once.

Thank you for letter and cheque!
All my fondest love to you & Eileen
Shivy
P.S. Tell Eileen & you I will ring on Sunday.
P.P.S. You and Eileen can never be old. Stop depressing yourself!

On November 22, President Kennedy was shot. I still have the November 23 *Guardian* insert covering the dreadful event. I was walking along the main road in Swiss Cottage and in a window with TVs running I saw the shock announcement. Who could believe it? I rang Sean when I got back to the flat: he was devastated, immediately sitting down to write to his American friends.

Sean's letter to David Krause:

22 November 1963

My dear Dave,

I mourn with you and all Americans. This bloody murder has stunned and horrified Eileen and me. President Kennedy's death is a disaster to mankind, this young, handsome, generous and enlightened spirit has snatched away from us a most noble gift from nature.

It is terrible the power for evil that lies hidden in the hands of bloody minded men.

God help us all

Sean

Sean's letter to Rose Russell*:

25 November 1963

Oh, my dear Rose,

What a terrible thing has happened to us all! To you there, to us here, to all everywhere. Peace who was becoming bright eyed, now sits in the shadow of death: her handsome champion has been killed as he walked by her very side. Her gallant boy is dead.

What a cruel, foul, and most unnatural murder!

We mourn here with you, poor, sad American People.

Sean

*Union leader, for twenty years legislative representative of the Teacher's Union of New York.

This letter was printed in the *New York Times* and the *New York Herald Tribune*, November 27, 1963. I was told it was also posted in the New York buses.

Sean's Autobiographies arrived by Special Delivery with a request from Mrs Rose Kennedy, John Kennedy's mother, if he would be kind enough to sign them: she had read his lament in the *NY Times*. He did, of course: I don't know what he wrote to her: they were duly sent back. He told American friends that he and Eileen felt the same way after my brother Niall died. "We were physically sick as well as emotionally upset; the belly

THE LAST LAP, 1962–1963

heavy as lead caused by the distension of the bowels. No wonder in ancient times, these were thought to be the centre of emotions; Gaelic mothers used to say to their babies 'M'aie istigh thu,' 'You are my bowels within'; and remember that passage in the scriptures which says 'If a man seeth his brother in want, and shutteth up his bowels in compassion against him, how dwelleth the love of God in that man?'"[12]

Sean's letter to me:

25 November 1963

Darling Shivaun,

... I'm glad ... you are beginning to sing. There are few things healthier or more cheering (even sorrowful songs) than singing. Good for the lungs, good for the Psyche. I hope we may hear you when you come home to us at Christmas.

We are still stunned by the stupid murder of President Kennedy; there was nor good nor evil nor any reason whatsoever for it. It was so aimless, so horribly aimless; utterly incomprehensible; and very sad; a bad blow to the cause of peace.

I enclose a check
And my love
As ever Sean

THE LAST CHRISTMAS

The first productions directed by Fettes of *Countess Mizzie* by Arthur Schnitzler and *Suddenly Last Summer* by Tennessee Williams were performed at the Jeanetta Cochrane Theatre London on December 16 and 17.[13] On December 18 and 19, the productions by John Blatchley of *The*

---

[12] Cited by David Krause in his *Letters of Sean O'Casey, Volume IV*, p. 455.
[13] The Austrian playwright Arthur Schnitzler (1862–1931) began his career as a doctor. His plays were controversially candid on the subject of sexuality and his works were banned by the Nazis. There have been English-speaking dramatic and film adaptations of some of his plays. *Countess Mizzie* was first performed in 1907. *Suddenly Last Summer* premiered off Broadway in 1958; Williams and Gore Vidal turned it into a screenplay for Joseph Mankiecwicz who directed Elizabeth Taylor, Katharine Hepburn and Montgomery Clift in the 1959 movie.

Maids by Jean Genet and *The Fire Raisers* by Max Frisch, were to take the stage.[14]

The time had come for my first public performance. John was directing *The Maids*. I played Solange, Deborah Norton was Clair, Nadia Atkin the Madam.[15] The Drama Centre had formed an alliance with the Central School of Arts and Crafts, where I had gone for a term seven or eight years before. The Theatre Design students were to design and make the sets and costumes. We came for a dress rehearsal on the morning before we were to open that evening – but sadly nothing was quite ready. We just had time for a quick "getting used" to the new furniture, etc. plus exits and entrances. Then it was time to make up and dress and perform. Not much time for reflection – bang, and you're on. Maybe that was a good thing; anyway we did it. And it was over. All that work for one performance. We had Blatchley's calm and knowledge; if he had been a panicky director I think we would have collapsed. The sets were a bit like a bordello – red and black. The maid's costumes and Madam's dresses for Clair to put on were all grand. I have no idea what the audience thought. I never actually liked the play but it was fun to work on with Blatchley and Deborah: John seemed to like the Theatre of the Absurd as much as did John Hale.

Sean's letter to me:

18 December 1963

Darling Shivaun,

Now you can rest for a spell from your labor, you have come out of a great adventure, and I hope you are pleased, & not too tired from the first public breaking of the ice. You will know now what it all is, & will be able to meet future trials with more certitude & coolness; but each attempt will mean an effort; but experience will make the effort easier.

I enclose usual, plus something more for Christmas, with my love

---

[14] Jean Genet (1910–1986) was a radical French writer and activist, and the son of a prostitute. *The Maids* dates from 1947. It was in his later career that Max Frisch (1911–1991), the Swiss playwright, became himself a radical writer. *The Fire Raisers* is a 1953 radio play that was adapted for the stage in 1958. This dark surreal allegory was first produced in London in 1961 at the Royal Court Theatre, translated by Michael Bullock.

[15] The stage career of Deborah Norton, born in Croydon in 1943, has seen her perform in, among other theatres, the Royal Court, Bristol Old Vic and National Theatre. She has 30 TV credits to her name, including *Yes, Prime Minister* (1986–1988). Nadia Atkin remains unidentified further.

As ever
Sean

Gordon and I drove down to Devon for Christmas. I think Gordon, who stayed at Claire's, left to go back to London before me and probably took my car. I know I did have time alone with Sean and Eileen. Before Christmas day came I had arranged a visit to Dartington to see if we could bring some productions from our Centre there. Sean with humorous acerbity turned our visit into a farce.

Sean's Notebook:

December 22, 1963

Shivaun ... and Gordon's visit to Peter Cox, Grand Secretary of Dartington Hall's Arts Center.

These two are members of a London School of Drama whose students had a few days before given a performance of Genet's "The Maids", Max Frisch's "The Fire Raisers", and a play by Schnitzler, which they were eager to do again before a wider audience, one of which they thought would be in Dartington Hall's Barn Theater. So Shivaun decided to ring up Mr and Mrs Elmhirst, to settle the matter pronto; but a sceptic at their elbow advised against it, saying they would not get any wave of a hand, or hear a voice cry "speak unto the children of Israel that they go forward". The sceptic was scorned (who was this fella, anyway?) Shivaun rang up, for she knew the parties well: The voices spoke to her, "Oh, yes; well Peter Cox arranges all these things; get in touch with Peter Cox; he knows. Peter Cox will deal with you". And Box ceased speaking. A murmur from the sceptic was heard to say, "Short is sending you to Codlin."[16] Apparently the cynic was wrong: Peter Cox rang up to speak with Miss Shivaun O'Casey. "He would be delighted to see her. Would she and her student companion come over tomorrow, Sunday?" Yes she would be glad to come.

---

[16] *Box and Cox* is a once popular one-act farce with two characters, James Cox and John Box. It was written by John Maddison Morton and produced in London in November 1847 at the Lyceum Theatre. Queen Victoria watched the play twice, in 1849 and 1850. (It was turned into a comic opera by F.C. Burnand and Sir Arthur Sullivan as *Cox and Box* and is performed to this day.) The *Oxford English Dictionary* defines "Box and Cox" as "applied allusively to an arrangement in which two persons take turns in sustaining a part, occupying a position, or the like." Sean has Codlin and Short, partners in a Punch and Judy show in Dickens' *The Old Curiosity Shop*, perform the same arrangement.

"Splendid". Said P. Cox, "I'll be glad then if you came between 4.0'c & 4.30 to take tea with me, then we can discuss all that is in your mind to say to me". "You see", said Shivaun, "he was very interested. He wants us for Tea, so we can talk quietly about our plan; and I'm sure he'll give us the chance of playing in his Theater". "Well", said the cynic, "You'll get a very nice tea anyway". With a tank bubbling with petrol, both set off on the 26 miles there and back, to see there the grand sec. of Dartington Hall's Arts Centre; full of hope and peace. Things promised well. Tra la la. The 2 young people came back in the late evening, and there was no tra la la in the way they looked. No one spoke for a time, for the 2 knew and we guessed. "Well?" asked Eileen. "Oh", said Shivaun, "buggerin awful! He said he couldn't, shouldn't, wouldn't – Um um, the theatre was, he feared, engaged for a long time ahead; yes, it was; coming here would, uhmmmummm cost quite a bit – £350 or thereabouts; maybe less, maybe more; his budget was ummm limited, and he had to keep it going. Sorry; oh he was sorry. Talked of the weather, brought out his little girl to 'show' to us; looked out of the window and murmured that there might be snow: and so we came out and came home". "Oh, well" said critic, "Just as I expected: but, anyway, you got a nice tea".

"We got no tea", said Shivaun's companion, "We didn't see a sign of cup, saucer or spoon, let alone a teapot. It was a frosty welcome, and we were hungry too. We squatted and listened to his mumbling, and listened to the call to tea that never came".

"After inviting you to tea he gave you none", queried the cynic: "well, we can add one more louser to the world's population. No tea, after promising tea? And at Christmas time, too! I write his name down in my psalter – Mr Peter Cox, of Dartington Hall: not a Devon man".[17]

---

[17] Peter Cox arrived to teach in the Arts Department at Dartington Hall in 1940. He was first Principal of the College of Arts from 1961 until his retirement in 1983. The College of Arts offered education in music and arts; courses prepared students for a teaching career and focused on a performative and multi-disciplinary approach to the arts. Cox died in 2015 at the age of 97. Cox's obituaries were highly complimentary about his development of the arts programmes at Dartington. See: https://www.dartington.org/peter-cox/

8
Sixteen Red Admirals
1963–1964

SPRING 1964

My time at the Drama Centre was coming to an end; our final shows would be in May and June. I had an idea of forming a company from the students of our year for a six-month tour of America, like the tour I had done with the Dublin Players. Instead of sitting around waiting for work, we would make work for ourselves as we wanted to do it. I still had the tour itinerary with all the contacts to the colleges we played, and also knew some others through Sean and Eileen. Carol Jenkins and Gordon were keen on the idea but Blatchley and the school definitely didn't want a company attached to the school. And who could blame them – they had just managed to build up a solid foundation for the new school and didn't need any more responsibilities.

I was continually worried about Sean, he was becoming ill so often now. Dr Doran came each day but hospital threatened, yet whenever a letter came saying he was up and about again I grasped at a hope that he would live into his nineties. A typed letter came from Sean (my second, which meant business) in which he poured cold water on the tour idea.

4 February 1964

My dearest Shivaun,

... I don't really know why you wrote your letter about the proposed 'tour' to me, for I'm sure you know, or have guessed, that I think it an impossible scheme, one fraught with impossible conditions of fulfillment. As I have already told you on the phone, I couldn't possibly become in any way any kind of sponsor for the scheme. As for asking Chancellor Murphy of the university to help you get a date or dates, in his other colleges, you cannot know what the Chancellor of a huge and populous University had to think and do.

But since you have sent me your 'prospectus', an action that seems to invite, and expect, comment, let me give you some advice and warning.

There is the cost – it would be very high indeed. There is no use quoting Josie Macavin, for her venture was done years ago, and then only under guarantee against loss by a rich woman [Lucille Lortel]. Since then costs have quadrupled, so much so that very very few London Companies travel even to Dublin because of the expense. You are unknown as a Company; her group with its name Irish Players had a psychological connection with the Abbey Theatre, world-known and world-famous; your lot are just a group of unknown attempters, unknown even to me. Again, you address your missive from your flat, showing the idea isn't from the School officially, but from the head of Gordon ... and S. O'Casey. ...

There is no use in continuing; I have said all I have to say, advised to abandon the idea. ...

Check enclosed adding a pound for a meal or two.

With my love as ever

Sean

Sound and valuable advice and advice that made Carol, Gordon, Patricia Grant and me sit back and think. I was sorry I worried him so much when he really was not well. He had bounced back from so many knocks I was often blind to how very weak he was becoming.

While this tour idea was brewing, the new school was going great guns. Because of the circumstances of the school happening so quickly, there wasn't an intake of new students this year. So it was only our two groups working together, and both sharing the history of recent events. This meant we knew each other better than we did when at the larger school at Swiss Cottage. With all our movement training we were less disjointed and our voices were clearer and stronger; and, most important, we were gaining in confidence, among ourselves at least. We were doing really interesting mask work. When we moved from Central we left the comic masks behind. We broke in to get them back but Blatchley told us in no uncertain terms to take them straight back. So we had no comic masks to work with, we had only the beautiful tragic, or full face masks. I now offered to make some, as I knew how to make props, etc. from my time at Bristol. I set to with clay, papier-maché and paint and made masks for us all to use. Group 2 performed *Hiroshima After the Bomb* in the full masks in the Methodist church, which was very impressive indeed. This was an improvisation with movement and sounds but no words or speech. They were all in black leotards. John Blatchley choreographed it and they all contributed ideas as to what to do with the theme of horror.

Our spring showings were to take place in our church hall. There were two large productions, *Medea* in February directed by Christopher Fettes and *Electra* in March directed by Dorothea Alexander, who none of us knew.¹ I was in the chorus in both. *Medea* was the more interesting as Fettes directed the movement to match the feeling using the Laban technique, which suited the Greek play with its abstract modern-dance style. It was fascinating learning the synchronization of the *Medea* chorus, beautifully choreographed by Yat. The extreme movement technique of the London Complicité theatre reminds me of the way we worked. Patricia Grant was excellent as Medea and Ian Hogg as Jason. Both these actors left for Canada during their acting careers. (They appeared at the Stratford Festival, Ontario in 1971; Patricia worked at the Guthrie Theatre with Robin Phillips.) Amaryllis was the Chorus leader. The young girl playing Electra had to be replaced when she became ill and Deborah Norton did a remarkable job of taking on the role at such short notice.

We also rehearsed one-act plays. The one I was in was *The Bald Primadonna* directed in April by John Blatchley.² I played the Maid; Blatchley praised me; I felt very good. What I had done was work very hard on the Stanislavsky technique: beats, intentions, climaxes, etc., worked out her story and her physical being as a maid; then I had done what Michael St. Denis had told Michael Redgrave to do — to throw it away and go with my main intention and the quick rhythm of the moment. We were to revive this with Blatchley directing later in the year.

Sean was ailing and my going home for Easter was an urgent need. He looked frail but better than I had imagined, and my stay was shorter than I had hoped. I looked after his well-worn eyes. I read aloud his letters, or whatever book or poem he wanted to hear. Often Eileen took the opportunity to go to London, or now St. Ives, while I was there.

During February 1964, Sean had lifted his ban on professional productions in Ireland, in order for the Abbey Theatre to bring *The Plough and the Stars* and *Juno and the Paycock* to the Peter Daubeny International Theatre Festival in London in April after staging them in Dublin in February, and for them also to take these productions to Paris. The London festival was to celebrate the 400th birthday of his beloved Shakespeare. There was a Souvenir Programme for the festival and the *Daily Telegraph* had asked Sean to write an article to be included in it.³

1 The actress Dorothea Alexander, born in Berlin, died in England at the age of 98. She had appeared in the BBC TV series (broadcast live), *Happy and Glorious*, dramatised episodes in the life of Queen Victoria.
2 *The Bald Prima Donna* – or *The Bald Soprano* (1950) was Ionesco's first play.
3 Christopher Murray has an account of O'Casey's unbanning in *Sean O'Casey*, pp. 432–433.

Thereby hung a tale. The *Telegraph* declined to publish it while liking it, the *Sunday Observer* declined, but the Sunday magazine of the *New York Times* snapped it up and paid Sean handsomely. The article in the Souvenir Programme was by [Micheál] MacLiammoir, Sean told Ron Ayling.[4] When I saw them I thought the productions but little better than those I had seen in Dublin before the ban: I slipped in and slipped out unnoticed.

Sadly Brendan Behan died in Dublin on March 20, 1964, aged 41. The few times Brendan had spoken to Sean over the phone, Sean had tried to coax him off the drink. In an April letter to Ron Ayling, Sean gave his verdict: "I suppose it was sad about B Behan, but it was the positive end of the too-gay lad. He has been one of many – either those who abandon work, and live off the little they've done; or, drink themselves to death like D[ylan] Thomas, Con O'Leary, [Louis] McN[eice], [Lennox] Robinson, and this morning comes the news of Seamus Kavanagh's death, who could have been a great comic actor. ..." Kavanagh was brilliant in *The Bishop's Bonfire* with his deep gravelly voice delivering lines with comic passion.[5]

SUMMER 1964

5 May 1964

Darling Shivaun,

Enclosed as usual, a cheque & One £ note.

I believe you are keeping the promise you made to me, not to overdo things for anyone Yatt [sic], Blatchley, or Gordon, however they may importune.

Your fair body and alert mind are all the property you have, and by God, they are valuable property! ...

Sleep well, sweet princess, remembering the ancient advice of Welsh physicians –

'A light dinner, a less supper, are the secrets of a long healthy life.' So they are.

MY love as ever.

Sean Dad

Such activity at the Drama Centre! The public showing of the last plays

---

[4] *The Letters of Sean O'Casey, Volume IV*, pp. 491–492.
[5] The Dublin actor Seamus Kavanagh (b. 1910) died on April 20, 1964. He starred in the movie comedy *Father Tim* (1957) and featured in *Broth of a Boy* (1959) with Barry Fitzgerald and June Thorburn.

was to take place at the Commonwealth Institute in South Kensington during May and June. A big barn of a place which was not bad for the Greek plays but not so good for *The Inca of Perusalem*, an intimate one-act in which my lovely part was a nervous, unsure princess. Alison Fiske played my Lady in Waiting, and Marc Karlin the Inca.[6] We had a lot of fun rehearsing it with George Benson.[7] George's surname reminded me of the Frank Benson Company that performed Shakespeare's plays in Dublin in the 1890s and according to Sean performed a different play each night. Sean's brother Archie was a prop maker at the theatre and although Sean was young his brother secreted him in and he sat in a half-full theatre in the middle of a row. He saw *Julius Caesar* to his full enjoyment: "The first Shakespeare play to present itself to me. Afterwards I and my brother used to play the quarrel scene between Brutus and Cassius; or I would give the speech of Brutus in the Forum, my brother acting the crowd, or he would give Anthony's speech while I acted the crowd".[8]

Medea was chosen to be performed again at the Institute, as an example of the best work done at the Centre. We performed it on May 27 and 29 and it was a success. *Medea* attracted the first review to praise Yat's movement principles of the Chorus: "Physical music, the complex geometry of the Chorus counterpoint to words ... in a finely balanced production, from which the Chorus, rightly, emerged as the true protagonists."

On June 23, also at the Commonwealth Institute, was our public performance of *The Inca of Perusalem*. Miriam Brickman was there, my old friend whom I had known since I used to hang out at the Wanamakers around the time of Niall's death: she was Sam's assistant then, now she was a famous casting director and was casting the film about Sean, finally

[6] George Bernard Shaw wrote *The Inca of Perusalem: An Almost Historical Comedietta* (1915) during the Great War; the comic, allegorical one-acter, despite its fairytale-like plot and setting, is really about the German Kaiser, Wilhelm II. Alison Fiske (1943–2020) and the future dramatist Stephen Fagan were part of the Central School breakaway group before they became wife and husband. Alison later joined the Royal Shakespeare Company and also became a television actress.

[7] George Benson (1911–1983) was a familiar figure in British movies from the 1930s until the early 1970s in which he often played a comic role. He began his career in revue followed by stage drama; it was when he was appearing as Polonius in *Hamlet* that he suffered the stroke that ended his career.

[8] As it happens, *Julius Caesar* was the second recorded Shakespearean play performed in Dublin, staged in Smock Alley in 1670. In Sean's time it was produced yearly 1888–1891 by Edmund Tearle's Co. and in 1893, 1894 and 1896 at the Gaiety Theatre by Frank Benson's Company.

called *Young Cassidy*. She said how good she thought I was and that she would suggest me to play Bella, Sean's sister, in the film. She did and I was asked to play it but I was already committed to organising and participating in the tour of the USA: all happening at the same time. So I had to turn it down. Siân Phillips was then cast for the part. Miriam was keen for me to be in the film and worked out that the early scheduled shooting of Lady Gregory's house would mean I only needed a week off if I played her maid. It would have been wiser for me to accept the part of Sean's sister and let the tour go ahead without me. So much happens by chance; I suppose the more we try the more we will gain and out of a hundred efforts one may happen.

When our last shows were over, the time came for some painful goodbyes. My three-year course had finished. We had signed up the actors for the proposed six-month tour of the American colleges, but it was definitely not a done deal. We were to go ahead with rehearsals after Blatchley had helped us choose a play. He had even agreed to direct us in John Gay's *The Beggar's Opera* and it was to be our main production. Wanting to have enough parts for all the actors on the tour, we also thought of some modern plays to do with *The Beggar's Opera*. I persuaded Sean against his better judgement to let us do *Figuro in the Night*, while Sam Beckett suggested a short monologue, *From an Abandoned Work*, and instructed us how to stage it. We also did The *Inca of Perusalem*. These three plays made up a very long triple bill. This meant we could draw up a proposal and send it out to the colleges we had earmarked with the hope of getting some acceptances and maybe promises of some money upfront.

Blatchley had told us a way of doing *The Beggar's Opera* very simply. The beggars come on stage, open three trunks, set up the props and furniture and get dressed on stage. He also suggested we should tour with a harpsichord to accompany the songs. Luckily for us, Julian Dawes agreed to tour with us with a harpsichord.[9] Daphne Dare, now living in London, agreed to design and get the costumes made for us. Another friend and great stage manager from Bristol, Mary Evans, now working for Peter Brook, agreed to manage the tour.[10] We obtained the rights for the Shaw

---

[9] Julian Dawes (b. 1942) is an English composer and musician who taught at the Drama Centre. He has written scores for numerous theatrical productions at the Royal Court Theatre and elsewhere. His compositions include concertos, sonatas, song cycles, chamber music and choral works.

[10] Mary Evans (b. 1934) 'was personal assistant to the famous director Peter Brook for seven years in the 1960s. She later co-founded Cygnet Theatre in Exeter in 1980 of which Brook was the patron. Evans retired from her administrative post at the theatre in 2014.

play from The League of Dramatists, an agency for playwrights founded by Shaw, which was also Sean's agent.

We started rehearsals in a church hall near Little Venice, London, Blatchley directing *The Beggar's Opera*, and someone else whose name I can't remember directing *Figuro in the Night*; *The Inca of Perusalem* was a revival. Our touring group of women actors was to be Deborah Norton, Alison Fiske, Patricia Grant, Amaryllis Garnett, Carol Jenkins, and myself, and the men were to be Stephen Fagan, Mark Karlin, Gordon Taylor, Alan Adams, Laurence Kenig, and Jimmy Maguire. All jobs other than directors, designer, stage manager and musician were to be done by the company.

YOUNG CASSIDY

When I was offered the part of Lady Gregory's maid in the movie of Sean's early career, I didn't know whether to take it or not. This was partly because I knew Sean didn't like the script, and although he had re-written some of the dialogue he was not in control of the rest. Nor did he like the concept of the film. I talked it over with Sean and Eileen. I had been in the Savoy Hotel suite with the two Bobs and my old friend Miriam Brickman the casting director: some interviews were taking place. Julie Christie came with John Schlesinger. She was beautiful and played Daisy Battles in the film. Sitting with Miriam on a sofa I asked her what the film would be like. She told me that at the first meeting about the film she had said, "This can be like the Gorky Trilogy", and was answered by a chorus of silence – so, no way.[11] I went on to ask how they were doing with the casting. Both Peter O'Toole and Richard Harris had turned down playing Sean and the Two Bobs were not keen to put Donal Donnelly or Norman Rodway in the lead as they were neither handsome enough nor well known enough, and that's how they ended up with Rod Taylor, a bulky Australian pin-up. Sean, if they wanted someone a little like him, was strong but always thin and wiry, and an actor and director could have worked on his bad eyesight as an interesting element. After all, when he played hurley he once hit a bird instead of the ball. In the end they cast as many well-known names as possible: Michael Redgrave, Flora Robson, Edith Evans, Maggie Smith, Julie Christie, etc. I feared the film was going to be sentimentalized

[11] *The Childhood of Maxim Gorky* (1938), *My Apprenticeship* (1939) and *My Universities* (1939) were a trilogy of Russian biopics adapted from the three volumes of autobiography by Gorky; the director was Mark Donsky.

SIXTEEN RED ADMIRALS, 1963-1964

in much the same way as John Ford's production of *The Plough and the Stars* (1936) had been, and to be an opportunity lost. In their search for a scriptwriter, the two Bobs had finally settled on John Whiting.

Now to be called *Young Cassidy*, the production was in full swing in Dublin. It had taken three years to get to this point.

Sean's letter to Teresa Sacco:

Sept 30 1963

Dear Teresa,

... The film you mention hits the story of "Johnnie [Casside]" here and there according to the written script even though Johnnie [Sean] himself changed considerable portions of the dialogue; but the photo scheme seemed to me to be good. All concerned with the production declare the script to be a splendid one, though I dont, but then I am not a script writer. No, my dear, it won't make me "very rich," not even rich. Between ourselves, I am due to get dollars to the value of 4,000 English pounds [£34,000 today], a fee which was two years ago a little larger, but the yearly fees for renewed options now leaves it the amount named; so minus tax, help to our boy, his wife, and two children, and help to our daughter at a drama school in London, will flip it down to a year's income or so. I have no desire to be very rich, or to be just rich, for riches are [a] sad and dangerous delusion. I have but one ambition which [is] to realize the many-year hope [that] Eileen (my wife) should be able to get herself a small house or bungalow where when she is older, and I'm gone, [she can] live in peace and charity with all men; and where she has room to accommodate her children or grandchildren whenever they may pay a visit to her. Throughout my life I had one burning ambition – that I and all might be able to live a full life. Getting ready for heaven in the only right way, as one might say. ...

As ever,
[Sean][12]

I decided to do the part of the maid; I would gain experience of filming and also some cash. The time came for me to leave rehearsals for a while and fly to Dublin for this small part in *Young Cassidy*. When I arrived as instructed at the Production Office, Miriam was there. I asked her where

[12] *The Letters of Sean O'Casey, Volume IV*, pp. 436–437.

the hotel was I had been allocated and how to get there, as I had never heard of it. "No, no", she said, "you are meant to be at the Shelbourne Hotel – to be in reach in case of interviews". So I just had to cross the road. As we were walking along with my case, Miriam told me there were two brothers with a very odd name who Bob Graff and Bob Ginna had hired to film the trailer for the film. She said she fancied the older one called Al. And there they were talking to the two Bobs in the Shelbourne foyer. I registered, got my key, and left my case with the porter, then Miriam introduced me to the two brothers Maysles. To my surprise I was immediately taken by the younger, David.[13] I was surprised because I had completely fallen out of love with Gordon, having faced the reality that he was untruthful and manipulative, and thus had no feelings for what I needed. I had started to gravitate towards the much more vital and intelligent Laurence Kenig, a good talker with a sense of humour and a political conscience. I wasn't looking for anyone else.

While I was in Dublin among the filmmakers, at home Eileen was busy trying to protect Sean from spending too much time with old friends that came knocking at the door. She was worried about his health and the weakness that she saw slowly creeping over him. In his Notebook, Sean recounts the final visits of some old friends:

> On the 18 or 14 of the month July Dr. Krause came to Trumlands Road, to sift and sort the letters he had gathered together over the time of many moons. He bore 4 bulky vols, each closely and beautifully clamping together well over 1000 pages of closely-typed m.s., enough, he said, to make 4 huge volumes of over 1000 pages each. For 8 days and nights he and I sifted, sorted, questioned, & tried to decide which of the letters could be taken out; and as fast as we rejected one, two others were found that must go in. Dave is a delightful companion, charming, and lovable; but when he has letters in front of him, he becomes a bloody tyrant. It was a hot and happy time, and when, at last, he packed the vols away to return to Dublin, we were no nearer deciding how the vols should be planned: 2 vols, or 4 vols? 2 vols of say 700 or 800 pages each; or; 1 vol of 1000 pages? My God! Why did I write so many letters? Counting all here, and all gone, musta written

---

[13] Albert Maysles (1926–2015) and David Maysles (1931–1987) were American brothers who made documentaries together. Of the thirty-odd movies they made, *Gimme Shelter* (1970), about the Rolling Stones tour that climaxed in the notorious Altamont concert, and *Grey Garden* (1975) were the most famous.

SIXTEEN RED ADMIRALS, 1963–1964

8 or 9 thousand of them! Let us face it!

But no – let us turn our back on them, and go to sleep, think of flowers and birds, or sing sweet hymns to God.

On the 21 July, same year, Gjon Mili, an old Albanian friend, the American Life Magazine's famous photographer. He came to take pictures, plain and colored, and O boy did he take them. Two hundred and more he took till I felt like the broad sunflower, bending over its grave in the earth so chilly, in the winter time. Leaning, standing, sitting, and reclining, he followed me in all positions: mid rapturous exclamations of fine, wonderful, splendid. God musta helped me through it all. Gjon was a very likeable lad away from the camera; but once the camera came into his hand, he became a fiend.

Gjon had no sooner gone with his cartload of pictures (as Dave had departed with his cargo of letters) than Richard Watts, Jr, and Tom Quinn Curtiss arrived; two old and valued American friends. Critics they were too; yet affection gathered us close together, showing that when the playwright and critic can love each other, that coexistence can be a real thing; and damn good for humanity.

A long time after we had heard the bells chime at midnight, our two friends left for their hotel, a short sleep, and an early morning rise to catch the first morning train from Torquay to London. A last visit? Maybe, for they have come many times, and I grow older, well, farewell, sweet friends, and if forever, then forever fare ye well! All that day, I had a slight pain in the side – one of the aches that ever assail the old; an hour after friends had gone. When I was making the bed, I got a stab in the side that doubled me in two, and all that night I waited for the day to come and bring the doctor with some salve for the pain.

Eileen had been right: the effort had weakened Sean and he was struck with acute bronchitis and had to go to the nursing home. He dreaded being away from the flat and especially his room where he knew exactly where everything was: every pen, every book.

Back in Dublin, Dave and Tom Curtiss would appear during the filming and it was lovely to see such good friends. When I arrived, a note was left for me with the concierge from John Ford, saying how much he was looking forward to working with me. I began to wish I had taken the part of Ella and let the tour go hang, but, as Sean said, decisions have to be made – and stuck to.[14] I was fitted for my maid's costume and a photo was taken of me in it – looking awful – to appear in a paper the next day. At a reception at the Shelbourne, while I am talking to Arthur Shields, Barry Fitzgerald's brother, I am aware of a man sidling up to me and I recognise him as Gaby Fallon, smiling and asking questions, trying to underhandedly interview me.[15] He had thrown so much hypocritical shit at Sean that I was not inclined to be very friendly. Civil, but that's all.

Then the news came that the filming had to be put on hold for two weeks! John Ford was plastered every night and incapable of working the following mornings: it is rumoured his drinking was led on by Rod Taylor. I had thought the Bobs looked worried but had put it down to the pressure of filming a large film, this one in partnership with MGM. Now the two Bobs were frantic. There were meetings in the office at the Shelbourne. Now a new director had to be found quickly as every day cost a lot of money.

During the hiatus I had to stay put. John Ford was removed and finally another director found, Jack Cardiff.[16] During this break the Maysles thought it would be a grand idea for them to film me talking to the Dublin people, some of whom remembered Sean. They also pressed me to let them come to Devon to film Sean but I said that was definitely a no-no as he was very frail now. They hired an open white Cadillac for us to drive around Dublin in – with me and David Krause in the back. Dave directed us to Sean's old living and working places. We filmed the people who came up to us who remembered Sean and the old times and talked and talked. One day, without Dave, we drove up to The Slads, in Howth, to see George Gilmore (whom I had run up and down the escalators with). His house was tiny and very neat. He asked us in but said they couldn't film inside. It was as sparse as Sean's room had been on the North Circular Road: very pleasing. We all went out, after a cup of tea was had, and they started filming as we looked out over the Irish Sea. We then went with

---

[14] Ella was played in the film by Siân Phillips who took over from Siobhán McKenna.

[15] Arthur Shields (1896–1970) was an Irish actor. The Shields family was Protestant. Arthur nonetheless fought in the Easter rebellion against the British in 1916. He had acted in Ford's 1939 film of *The Plough and the Stars*; he lived in California and appeared in several more Ford movies, including *She Wore a Yellow Ribbon* (1949) and *The Quiet Man* (1952).

[16] Jack Cardiff (b. 1914) had directed *Sons and Lovers* (1960) and *The Long Ships* (1964) before being brought in to direct *Young Cassidy*. Before directing, he was the award-winning cinematographer for such films as *Black Narcissus* (1947), *The Red Shoes* (1948) and *The African Queen* (1951). He died in 2009 at the age of 94.

George to the harbour and climbed into his rowing boat. With Al filming and David recording, we headed to Ireland's Eye. What a beautiful day it was. We looked for seals but saw none. On the way back it started to rain and before John Reid, the charming man whose car they had hired, could get the hood up, we were drenched. Then David and I fell in love.

The next day I talked to Arthur Shields on the set at Mountjoy Square, where Sean had shared a room with his friend and Gaelic teacher on whom he based the character of Seamus Shields in his first play that was accepted by the Abbey, *The Shadow of a Gunman*. We spoke of his brother, Barry, and he described to me what the living conditions would have been like in those days, in such a place. Arthur was a consultant on the film and a lovely man.

The new director arrived. And filming swung into action again. The very next day I was driven outside Dublin to a Georgian house, similar to the one that used to stand in Coole Park. (Lady Gregory's house had been pulled down by the nationalist Government, a scandal according to Sean and many others. The grounds were left when the house was demolished. Lady Gregory's daughter-in-law had let the roof fall into disrepair and by law this enabled demolition to go ahead. A man whom I met in Galway told me that he was one of the demolition workers; he stood in the large attic, that had all the old Abbey Posters pinned to the walls, and many other things. "Should I go ahead?", he thought, and then the command came to "Hurry up for Christ sake", and his hammer smashed through the top walls of the attic. He said later all the Old Lady's possessions, those not wanted by the daughter I presume, were auctioned off for practically nothing: books, suitcases, linen, etc.) I was shown into a room where I was made-up and dressed and then taken to a front room fitted out as a green room for the actors. The only other person in the room was Edith Evans, who was playing Lady Gregory. I was overawed, I thought she was such a brilliant actress. She quickly put me at my ease as we licked ice creams together. I asked her what to do with my long skirt as I ran up the stairs carrying Sean's small suitcase. She told me to do what came naturally to me, pick my skirts up as best I can – or not. We continued to lick our vanilla ice creams together. She told me how lonely she was since her husband had died, living alone at such an old age; she said she loved her old house but simply couldn't get rid of her loneliness. She invited me to visit her, but I never got her address and was far too shy to ask for it.

It was a balmy evening and David asked me to walk with him in

Stephen's Green. We walked and he took my hand, and on we walked, until the park gates were to be shut; as they closed we left and kissed against the railings. He walked me, arms around each other, to the closed doors of the Shelbourne and asked me my room number. "I'll see you", he said. In my room I undressed ready for bed. A gentle knocking at the door. He had got there through the kitchens. We made blissful love and fell fast asleep. The next morning we woke up late for him, so he left quickly. When I saw him as I watched the filming outside the hotel, he ignored me. So I thought, blast him. As I was feeling let down a young assistant handed me a note to say I should ring home immediately. It was Geoffrey Dobbie who answered the phone first; he said Sean and Eileen wouldn't say it, but Sean wasn't at all well and he thought I should come home immediately. I ran to the production office, where, after making sure that I was cleared and done all I was meant to, they arranged a flight back that very day. I packed my bag and took a taxi to the Dublin airport. From London I took the first train home to Devon. I rang Carol and Gordon to say not to expect me for at least a week.

OLD CASSIDY

Eileen hadn't told me Sean had been taken into the nursing home, a thing he dreaded. She didn't want to worry me while I was working. While in the nursing home and with the volumes of letters on his mind, Eileen told him that she wouldn't let Dave use her letters from Sean. "Would he let him just put one or two in?" he asked. She said she would. Then in August, Sean wrote a letter to Eileen that was his testament to her above all others, started in the Torbay Clinic

12 August 1964

Dearest and sweetest girl of my life; dear dear Eileen, here I am like a cooped-up Cock, ragged in feather, drooping in comb, the crow gone off into a cough. I have tried to let myself be absorbed by the clinic, tried to fit in, but my whole being refuses to do away with my wish to be home, to be back again where you are.

 That is my only home, has been so for many, many years – where you, my darling, are: where you get up in the morning, go to sleep o' nights; where you come and go, where we eat together and talk together, and walk the well-worn paths, still bordered with many bright flowers, & many blossoming bushes. When I first set eyes on you, [I] thought you the loveliest lass I had ever seen; but bred straight out of the workers' way & suddenly plunged into the world of literary & drama society, I thought I had become "a man of the world" & so girls were but pretty and gay things to play with, – impudent and barbaric idea. Yet as I got to know you more, & the dog, Bobbie; as we laughed together so readily over many things – including "Bobbie", I began to like you for much more than your lovely face and handsome figure. I failed as "a man of the world" for I couldn't stop myself from talking of serious things, and your interest in the talks and your quick and sensitive responses, showed me a girl with a most active sensitive, and kindly mind, and the "girl for a gay time," vanished; and a lovely companion took her place. Then companionship was linked with marriage, so you set to create the first O'Casey home in 19 Woronzow Road, St. John's Wood, making it very colorful with much ingenuity and imagination, and damned little money. Within a year, the first baby, Breon, came, and here were we. I with as little idea of what fatherhood was, and Eileen with a natural instinct, having a far bigger idea of all that motherhood meant; a hard time, a colourful time, but a testing time for both of us.

And so it has gone on for nigh on forty years, your hands alone moulding the life of the little household, solving all problems, dealing well with practical affairs, and wisely with the Education of our boy, a matter in which I could give no hand, for I had had no jot of Knowledge or experience on the way a child should be educationally brought up; and, darling, you gave all our children a sensible & artistic entrance into life. ...

Sean completed the letter at home, sitting in his own chair at his own table, and Dave later published it in his last volume of Sean's correspondence.

You are, and have been, indeed, Cuisle mo Chroidhe – the Pulse of my heart; and this heart of mine loves you, & will love you unto the last. Oh my darling girl.

Sean[17]

I climbed the cement steps and opened the door: there in the little hall was the old mock-Tudor oak chest they had bought from Harrods for

[17] The letter is on pp. 505–507 of *The Letters of Sean O'Casey, Volume IV.*

Woronzow Road, the mahogany umbrella stand, the bright orange wall behind the chest and, as always, flowers on the chest, this time a pot of white cyclamen. As I straightened up from putting down my case, there was Sean dressed and standing. We hugged and kissed. How thin he was. He took my face into his fine cold hands and studied my face closely, looking into my eyes. "Darling, how lovely to have you back again". Eileen was there, smiling, but with a worried brow above the smile; I only knew a little of what had just happened to Sean, and the toll it had on Eileen. The tapes had been set aside – on them a rich supply of Sean talking and singing – as he was not strong enough for that now. His lungs were really in a chronic state, although beginning to ease from the last infection, they had taken another battering. In Sean's room as we all had a cup of tea – the O'Casey elixir – he lying on the bed and Eileen and I in the chairs, I told them about the filming, the two weeks of nervous activity as they searched for a new director who was willing to take over from John Ford, the trickiness of getting rid of John Ford who had turned out to be such a liability and must have cost them a small fortune, with two weeks added to their budget. I told him about Gaby slithering up to me through the long grass of the other journalists and film actors, to try to twist me into an interview; he had organised his cameraman friend to take a photo of him with me and Arthur Shields before I knew it was happening, and there it was in the paper: Tuesday August 11, 1964, captioned: "At a reception held in Dublin, yesterday for Mr. Arthur Shields were (left to right): Miss Shevaun O'Casey, Mr. Gabriel Fallon and Mr. Arthur Shields" "Friends still", I think he wanted the photograph to say.

We spoke of Barney Conway and of my time with George Gilmore, and I mentioned the Maysles brothers who wanted to make a documentary of him, quickly adding I had told them that it was completely impossible.

Even though he couldn't read anymore, I often saw Sean sitting in his armchair with a book on his lap, his hands resting on top of it, as if by holding it he could imbibe all that was inside the covers. When I offered to read some, his face lit up. We tried again to work out T.S. Eliot's *The Waste Land*. I found it and read it, me puzzled and him puzzled. "I hope I won't die with a whimper", Sean said. He was gaining health by the day but had a long way to go to get anywhere near his old strength: so weakened now, it was clear, if you could bear to admit it, that he wouldn't get that much better.

A week had gone and they needed me up in London for rehearsals. I argued that I wasn't needed for *The Beggar's Opera*, as I was only playing one of the whores, and stayed another week, giving Eileen time to go out and visit friends, while I did some of the shopping and cooking. Sean told me that I couldn't stay forever, my work was also important. I knew this, but I didn't want to leave. Then the time did come. A taxi came to take me to the station. As we hugged I had to force myself not to cry out: he took my head between his firm hands and said, "You have to go and live your own life now, my darling girl. You will always be in my mind." I said the same to him, that I would ring every night, and day if need be. As the taxi drew away from the home, through the back window I saw Sean and Eileen waving: I knew, I felt, I would never see him alive again.

Sean's letter to David Krause:

27 August 1964

My dear Dave,

Jim [Plunkett] told me you leave Ireland on Sept.1st. When you come to London, I'd like you to phone us. I'd like you to come down here for a day or two so's I could answer any last remaining questions, which would be better than leaving them to be answered in subsequent letters for it is harder than ever for me to write now.

I've had a nasty time with a torn muscle in the side, and afterwards, with a ghastly virus infection in the lungs, which made me semi-delirious for a time; and am still a little toxic from the effects; but sensible now, and fling no bricks.

As ever,
Sean[18]

I rang every night, often in the day as well, and sent letters and received notes he managed to write, always including the £1 cheque and £1 note. His writing in these last letters became weaker and weaker.

September 1964

Darling Shivaun,

Enclosed are the usual items:-
  1 Cheque
  1 £1 note
  I hope you are seeing after yourself, taking rests and sleeping well.

[18] *The Letters of Sean O'Casey, Volume IV*, pp. 507–508.

Eileen seems to be much better.
Very windy here. My fond love as ever Sean
With LOVE Sean

While back rehearsing and working in the flat, David Maysles came to London to see me. We met in a coffee bar in Chelsea, and we talked and laughed. He apologized for ignoring me. But we decided with some difficulty that, as he had a girlfriend in New York and maybe I had someone here, it was impossible to be so far apart and remain anything more than friends – great friends. I did have to walk away crushing my feelings inside me. We were close friends until his death at 55 in 1987, now and again spending moments together; and I, foolishly maybe, used to imagine that when we were very old we would sit and laugh together, holding hands and watching the sun set.

THE LAST OF THE BLOSSOMS

Eileen fell ill. It was worrying when Eileen was ill, not only for her, but also because we all feared she would pass her 'flu or cold on to Sean. Eileen was worn out. Her nights were often disturbed for she was the kindest nurse, caring for Sean now as she had cared for us all when we were young, and when tending her handsome Niall when he was sick and dying. She had a delicate warm touch that soothed immediately and a soft lilt of her beautiful resonant voice. She and I spoke often on the phone now, sometimes twice a night. Now and again Sean would chat too. On September 16 Eileen told me Sean was having some very bad nose bleeds and that Dr Doran was seeing to them.

On September 18 the phone rang; I sensed what she was going to say – "Sean has died, dear."

Carol and Gordon and some other members of our new theatre company were in the flat. By my gasp they knew something serious had happened and silence fell. I had to be with Eileen, I could not leave her alone "I am coming right away, Eileen. I'll be there in about four hours." To his credit Gordon insisted on driving me down to Devon in my sports car: he wouldn't let me drive myself. During the journey I said practically nothing. As I looked out at the dark night I remembered the desperate drive down with Niall and I thought of life without Sean, the kindest, funniest, cleverest person in my life. My bowels were in a tight knot and my face was wet with tears, silent tears.

SIXTEEN RED ADMIRALS, 1963–1964

Eileen describes in her book, *Sean* (pp. 296–297) how a young doctor drove her home after Sean had died in the nursing home: "... the doctor [Dr Haskins] did not like to leave me at the flat; it seemed so still, Sean's room so quiet; I do not think that I realised entirely that Sean was dead. Then, trying to concentrate, I found myself doing so calmly, and Sean's own words returned to me that, whenever I was really in stress or grief, I became still and practical. ... As a rule I hated being alone, but at this moment I wanted nothing more".

Gordon and I arrived and drove down the familiar short driveway with the tall sombre fir trees sturdy to the left, black and funereal in the dark of the night. The outside light was on at the top of the steps, and lights were on in Sean's room, and in Eileen's room at the side. Gordon climbed out of the car as if to come in with me. I stopped him, rather curtly I think, and told him he had to go: "Please, take the car and just go". After some hesitation he did so. I raced up the steps, opened the door and Eileen and I flung our arms around each other and wept. We sat on Sean's bed clutching hands. "He had a wonderful death", she kept on saying. I made a pot of tea and we drank it together. Then she told me what had happened to my dad and her lovely old man.

That evening Sean had a terrible pain in his chest that doubled him over. Unfortunately for Sean and Eileen Dr Doran had gone on holiday and there was a young intern holding the fort. Eileen knew that Sean would not live for many more years but didn't think this was the time. The young doctor came and gave Sean an injection for the pain, telling Eileen to make him lie down and rest and to ring if he became any worse. Then he left. Soon after, another greater pain cramped his chest and surged over his whole body. It took a while to get hold of the doctor as he was on his way back to the surgery. Finally he came and gave Sean another injection and they waited for the ambulance. Eileen told me Sean talked quietly to her a little before the ambulance arrived but that in the ambulance they did not speak. She held his hand. Sean always had a tremendously firm grip. As they approached the nursing home she noticed his grip had lessened and she thought he was falling asleep. They carried him into the hall and into his room that was to the left of the hall. When he was safely in bed she turned to the doctor and said "I don't want Sean to suffer any more, he has suffered enough in his life". In a very soft voice the doctor replied, "He will have no more pain. He is dead, Eileen." He had fallen into the endless sleep of death holding her hand. It was the final icy word; she had heard it when Niall died. "Sean's little cap was on the side-table; his coloured cap. Neither the doctor nor I could speak. He put the cap gently on Sean's head and left us alone. Sean had gone after his long and wonderful life, his life of fighting, integrity and love. He died between the sunset and the evening star."

As the sun began to rise we lay down for a short while, still, on his bed. In the early morning she asked me if I would like to see Sean. I had never seen a dead person and I still missed not being with Niall as he died; seeing Sean would maybe make me believe he had actually gone. The word "closure" may have a meaning. I went with her to the clinic. I drove her; it was the clinic where he had his operations for his prostate and his kidney stones, where I had visited him; and where he had been just a week or so ago. An Edwardian building with big generous windows. We were taken into the room to the side of the hall; the green curtains were drawn closed and a simple light shone by his face.

There he was, lying in front of both of us, unable to jump up and embrace us. Gone. Taut and thin: his face still determined in death, an image etched in the pale-yellow hardening flesh. A fly landed on his cold forehead. Nothing moved. I shooed it away, indignant at its presence. There he lay still, yet singing now with God, maybe, and doing a jazz dance with our darling Niall: that was a thing devoutly to be wished. He was looking death squarely in the face as he had life. Eileen was next to me and we squeezed hands until it hurt. I had had a quiet kind of life, together with Sean and Eileen – too ordinary, maybe, to write about. I had known an idyllic childhood. The sudden death of our Niall had shattered us all, but mostly it struck Sean and Eileen, but we all dealt with the hidden pain we had never dreamt would touch us: the worries of Sean's last years, the great unbounded strength of love between Sean and Eileen; I had lived with them through it all. Now he had finally left us. We kissed him, Eileen last, and left.

Back in his room it was deathly quiet – the life had left here too and imperceptibly a thin layer of white dust seemed to cover everything. A deep longing to hear his voice again crept over me and I fought back the emotion that tightened my chest and grabbed my throat. "I am an old man," he would say, "You have a life to live of your own – don't mind me – go and live it". But how I did mind him.

Breon arrived in the afternoon and the funeral was arranged for as soon as possible. Before we left for the crematorium, Breon put on Eileen's hat and said, "Here he is, his simple son". For some reason we laughed and laughed – laughter can be so near to crying.

Eileen had stipulated that no one except us should be at the funeral. I saw poor Dobbie standing outside as we drove up, looking wretched, and I felt very sorry for him. Maybe we should have had some people inside with us: but the decision had been made and we were in no condition to do anything except get through it: just us three.

It was a dark sombre church. Eileen had chosen some prayers. The priest asked us to follow him in saying them. Eileen did brilliantly, but I looked down and noticed that his surplice was rather short and he had brown shoes on. Then Eileen jumped a line and a short flurry of confusion followed. Why that was funny I don't know but I got the giggles, and then Breon caught them. Eileen gave us such a furious look it froze us to silence. Then the coffin was carried to the side and put on some rollers; two small dull curtains opened and the coffin jerked through the hole; the curtains closed, so no one should see Sean's body incinerated in the fierce flames of the furnace. His body was gone, empty of the father I knew, gone to ashes now.

The next day Breon left to get back to his family. I stayed another few days to be with Eileen and then went back to the company and rehearsals. A few days later a letter arrived on the doormat:

15 September 1964

Darling Shivaun,

The usual check
1 £1 note.
Love Sean

Enclosure: returned cheque for £4 'Drawer deceased' written across it.

I had sent it to the bank before he died, and here it was back again. I still have it.

Letters came to Eileen from all over the world. We both had notes from Sam Beckett.

Dear Eileen,

I only heard this evening and have no words for what's in my heart for you all.

Affectionately
Sam Beckett

Dear Shivaun,
Very deep sympathy
Love Sam

David Krause's letter to me:

October 4 1964

Dear Shivaun,

And now it will never be the same again, we will never be the same without him, even though he will live on for us. I suppose I knew it would have to happen one day, but I know now that the inevitable loss comes mercilessly when it comes, the shock no less for the knowledge that Sean lived a full and good life. So I send you my dearest sympathy and love. I do hope Eileen and Breon and you are coming through the whole thing, with the part of him that is in all of you keeping firm and safe.

Soon again I will write to you about other things; but meanwhile, know that I am with you always in the thought and memory of that great and grand fella, the father of the best in all of us.

Dave Krause

Sean wrote his last will two years to the month before he died. Eileen reproduced it in her book, *Sean* (p. 285).

Written on 15 September 1962
I bequeath and leave to my beloved wife, Eileen O'Casey, all I have and hope to get: all royalties due, all contracts, all manuscripts and typescripts, all royalties to come, fees of every sort – in short, all I am possessed of, and all moneys my work may earn in future years. I give all my goods, estate valuation, and all else, to her in gratitude for many, many years of happy and fruitful companionship; and with all I bequeath to her my deep love, as deep now, deeper indeed, than the love I felt for her in our earlier years.

Witness my signature this day, 14 September 1962

SEAN O'CASEY
(Witnessed by Geoffrey Youngman Dobbie and Ronald Frederick Ayling)
Eileen wanted his ashes to be scattered at the Golders Green Crematorium, next to Niall's. It was an overcast day and I was spending the night with Eileen at Ella and Don's. Eileen didn't want to face any of the group of students who were working at the flat on our American tour: it was now "the office" for what we called "Theatre Group 20" – God knows why.[19] Ella left us alone to wait to be collected by a car sent for us by Sidney Bernstein. We didn't have to wait long before this grand black car and driver pulled up in front of 103 Frognal. Eileen and I sat in the back holding hands, still shell-shocked as we passed through Hampstead to the crematorium.

After formalities a man arrived carrying the urn with Sean in it. He asked us to follow him up the slope to the Shelley and Tennyson rose gardens, where Eileen and Breon had followed Niall to be scattered. There were still a few last blossoms of shrub roses hanging on to their woody branches. When he stopped, he signalled to us to stand back slightly to where the gentle wind would blow the ashes away from us. He then asked if we were ready. Eileen said, "Yes, thank you," as her cold hand tightened in mine. Then he pulled the bottom of the flask away and a huge mass fell to the grass with a thump – so much like a body, I saw Sean for a moment and felt faint. I looked at Eileen who was ashen white and who gasped, "I have to sit down". We made our way to a bench and collapsed together, hugged and cried. The man discreetly left, his duty done.

Thirty one years later, I was there alone with the ashes of Eileen. I was told no-one was scattered now in the Shelley and Tennyson rose gardens; not scattered, indeed, in any part of the gardens, so she couldn't be scattered where Sean and Niall had been cast to the winds; she had to go to the designated spot for this month. I think the official said it was because cremation had become more popular since 1964 and too much ash damaged the grass. I was sorry for Eileen but she wouldn't be too far

[19] In *After the Revolution: A Critical History of Drama Centre* (p. 52), Vladimir Mirodan gives a brief account of the U.S. university tour by Group 20 organised by Shivaun, Carol and Gordon. The Group's financial assisters included Marcel Marceau, David Deutsch and Prince Philip. From January to May 1965, the company travelled over 15,000 miles by bus, performing on 35 campuses. The Group also staged a "Demonstration Programme" showing in action Drama Centre methods developed by Rudolf Laban, Michael Chekhov and Yat Malmgren.

away. So there I stood at the bottom of the slope we had climbed together to scatter Sean and where she had scattered her Niall, standing by a square patch of newly-laid turf. Again, the thud as Eileen landed as near as was allowed to her great loves, Sean and Niall. I felt very alone. I walked back to Hampstead through the back streets, and then down to Eileen's garden flat at 8 Parkhill Road, in Belsize Park. She had told me before she died, in a questioning way, that I would miss her when she was gone. I said "I know – I will, I know" – and I sure have.

I am the last of the bunch called the O'Caseys, as my brother Breon died in May 2011: the last person to talk to within the family. We were a close-knit crew, with a big unravelling after Niall's death. Breon and I talked a lot before he too died, as the memories all came back to us again and as we relaxed and talked of the past we had shared together, and laughed at our foolishness. A red admiral fluttered through the open window.

Sean's Notebook:

> The other day a friend, breathless with remembrance adorations, he told me that on the path of waste ground, its meanness hidden by thistle, dandelion, dock, common poppies and moon daisies, he saw 16 Red Admirals resting from the heat and burden of the day. 16 Red Admirals on the same bush at the same time! 'Try to imagine it Sean; there they were in all their colors – 16 beauties together, sunning themselves on the same bush: a humble old bush gemmed with a crowd of glittering butterflies what duchess or film star could gem throat or breast with such living jewels as these Red Admirals! Never before in my life have I seen such a sight, and I never expect to see them again. I lingered while they were there, till one by one or two by two, they fluttered away, &, when I went my way I was regardless of customers' complaints that I was late in delivering the milk for their breakfast'.

Sean, 1954
PHOTOGRAPH: Gjon Mili

ACKNOWLEDGEMENTS

The first person who read my book was Anne Krause – who I had met many years before with her husband Professor Emeritus David Krause and intrepid Sean O'Casey letter hunter. It was Anne who gave me the courage to proceed and approach publishers. My friend Professor John Fairleigh encouraged me and introduced me to the first possible publisher, who in turn introduced me to the editor John Wilson Foster. David Gothard CBE has been my trusted advisor throughout the long process. Down the path many others wished me well and gave good advice: Des and Rosheen Geraghty, Paul O'Brien and locally in Devon, Mark Burley, who gave me invaluable help with the images. I thank my close friend Nella Opperman for her unwavering support. For his help I am also indebted to Adrian Barr-Smith. Then of course to family. But most of all John Wilson Foster (Jack) whose knowledge and friendship is a rich reward.

Thanks everyone ... Shivaun